THE PEOPLE WHO
OWN THEMSELVES

THE PEOPLE WHO

Aboriginal Ethnogenesis in a Canadian Family, 1660–1900

OWN THEMSELVES

Heather Devine

UNIVERSITY OF
CALGARY
PRESS

© 2004 Heather Devine
Published by the
University of Calgary Press
2500 University Drive NW
Calgary, Alberta, Canada T2N 1N4
www.uofcpress.com

We acknowledge the financial
support of the Government of
Canada through the Book Publishing
Industry Development Program
(BPIDP) for our publishing activities.
We acknowledge the support of the
Alberta Foundation for the Arts for
this published work.

Canada

Canada Council   Conseil des Arts
for the Arts   du Canada

This book has been published
with the help of a grant from
the Canadian Federation for the
Humanities and Social Sciences,
through the Aid to Scholarly
Publications Programme, using funds
provided by the Social Sciences and
Humanities Research Council of
Canada.

National Library of Canada Cataloguing in Publication

Devine, Heather
    The people who own themselves : aboriginal ethnogenesis
in a Canadian family, 1660-1900 / Heather Devine.

Includes bibliographical references and index.
ISBN 1-55238-115-3

    1. Desjarlais family. 2. Métis--Ethnic identity. 3. Métis-
-Genealogy.

I. Title.
E99.M47D48 2003   971'.00497   C2003-905787-9

Printed and bound in Canada by Friesens

∞ This book is printed on 100% Recycled, acid-free paper
Cover, page design and typesetting by Mieka West.
Production by Samuel Smith Esseh

Table of Contents

Illustrations

Preface

....

In the early 1980s, after several years of searching, my mother finally made contact with her biological family. She had been given up for adoption in the 1930s, and raised to adulthood by a farm family in southwestern Saskatchewan. Although her ties to her adoptive family were, and remain, close, she still wanted to know about her real heritage. Born with jet-black hair, brown eyes, and a dark complexion, she stood out from the other children in the community where she was raised.

Eventually she discovered the source of her striking looks – a Métis father, now deceased. Although he had passed away before she could meet him, she was able to meet his sisters, who lived in Regina. They had known of her existence, and they graciously welcomed her into their homes and shared with her information about her father. They also directed her to the tiny village of Lebret, about an hour's drive away, where she would be able to look at the parish records of their mother's family, surnamed Desjarlais.

During the mid-1980s, I began researching the genealogy of my mother's family, which had miraculously revealed itself. When my mother phoned to tell me about her visit to the Roman Catholic Church at Lebret, she was excited about finding my great-grandmother's baptismal records. She was able to give me the names of Rosine Desjarlais' parents (Thomas Desjarlais and Madeleine Klyne), the sponsors at her baptism (Veronique Klyne and Joseph Bellegarde), and the officiating priest (Father Joseph Hugonard, O.M.I.).

This handful of names, and a healthy curiosity and interest in the past, started me on a quest that became almost an obsession, occupying most of my free moments and causing my family no end of puzzlement and, at times, consternation.

As it turned out, there was a local chapter of the Alberta Genealogical Society (A.G.S.) in the city of Edmonton, where I lived. Edmonton was also the home of the founder of the A.G.S., Mr. Charles Denney. Mr. Denney (now deceased) was a former provincial Archivist of Alberta. In his younger years, he had begun the task of researching the ancestry of his first wife, who was descended from some of the earliest Scots and Métis settlers at Red River. His initial interest in his wife's ancestry blossomed into a consuming interest in the genealogy of the Métis people of Western Canada. His extensive collection of genealogical records, compiled from parish records, scrip affidavits, and historical documents, and supplemented with correspondence from descendants throughout Western Canada, now resides in the Glenbow Archives, to which it was donated by Mr. Denney in the 1980s. Mr. Denney continued to work on Métis genealogy after the bulk of his collection moved to Calgary, however, and he kept the working copies of the collection at the Edmonton Branch Library of the Alberta Genealogical Society, housed in Edmonton. I became a regular visitor to that library, meticulously compiling the family tree of Rosine Desjarlais and her numerous ancestors, and learning a great deal of early Western Canadian history along the way.

As I continued to investigate my Métis heritage through the relatively 'safe' lenses of genealogy and history, I also got to know my relatives a little better. I began corresponding with my mother's cousin, who was teaching in northern Saskatchewan on an Indian reserve at the time. We soon found that we shared a common interest in our family history, and swapped information, recipes, and observations about the world in general, and the Native world in particular.

By 1990, my government duties involved close work with aboriginal communities interested in preserving and interpreting their heritage. I found myself dealing with contemporary aboriginal issues on a daily basis. After the siege at Oka, I found myself increasingly conflicted about my role as a government worker and my evolving perceptions of Native issues, influenced not a little by the unanswered questions about my own heritage. Why, for example, did my great-grandmother not teach Cree and Saulteaux to her children, when she spoke those languages herself? Why had she sought to distance herself from her own background during much of her life? These questions nagged at me.

Since 1993, I have applied myself to answering the questions that my great-grandmother's life elicited in me. I have tried to frame my enquiry so that the observations and the conclusions have historical and cultural relevance for a broad audience as well as for my family and friends. Hence this study, now completed.

Definitions

Several terms used in this study are defined below. Some are French terms that were commonly used in the fur trade. Others refer to geographic locales whose names and boundaries changed over the course of time.

à la façon du pays ("according to the custom of the country"): an expression used to describe marital unions in the fur country that were not solemnized in a Christian church.

Athabasca: the region comprising the watershed of Lake Athabasca, including the Athabasca and Peace River drainage systems. By 1885, the term referred to the northern half of Alberta.

Bourgeois ("middle-class person"): in the fur-trade context, this term referred to district officers in the North West Company. They administered one or more posts in the fur country, and were often partners. North West Company partners who were working in the fur country were known as "wintering partners."

censitaire: a tenant farmer in the seigneurial system of New France.

coureur de bois ("runner of the woods"): a term used during the French régime to refer to independent fur traders, who were often operating illegally.

Creole: used to describe people of French or Spanish ethnic extraction born in North America and the Caribbean. Commonly used to refer to ethnic French people in the pre-1760 region of French Louisiana and later to refer to Franco-Americans in the southern portion of the United States.

en derouine: a term used to describe the pattern whereby traders travelled to (and lived in) Native camps to trade for furs, rather than having the Natives bring furs to a post.

engagé: a lower-level employee (i.e., a servant as opposed to clerk) under contract to a fur-trading company.

Indian: a collective term used to describe Canadian aboriginal people who are not legally defined as Métis or Inuit. In modern parlance this is a legal designation used to refer to members of Indian bands under treaty. Historically, the term "Indian" is believed to have originated from the misidentification of the indigenous people of the New World by European explorers, who thought they had reached India. Although the colonial origins of the term caused the usage of "Indian" to fall into disfavour briefly, it is widely used today by Natives and non-Natives alike as a useful collective term. When more specificity is required, the terms used by various aboriginal groups and subgroups to describe themselves (e.g., Siksika for Blackfoot; Dakota for eastern Sioux), are generally employed.

Louisiana: the French territories south of the Great Lakes to the Gulf of Mexico between 1702 (the date when Fort Mobile was established on the Gulf coast) and 1763. During this period, the French territories consisted of the Mississippi-Missouri watershed; more precisely, the lands on the east side of the Mississippi extending to the western boundary of the British colonies, and the lands extending one to two hundred miles from the west bank of the Mississippi River. After the Treaty of Paris was signed in 1763, the French territory west of the Mississippi River was ceded to Spain, while the territory east of the Mississippi came under British jurisdiction.[1]

mangeurs du lard ("pork eaters"): voyageurs transporting goods between Montreal and Lake Superior, who subsisted on salt pork, sea biscuit, and dried peas or beans. These canoemen were seasonal labourers, who did not travel into the fur country beyond the Great Lakes.

négociant: an independent merchant.

North-West Territories: Historically, the term "North West Territory" was loosely applied to the vast region north and west of Lake Superior. In 1870, the Hudson's Bay Company ceded title of Rupert's Land to Canada. The Red River Settlement and adjacent southern areas became the new Province of Manitoba. The remaining British territories between British Columbia, the Arctic Ocean, and Alaska were merged with what remained of Rupert's Land to form the Canadian North-West Territories. In 1881, Manitoba's provincial boundaries were extended further north, decreasing the size of the North West Territories. In 1882, districts called Assiniboia, Alberta, Saskatchewan, and Athabasca were created within the area of the North-West Territories. By 1895 the North-West Territories consisted of the following districts: Yukon, Mackenzie, Franklin, Athabaska, Alberta, Saskatchewan, Assiniboia, and Ungava. In 1898 the Yukon Territory was established as a separate territory, and Quebec's boundary was moved north the same year. In 1905 Alberta and Saskatchewan were created from the southern portions of the North-West Territories.

Ojibwa: the standard term used to describe a group of woodland aboriginal people who migrated westward from the region of the Great Lakes into western North America. As they migrated, different groups of Ojibwa became known under different terms. The eastern Ojibwa are commonly known as Ojibwa or Anishinabeg, while western Ojibwa are referred to as Plains Ojibway or more commonly, Saulteaux. Western Ojibwa have also been referred to as Bungi (Bungee), a term which has fallen into disuse. Western Ojibwa living in the United States also use the terms Anishinabe or Anishinabeg, but are more commonly known as Plains Chippewa or simply, Chippewa.[2]

Otipemisiwak: Several words were employed by different aboriginal groups to describe the Métis. The term *Otipemisiwak* comes from the Cree, which, loosely translated, means "the people who own themselves," "their own boss," "the people who govern themselves." These descriptions refers to the fact that, historically, most Métis people were not employed as servants of fur trade companies but operated independently, coming and going as they pleased. In aboriginal cultures, personal autonomy was paramount; an individual who worked for someone else was considered to be a slave, and not truly human.

pays d'en haut ("the upper country"): the term used to refer to the regions north and west of the settlements along the St. Lawrence River. In time, it came to refer to the western country beyond the Great Lakes.

Rupert's Land: the territory encompassing the watershed of Hudson's Bay, the exclusive monopoly of which was granted to the members of the Company of Adventurers by the British king in 1670, and which was ceded to Canada in 1869–70. Rupert's Land consisted of large parts of present-day Canada, including what is now southern Alberta, Manitoba, Northern Ontario, Northern Quebec, parts of today's Northwest Territories and most of Saskatchewan.

scrip: certificates issued to eligible Métis residents of Western Canada by the Canadian government in recognition – and extinguishment – of their aboriginal rights. The certificates could be redeemed for cash, or for land of equivalent value.[3]

voyageur: canoeman. This term was used after 1763 to refer to canoemen hired on contract by fur trading companies. As servants on contract, they were also known as *engagés*.

One definition that requires special attention is the dual usage of the word "Métis/métis." The Métis National Council stated in 1984, "Written with a small 'm,' métis is a racial term for anyone of mixed Indian and European ancestry. Written with a capital 'M,' Métis is a socio-cultural or political term for those originally of mixed ancestry who evolved into a distinct indigenous people during a certain historical period in a certain region of Canada."[4] The usage of the term continues to be problematic. As the co-editors of *The New Peoples: Being and Becoming Métis in North America* observed in 1985,

> To attempt a dual usage (Métis/métis) would be to take it upon ourselves to decide who belongs to socio-political cat-egories that are still subject to redefinition and evolution.[5]

As I have discovered in my research, the ethnic labels arbitrarily assigned by outsiders may be quite different from the personal and familial understandings of their own identity that individuals and groups share.

Like Brown and Peterson, I am reluctant to impose arbitrary ethnic labels on groups of people, whether historical or contemporary. However, the entire thrust of this study is an exploration of how groups of aboriginal people have come to acquire the ethnic labels by which they and their descendants are known to outsiders. I shall therefore apply the terms "métis" and "Métis" based on the following criteria. When the spelling "métis" is used, it refers to individuals or groups who are simply of mixed ancestry (e.g., French/Native). In contrast, the use of "Métis" signifies that the individuals or groups involved are a distinct ethnic entity as perceived by others and/or by themselves. My application of these terms is based on my historical analyses of individual and group situations, recognizing that these identities are contextually defined and in constant flux.

Acknowledgments

Many individuals have given me inspiration and assistance along the way. The first of these were Dr. Jennifer Brown of the University of Winnipeg and the late Dr John Foster of the University of Alberta. They were ably supported, in various capacities, by Drs. Michael Asch, Lesley Cormack, Gerhard Ens, David Hall, Kenneth Munro, Burton M. Smith, Donald Smith, Susan L. Smith, and Frances Swyripa. Research funding was provided by the Social Sciences and Humanities Research Council, the University of Alberta, and the Government of Alberta.

Various research facilities provided access to documents over the years. Father Lucien Casterman, Oblate Archivist, granted me permission to study the Oblate parish records in the Oblate Archives, the bulk of which are now housed in the Provincial Archives of Alberta in Edmonton. I also received assistance and permission to cite material from the late Alfred Fortier and his staff at the St. Boniface Historical Society Archives, Winnipeg; the Hudson's Bay Company Archives in Winnipeg, courtesy of Judith Hudson-Beattie, former Keeper of the Archives; and the Dawson Creek Public Library, holder of the Dorothea Calverley oral history collection. I would like to acknowledge all of these institutions, and their employees, for their help.

Wendy Johnson of Johnson Cartographics, Edmonton, Alberta, supplied the maps featured in this publication. Christi Belcourt, a Metis artist from Ontario, provided one of her pieces, "Infinity" for the cover. A variety of different archives supplied photographs, including the Glenbow Archives in Calgary, Alberta; the Provincial Archives of Alberta in Edmonton; the Saskatchewan Archives in Regina; and the St. Boniface Historical Society Archives in Winnipeg.

Several individuals shared their expertise with me over the course of my research, providing interesting and helpful information during our conversations and/or correspondence. They include Patricia Bartko, Ted Binnema, Geoff Burtonshaw, Olive Dickason, Harry Duckworth, Martha Harroun Foster, John Jackson, Ian MacLaren,

Elizabeth Macpherson, Tom Maccagno, Peter Melnycky, Gail Morin, Diane Payment, Carolyn Podruchny, Sherry Farrell Racette, Neil Reddekopp, Gordon Sinclair, Donald Smith, Tanis Thorne, Frank Tough, and Carl Urion.

There is a special group of people to whom I'm very grateful: a selection of Desjarlais family descendants from across Canada and the United States. Some have sent me family information, articles, genealogical charts, and photographs. Others have written across the Internet just to say "hi!" All have been interested in my progress. They include: Dick Boucher, northern California; Tom Bushery, Des Plaines, Illinois; Jack Chalais, Sacramento, California; Cindy Collins-Hogg, Livingston, Montana; Frank DeChalais, Rochester, New York; Michael Desjarlais, Albuquerque, New Mexico; Fred DeJarlais, Walnut Creek, California; Phil DeJarlais, Champlin, Minnesota; Dan Diserlais, Edmonton, Alberta; Dan DeJarlais, Minnesota; John P. DuLong, Berkeley, Michigan; Thérèse Lavigne, Orleans, Ontario; Hugh M. Lewis, U.S.A.; Sandy MacDonald, Edmonton, Alberta; Arthur Milot, Louiseville, Quebec; Anton Pregaldin, Clayton, Missouri; Larry Quinto, Ottawa, Ontario; Howard K. Thomas, Washington, D.C.; and Doreen Wabasca, Edmonton, Alberta.

Although the impetus for this book comes from my own research interests and personal background, I was hopeful that other people of Métis ancestry might also find it useful. I would like to thank Muriel Stanley-Venne, a long-time activist in the Alberta Métis community, for encouraging me to pursue this line of enquiry.

In some instances, the genealogical information presented in this study contradicts secondary sources that have been considered accurate in the past.[6] These revisions to standard genealogical understandings are based on my research and analyses of the primary and secondary documents cited in the notes and bibliography of the study. Any errors and omissions made in this regard are my responsibility.

My research has involved several years of effort that could not have been completed without the support of my family. I would like to thank my parents, my sisters Mary Lou and Lori, my cousin Art Fisher, and especially my husband Andy and daughter Lindsay.

Approaching the Stories of the Desjarlais Family: Methods and Goals

In 1985, Robert K. Thomas, in his afterword to the anthology *The New Peoples: Being and Becoming Metis in North America*[1] drew attention to the problems inherent in attempting to define who, or what, constitutes a Métis person. He delineated two important aspects of cultural identity:

> The first has to do with the content; the "what" of the "we" that which anthropologists generally call culture. The second concerns the more abstract dimension of collective identity, the question of nationality, that sense of common origin and common destiny felt even between strangers who live many miles apart.[2]

These issues of identity are not simply the stuff of scholarly debate, but have been of real importance to both historical and contemporary mixed-blood populations.

The process of Métis ethnogenesis, both historically and in the present day, remains poorly understood,[3] despite the efforts of researchers working in various regions of North America. Although new approaches to data analysis are being used, researchers still rely largely on a limited pool of documentary sources which suffer from their own intrinsic shortcomings. For example, few Métis-authored materials exist which address Métis history and origins. Most documentary sources were created by outsiders whose recording of events was influenced by their own economic preoccupations and cultural biases.[4] In these writings, the lives of the working classes of the fur trade are often almost invisible. As a result,

> ... dependence upon sources skewed in favor of literate and white or high-ranking employees has limited investigation and understanding of lower-ranking personnel and particularly of large numbers of seasonally or irregularly employed freeman

and native and Métis transporters, middlemen, provisioners, guides, and servants.[5]

Grace Lee Nute's *The Voyageur* was perhaps the first attempt to examine the social history of *Canadien engagés*.[6] Although Nute amassed a great deal of detail about the ordinary lives of voyageurs, too often the primary sources she quoted portrayed stereotypic, one-dimensional depictions of these men. Nute's uncritical acceptance of these descriptions has served to reinforce and entrench these stereotypes in the literature where they have persisted to the present day. More recent scholarship does address the topic of indentured labour in the fur trade, but these studies, with some exceptions, tend not to focus on *engagés* exclusively, but deal with them in the broader context of the social and demographic history of New France.[7]

What would prompt a *habitant* such as Joseph Desjarlais to enter the fur trade in the first place? What *Canadien* values, attitudes, and behaviours did *engagés* such as Desjarlais take with them into the interior? What cultural characteristics did they retain, and which did they discard? What social practices and cultural values did they and their Indian and métis wives pass on to their children? What factors motivated an *engagé* such as Desjarlais to remain in the interior rather than return permanently to New France or Lower Canada? Occasional descriptions of *engagés* can be found in the contemporary accounts of the merchants, military officers, and government officials who employed them. One of the earliest of these comes from Buade de Frontenac, Governor of New France, who defined an *engagé* in 1681 as "a man obliged to go everywhere and to do whatever his master commanded like a slave."[8]

Unfortunately, Frontenac's description of the experience of *engagés* fails to provide the familial context that governed the relationship of servants to those around them. Chapter 2 is devoted to examining the "psychological terrain" governing family formation in Europe and New France. More specifically, it examines the sociocultural milieu that prompted the enlistment of Jean-Jacques De Gerlaise as a soldier with the Carignan-Salières Regiment in France, and his subsequent migration to Canada in

1666. This overview is followed by an examination of the social and economic alliances that he and his family established in New France through marriage, friendship, and commerce during the French régime, and an investigation of the economic and social factors that influenced the Desjarlais family's involvement in the Montreal-based fur trade prior to 1760.

During the French régime, the settlement of the North American interior by *Canadiens* was a by-product of the imperial activities of the French government. The French authorities established diplomatic and economic (i.e., trading) relations with aboriginal groups in the Great Lakes and Illinois regions in the latter half of the seventeenth century and administered these territories from military outposts whose commanders were licensed to control the fur trade. *Coureurs de bois*, *engagés*, and soldiers established marital relations *à la façon du pays* with Native women in these regions, alliances that were monitored and regulated where possible by their religious and military superiors. Within one or two generations small settlements surrounded the colonial outposts, inhabited by *Canadiens*, their Native wives, and their children, who subsisted on seasonal small-scale agriculture, hunting, fishing, and fur trading with their aboriginal kin. As these communities became more established, their inhabitants were joined by *Canadien* friends and relatives from the parishes along the St. Lawrence River, a pattern of migration that did not alter appreciably until the British conquest of Quebec in 1760.

As early as the 1730s, French expeditions to the region which now comprises Western Canada were undertaken. Although individual soldier-adventurers such as La Vérendrye established forts, the French were not successful in establishing a permanent economic or political presence in this area. Conflicts with the Dakota, the defeat of the French in the Seven Years' War, and the assumption of control over the inland fur trade by the Hudson's Bay Company after 1760, disrupted the pattern of military penetration, aboriginal diplomacy, *métissage*, community formation, and migration from Quebec which had characterized French domination of the North American interior heretofore.

Chapter 3 investigates the individual and collective decisions of Desjarlais family members to migrate deeper into the *pays d'en haut*, placing them in the context of economic and social conditions in Quebec (later known as Lower Canada) between 1760 and 1830. During this period, out-migration of family members became a necessary and accepted part of rural life in Quebec, a response to overpopulation and diminished access to fertile agricultural land. Some branches of the Desjarlais family moved after 1763 to French settlements in the former French territory of Louisiana, and established themselves in the social and economic milieu of the St. Louis-based fur trade. The multiracial families that they and their relatives formed would be irreparably undermined, however, by the Anglo-American expansion westward.

Canadiens were involved in the northwest fur trade after 1760 as *engagés* with small trading companies based in Montreal or St. Louis. As the nineteenth century approached, increased competition between these companies and the Hudson's Bay Company offered opportunities for *Canadiens* who wanted to establish themselves as independent entrepreneurs in the *pays d'en haut*. The key to achieving this goal was to become a freeman.

A freeman was a former employee of a trading company who, having established a familial relationship *à la façon du pays* with a woman from a local Indian band, left the control of the trading firm to operate in a broker capacity among various Native bands and the different trading establishments in the *pays d'en haut*. During the period of intense commercial competition in the fur trade, between 1783 and 1821, *Canadien* freemen such as Joseph Desjarlais played an influential role in securing the trade of Native bands, achieving and enjoying a degree of personal and economic autonomy hitherto denied them as *engagés* in the British-controlled fur trade.

John E. Foster suggested that the behaviours and social relationships which gave rise to the Plains Métis occurred in the context of wintering, "as it was practised by Montreal-based fur traders in the last quarter of the eighteenth century." Foster argued that the origins of the western Plains Métis in the latter quarter of the eighteenth century were a function of "wintering" in the Montreal-based fur trade. Wintering laid the basis for relationships that, with the emergence of the freeman, would establish the "enculturation circumstance" necessary for some Native children to be raised apart from residential Indian bands. When these children married amongst themselves and established their own family units apart from Indian and Euro-Canadian communities, the Métis emerged as a distinct people.

Foster argued that three critical relationships had to be established in the context of wintering before Métis ethnogenesis could take place. These relationships were (1) the country marriage between an outsider adult male and an Indian woman of the band; (2) an alliance between the outsider male and the woman's extended male kin; and (3) friendships that bound outsider males in an economic and social relationship. Step (2) involved the outsider male making a conscious decision to go free – to separate himself from the trading establishment, and separate his wife from the Indian band. This enabled the enculturation of the freemen's children in an environment separate from both the trading establishment and the band. Although wintering was also practised by ethnic British or American traders and clerks, it was the *Canadien* and Iroquois *engagés*,[9] by and large, who chose to end their employment in the direct service of these trading companies and live independently. It is these labouring-class groups from which most Métis populations are derived.[10]

What would prompt an Indian band to consider an *engagé* as a potential kinsman? What characteristics of hunting band formation and dissolution influenced the manner in which Aboriginal peoples incorporated *engagés* and mixed-race children into their communities?[11] Answering these questions requires an understanding of how aboriginal kin groups work.

> Kin groups do not exist as things in themselves without regard to the rights and interests which center in them. Membership of such a group is not established by genealogy alone. Properly speaking, two individuals can only be said to be of the same kinship group when they share some common interest

– economic, legal, political, religious, as the case may be – and justify that sharing by reference to a kinship nexus.[12]

The determination of one's "group of orientation" is not based solely on biological descent, particularly in hunter-gatherer populations which have developed flexible kinship systems in response to their subsistence needs. Research on Dene kinship, for example, suggests that maintaining one's length of residence with a particular group during one's formative years, and maintaining one's residence with same-sex siblings throughout one's life, have a more significant influence on an individual's ethnic identification than mere biological ties.[13] Can these theories be applied to understanding the process of Métis ethnogenesis, and, more specifically, the experiences of *Les Desjarlais*?

Foster's article posited a framework for addressing several of the questions stated above. However, the scope of the article did not permit him to pursue his premises extensively. In order to do this successfully, it is necessary to identify an *engagé*, trace his migration into the interior, document his relationships with aboriginal women, and then study, in turn, the lives of his descendants to determine how social, political, and economic factors influenced the development of their ethnic identities. Chapter 4 takes on this task by tracing the involvement of various male members of the Desjarlais family in the Rupert's Land fur trade, first as *engagés*, and then as freemen in the Athabasca region between 1810 and 1821.

After the coalition of the Hudson's Bay and North West companies in 1821, a period of commercial monopoly existed in the northerly regions of Rupert's Land, far from American competition to the south. For many *Canadien* freemen and their Native families, the Hudson's Bay Company monopoly signalled an end to the opportunities they had experienced as brokers in a competitive milieu. Several families of freemen, among them members of the Desjarlais family, chose to leave the Athabasca region and migrate eastward. Some of these families settled in the newly established métis communities along the Red and Assiniboine Rivers, where they received their first exposure to Christianity.

From 1760 to 1818, the British authorities had steadfastly refused to permit Christian missionaries access to the *pays d'en haut*, for two reasons. One reason was that prevailing government policy in Quebec after the Conquest was to reduce the influence of the Roman Catholic Church, which was viewed as a threat to British authority that needed to be neutralized. Part and parcel of this policy was to deny the appointment of a Roman Catholic archbishop in Canada, which would have permitted the establishment of a Roman Catholic hierarchy in the settlements and frontier regions of British North America – this despite the fact that the British government promised to preserve religious freedom in Quebec.[14]

The second reason for discouraging access to missionaries – of all denominations – was the belief that Christianity was bad for business. Christianity led to a curtailment of activities (i.e., unions *à la façon du pays*, trade in liquor), which, while morally questionable, also benefited the trade. Christianity also led to increased agricultural settlement, which in turn diminished game populations and led to increased tension between Natives and Europeans. However, the violence and other social disorder that resulted as a consequence of commercial competition and the traffic in liquor prompted the officers of the Hudson's Bay Company to permit the establishment of missions at Red River, starting in 1818.[15] The presence of these missions, both Roman Catholic and Protestant, was instrumental in the development of distinct and separate corporate identities for the biracial people of Red River, whose social, economic, and political activities and interests evolved further and further away from those of their aboriginal relations in Native bands.

In the meantime, the lives of the members of the Desjarlais family still resident in Athabasca continued to be based on a boreal-parkland subsistence round of hunting and trapping in winter, fishing year-round, and buffalo hunting on the plains in spring and fall. Despite the presence of several individuals of biracial descent, the métis children of the Desjarlais family did not necessarily choose mates from other freeman families; some continued to select spouses from resident Indian bands.

A permanent Christian influence did not make its presence felt in the Athabasca region until the mid-1840s, a full twenty-five years, or one generation, after the arrival of missionaries at Red River. Chapter 5 details how the involvement of the Desjarlais in regional kinship alliances with aboriginal groups, and the migration patterns of Desjarlais siblings, influenced the ethnic identification of their descendants. It compares and contrasts the development of aboriginal identities in Athabasca with those of Red River between 1821 and 1869, explaining how ecological and religious factors dictated the economic, social, and political choices of family members.

After Canada took firm control of Rupert's Land following the Red River Resistance of 1869–70, the government sought to ensure a peaceful transition to agricultural settlement by negotiating land settlements with the various aboriginal groups. The government negotiators responsible for making treaties and awarding scrip were hampered, however, by their lack of knowledge and understanding of aboriginal cultures. In particular, they did not appreciate aboriginal perspectives concerning kinship, and the fact that treaty-making was viewed by Native peoples as a means of establishing and maintaining kin relations with outsiders – with all of the obligations and privileges that kinship entails.[16] Even more incomprehensible to the government representatives was the relationship between various métis groups and Indian bands. In Manitoba, numerous métis groups had evolved separate and distinct ethnic identities from their aboriginal cousins in residential Indian bands. However, the situation was different in parts of the North-West Territories and Assiniboia, the areas now encompassing Saskatchewan and Alberta. In these regions, particularly in the boreal forests of the north, métis people lived as part of aboriginal hunting bands, spoke aboriginal languages, and continued to choose spouses from either aboriginal or métis groups, as inclination or circumstance dictated.

When government representatives came to these regions to negotiate treaties, they did not enumerate métis groups separately, as it was not their initial intention to extend the offer of scrip to métis living outside of Manitoba. As a result, many métis living in Indian bands became signatories to Treaties Four, Five, and Six, and some became chiefs and headmen in these newly formed treaty bands.

Chapter 6 compares and contrasts the social, political, and economic responses of Desjarlais families in Manitoba to those resident in the North-West Territories *vis à vis* their signing of treaties or acceptance of scrip. In particular, Chapter 6 focuses on the response of various Desjarlais families to the 1885 Northwest Rebellion, exploring how their kinship obligations dictated the nature and extent of their participation in the conflict.

After the Canadian government successfully put down the North-West Rebellion of 1885, it implemented policies designed to subdue and pacify Western Canada's aboriginal population. One of the effects of government policy was the removal of métis people from Indian bands, and the enforced partition of Métis and Indian aboriginal claims in the North West Territories – a process reinforced, and refined, by the simultaneous negotiation and signing of Treaty Eight and the issuance of Métis scrip in 1899–1900. Chapter 7 focuses on how Indian Department regulations and judicial practices in Northern Alberta in late 1885 served to manipulate the decision-making process of mixed-race treaty Indians, inducing them to withdraw from treaty voluntarily and accept scrip, and explores the experiences of different members of the Desjarlais family who withdrew from treaty after 1885. Their subsequent attempts at agriculture and their migration westward and northward into the Peace River country to take treaty or scrip is documented.

Chapter 8 concludes that the divergent ethnic identities of various mixed-race branches of the Desjarlais family arose from diverse adaptations to changing ecological, social, political, and economic circumstances over time. Their diverse experiences illustrate a broadly based phenomenon of aboriginal ethnogenesis across Western Canada, where individual and collective identity formation evolved from a relatively fluid and self-directed phenomenon based on kinship to a more rigid, ascribed process shaped by Euro-Canadian government, religious, and economic policies.

Appendix 1 which follows is a brief overview of the primary and secondary sources used in this volume to reconstruct the Desjarlais family genealogy. Where appropriate, a critique of the strengths and weaknesses of these sources is provided, making reference to specific family branches. Appendix 2 is a detailed discussion of naming practices. Métis naming practices are an amalgam of Euro-*Canadien* and First Nations approaches to naming. For this reason it is important to elucidate the steps involved in accurately determining the identity of various Desjarlais in the historical record who share identical given names and surnames.

Appendix 3 explains how readers can access an on–line collection of genealogical charts, focusing on various Desjarlais families. This information, which also feature Appendices 1 and 2, will be posted to a website specially constructed for this purpose.

The issues investigated in this book parallel some broader currents of historical research on the family. Contemporary scholarship on families is concerned with the interaction of family groups with wider kinship networks, and with familial responses to religious, industrial, and educational institutions. Recent studies emphasize the agency of families in strategizing and pursuing varying courses of action in response to external forces, as opposed to their passive acquiescence to changing circumstances.[17]

Then there is the matter of considering aboriginal ethnicity.[18] Scholars of the "new" western history suggest that there is a "need to place the Native American experience within the context of ethnic history, considering tribal people as similar to emigrants exploited and oppressed by the Anglo-American majority."[19] Whether one agrees or disagrees with the idea of viewing aboriginal peoples as "exploited and oppressed," a perspective that treats *Canadien* freemen and their métis offspring as members of ethnic groups, negotiating and competing with other ethnic groups (both aboriginal and non-aboriginal) for power and resources, leads to a much more dynamic approach to the study of inter-group relations.

Another topic germane to both kinship and ethnicity is the role of gender in the process of forming ethnic identities. How are individuals' ethnic identities, and those of their children, influenced by choice of marital partner? Which parent has more influence in enculturating children? And how does gender complement or counteract the influences of race, social class, and proximity of kin in determining how (or whether) children identify themselves ethnically?

This book provides a bridge between the studies of the fur trade of pre-Conquest New France (which tends to focus on the activities of the French in the Great Lakes/Mississippi region), and those of the fur trade of Rupert's Land, or Hudson's Bay watershed. By and large, Quebec historians have chosen not to focus on *Canadiens* involved in the fur trade after 1760, particularly those situated in the west. English-Canadian researchers have tended to study the family and business relationships of the officer class involved in the post-Conquest fur trade of the Northwest. Until recently, few studies concentrated on *engagés*, or traced the progeny of *engagé* families over time and across regions either before or after 1760.[20] More broadly, the development of aboriginal ethnic identity among these families and their descendants has received little attention. This book seeks to remedy these problems and to contribute to new literature that addresses these concerns.

Data Collection and Analysis

One of the problems associated with Métis research is the difficulty in documenting the Métis working classes. Fur trade records were generated, for the most part, in a corporate context and deal primarily with business. The activities of Indian and Métis were selectively recorded based upon their relevance to the business at hand. The result is that there is a great deal of data on men's work activities, some discussion of the work of women, and little or nothing about the lives of children.

A second limitation of these sources is that the writers recorded what they saw from a Euro-Canadian, Christian, male, literate perspective. Rarely are the words of Indians and Métis quoted in these texts. Even more unusual is any discussion of the daily lives of the working classes as told by the participants themselves. We are forced to rely on the analyses of traders and missionaries who may have had little understanding of the values, attitudes, or behaviours of the people they describe.

A third barrier facing researchers is the restricted number of texts available from the Anglo/French period in the Canadian West. Compared to the Hudson's Bay Company records, relatively few documents survive from the North West Company because of the loss and destruction of many business records prior to the amalgamation of 1821.

After 1821, the organizational changes brought about as a result of the HBC-NWC coalition caused many *Canadien* and Métis employees to leave the concern. For example, when the Hudson's Bay Company revamped its transportation network, several hundred *Canadien* voyageurs lost their company positions. Many of the progenitors of Métis families became freemen after 1821, and maintained only sporadic connections to the Hudson's Bay Company. Consequently, researchers wishing to document the Métis encounter difficulties when tracing the activities of individual Métis freemen and their families outside the company context.

Families such as the Desjarlais were highly mobile. The social upheavals resulting from economic and political unrest, and the travel dictated by seasonal subsistence activities such as buffalo hunting, trapping, and freighting leave us with fragmentary and highly variable evidence about specific individuals or groups scattered across a wide geographical range, and recorded under a variety of circumstances. The areas occupied by the Métis ranged from the Great Lakes region westward and northward into the areas that became Alberta, Saskatchewan, Manitoba, and the Pacific Northwest. Biracial populations also emerged south of the Great Lakes, in what are now the American Midwest, southwest, and Great Plains regions of the United States. People researching

Métis populations are compelled to trace their subjects across immense areas.

A remarkable amount of primary data on these people can be derived from genealogical sources. The notarial records and church documents from Quebec, Ontario, the midwestern United States and Britain, combined with fur trade documents from the pre-coalition period, provide ample documentation for the French-Canadian and British patriarchs of Métis family lines. This information, combined with post-coalition HBC records, travel accounts, scrip affidavits, and the extensive church records amassed by Roman Catholic priests and Protestant missionaries in Western Canada provide an abundance of genealogical data spanning a period of well over two hundred years. Also, a number of genealogical collections devoted to Métis families are housed in several different repositories in Canada and the United States, prompting one historian to note that "for a largely illiterate people, the Métis are astonishingly well-documented for genealogical purposes."[21]

Genealogical reconstruction provides a framework for detailed study of families such as the Desjarlais, and enabled me identify kin groupings, to postulate sociopolitical alliances, to track the migrations of métis individuals and extended families into different regions, to examine the socioeconomic status of these families over time, and to trace the process of acculturation as they responded to changing socioeconomic circumstances and adopted Indian, Métis, or Euro-Canadian modes of behaviour to survive.

There are drawbacks, however, to relying solely on these compilations of data to generate assumptions about individual and group behaviour. Unlike the officers of the fur trade and their mixed-blood descendants, who generated business and private correspondence, diaries, books, and later, photographs, working class Métis operated, by and large, in an oral tradition. Therefore, the family recollections and heirlooms available to validate the data derived from compiling and processing masses of genealogical data are limited. In order to address this shortcoming, the research methodology consists of two components – genealogical reconstruction and historical analysis.

The genealogical reconstruction was necessary in order to accurately identify individual Desjarlais family members, differentiate between specific descendant branches of the family, and to place these individuals and family branches in specific geographical locales at different points in time. Once the family members were located in time and space, their activities were analysed using primary and secondary sources which placed these activities in cultural, economic, and political context.

Genealogical information – like other primary and secondary source data – must be gathered and interpreted with care. In genealogy, the approach to reconstructing family groups is to work from the present and move into the past.[22] The researcher begins by gathering as much information as possible from contemporary sources – surviving relatives and other informants, and various vital statistics – compiling enough data to establish a documented link between the living generation and past generations, whose ancestry can be further documented using various sources.

For this study, Métis scrip records, treaty paylists, and Roman Catholic parish records from Western Canada, Quebec, Missouri, and the French régime forts of the Great Lakes and Illinois region were used to identify family members and reconstruct the genealogy of the various family branches. To link the Desjarlais family branches in Rupert's Land, pre-1760 Louisiana, and Missouri to those of Quebec, the indexed notarial records of Quebec were consulted in order to identify specific male members of the Desjarlais family who signed engagement contracts for the *pays d'en haut* with various Montreal-based trading firms. Because the contracts in several notarial records identify the *engagés'* parish of origin, it was then possible to find the birth record for the *engagé* in the parish records, and continue the reconstruction of the family's genealogy back in time to the arrival of the first Desjarlais in New France.[23]

The genealogical information was compiled and entered into a genealogical computer software program called Reunion®,[24] which could generate family group sheets, ascending and descending pedigree charts, and statistical information. Once the genealogical reconstruction was more or less complete, it was possible to identify the geographical location of different descendant branches through time. Various historical, sociological, and anthropological sources were then used to document the various activities of the family members, and to place this information in a broader social, political, and economic context.

Although our understanding of the motivations of aboriginal populations is generally limited to the biased and selective ob-servances of non-Native writers, it is possible to make reasoned inferences concerning past human behaviours by an approach to analysis known as "controlled speculation." According to ethno-historian Frederic Gleach,

> ... controlled speculation involves the use of comparative material from other cultural or historical situations to infer crucial information that may be missing or obscured in the historical record of a particular situation; the comparative material is selected from contexts that appear closely analogous. The speculative inferences are thus controlled by being carefully and explicitly grounded in the ethnographic, historical, and/or archaeological records.[25]

Gleach observes that controlled speculation is inherently subjective, relying on the historian's knowledge of, and experience with, relevant ethnohistorical sources. However, in order to be truly authoritative, and gain some validity, ground rules must be established for speculation. Speculation must be based, wherever possible, on clearly identified, documented sources. These sources must not only have a reputation amongst scholars for reliability, but must be contextually relevant to the historical situation to which they are being applied. Criteria governing the use of comparative sources for controlled speculation include (a) the existence of a cultural practice or institution in the historical situation under study which lends itself to comparison with other contexts; (b) the existence of other human groups, preferably close in both physical and cultural proximity, for comparative purposes; (c) the existence of a similar phenomenon documented in a comparable context; and (d) the existence of contradictory evidence which might render the speculation invalid.[26] Controlled speculation permits a researcher to interpret, and draw conclusions regarding individual and group behaviour based on comparable cultural contexts elsewhere. This is particularly valuable when it comes to interpreting the behaviour of people who are given minimal attention in documents, such as aboriginal women or *engagés*. In this study, for example, understanding the responsibilities of kinship in aboriginal communities enables one to make valid inferences about the occurrence of certain types of behaviour (e.g., revenge killings or raids) based on kinship obligation, because these responses are well-understood, and practiced consistently, across a wide cross-section of aboriginal groups.

Conclusion

This book focuses first on how the kinship networks of the Desjarlais – in Euro-Canadian and Aboriginal contexts – influenced the social, economic, and political decisions of their members, and second, on how these networks and decisions ultimately shaped the ethnic identity and related collective rights that their descendants inherited as members of Indian or Métis communities.

In the *Canadien* settlements of New France, kinship influenced one's social class and occupation, and, in turn, one's choice of spouse and resultant acquisition of affinal kin. In Aboriginal hunter-gatherer groups, where authority was decentralized and personal autonomy prevailed, kin choices were flexible in order to adapt to the vagaries of the physical environment in which they lived. But in both the Euro-Canadian and Aboriginal communities, an individual's responsibility to ensure the protection and well-being of his family was of primary importance. Kin obligations generally superseded other commitments, resulting in social, economic, and political behaviours that, to the modern observer, may seem at times to be unfair, counter-productive, and even illogical.

Understanding how privileges and obligations of kinship operate in societal contexts, and accepting the idea that the actions of people in the past were often motivated by kinship obligations, is key to understanding Euro-Canadian and Aboriginal behaviours in the period prior to the twentieth century. That many of the descendants of both Euro-Canadian and Aboriginal groups continue to operate in the context of kin-based "communities of interest" today, makes this study both timely and appropriate.

2

·····················

The Social Contexts of Europe and New France

A full understanding of the process of Métis ethnogenesis is impossible without a thorough familiarity with the *mentalités* of the aboriginal and European groups that engendered Métis populations and with the contexts in which they arose. This investigation begins with an overview of the social, political, and economic contexts that influenced life in Europe, and prompted individuals such as Jean-Jacques De Gerlaise to migrate to the settlements of New France, where they reconstituted their interpersonal relationships in the North American context. The demographic profiles drawn from this information provide a basis for understanding the social values and economic strategies that prompted young men to engage in the fur trade, and encouraged some to remain in the *pays d'en haut*.

The Psychological Terrain of Early Modern Europe[1]

For individuals living prior to the onset of nation/state formation and widespread industrialization, the social world was narrowly defined, consisting of kin relations in home and village-based settings. One's country, or *pays*, was the "fatherland"; literally, the land of one's forefathers. The nature and extent of the "fatherland" changed over time, but originally it referred to one's village, the local working group, or the rural estate, and its limits were usually the distance an individual could walk overland in one day – approximately forty to fifty kilometres, or the area encompassing a mid-sized town and the land surrounding it. Transfer of elite control of different regions through inheritance or grants was common during the medieval and early modern period, and the local common people did not object – as long as local governing structures remained constant.[2]

To the people who fought, studied, bought and sold – the nobles, clerics, and merchants of early-modern Europe – the concept of the *pays* began to broaden to incorporate diverse peoples and distant regions, particularly after their discovery of the Americas. Rulers sought to consolidate their holdings in Europe, while extending their influence to Asia and North and South America. Increasingly their concept of nation – or *pays* – began to outstrip that of their subjects, who continued to view their world from a localized perspective. Even as local villagers and regional nobility entered "national" armies and travelled overseas to fight, their primary loyalties continued to be directed towards their immediate families, their neighbours, and their communities.

Between 1348 and 1354, an estimated one-third of the European population died from bubonic plague.[3] In the decades that followed, the population of Europe stagnated, but began a rapid recovery in the latter half of the fifteenth century. The end of the medieval period and the discovery of the New World broadened conceptual horizons and held forth the prospect of widespread economic prosperity in Western Europe. Between 1450 and 1600, Europe's numbers grew from fifty million to ninety million people without, unfortunately, a corresponding increase in agricultural productivity.

Between 1560 and 1600, a cooling of the climate in Europe resulted in harsher winters and cooler summers. This deterioration in the weather resulted in a series of crop failures, which in turn precipitated famines throughout western and central Europe.[4] The result was massive inflation affecting prices of basic foodstuffs and raw materials such as wheat and lumber. The influx of Spanish silver from the Americas further destabilized the economies of Europe by increasing the volume of money in circulation which, combined with crop failures, drove prices even higher. The amount of money available to the poor did not increase, however, resulting in widespread starvation.

Nor was Europe free from the devastation of disease. Since the fourteenth century Europe had been free of widespread pandemics, but near the end of the sixteenth century the bubonic plague appeared once again in force. The first was the most serious, spreading along the Atlantic coast from southern Spain to Northern Germany between 1596 and 1604. Then two lengthy epidemics struck in the years between 1625 and 1637, and 1647 and 1652. In France alone, it has been estimated that between 2,300,000 and 3,300,000 people died from plague between 1600 and 1670.[5]

After 1600, despite the plague, the population began to stabilize and increase once again. The importation of Spanish silver had decreased, but prices continued to outpace wages. These economic difficulties were further aggravated by political turmoil brought about by warring states attempting to enforce religious uniformity upon their peoples. Because the development of the printing press enabled ordinary people to produce and distribute printed material, the Roman Catholic Church was unable to impose its doctrines uniformly or prevent the spread of unorthodox social and religious ideas. The proliferation of competing religious and social ideas, printed in vernacular languages, accentuated cultural differences and prompted violent clashes between various factions throughout Europe. Sovereigns, in concert with various Protestant and Roman Catholic groups, responded by attempting to impose uniformity of belief in their subject populations during a period when political boundaries remained in a constant state of flux. The period of 1560–1660 has been described as Europe's "iron century" – a time when economic crises, religious strife, political turmoil and challenges to prevailing intellectual and moral assumptions created conditions for an almost constant state of war. Hostile armies crisscrossed the continent, killing, sacking, and burning with a ferocity that permanently imprinted itself on the family and community structures of early modern Europe.[6]

In modern times, the systematic collection and analysis of data from censuses, cadasters, and church registers has enabled demographers to reconstruct a persuasive portrait of the inherent instability of the European family during this turbulent period.[7] Intermittent wars, disease outbreaks, and famine killed large numbers of marriageable adults, which served to delay the onset of marriage, cut short existing marriages, and limit the numbers of children. Indeed, as Burguière and Lebrun conclude,

> One of the consequences of this high death rate for adults of all ages was that marriages were frequently curtailed. Widowhood and remarriage, the lot very often of the survivor, were common experiences: in the seventeenth and eighteenth centuries at least one marriage in four was a remarriage. In the absence of divorce, which did not exist either in Catholic countries or *de facto* even in Protestant ones, most marriages were terminated by death, which turned the family into a far less stable and protected unit than one might imagine. Quite the contrary. The chief feature of the traditional European family was its instability, the successive blows dealt it by death: the loss of infants whom their brothers and sisters could scarcely have had time to know, and the frequent ending of marriages by a husband's or wife's death.[8]

A typical woman of the period would have given birth to her last child by the age of forty; on average, she would have given birth to seven children in her lifetime. However, inherited defects, accidents, and infections would kill one child in four before its first birthday. Only two children out of four would survive to their fifteenth birthday. Of those individuals fortunate enough to survive to adulthood, poor diets would leave them vulnerable to death by disease.[9]

Emotional detachment was a by-product of unstable family relations. Serial marriages created "blended families," which generated the same kinds of familial conflicts associated with more modern varieties: tensions between step-parents and step-children, disputes over inheritance, and complex kin relationships.[10] The regularity of death created emotional estrangement between parents and children, and between siblings. Emotional detachment was further heightened by the frequent incidence of violence in peoples' daily lives, whether it be the casual application of corporal punishment to children and servants, or the sustained, public displays of torture and execution which were an integral part of institutionalized religious and civil doctrine.[11]

Despite the privations that characterized the lives of people, families and communities managed to survive amidst the chaos of sixteenth- and seventeenth-century Europe. For those individuals able to reach adulthood physically whole and emotionally resilient, patriarchal, hierarchical religious doctrines and civil codes had evolved to provide a measure of stability in the face of social upheaval.

Not all individuals sought after, or welcomed, the imposition of structure and authority, however. Many were able to thrive in an environment where traditional boundaries were permeable. Hitherto-unimaginable social and economic opportunities existed for those with the ambition, initiative, and courage to exploit them. Perhaps one of these people was Jean De Gerlaise – *déclassé* bourgeois, itinerant soldier, and early migrant to New France.

Enter Jean-Jacques De Gerlaise

The beginnings of the Desjarlais family in North America can be traced back to the arrival of one man, Jean-Jacques de Gerlaise dit St.-Amant (b. 1643), a soldier in the La Fouille Company of the Carignan-Salières Regiment, and the son of Ferdinand de Gerlaise, seigneur des Hameteaux and Dorothée Cona, residents of the parish of St.-Paul in the principality of Liège, now part of Belgium. Other than these sketchy biographical facts gleaned from his marriage contract, little is known about the origins of Jean de Gerlaise. His literacy, however, as well as the family and estate patronymics of himself and his father, indicates the likelihood of a respectable, landed family background.[12] Through the application of more general demographic and historical data, it is possible to recreate the "conceptual terrain" that governed his life, that of his family, and that of his associates in New France.[13]

Unlike that of De Gerlaise himself, the history of his military company, the Carignan-Salières Regiment, is well known to students of New France. Past historians, among them Abbé Lionel Groulx, Benjamin Sulte, Gérard Malchelosse, and Régis

Roy, have painted an idealized picture of the role of the regiment in saving New France from Iroquois annihilation, in the process transforming its soldiers into heroic knights fighting for France, for Catholicism, and for civilization. A more recent, revisionist study of the regiment portrays them for what they actually were – "a workaday seventeenth-century infantry unit sent to fight overseas" – comprised of ordinary foot soldiers who managed to prevail against the Iroquois despite the dangers, hardships, and incompetence they faced.[14]

The Carignan-Salières Regiment was formed in France in 1658 from the amalgamation of two regiments that had seen service during the Thirty Years' War and the war between France and Spain. By 1665, the regiment, comprised of twenty battalions, had been assigned defensive duties, being deployed along France's northeastern frontier. It is uncertain exactly when, or where, Jean de Gerlaise joined the Carignan-Salières Regiment, but it is probable that he enlisted at one of the garrisons on the northern French frontier, which abutted the neutral Principality of Liège, Gerlaise's home province, to the north.

Young men joined military regiments for a variety of reasons. Some came from a family tradition of military service, and enlisted because it was expected of them. Some recruits were debt-ridden, and trying either to meet or to flee from their financial obligations. Others, particularly rebellious young men, sought personal freedom from the social pressures of their families or villages. Protestants and other persecuted minorities sought the relative freedom and anonymity of the secular army ranks to minimize, if not avoid, discrimination. Still others were rootless individuals – orphans, vagrants, or widowers with no family network and no permanent home. And always, there were those who could satisfy their taste for violence and excess in the course of a military life.[15]

During this period, the sovereign would contract with members of the nobility to recruit regiments or companies on the Crown's behalf, providing each captain with a stipend for this purpose. Since the captain of the company was responsible for recruiting, feeding, clothing, housing, disciplining, and paying his soldiers, he assumed a form of ownership over his troops, and controlled virtually all aspects of their lives.[16]

Given the personalized nature of recruitment, and the diverse origins of the soldiers, it is not surprising that these companies developed an *esprit de corps* that reflected the personal loyalties and tastes of the captains rather than those of the king. Although French authorities took steps to dilute the influence of individual commanders by centralizing certain aspects of military administration,[17] it is probably true that the loyalties of individual soldiers were ultimately directed towards their captain and fellow soldiers, rather than to a distant ruler.

These conflicting loyalties became particularly apparent when Louis XIV, in response to repeated pleas from colonial officials to provide some defense against Iroquois attacks, assigned the Carignan-Salières Regiment to overseas duty in New France.[18] This decision was greeted with widespread disapproval by both the officers and the soldiers of the various companies that comprised the regiment. The officers in particular resented the prospect of overseas service in an isolated wilderness outpost, far from creature comforts and the spheres of political and social influence. Their response was to delay or avoid reporting for duty. Those officers who did muster troops did so reluctantly. Their negative attitudes infected the ranks, undermining soldier morale and weakening discipline. The result was a series of violent incidents between soldiers and townspeople as the various regimental units travelled across rural France towards their embarkation point of La Rochelle.

Jean de Gerlaise's unit, the La Fouille Company, was one of the army cadres in the regiment which gained notoriety through its bad behaviour in transit. Under the command of Jean-Maurice-Philippe de Vernon, Sieur de La Fouille, the company was below its fighting strength and needed additional recruits. When the company drummer, under orders from his commanding officer, attempted to attract potential recruits in the town of La Mothe-Saint-Héray, he was assaulted by the local magistrate and his drum confiscated. That night the drummer and some of his comrades responded by ambushing the magistrate and his companions in the street. Both sides were well armed, and in the street brawl that followed, the magistrate was killed outright and one of his companions later died of his wounds. As a result of the battle, five members of the company, including Lieutenant Philippe Gaultier de Comporté, Captain de Vernon's nephew, were sentenced to death *in absentia*.[19]

Other Carignan-Salières companies got involved in similar scrapes, prompting the French authorities to post armed guards in any villages through which the regiment was to pass in order to prevent further trouble on the way to the coast. Finally, the motley assortment of companies reached La Rochelle, where they were encamped on two offshore islands until their departure, a strategy intended to prevent desertions and keep the volatile soldiers and townspeople apart.[20]

In the spring of 1665, six shiploads of soldiers from the Carignan-Salières Regiment crossed the Atlantic, the first vessel disembarking at Quebec on 16 June 1665. By all accounts, the beleaguered residents greeted the troops with a great deal of enthusiasm, no doubt an unusual reception for the erstwhile delinquents.[21]

At the time of De Gerlaise's arrival, the population of New France was small; barely 3,500 French residents, including residents of Acadia.[22] Prior to 1663, settlement in the colony had been conducted under the auspices of commercial proprietors who were responsible for recruiting, transporting, and settling colonists in exchange for exclusive commercial monopolies.[23] Unfortunately, these settlement schemes were largely unsuccessful. Canada's harsh winters, the constant warfare with the Iroquois, and a limited economy based on the fur trade did little to attract colonists. Moreover, the French authorities never aggressively promoted emigration, because of a fear that mass migration to the colonies might depopulate France itself.[24]

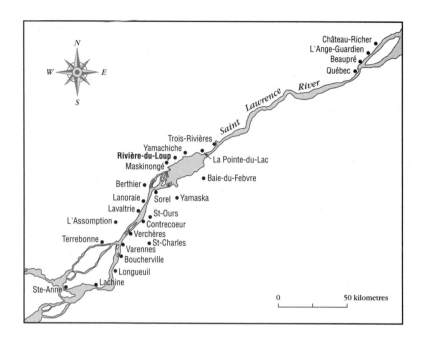

2.1. *Canadien* parishes on the St. Lawrence where Desjarlais family
members lived and worked

It has been estimated that no more than fifteen thousand
French immigrants came to New France before 1700. Of this
group, 10 to 15 per cent died in Canada without marrying, and
over half of the migrants eventually returned home to France.
Slightly over five thousand individuals remained in the colony to
start families.[25]

Those colonists who settled permanently in Canada were
those who had migrated with family members, or who established family ties with people already resident in the colony. The
other colonists who opted for permanent settlement in Canada
were those who lacked meaningful social and economic ties in
Europe.[26] This profile certainly describes the orphans and spin-
sters who comprised the *filles du roi*:[27] it also fits the religious
dissidents, disinherited sons, and worn-out career soldiers who
populated the companies of the Carignan-Salières Regiment.

When not constructing fortifications or raiding Iroquois
villages, the officers and the soldiers of the regiment remained

in the now-overcrowded settlements of Québec, Trois-Rivières, and Montréal. The officers performed the social duties expected of their class, which included their official presence at religious and legal functions. They also found time to engage in a variety of business ventures, including the sale of excess liquor, tobacco, clothing, and ammunition brought into the country for military use. The profits of this lucrative trade were used to purchase furs for resale in France. The common soldiers had neither the time nor the money to participate in these activities. Instead they lived and worked alongside the civilians, clearing land, bringing in the harvest, and constructing dwellings and fortifications.[28]

Although the king's intentions were never clearly communicated to the soldiers of the regiment, it was his desire to have the men stay in Canada. Not only would they be able to function in a fencible capacity, but also they would bolster the meagre population with their numbers and those of their children, should they marry and settle on a grant of land. Moreover, existing settlers were less likely to return to France if their daughters married soldiers and started families. Marriage was therefore actively encouraged between local women and soldiers.[29]

It is unlikely that Jean de Gerlaise's courtship and marriage to Jeanne Trudel, a *Canadien*-born resident of L'Ange le Guardien, was a love match. Although it was forbidden by both the church and state to force people to marry, nonetheless, considerable pressure could be brought to bear on a young couple when their union was seen to be in their families' best interests. Such was likely the case when Jean de Gerlaise, aged twenty-four, was betrothed to Jeanne Trudel, aged eleven, in 1667.

In 1666 and 1667, Philippe de Vernon, Sieur de La Fouille, was responsible for commanding the local militia of the Côte de Beaupré as well as captaining his own company, the La Fouille Company, within the Carignan-Salières Regiment. While stationed in the area, de Vernon acted as sponsor for the baptism of one Philippe Trudel, son of Jean Trudel and Marguerite Thomas, who were two of the *censitaires* resident on merchant-colonizer Robert Giffard's seigneury. It is probable that de Vernon took steps to introduce his young Liègeois recruit, Jean de Gerlaise, to Marguerite (Thomas) Trudel once he discovered that she came from the village of Stavelot, in the Principality of Liège.[30]

In the seventeenth century there were but a handful of Belgians in New France. Only twenty-seven individuals from the Belgian provinces were present in Canada by 1700, the bulk of them military personnel like Jean de Gerlaise, followed by a lesser percentage of clergy.[31] At a time when village and regional affiliations were virtually synonymous with kinship, the arrival of Jean de Gerlaise must have been the answer to a mother's dreams; in this case, those of Marguerite Trudel.

It is probable that Marguerite Thomas Trudel was already familiar with the de Gerlaise patronym, an old, extended, and respected family in the Principality of Liège.[32] Although de Gerlaise probably lacked the necessary documentation to establish his links to titled members of the de Gerlaise family, he was undoubtedly respectable, as evidenced by his literacy. He had the direct endorsement of his commanding officer, the man who had recruited him for overseas service. There were no known blood ties to complicate the union. Moreover, he would receive money from the king and a plot of land once he agreed to stay in Canada.[33] What more could a mother ask?

The purpose of marriage in most early modern families, from the landed aristocracy to the peasantry, was to establish alliances that would accumulate, manage, divide, and transfer property in the most efficient and equitable way, for the purposes of maximizing the fortunes of one's immediate and extended family. The ideal union provided upward social or economic mobility as a "trade-off" for the spouses, and did not violate social or religious taboos.[34]

Because the economic, social, and political implications of marriage were so significant, the authorities sought to exercise as much control over unions as possible. By the beginning of the six-teenth to the end of the eighteenth century, the process of family formation in France and its possessions was covered under royal legislation, which sought to regulate marriage and inheritance practices in order to protect individual and community interests and honour the teachings of the Roman Catholic Church.

According to Maureen Molloy, "the social organization of kinship and marriage in New France was produced from a cultural template drawn from the Old World."[35] Marriages in the settlements did not take place without the consent of the authorities.

> Louis XIV, by ordinances of 1649 and 1667, confirmed the basic requirements insisted upon by the church: reciprocal consent of the contracting parties; consent of the parents or guardians; public celebration of marriage with witnesses and the benediction of the priest at the exchange of the marriage vows; and proper registration of marriages. The church, for its part, insisted on parental approval, on the observance of the canons respecting consanguinity and affinity, on the publication of banns over three successive Sundays prior to the nuptial Mass, and on having the bride and groom inter-rogated and instructed in their duties and responsibilities by a parish priest beforehand. The Seminary of Quebec gave its priests a list of points to discuss with young men planning to be married. This advice to prospective bridegrooms included the admonition to set aside all desires of fortune, ambition, and sensuality; to choose a partner whose piety, gentleness, modesty, cleanliness, frugality, and obedience to her parents were well-known; not to court several girls at once and not to make rash promises; to obtain the consent of both sets of parents and, in case of opposition, to avoid threats and schemes; never to remain alone with the intended spouse "for only those who wish to do evil seek out darkness"; to pray frequently for guidance; and to beware lest human affections should replace the first love due to God.[36]

Irregular unions were considered a scandal, and the vast majority of couples did not resort to these practices. To do so would be to violate the most important bonds of all, those of family obligation. As J. F. Bosher has noted, the family unit was "a business or agricultural unit with every member expecting to live on the family wealth and in turn expected to take part in the family enterprise. It was also a social enterprise in which every member tried to assist in the advancement of the whole. Families climbed socially like ivy up a wall."[37]

For families with daughters, the onus was on the parents to provide an attractive dowry to lure a prospective spouse. Without a dowry, a woman was likely to remain unmarried. But although the woman's family was expected to supply the dowry, the actual value of the dowry itself was always open to negotiation. Trade-offs were made in the bargaining between families; a certain degree of wealth was worth a certain level of social respectability or patronage in return.[38] The culmination of these business deals (for that is what they were) was the preparation of the marriage contract, which would be drawn up and signed in front of a royal notary by the betrothed, in the presence of their parents and assorted other witnesses prior to the church ceremony itself.

The contract itemized all of the movable property owned by each party on the day of the marriage, which became part of the "community of goods" or total assets, movable and immovable, acquired and owned jointly by the couple during their marriage. Although the husband managed the joint property during the marriage, he was expected to do so in an honest and prudent fashion. The wife could renounce the "community" as detailed in the contract, and take back any property she acquired before or during the marriage, together with the dowry paid to the groom by her parents before the marriage and the *préciput*. The *préciput* was a fixed sum of money, stipulated in the contract, which was payable to the wife at her husband's death or as annual installments during her lifetime. Contracts would also stipulate the division of property amongst children of the couple's union, as well as the inheritance of children from either spouse's previous marriages.[39]

The marriage contract between Jean de Gerlaise and Jeanne Trudel was witnessed and signed on 12 September 1667 in the presence of Claude Auber, the royal notary of New France. It was a sign of social distinction to have individuals of rank attend the signing of the marriage contract.[40] It also symbolized the official sanction of the marriage by the community at large.

The guests representing the groom's "side of the family" were the officers of the La Fouille Company of the Carignan-Salières Regiment.[41] They included Jean-Maurice-Philippe de Vernon de La Fouille, captain of the La Fouille Company; Pierre Ferré de Lespinay, lieutenant of the La Fouille Company; and Charles du Jay,[42] knight, Sieur de Manereuil, Seigneur de Grand Rosoy, and ensign of the La Fouille Company. The bride's witnesses were a cross-section of the nobles and *censitaires* of the Beauport Seigneury originally established by Robert Giffard. They included her parents, Jean Trudel and Marguerite Thomas; Joseph Giffard,[43] knight, Seigneur de Beauport; Jean Juchereau, knight, Sieur de La Ferté,[44] Nicolas Juchereau, knight, Sieur de St. Denis[45]; Demoiselle Marie Giffard, wife of Nicolas Juchereau; Demoiselle de Carion[46]; Jacques Vésina; Charles Grenier; Jacques Maret dit Lépine; René Brisson; René Oudain; and Nicolas Le Roy.

In addition to the shared property itemized in the document, the contract stipulated that the bride's parents would support the couple for a period of one year, and that Jeanne Trudel's father would work for a period of six weeks on the couple's house. The groom responded in kind, presenting his intended spouse with a wedding ring of solid gold. In order to satisfy the authorities of the validity of the union, the contract further stipulated that the bride (who was considered to be extremely young for marriage even by seventeenth century standards)[47] was "big and strong" for her age![48]

Despite the sanctioning of the union, it should not be assumed that the marriage was consummated immediately. It was not uncommon in the late medieval and early modern period for betrothals of infants to take place, with the understanding that the sexual aspects of the union would occur when both partners had reached a suitable degree of maturity. The prolonged absences of the groom, who continued his military career after the wedding, would have prevented the young couple from establishing a separate home from the Trudel family for some time after their church union.[49]

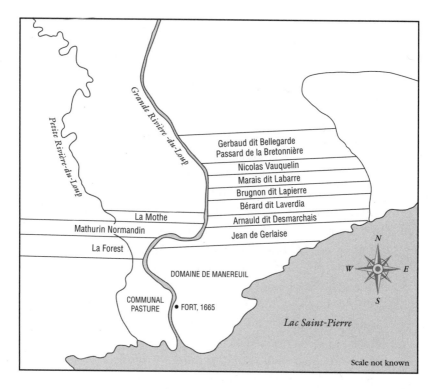

2.2. Riverlots at Rivière-du-Loup (Seigneurie de Manereuil, ca. 1671)

De Gerlaise's plot of land was situated on the seigneury at Rivière-du-Loup, a settlement approximately twenty kilometres west of Trois-Rivières.[50] It was here that Charles du Jay, Vicomte de Manereuil, the ensign of the Carignan-Salières Regiment, had been granted the fief and seigneury of Rivière-du-Loup, and where several former soldiers from the regiment received concessions.[51]

Unfortunately, conditions on the seigneury did not lend themselves to the pursuit of agriculture by its *censitaires*. A problem that plagued the seigneurial system from its beginnings was the frequent absence of its seigneurs. Although the French government was extremely generous in its land grants to former military officers, the isolated colony offered few other attractions that might retain ambitious men. Consequently, many officers returned to France rather than settle in a harsh wilderness with few creature comforts and almost no marriageable Frenchwomen.

Both Jean-Maurice-Philippe de Vernon de La Fouille, captain of the La Fouille Company and Pierre Ferré de Lespinay, lieutenant of the La Fouille Company, chose to return to France after the Carignan-Salières Regiment was disbanded. The next officer eligible to be granted land was the company's ensign, the Vicomte de Manereuil. He, too, sailed for France by 1692, the year when the king officially granted his fief. Although his visit to France was probably intended to be a temporary one, Manereuil did not return to New France. Without a resident seigneur, no new concessions of land could be granted to incoming *censitaires*, nor could existing settlers receive additional agricultural land.[52] Therefore, the population remained low for several years, and agricultural development was minimal.[53]

However, this did not discourage other sorts of economic activity. The fur trade continued to provide a steady source of income for those individuals who could acquire the needed licences and trade goods. Like most economic activity in Rivière-du-Loup, the grassroots fur trade was a community-based, family-oriented enterprise, administered at a distance by a succession of powerful trading companies who had been granted monopolies by the French government to purchase furs from traders.

By the 1690s, the French trading territories extended to the far western edge of the Great Lakes and south to the Mississippi delta. This vast region was administered from a handful of military forts situated at strategic points along lakeshores and river junctions. In some cases, the government authorities traded directly with Native people from the posts. In other cases, the military commanders placed in charge of distant posts were those who were conceded control of a specific trading territory, thereby controlling the fur trade in their jurisdiction in addition to their military responsibilities. However, small local trading companies and individual merchants could also enter the *pays d'en haut* and trade directly with the Indians – providing, of course, that they possessed a valid *congé de traite* – a trading passport, which permitted the bearer to send a canoe with trade goods and *engagés* into the hinterland to trade.[54]

The fur trade required strict regulation by the authorities. As the only truly profitable industry in New France, it provided the disposable income needed to purchase imported luxuries from France. It enabled young men to accumulate the money needed to establish households apart from their parents – a necessary precursor to marriage. It also provided a means of redistributing income to those in need. Trading passports were issued to poor families (often widows with children) who could then dispose of the passport as they saw fit. They could choose to sell the *congé*, which was worth one thousand pounds, or they could keep the *congé* and outfit a trading expedition in partnership with close relatives and friends.[55]

In the early days of the French régime, the fur trade was viewed as a lucrative and effective instrument of diplomacy. Because the authorities were confident that their culture and religion would prevail over that of the Amerindians, they failed to anticipate the possible negative consequences of closer economic and social relations with Amerindians, particularly those of *métissage*. Intermarriage was promoted, initially, by both the civil and religious authorities as a means of creating "one people" through church-sanctioned unions, a non-violent approach to conquest and occupation of foreign territory. Because marriages could not be consecrated between Christians and infidels, baptism of Amerindian brides contributed to achieving the Christianizing goals used to justify France's presence in North America. A policy of intermarriage also addressed the need to provide a sanctioned outlet for sexual activity in a society with few European women. If the colony was to survive, its population needed to stabilize and expand. This goal could only be achieved if colonists married and established families.[56]

Unfortunately, the authorities underestimated the appeal of Amerindian life. The young men who went to live with the Natives often contracted marriages *à la façon du pays* without church sanction. Such unions were attractive because they provided the economic and personal functions normally provided by a wife without the permanence demanded by church doctrine. The responsibility for the children was, more often than not, assumed by the Amerindian woman and her extended family, though the French father could acknowledge and support his métis children as individual circumstances and inclination dictated.

Although the local authorities were well aware of the diplomatic and economic benefits to be had from French interpreters and traders who chose to live *en derouine* with Native groups, they were not pleased with the detrimental impact of the trade on social order in the colony. The vast uninhabited spaces, the scattered population, and the physical and social demands of life in the wilderness contributed to an unseemly and dangerous lack of social conformity and a tendency to defy authority. The colonists adopted "uncivilized" forms of dress and diet. Others chose to defy the government more openly, ignoring the threat of fines or imprisonment to trade illegally in the interior. Voyageurs cohabited openly with Native women in the remote settlements, in defiance of clerical teachings.

Marriage, children, and a sedentary agricultural life in a traditional Christian community were the ideals in a society where family relationships were inextricably tied to work and the accumulation of property.[57] Although the marital connections with Indian women and their extended families were essential to the fur trade (and therefore did contribute to the economic prosperity of *Canadien* fur trading families) such unions did not fulfil the social functions of marriage – one of which was increased respectability through enhanced social status. Marriages *à la façon du pays* (even those which were later "regularized" via a church ceremony), and the adoption of aboriginal customs and practices that came as a by-product of fur trading, were tolerated for the sake of commerce and diplomacy. They rarely, however, achieved any degree of social respectability or acceptance.[58] Indeed, they were considered a threat to the social fabric of the nation. Consequently, the French authorities sought to implement regulations that would permit the fur trade to proceed but limit the amount of irregular behaviour that accompanied it.

Prior to 1666, for example, only *censitaires* permanently settled on concessions were permitted to engage in the fur trade for their private profit. This restriction was based on the belief that the demands of a farm required the assistance of a wife and children, who in turn required the regular presence of a husband and father for support and protection.[59] After 1666, a regulation forbidding unmarried single males from engaging in trade was also enacted. When expeditions of exploration or trade were launched into the *pays d'en haut*, every effort was made to establish a religious and administrative presence on-site, to prevent, or at least discourage, social excesses from occurring.

The fur trade was an almost irresistible attraction to ex-soldiers who had received land grants for military service, particularly at Rivière-du-Loup. The opportunities for money and excitement overshadowed the obvious hardships and risks involved. Veterans with combat experience and exposure to wilderness conditions made ideal trading personnel, and they eagerly sought trading capital and employment from their former commanding officers, many of whom were already active in business.

The closest large settlement to the Maneureil concession, Trois-Rivières, was one of the major centres for the seventeenth-century fur trade, being one of the sites where annual Indian trading fairs were held.[60] It was also the home of the earliest and most prominent *coureurs des bois* and explorers active in the interior.[61] Many former soldiers chose to be part-time farmers, working their small plots of land for a brief part of the year and trading furs the rest of the time, leaving their wives and children to manage the farm. Needless to say, the absence of a seigneur to demand agricultural dues did not encourage these *censitaire*-traders to practise agriculture seriously.[62]

Several of the nine households resident in the siegneury at Rivière-du-Loup in 1681 avidly participated in the fur trade, as part of a closely-knit network that revolved around the LeMaître family, a large and extended merchant family headed by its controversial matriarch, Judith Rigaud. Judith Rigaud, born in 1633, was an educated servant of Huguenot ancestry who crossed the Atlantic to enter the service of Marguerite LeGardeur, wife of Jacques LeNeuf de la Potherie, governor of Trois-Rivières, and acting governor of New France, in 1652. By the spring of 1654, Judith Rigaud had married François LeMaître dit Le Picard, a soldier of the Trois-Rivières garrison. Witnesses to their wedding included the Godefroys, one of the most influential families in Trois-Rivières, and the bride's employers, the LeNeufs. The groom was represented by his military commanders and comrades, including one Sieur Médard Chouart des Groseilliers, a sergeant-major at Trois-Rivières who also acted as a voyageur and interpreter, and was soon to become one of the best-known fur traders of his era.[63]

At the urging of his wife and his friend Médard Chouart, François LeMaître left the army and entered the fur trade. The profits enabled the couple to raise their growing family of seven children in relative affluence. In 1665, Judith Rigaud, pregnant with her eighth child, left Quebec for the French port of La Rochelle to establish commercial relations with the financiers and wholesale merchants of that city.[64] In her absence, her husband was murdered, and her children taken in by their uncle, Antoine LeMaître dit Lamorille. Rigaud quickly found a new husband, Jean Therrien du Ponceau dit Duhaime, and proceeded to sell assets to repay a mountain of debt.[65]

By 1670 Judith Rigaud was a widow again, having lost her husband after his accidental death on a trading expedition in the fall of that year. Left with three small Therrien sons, she remarried a third time, in 1675, to Jean LaPlanche, a surgeon who had recently arrived in New France.

In early 1676 Judith Rigaud's daughter, Marie LeMaître, married Jacques Passard, Sieur de la Brettonnière, a *censitaire* at Rivière-du-Loup. Passard was a veteran of the DuGué Company of the Carignan-Salières Regiment. He entered the fur trade with two other former soldiers; Paul Guyon dit Letremblade of the La Fouille Company, and Christophe Gerbaud dit Bellegarde, another La Fouille veteran who had also married a daughter of Judith Rigaud and settled at Rivière-du-Loup.[66] By 1678 Jean Laplanche had returned to France after Judith Rigaud, his wife, deserted him to live with Pierre Cavelier, a man to whom he had leased some farmland. The illicit couple was hounded by creditors, whose agents were threatened and chased off the farming lease by Judith Rigaud, wielding a pitchfork. In 1679, the scandalized authorities in Montreal banished Judith Rigaud from Montreal for ten years, on pain of corporal punishment.[67]

Rigaud prudently left Montreal to live on the seigneury at Rivière-du-Loup, where two of her sons already had grants of land. She resumed her fur trading activities in concert with her sons, and her sons-in-law, who had as much difficulty staying on the correct side of the authorities as Rigaud did herself. In 1681 Jacques Passard and Christophe Gerbaud dit Bellegarde were both arrested by the authorities for illegally trading with the Indians. They were fined two hundred pounds and had their weapons and canoes confiscated and sold. This did not deter the two, who purchased provisions from the merchant Joseph Petit dit Bruno and carried on with the trade shortly thereafter. Later, Gerbaud dit Bellegarde entered a clandestine partnership with Petit dit Bruno, Médard Chouart des Groseilliers, Pierre Esprit Radisson and other prominent merchants to trade furs illegally in the Gaspé Peninsula, launching their vessels from the coast of France.[68]

Because of Judith Rigaud's multiple marriages and her considerable involvement in the fur trade, few, if any, of the *censitaires* at Rivière-du-Loup were free of her family's influence. Most of the residents of the seigneury, including the de Gerlaise family, became connected to the LeMaîtres by marriage as time went on. The commercial opportunities in the fur trade created by Judith Rigaud and her associates offered a source of extra prosperity, if not notoriety, to the community as a whole.

Unlike many of his former comrades-in-arms, Jean-Jacques de Gerlaise left no evidence that he participated in the fur trade. It is curious that de Gerlaise turned his back on the trade and ignored this potential source of income, especially when military and commercial endeavors offered the only real opportunities for economic and social mobility in this stratified society.[69] However, it appears that this is precisely what he did. Content to farm his concession and stay close to home, de Gerlaise, as one of the few full-time farmers in the area, rented the concessions of other *censitaires* who were involved in trade, and farmed their land in their absence.[70] In the spring of 1683, when a new seigneur, Jean Le Chasseur, was conceded the fief of Rivière-du-Loup,[71] De Gerlaise was granted two river lots, perhaps in recognition of his agricultural efforts.

Although the new seigneur was active in administering his fief, his tenure was short. In 1686 Le Chasseur was appointed to oversee the administration of civil and criminal law in Trois-Rivières, a responsibility that took him away from his seigneury. By May of 1688, Le Chasseur had sold his fief and its associated judicial rights to the famous fur trader, interpreter, and diplomat Nicolas Perrot, for four thousand livres worth of beaver furs.[72]

Prior to and during his tenure as seigneur of Rivière-du-Loup, Nicolas Perrot gained prominence in New France as a result of his talents in aboriginal diplomacy. He was one of those responsible for negotiating the entrance of France's native allies into the war against the Iroquois, who, with backing from the British, had resumed their war against the French in 1684. He was the mediator in peace negotiations between the Fox and the Ojibwa. He opened a trading post in the country of the Sioux, and served as interpreter when the French negotiated peace with the Onondagas. Unfortunately, Perrot's purchase of the Rivière-du-Loup seigneury coincided with a particularly vicious upsurge in Iroquois attacks along the St. Lawrence. Perrot was compelled to spend his time in the west, maintaining peace among France's allies while the French fought a bitter defensive battle against Iroquois raiding parties who kept the settlements under constant siege.[73]

While their absentee seigneur negotiated, his long-suffering *censitaires* at Rivière-du-Loup defended themselves as best they could. The men of Rivière-du-Loup had already spent the summer of 1687 away from their concessions, fighting under the command of the Marquis de Denonville, whose clumsy attempt at a counteroffensive against the Iroquois served merely to intensify their raiding activity. By the summer of 1688, the situation had grown so desperate that several families fled temporarily to Trois-Rivières and Montreal after two *censitaires* were ambushed and killed, and the seigneur's manor burnt. By the fall of 1688 only four *censitaires* remained with their families; Jean De Gerlaise, François Bergeron, Marin Marais, and François Banhiac.[74] These families, who engaged in agriculture full-time with farm buildings, animals, and crops to protect, had much more to lose than those whose primary occupation was trade.

The years that followed held more of the same. In August of 1689 the Iroquois destroyed the settlement of Lachine and immolated many of its inhabitants within view of the ramparts of Montreal. In the summer of 1690 at Sorel and the island of Montreal, Iroquois raiders took captives whom they killed in sight of pursuing French militia. The following October, the British admiral Sir William Phipps laid siege to Quebec City, an assault repulsed by Frontenac. The following spring the Iroquois raids resumed on both sides of the St. Lawrence River. The settlements of Saint-Ours and Contrecoeur were burnt, and war parties penetrated the islands near Verchères. The settlements of Boucherville, Yamaska, and Trois-Rivières were all attacked.[75]

During this period, agricultural work came to a virtual standstill, resulting in shortages of corn and wheat. It was impossible to venture outdoors to work in the fields without armed guards. *Censitaires* were forced to move from one fortified building to another. During the summer of 1692, despite all of their precautions, six young men were captured by Iroquois raiders at Rivière-du-Loup.[76] Surprisingly, a semblance of normalcy still managed to prevail. In the face of dislocation, food shortages, and the threat of attack, the tiny population of Rivière-du-Loup continued to grow, as the *censitaires* took wives and children were born.[77] Some absentee settlers, defying the odds, continued to traffic in furs from their temporary bases in Trois-Rivières and Montreal![78]

By November of 1698 the French finally prevailed against the Iroquois, and a treaty was negotiated, followed shortly thereafter by the death of Governor Frontenac. In the wake of the treaty, the former seigneur of Rivière-du-Loup, Jean Le Chasseur, launched a lawsuit against Nicolas Perrot due to his failure to pay the four thousand-livre price promised for the seigneurial fief in 1688. The court at Trois-Rivières ruled in Le Chasseur's favour, and declared the 1688 contract null and void.[79]

The onset of peace and the return of Jean Le Chasseur as seigneur of Rivière-du-Loup signalled a return to relative calm. Although a couple of families chose not to return to their concessions, the majority of *censitaires* returned, joined by new settlers who were awarded the river lots vacated by those who had died or left the region. By 1701 Jean Le Chasseur sold his seigneury once again, but this time to a younger man, Michel Trottier dit Beaubien, who was able and willing to maintain permanent residence.

Michel Trottier dit Beaubien (b. 1672) was the son of Antoine Trottier dit Desruisseaux, a merchant and seigneur, and Catherine Lefebvre. While Michel Trottier chose to purchase and develop a parcel of land as a seigneur, three of his brothers worked for various periods in the fur trade.[80] Although two of the brothers began as lowly *engagés*, they eventually became merchants in their own right, establishing a firm foothold in the business community for the Trottier family. By the mid-eighteenth century, five of Michel Trottier's nephews numbered among the largest outfitters in Montreal.[81]

The Seigneurie Beaubien, as the small settlement of Rivière-du-Loup was officially called, was a closely-knit community. Although the lack of a resident seigneur in its formative years, combined with the isolation and hardships imposed by more than a decade of warfare, had limited its physical expansion, the community had survived virtually intact. With the exception of a handful of newcomers introduced by Seigneur Trottier dit Beaubien, the settlement retained most of its original *censitaires*, their wives and their children, who had now reached marriageable age. In keeping with local tradition, Jean-Jacques de Gerlaise and Jeanne Trudel did not venture far afield in search of marriage partners for their children. Instead, they established

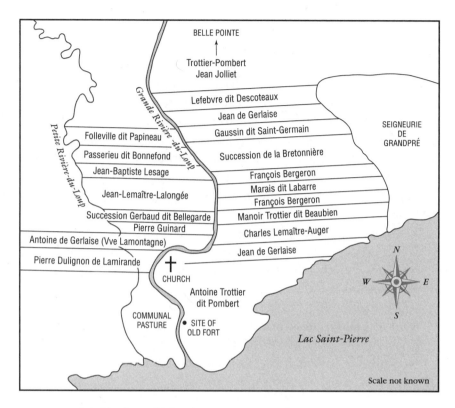

BELLE POINTE

Trottier-Pombert
Jean Jolliet

Grande Rivière-du-Loup

Petite Rivière-du-Loup

Lefebvre dit Descoteaux

Jean de Gerlaise

Folleville dit Papineau

Gaussin dit Saint-Germain

SEIGNEURIE
DE
GRANDPRÉ

Passerieu dit Bonnefond

Succession de la Bretonnière

Jean-Baptiste Lesage

François Bergeron

Marais dit Labarre

Jean-Lemaître-Lalongée

François Bergeron

Succession Gerbaud dit Bellegarde

Manoir Trottier dit Beaubien

Pierre Guinard

Charles Lemaître-Auger

Antoine de Gerlaise (Vve Lamontagne)

Jean de Gerlaise

Pierre Dulignon de Lamirande

✝
CHURCH

Antoine Trottier
dit Pombert

COMMUNAL
PASTURE

● SITE OF
OLD FORT

Lac Saint-Pierre

N
W   E
S

Scale not known

2.3. Riverlots at Rivière-du-Loup (Seigneurie de Beaubien), ca. 1709

even closer ties to the neighbours and friends with whom they had fought, farmed, hunted, and traded.[82]

By the third generation of the Desjarlais family's presence in Canada, the marital connections made by Jean De Gerlaise's daughters facilitated the entrance of their Desjarlais nephews into the fur trade.[83] Jean De Gerlaise's eldest surviving daughter, Jeanne (b. 1679, d. 25 November 1771) married Pierre Benoist dit La Forest in 1705. Son of Gabriel Benoist dit La Forest, a concessionnaire-turned-landowner near Trois-Rivières, Pierre Benoist and his elder brother Gabriel had moved to Baie-St. Antoine to take a farming concession in 1687 after the death of their father. However, both entered the fur trade shortly thereafter. In 1693 Benoist's brother Gabriel engaged as a voyageur for the Mississippi explorer and trader Henri de Tonty,[84] an associate of La Salle. He later contracted to trade in the Ottawa country. Pierre followed suit, farming and contracting with a number of different trading concerns for a period of close to ten years. In the interim their widowed mother, Anne Guesdon, had married Marin Marest dit Labarre, a former soldier of the La Fouille Company of the Carignan-Salières Regiment who lived as a *censitaire* at Rivière-du-Loup. It is probable that his mother's remarriage and settlement in Rivière-du-Loup provided the opportunity for Pierre to meet and to marry Jeanne De Gerlaise by 1705.[85]

Another daughter, Marguerite De Gerlaise, married Pierre Dulignon de Lamirande, a sergeant of the Cabanac Company who had recently been granted a concession at Rivière-du-Loup by Michel Trottier dit Beaubien. Pierre Dulignon de Lamirande was the elder brother of Huguenot nobleman Jean Dulignon, Sieur de La Mirande.[86] Jean Dulignon had been part of LaSalle's expedition to the Gulf of Mexico, having participated in the erection of a column and cross at the mouth of the Mississippi near the Gulf of Mexico on 9 April 1682, whereby the region was formally claimed by France.[87] Jean Dulignon's wife, Marie Testard de Folleville, came from one of the most prominent military families in New France.[88]

The two remaining daughters, Marie-Anne and Marie-Josephte, also married *censitaires* at Rivière-du-Loup.[89] Marie-Anne De Gerlaise married Jean Brisard dit Saint-Germain, a former soldier with the La Durantaye company of the Carignan-Salières Regiment. Marie-Josephte De Gerlaise married Jean-Baptiste Lesage, a former resident of Quebec City.

Of the two surviving sons in the De Gerlaise family, only one, Jean-François, left descendants to carry on the family name. Antoine, the elder surviving son, married Marie-Angélique Pelletier. She was the widow of François Banhiac de Lamontagne, a veteran of the La Fouille Company of the Carignan-Salières Regiment who had settled at Rivière-du-Loup. She was the daughter of a family noted for its activities in the fur trade.[90] She and Antoine had no children from their union. However, the marriage of his brother Jean-François to Marie-Catherine Aubert, great-granddaughter of the royal notary of the seigneury of Beaupré, produced fourteen children.[91]

The marital alliances of Jean-François Desjarlais' offspring continued to link the family to the fur trade and military families of Riviére-du-Loup and Trois-Rivières, although Jean-François, like his father, chose farming as his primary occupation.[92] Five of Jean-François Desjarlais' children, Marie-Madeleine (b. 1725), Charles (b. 1735), Madeleine (b. 1743); Pierre-Amador (b. 1740); and Louis (b. 1730) married descendants of the LeMaître family, by now a prominent and extended merchant clan based primarily in Trois-Rivières. Given these connections, it was perhaps inevitable that third-generation male members of the Desjarlais family would later involve themselves in the fur trade.

On 20 December 1722, Jean Jacques De Gerlaise dit Saint-Amant, aged seventy-nine years, passed away at Rivière-du-Loup. As a young man he had severed his ties with his family in the Principality of Liège, to cast his lot with a company of soldiers bound for an uncertain future in a new land. When he arrived in New France he had nothing but his name, his education, and his youthful strength. Cast adrift from the family and community ties of his childhood, he established new relationships to take their place. For a brief time, his army unit became his family. Through the patronage of his commanding officers and his military duties, he was introduced to and established himself in another family unit firmly rooted in Canada, and saw his own family name take root in his new home.

In the isolated settlement of Rivière-du-Loup, he and his fellow veterans established themselves as *censitaires*, and started families of their own. The hardships of the Iroquois wars, combined with the benign neglect of the French authorities and a succession of absentee seigneurs, served to create an autonomous, self-reliant community whose loyalties were to its members and their social and economic well-being, whether inside or outside the law. The increasingly endogamous nature of the marriages at Rivière-du-Loup over the remainder of the seventeenth century, combined with the network of business and social relationships created through the fur trade and the military campaigns, strengthened these bonds of friendship and kinship. This pattern of community building was duplicated in all of the small communities along the St. Lawrence River. Together, they formed the basis of a distinct and uniquely *Canadien* society, built on common origins and the shared experience of survival in a hostile land.

After almost fifteen years of marriage, Jean de Gerlaise paid a visit to his parents-in-law at the Beaupré seigneury. In a short but poignant note, he acknowledged his *Canadien* family:

> Je soussigné, moi, Jean Gerloisse dit St-Amant, (époux) de Jeanne Trudel, ma femme, (confesse) d'avoir reçu de Jean Trudelle et Marguerite Thomas nos père et mère, ce qu'ils nous avaient promis en mariage, duquel je suis content.
>
> Jean Gerloisse[93]

Les Desjarlais and the Fur Trade Prior to the Conquest

By 1722 a single firm, the Compagnie des Indes, was granted the trading monopoly for New France, and held it until the end of the French régime in 1760. All traders who had acquired pelts in the territory controlled by the French were required to take their furs to the Compagnie des Indes trading offices in Montreal and Quebec City, where they were purchased for fixed rates.[94] The change in monopoly control also heralded the decline in Trois-Rivières as a centre of the Indian trade, and the ascendancy of Montreal as the major commercial centre.

The shift to Montreal had actually begun much earlier, with the economic stimulation brought about by the arrival of the Carignan-Salières Regiment in 1666. The suppression of the Iroquois, if only for a brief time, renewed the flow of furs into the French settlements along the St. Lawrence. But it was the influx of over a thousand soldiers, needing food, clothing, and shelter, and bringing with them specie and goods for sale and barter, that brought New France out of the economic doldrums.[95]

Although Montreal was founded in 1641 as a base from which missionaries could proselytize to the Indians, these motivations were soon eclipsed by the potential for profit from the fur trade. The earliest settlers in Montreal focused their energies on trading furs and acquiring additional grants of land along the St. Lawrence River, particularly at Lachine, west of Montreal. These *seigneurs*-cum-traders were in an advantageous position, able to intercept Natives laden with pelts on their way to Montreal, getting the best furs at the cheapest rates before they reached the main market there. Soon other merchants, in partnership with government officials and military commanders, were establishing posts upriver to intercept trading Indians. When posts could not be built, the merchants engaged individuals to enter the country to trade in the Indian settlements themselves. Gradually a number of competing business networks established themselves in Montreal, vying for control of the up-country posts that handled the inland trade.

By the 1680s the commercial landscape of Montreal was dominated by two opposing cliques of merchant-adventurers who battled for control of the interior trade. One clique, consisting of Henri de Tonty and Robert Cavelier, Sieur de La Salle (d. 1687), flourished under the patronage of the governor of New France, Buade de Frontenac. Charles Le Moyne and Jacques Le Ber, who had acquired large landholdings at Lachine by 1670, enjoyed the patronage of the governor of Montreal, François-Marie Perrot, who operated a commercial network in opposition to that of his commanding officer, Frontenac.[96] Both governors were active in establishing posts upriver with their partners, which served to move the locus of the actual trading activity far from the city itself. Eventually the Natives stopped travelling to Montreal to trade. Instead Montreal became a staging ground for the business of inland trading.[97]

By 1754 the population of Montreal had grown to an estimated four thousand, of which 160 were merchants or master tradesmen, and 540 were day-labourers.[98] By the mid-eighteenth century the military officers, government officials, merchants, and outfitters had formed tightly knit, occupationally stratified groups. Intermarriage was the "glue" that bound these disparate groups together. As W. J. Eccles observed,

> Large amounts of capital were required to provide the trade goods needed at the posts, and to transport both goods and furs to and from Montreal. The officers who obtained posts formed companies, consisting mainly of relatives, to raise the capital and handle the trade. Business alliances were cemented by marriage alliances; the family of one post commander married into the family of another, the better to protect their trading interests. The lion's share of the western fur trade was controlled by a coterie of interrelated, wealthy families forming a military and commercial colonial aristocracy with the governor general and the intendant at its head.[99]

Importers and wholesale merchants, some of whom also engaged in retail selling or fur trading, were at the top of the hierarchy. Immediately below them were the outfitters, who were responsible for hiring *engagés* and servicing the inland posts in partnership among themselves or with wholesalers. Next in status were the independent traders, or *négociants*, who conducted their own trading; the merchant-artisans who retailed their crafts to the traders; the shopkeepers; and the moneylenders.[100] The importers tended to marry the daughters of other import merchants or, very rarely, the daughters of outfitters, the occupational category immediately beneath them in socioeconomic status. The outfitters also tended toward endogamy, marrying into the families of other outfitters, or the daughters of shopkeepers, but very rarely the daughters of import merchants.[101]

These patterns suggest that the maintenance of social status was a primary concern among the import merchants at the top. Marriage, particularly for outfitters, was not a means of social ascent. But it did tend to influence from whom the outfitters would purchase trade goods or borrow money, or whom they might engage as canoemen.

By 1745 the names of Jean-François Desjarlais' sons began to appear in the notarial records of fur trade contracts. In commenting on this generation of Desjarlais, one genealogist noted that "Les Desjarlais dit St.-Amant, de Louiseville, étaient de grands voyageurs. Plusieurs des fils partaient annuellement pour faire la traite avec les Indiens de l'Ouest Américain."[102]

The involvement of the Desjarlais brothers in the fur trade was, in all likelihood, the result of their sponsorship by relatives already active in the trade. Their grandfather Jean De Gerlaise, the seventeenth-century founder of the family, and his only surviving son, Jean-François de Gerlaise, evidently never traded furs. Their landholdings required them to farm full-time. But Pierre Dulignon de Lamirande, Jean de Gerlaise's son-in-law, came from a family with strong military and commercial connections that virtually ensured access to the inland fur trade for his sons and his Desjarlais nephews.[103]

On 1 and 2 June 1745, a total of eight *congés* (trading passes) were awarded to four Montreal partnerships for the purposes of conducting the fur trade at the post of La Baie (Green Bay, Wisconsin). Sieurs d'Ailleboust, Auger, and Texier,[104] forming one partnership, were issued *congés* for four canoes to be manned by a total of twenty-eight *engagés*. Another partnership, represented by Paul Leduc, was permitted trading passes for two canoes carrying twelve *engagés*. The outfitters Jean-Baptiste Lefebvre and Louis Ducharme received one trading pass apiece.

Jacques La Mirande of Rivière-du-Loup, a nephew of Jean-François de Gerlaise, was *conducteur* of one of the canoes for d'Ailleboust, Auger and Texier, and had been issued the *congé* on their behalf. Zénon Auger, another resident of Rivière-du-Loup and a member of the LeMaître-Auger family, acted in the same capacity for another of the firm's canoes. Both men used their positions as *conducteurs* to man the canoes with some of their siblings, cousins, and friends from Rivière-du-Loup, including Antoine Augé, Jean-Baptiste Lamirande, Pierre-François and Joseph Desjarlais (Jacques Lamirande's first cousins), and Pierre and Joseph Trottier Desruisseaux dit Pombert.[105]

After their initial sponsorship as *engagés*, Pierre and Joseph Desjarlais were able to obtain regular employment as *engagés* without the overt assistance of relatives. Their younger brother Louis Desjarlais (b. ca. 1730), the seventh child and fifth son in the family, later engaged with Sieur Raymond Quesnel to go to a post in Illinois in May of 1749.[106] By 1750 Joseph Desjarlais had also contracted his services again, this time to Sieur Marin de la Marque to go to Michilimackinac.[107] Louis Desjarlais re-engaged 1 June 1752 with Sieur Saint-Dizier,[108] and 18 January 1753 with Toussaint Pothier to go to Michilimackinac.[109]

Eventually, however, Pierre-François, Joseph, and Louis Desjarlais returned to Quebec to settle permanently. Pierre-François appears to have remained single.[110] Joseph Desjarlais married on 28 May 1752 and moved to Contrecoeur with his bride, but engaged with Toussaint Pothier on 12 April 1753, the day before the birth of his first child, for one last voyage to Michilimackinac. In 1754, Louis Desjarlais engaged for one last trip to Michilimackinac; he married on 25 August 1755.[111] In 1756 yet another brother, Jean-Augustin-Baptiste (b. 1733) engaged with Sieur Alexis Le Pelé Mésière for the same destination.[112] However, his was the last fur trade engagement by this group of brothers. The expansion of the Seven Years' War onto North American soil in 1755 brought about the suspension of most trading activities in the Great Lakes and elsewhere, until the mid-1760s.

Conclusion

The fur trade of New France was a family-centred, endogamous enterprise, where an individual's occupation, choice of spouse, and social standing reflected one's position in the larger network of patronage. Patronage radiated outward, from influential merchants and military officers at the heart of the business, to their distant relatives and friends at the periphery.

The Desjarlais family first entered the fur trade through the marital connections made by its second-generation female members in Canada. The family's founder, Jean-Jacques De Gerlaise, had focused on farming his two concessions of land on the Rivière-du-Loup seigneury. His eldest son, Jean-François, chose to farm as well. Jean-François' sons might also have limited themselves to farming or the skilled trades, had their aunts not made marriages which brought the Desjarlais family within the fur trade sphere of influence.

Jean-Jacques' eldest daughter, Marguerite, married into the Du Lignon family, a clan with not only impeccable military and commercial connections, but one with bona-fide noble origins in France.[113] Marguerite's marriage not only enhanced her family's social respectability, but may have provided her De Gerlaise nephews with the familial connection needed to gain admittance to the lower rungs of the fur trade.

By the 1750s four male members of the Desjarlais family had gained considerable experience as *engagés* in the Great Lakes-Illinois fur trade.[114] However, the Seven Years' War curtailed the inland fur trade from 1755 until hostilities ended with the Treaty of Paris in 1763.

The Desjarlais family, and other individuals who relied on the fur trade for employment, found their world irrevocably altered by the British victory over France. The colonies of Quebec and Acadia became British possessions. Louisiana became British territory to the east of the Mississippi River, and Spanish territory to the west. Almost immediately, the fur trade began its evolution into a British-controlled enterprise, with British bankers and manufacturers supplying the capital and the goods, and Anglo-Scots traders from the British colonies and Scotland moving to Montreal to re-establish themselves in this promising new environment.

The French and *Canadien* import-export merchants, on the other hand, experienced a reversal of their fortunes. Cut off from their traditional sources of working capital and manufactured goods in France, those who did not migrate to Europe were forced to scale back their businesses in order to preserve what was left of their families' wealth.[115]

In the meantime, their former *engagés* also adapted to the changing political and economic landscape. Some remained in their rural parishes along the St. Lawrence where the traditional rhythms of life remained virtually unchanged, save for seasonal employment with British, rather than French, fur trading companies, Others chose to migrate southward to the French communities west of the Mississippi, where there was still abundant agricultural land available. An additional inducement to travel south was the lure of the settlement of St. Louis, a thriving outpost where the fur trade continued largely under the control of the French.

3

·················

From the St. Lawrence to St. Louis: The Desjarlais Migration to the Mississippi and Beyond

After 1763, Anglo-American, English, and Highland Scots merchants increasingly dominated the Montreal trade. The newcomers had their own social networks and community loyalties. *Canadien* merchants and outfitters had few avenues for entry into the upper echelons of the British colonial business establishment. Basically the *Canadiens* had three alternatives available, to (1) migrate southward to the French communities in Louisiana to farm or work for French trading companies, (2) continue operations as small-scale, independent traders in competition with British firms, or (3) join the British firms and work as *engagés*, interpreters, or clerks until they could acquire the resources needed to become independent *négociants* in the fur country.

Unfortunately for the *Canadien* merchants, their century of trading experience in the *pays d'en haut* gave them but a few years' advantage over their British competitors. In a relatively short time they were supplanted by the British, who made up for their relative inexperience in the Montreal trade by their willingness to forge alliances based on shared business interests as well as ties of kinship. Rising costs for transportation, labour, and merchandise put family-based businesses at risk. Because of the increased numbers of merchants competing for business, trading companies were forced to provide greater numbers of gifts to their Native customers, and goods at more attractive rates. The need to transport larger amounts of merchandise, coupled with the need to travel farther inland to exploit new hunting territories, required greater numbers of canoes, which in turn required more *engagés*. Demand for *engagés*, in turn, placed inflationary pressure on wages.

The British merchants responded to these pressures by amalgamating with businessmen of several ethnic stripes – Swiss,

Germans, and Anglo-Americans – in order to consolidate holdings and reduce costs. Moreover, the British were quick to embrace technological innovations that would save money, in particular the adoption of bateaux rather than canoes in the waterways of the Great Lakes and Mississippi.[1]

The Fur Trade of the Mississippi Valley

In 1763, when the Illinois country became British territory, the bulk of its French population was concentrated in five villages situated in a 120-kilometre belt along the east bank of the Mississippi River. Although some of these communities began their lives as renegade outposts – homes for *coureurs de bois* and other miscreants on the run from the French authorities[2] – the villages of Kaskaskia, Prairie du Rocher, Nouvelle-Chartres, Sainte-Philippe, and Cahokia, had evolved into thriving settlements whose lifestyles and customs mirrored the society of the *Canadien* parishes along the St. Lawrence River. Supported by an economy based primarily on fur trading and secondarily on subsistence agriculture, the residents of the Illinois settlements, like their relatives in Quebec, were a closely-knit people whose social organization reflected their Roman Catholic spirituality and values. The social hierarchy of the Illinois settlements placed missionaries, military officers, and merchant traders at the top of the social ladder, habitants, soldiers, hunters, trappers, and labourers, in the middle, and Native people and African-American slaves at the bottom.[3]

3.1 French Settlements on the Great Lakes and Mississippi during the French
Régime

This lifestyle was abruptly altered by the British conquest. When word of the fall of New France reached the Illinois settlements, a considerable portion of the population packed their property and moved westward across the Mississippi River into Spanish territory. When the British troops arrived to inspect the French villages in 1765, two years after the Treaty of Paris, they found Nouvelle-Chartres and Sainte-Philippe largely deserted.[4]

The destination of choice for the Illinois migrants was the new settlement of St. Louis, which was to become the principal headquarters of the fur trade of the American west. St. Louis was founded in 1764, immediately south of the junction of the Mississippi and Missouri Rivers, by Pierre Laclède Liguest and his stepson Auguste Chouteau on behalf of the New Orleans business firm Maxent and Laclède. The French governor of Louisiana had granted the firm a six-year monopoly over the Indian trade west of the Mississippi River and in the territory bordering both banks of the Missouri River. Although the trading post and the surrounding territory came under Spanish domination shortly thereafter, the community established there was permitted to flourish for forty years as an ethnically French settlement, in which virtually all of the males were employed in some aspect of fur trading.[5]

Although Maxent and Laclède had an initial monopoly over the trade, this situation was impossible to maintain, and the Spanish governor of Louisiana later chose to grant traders exclusive licences for trading with individual Native groups.[6] Competition between the different trading partnerships was brisk, and the bustling community of St. Louis and its satellite settlements of New Madrid, Little Prairie, St. Charles, Carondelet, St. Ferdinand de Florissant, and Portage des Sioux soon attracted *Canadien* merchants, outfitters, and labourers who had been marginalized in the now British-dominated Montreal trade, and who found the ambiance of St. Louis to their liking.

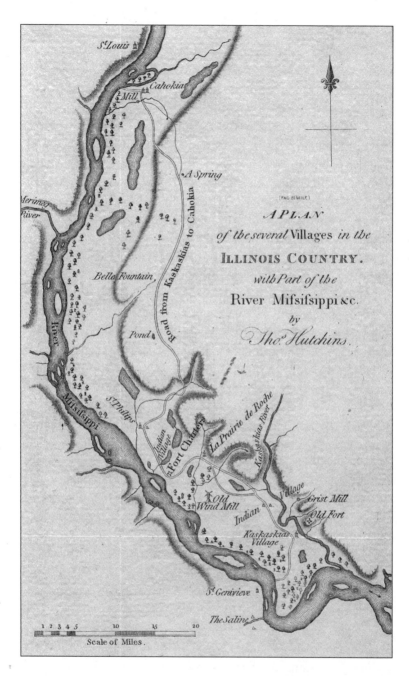

3.2 Engraved map by Thomas Hutchins depicting the French villages of the Illinois country in the 1770s, from *A Topographical Description of Virginia, Pennsylvania, Maryland, and North Carolina* (London, 1778).

Many of these new arrivals were members of merchant families who had established themselves in the Illinois country as traders decades earlier.[7] Upon the transfer of the lands east of the Mississippi to the British the *Canadien* merchants simply pulled up stakes and moved downriver, crossing the Mississippi to settle on its western banks, then in Spanish hands. Others came directly from Canada, bypassing the Illinois communities altogether.

Migration to Missouri was not simply a reaction against British or American rule. It was also part of a well-established practice of out-migration – a response to economic and social pressures in overcrowded *Canadien* communities. During the French and British régimes and even to the time of Confederation, Quebec society was largely rural in its orientation. Land was abundant and accessible, and offered a wider variety of economic pursuits than those available in the cities. Markets for surplus grain and other agricultural commodities had developed, and seasonal labour in the fur trade, in lumbering, and in the fishery provided supplemental income for families when farming income faltered. Gradually, however, population growth resulting from a high domestic birth rate, coupled with immigration from Britain and its former American colonies, reduced the amounts of arable land available for farming. By the early nineteenth century, noted Alan Greer, "it was no longer possible for the majority of young adults to acquire farms in their home parishes or in the immediate vicinity."[8]

The response of farming families in rural Quebec, like their contemporaries in Europe, was to have some of their younger members leave the parish to live elsewhere. As Jacques Mathieu's research into the history of *Canadien* out-migration reveals, the rural family unit had to divest itself of half its descendants each generation in order that the core family could survive. Because of this necessity, the need for leaving preceded the decision to leave; male *and* female children grew up with the knowledge that at some point in the future, some of them would be forced by economic circumstances to move far away from their families.[9]

For younger sons in large families, the most promising future lay in contracting a good marriage with the daughter of a local family with farmland to spare. Failing that, a young man might extend an apprenticeship in the fur trade into something more permanent, as a trader or soldier at one of the inland posts. During the French régime, it was still possible to find opportunities close to home. For most migrants, their final destination was likely to be a neighbouring parish fronting the St. Lawrence River. However, as arable land disappeared, the migrants took lands in areas farther inland, north, and south of the parishes on the banks of the St. Lawrence. After the British conquest of Quebec, they moved westward towards what became the colony of Upper Canada and south to the French settlements along the Mississippi River.[10]

Among the *Canadien* migrants to the St. Louis region were members of the Desjarlais family of Rivière-du-Loup, Quebec. Although the family patriarch, Jean-Jacques De Gerlaise and his only surviving son, Jean-François, had been diligent in acquiring farmland, the arrival of seven sons to Jean-François, out of a total of fourteen children,[11] would have strained the family's resources considerably. It is not surprising that after 1785, at least nine Desjarlais grandchildren (all children of Jean-François' younger sons) migrated to the Illinois country, and from there to St. Louis, Missouri to establish farms and participate in commerce.[12]

It is debatable which branches of the Desjarlais family migrated first. Earlier in the eighteenth century, male cousins from the Lamirande family had migrated to the Great Lakes and beyond. Jean Dulignon de Lamirande, a son of Pierre Du Lignon and Marguerite De Gerlaise, was living at Michilimackinac in the 1730s with his Indian wife Angélique and their children, and at Sault Ste-Marie in the 1740s. His brother Joseph ventured farther south into the Illinois country, marrying at Kaskaskia in 1750.[13] By 1780, members of the Lamirande family had reached St. Louis. In the roster of the First Company of the San Luis de Ilinueses Militia, recorded 22 December 1780, one Juan Baptista Lamarina, aged twenty-five, a rower from Canada, appears.[14]

The majority of Desjarlais family members who migrated southward appear to have bypassed the Illinois communities entirely, however, moving directly to the St. Louis area. Three children of Charles Desjarlais and Madeleine LeMaître Auger dit Beaunoyer of Rivière-du-Loup moved to the region. Their son Antoine Desjarlais (b. 22 May 1769 at Rivière-du-Loup, Quebec) was a resident of Florissant, a small settlement in the St. Charles district by the time of the 1787 Spanish census. His sister Marie-Anne was in Florrisant ca. 1801, when her marriage to her first husband was recorded in the parish records.[15] Another brother, Paul Desjarlais, also settled on the Cuivre River by 1790. He apparently returned briefly to Quebec in 1799 to marry Rosalie Hardy dit Chatillon at Yamachiche on 22 July.[16]

On 29 September 1795 Antoine married Thérèse Gagné, the métisse daughter of Antoine Gagné and Dorothée Desgagnées, former residents of Kaskaskia and Cahokia, Illinois.[17] Following her death he contracted a second marriage to Thérèse Pelletier, daughter of André Pelletier and Angélique Lacoste dit Languedoc of Vincennes, Indiana. This marriage, which produced eight children, ended with Thérèse's death sometime after 1818; the birthdate of her last surviving child was recorded as 14 January 1818.[18] On 10 May 1828 Antoine Desjarlais married a third time, to Eulalie Dubreuil, the daughter of Louis Dubreuil and Marie-Anne Laroche, and the widow of trader Joseph Calvé. By 1800 another relative from Lower Canada – via Kaskaskia – had settled in St. Ferdinand; Joseph Lamirande, "from St. Antonio Parish, lower Canada" [sic].[19]

Antoine Desjarlais appears to have settled initially into an economic and social routine that differed little from that left behind in Quebec – small-scale agriculture and seasonal fur-trading, all facilitated by an ever-widening circle of kin connections that linked him to established families and the commercial elite.[20] Records of cash advances to Antoine Desjarlais appear in the private papers of the Chouteau family, as does a document identifying him acting as attorney on behalf of his minor brother and sister-in-law André and Suzanne Pelletier, in the settlement of their deceased father's estate.[21]

However, Antoine Desjarlais does not appear to have been employed by the half-brothers Auguste and Pierre Chouteau, who were awarded exclusive trading privileges with the Osage by the Spanish authorities after 1794.[22] Instead, oral accounts from descendants describe him as a farmer, a store and saloon-keeper, and the operator of a steamboat-landing on the Illinois River, in Calhoun County north of Hardin, Illinois. Here he catered to the needs of "woodboats" that transported lumber for building and fuel downriver to St. Louis. Both Antoine Desjarlais Sr. and his namesake, Antoine Desjarlais Jr., acquired land by purchasing land grants from military veterans who had logged their holdings and moved on.[23]

One of the sons of Antoine Desjarlais and his second wife, Thérèse Pelletier, did not settle down to a life of farming. Joseph DeGerlais (b, 29 January 1810) was to have a different life course. Fur trade documents suggest that Joseph entered the employ of Bernard Pratte and Company, the western agent of the American Fur Company, in 1830. Joseph engaged for one year as a "voyageur, hivernant, chasseur" with the Upper Missouri Outfit, then under the control of his second cousin, Honoré Picotte, who had become the general agent of the Upper Missouri Outfit the same year. Joseph did not come back for a long time.[24]

> He lived among the Indians for some 24 years and produced métis children. On December 14, 1847 he married Sophie (a Bannock Indian) at the St. Louis Mission in Oregon, who was baptized the same day, aged ca. 40 (however, she was ca. 33 according to the 1850 census), and she died by 1857. She was the mother of several, if not all, of his children mentioned in the St. Louis Mission records.[25]

Eventually, Joseph Desjarlais returned to Missouri, marrying a white woman in Kansas City in 1855.

> According to my father, Joseph had homesteaded in Kansas first, and during the troubles there during the Civl War era Quantrill's Raiders came by, seeking the $4000.00 proceeds of a land sale they had heard that Joseph had made. When he either didn't have the money or refused to give it up if he did have it, they hung him and rode off, at which point his wife ran out, cut the rope, and revived him.... According to my

father, when Joseph DeGerlia left Calhoun Co. for the last time (in the 1870s?) someone else's wife ran off with him.[26]

Members of a second branch of the Desjarlais family, the children of Joseph Desjarlais and Marie-Josephte Hervieux dit Lesperance of Contrecoeur, Quebec, also chose to move to Illinois, possibly to join their cousins, but more likely in pursuit of abundant, fertile farmland and the potential for involvement in the fur trade, prospects made possible through their marital connections to the Gélinas dit Lacourse family.

The Lacourse family of Trois-Rivières were no strangers to the Illinois country; some family members had established themselves at Kaskaskia as early as the 1740s.[27] But it was not their longevity in Illinois that enhanced their commercial prospects, but rather their extensive intermarriage with another Trois-Rivières family, the Lesieurs.

The Lesieurs were a prominent family who had held the seigneury of Yamachiche, near Trois-Rivières, Quebec for several generations. Charles Lesieur, the seigneur of Yamachiche during much of the eighteenth century, presided over a large family active in the fur trade. One of his sons, Toussaint, was one of the earliest *Canadien* traders in the Athabasca region, an associate of Peter Pond, and later Benjamin and Joseph Frobisher.[28] However, two other Lesieur sons, François and Joseph, chose to seek their fortune in Missouri.

By the early 1780s both men were in the employ of Gabriel Cerré, the principal merchant in St. Louis at the time. In 1783 Cerré sent the brothers to a Native settlement on a large bend in the Mississippi River known locally as L'Anse la Graise – "cove of grease" – because of the processing of large quantities of bear and bison meat that took place there. Although the abundance of game had attracted itinerant traders to the area for generations, the Lesieurs established themselves permanently in the area after several successful trading seasons. Consequently, they were credited as the official founders of the trading post and satellite community later known as New Madrid. By 1794, François Lesieur had married and moved south of New Madrid to establish a new trading post known as Little Prairie. Onearpent lots were laid out, and the new settlement began to attract agricultural settlers.[29]

Among these settlers were relatives of the Lesieurs from Quebec. Michel Gélinas dit Lacourse and his wife Marie-Josèphe Desjarlais of the parish of St.-Antoine-sur-Richelieu migrated to the area shortly after the establishment of Little Prairie. Lacourse is recorded in 1797 as owning a lot on Open Lake near Portage Bay, which was a short distance from Little Prairie. His wife Marie-Josèphe was recorded as being settled at Little Prairie in 1801, along with one Eloy Desjarlais, possibly her brother.[30]

Unlike the fur trade of the Great Lakes or Rupert's Land, the Missouri fur-trading territories were notable for their close proximity to the Mississippi and Missouri River settlements. The aboriginal groups with whom the St. Louis companies traded were accessible by horse or keelboat. Steamboats, which were introduced on the Missouri before 1820, reduced travelling time considerably, could carry a great deal more freight, and were infinitely more comfortable.

The close proximity of St. Louis to the Indian country meant that many of the local French-Canadians and Americans involved in the Missouri fur trade were already formally married to Euro-American or acculturated métis women before contracting country unions with Native Americans. This juxtaposition of colonial settlements to the fur country was conducive to kin relations that became increasingly complex, and even awkward, for many traders of St. Louis were connected simultaneously with one creole family in St. Louis and another family domiciled in whichever Indian group the trader was doing business with.

As Tanis Thorne observed, despite the continued presence and influence of the Roman Catholic Church in regulating family life within the environs of St. Louis, "the eighteenth century fur trade in the Old Northwest clearly engendered a variety of marital and familial forms – polygamy, serial monogamy, sororal polygyny, monogamy, patrilocal-patrilineality, matrilocal-patrilineality, and foster-parenthood – to name a few of the prevalent patterns." Traders would bring their métis children by Osage, Fox, Sioux, or Ponca country wives to St. Louis for baptism, and often made financial provisions for them in their wills.[31] But while these extramarital unions were common, these practices and the children who resulted were barely tolerated by the colonial community. For example, in two instances where mass baptisms of Osage mixed-blood children took place in St. Louis, the parish records suggest that the ceremonies took place in private residences rather than the Roman Catholic Church.[32]

It is probable that despite the necessity of country unions for advancing the fur trade, the creole ladies of St. Louis held the sentiments of most wives forced to share their husbands with other women. Given the financial affluence and social respectability most of them enjoyed, however, they chose to discreetly ignore infidelity as long as their husbands compartmentalized their Indian family lives away from St. Louis.[33]

One of the St. Louis traders who demonstrated a typically complex St. Louis family life was Honoré Picotte,[34] a transplanted *Canadien* trader who joined the American Fur Company in the 1820's. Honoré Picotte was born in 1796, the son of Jean-Baptiste Picotte and Hélène Desjarlais of Rivière-du-Loup, Quebec.[35] Like many young men of that community, Honoré and his elder brother Louis initially joined the North West Company. Unlike most of their Desjarlais relatives, however, who had entered the fur trade as *engagés*, both Honoré and Louis joined the company as clerks.[36]

Few details of their service survive. Honoré Picotte demonstrated a familiarity with the Native groups around the region of Lakes Superior and Winnipeg, and had travelled in the subarctic regions as well. He had also visited the Mandan earth lodges on the Missouri River as early as 1820.[37]

By 1818 Louis Picotte had returned from the fur trade and married his second cousin, Archange Desjarlais, the daughter of Jean-Baptiste Desjarlais and Madeleine Pratte of Rivière-du-Loup. There he established a successful farming operation and later became the local representative to the Lower Canada House of Assembly.[38]

Honoré, however, did not choose to leave the fur trade, even after the amalgamation of the Hudson's Bay and North West companies in 1821 jettisoned several superfluous junior officers, including himself. Instead of returning to Lower Canada, he left the Selkirk Settlement by dogsled in January of 1822, travelling via Fort Snelling to Prairie du Chien, Wisconsin. He was in the company of three other disaffected former clerks; Kenneth McKenzie, William Laidlaw, and Daniel Lamont. By February 1822, the party of migrants had arrived in St. Louis, Missouri, where McKenzie, Laidlaw, and Lamont registered for naturalization as U.S. citizens.[39]

Shortly thereafter, Picotte, McKenzie, Laidlaw, and Lamont entered into partnership with James Kipp. With Joseph Renville, William B. Tilton, and S.S. Dudley, the group established the Columbia Fur Company. The firm obtained a trading licence on 17 July 1822 from Indian Superintendent William Clark, which permitted the company to trade with the Sioux on the Minnesota River, and the Mandans and other tribes on the Missouri River. By 1827 the company had expanded its operations across Minnesota and Wisconsin, competing successfully with several rival firms also based in St. Louis.[40]

However, the subsequent merger of the Western Department of the American Fur Company with Pierre Chouteau's French Fur Company resulted in the absorption of the Columbia Fur Company by its stronger rival in the summer of 1827. The Columbia Fur Company's posts in Minnesota and Wisconsin were taken over by the Northern Department of the American Fur Company, and its Missouri operations were subsumed under those of the American Fur Company's Western Department, which was renamed the Upper Missouri Outfit.[41]

Unfortunately, Honoré Picotte was not invited to join the American Fur Company, although his former colleagues McKenzie, Laidlaw, and Lamont were all contracted to manage the Upper Missouri Outfit. Picotte subsequently went into partnership with two other traders of French extraction, Pierre D. Papin and Pascal Cerré, to form a new company, called P.D. Papin and Company, in 1829. However, the American Fur Company (operating as Bernard Pratte and Company), preferred a monopoly situation, and bought out its rivals when it could not defeat them economically. In 1828, Bernard Pratte and Company had bought out erstwhile partner Joseph Robidoux paying him one thousand dollars not to trade for an entire year. By 1830, the American Fur Company had also purchased P. D. Papin and Co., then only a year old, for twenty-one thousand dollars.[42]

In August of 1831 Picotte, now the American Fur Company agent for the Upper Missouri Outfit, married Thérèse Duchouquette, the daughter of Jean Baptiste Duchouquette and Thérèse Brazeau, themselves from local *Canadien* fur trading families. However, Picotte already had a country wife, a sister of the principal chief of the Yankton Sioux, Struck-By-the-Ree, who had given birth to their son Charles one year earlier. By 1837 Picotte had taken a second Sioux wife, Wambdi Autopewin ("Eagle-Woman-That-All-Look-At"), the daughter of Two-Lance, a chief of the Hunkpapa Sioux. She was later baptized with an English name, Matilda, and she bore Picotte several children. In 1848, prior to his retirement, Picotte made arrangements for Matilda and their children to be placed under the care of one of his employees, Charles E. Galpin, who later married Matilda.[43]

Honoré Picotte was remembered by his relatives as a devoted family man. He was generous to his Desjarlais and Picotte kin, giving loans to his young *Canadien* nephews to seek their fortunes in the California gold fields.[44] After his retirement until his death, he made frequent visits to his niece Aurélie Picotte Lottinville and her family, who lived near Kankakee, Illinois.

> Descendants of this branch of the family retain the tradition that their parish priest had dispensed a separation of Honoré from an Indian wife. Ever thoughtful, the old gentleman undoubtedly sought this separation to regularize not only his own church marriage, but Matilda's second marriage to Charles Galpin, who has proved to be a devoted stepfather to Honoré's Indian family.[45]

Marriage as Business: The Robidoux Family

Not all St. Louis women chose to tolerate their husbands' parallel lives. Julie Desjarlais, daughter of Eloi Desjarlais and Marie-Amable Leblanc of Cahokia,[46] enjoyed a relatively affluent existence as the wife of Pierre-Isidore Robidoux, one of the famous, and notorious, Robidoux brothers of St. Louis.[47]

The Robidoux family migrated to St. Louis from their home in the concession of St. Lambert, in the parish of LaPrairie, Montreal, in 1770. Joseph Robidoux, the family patriarch and a widower, established himself in the St. Louis fur trade with his son Joseph Robidoux II. Robidoux Sr. died shortly thereafter, leaving his estate to his son Joseph, then twenty-one, who promptly used his inheritance to establish himself as a trapper and trader.[48]

In September of 1782 Joseph Robidoux II married Catherine Rollet dit Ladéroute of Cahokia. They lived in St. Louis until 1794, when Robidoux received a grant of 1,725 acres of land at St. Ferdinand de Florissant. Here the family lived until 1806, when Joseph moved his family back to St. Louis and established a home at the junction of First and Elm Streets, adjacent to the banks of the Mississippi River.[49]

In 1809 Joseph Robidoux II died at St. Louis, leaving behind a large family of children, mostly boys. Under the leadership of the eldest son and namesake, Joseph Robidoux III, the brothers Robidoux took over the family business. They expanded their operations, and rapidly carved out a chunk of the St. Louis fur trade for themselves, even while working for other traders, like old family friend Auguste Chouteau, a leading partner in Bernard Pratte and Company, and the executor of their father's estate.[50] The Robidoux brothers used the trade goods, financing, and other benefits available through Pratte and Company while conducting clandestine business for the sole benefit of themselves. Despite the complaints of other partners such as Jean Pierre Cabanné, who heartily detested Joseph Robidoux and his brothers, Auguste Chouteau kept the Robidoux family affiliated with the firm, even when compelled to buy out Joseph Robidoux stake in the company and paying him one thousand dollars to stay home for a year.[51]

The fur-trade elite of St. Louis has been described as "one big extended family," whose complex kin connections often contributed to poor business decisions. All the members of the larger firms were involved in smaller business enterprises, making up partnerships within partnerships, which sometimes resulted in competition between family members, and even with the company with which their primary loyalties were expected to lie. As was customary in the French fur trade, traders with influence were expected to provide employment opportunities for various sons, nephews, brothers-in-law, cousins, and family friends, regardless of their ineptitude or lack of fidelity.[52]

The endogamous nature of marriages contracted among the St. Louis elite further contributed to the extension of these kin ties. All marriages were strategic in nature, designed to increase family fortunes economically, socially, and politically. Traders married the daughters of other traders; brothers of one family would marry the sisters in another family, and so on. Remarriage, a common occurrence during this period, further complicated kin ties.[53]

Most of the Robidoux brothers followed St. Louis tradition, contracting marriages[54] with the *creole* daughters of local French fur-trading families, who raised their children and managed their households, farms, and other businesses while the men were trapping and trading in the far-flung reaches of Missouri, Iowa, Colorado, New Mexico, and California. Julie Desjarlais Robidoux, who married Pierre-Isidore Robidoux at Cahokia in 1814, managed a large household that included six slaves, who were probably used as field hands on their farm.[55]

Despite their married state and their considerable assets in St. Louis, the Robidoux brothers did not make undue efforts to stay close to home, nor did they avoid contracting extramarital alliances *à la façon du pays* in whatever region they happened to be trading. Joseph Robidoux III had fathered his first child by an Indian woman as early as 1805, at a post in the Blacksnake Hills of northwestern Missouri,[56] which became a home base for the Robidoux brothers and their sons while doing business, and where the Robidoux men fathered "dozens" of mixed-blood children.

> As his own father had apprenticed him in the trade, Joseph Robidoux brought his brothers and white sons from St. Louis to assist him around his trading establishment. Joseph Robidoux had Ioway and Otoe wives. His sons Ferron and Joseph had children by Indian and French-Indian women. His younger brother Michel had an Otoe wife. Joseph was perhaps the most prolific of all the fur-traders, having fourteen children by his different Indian and white wives before 1830. The Indian agent Hughes complained of sales of Indian girls to traders, singling Joseph Robidoux as one of the buyers. These young girls were debauched and abandoned, "forever wretched and ruined," said the agent. Joseph Robidoux unquestionably exercised considerable licence in his romantic affairs and had many children by Indian women. A visitor to his post in November 1839 said that behind the trading house were five scaffolds supported by poles on which the bones of Robidoux's children by his various Indian wives were laid according to Indian burial customs. Both the Catholic and Protestant missionaries who visited Robidoux's establishment disapproved of moral laxity and debasement, the key offenses being polygynous relationships, gambling, and heavy drinking. By one report, Joseph Robidoux had sixty 'papouses' in 1850.[57]

Although Joseph Robidoux III and his brothers had established themselves in trade in the Missouri River region, they wanted to expand their business to the areas of California and New Mexico, then under Mexican rule. Joseph Robidoux supplied his brothers Antoine and Louis with trade goods for the Rio Arriba (the expanse of Mexican territory between Santa Fe and Taos, New Mexico) as early as 1823. By 1824, Joseph Robidoux sent a second expedition to Santa Fe, this time with two other brothers, François and Pierre-Isidore.[58]

Unfortunately for the Robidoux brothers and other traders from the United States, these men were *los extranjeros* –

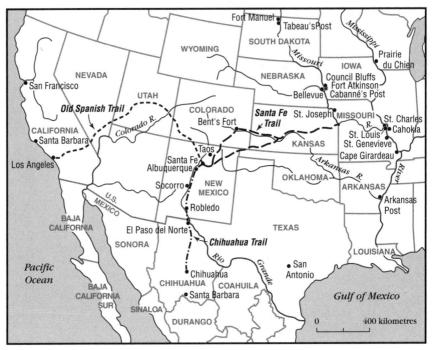

3.3 The American Southwest and Spanish trading communities, early nineteenth century

foreigners. Only Mexican nationals could be granted trapping and trading licences. However, there were ways to circumvent these restrictions. Between 1823 and 1828 the Mexican government developed criteria for granting citizenship to foreigners in its territories. Basically, *extranjeros* could become citizens if they had been a permanent resident of Mexico for two years, were Roman Catholic, were employed, and responsible. Those who were married to or living common-law with Mexican women and had families were given special consideration.[59]

Establishing oneself as a permanent resident, with a Mexican wife and children, became imperative as time went on. By the 1830s and 1840s the Mexican government began to implement laws which forbade foreigners from engaging in retail business. However, a clause exempted foreigners who were naturalized citizens, were married to Mexicans, and/or were residents of Mexico with their families.[60]

Both Antoine and Louis Robidoux, the sole remaining brothers who were not formally married, were living with common-law Mexican wives by 1828: Antoine Robidoux with Carmel Benevides, and Louis with Guadelupe García. By 1829 both men were granted Mexican citizenship. By 1830 Antoine had been elected president, or *alcalde*, of the *ayuntamiento*, or municipal council, of Santa Fe. Louis followed in his brother's footsteps, being elected as a *regidor*, or alderman, in the Santa Fe municipal council. By 1839, Louis Robidoux had been chosen *alcalde* of the *ayuntamiento* in Santa Fe, where a visiting American journalist, Matt Field, observed that Louis Robidoux appeared to "share the rule over the people almost equally with the governor and priests."[61]

One other Robidoux brother, François, had also established a common-law relationship with a local Mexican woman, Luisa Romero,[62] and had fathered a daughter by her in January of 1836[63] although he had a large family living in St. Louis.[64] Pierre-Isidore Robidoux, who handled minor trading in Chihuahua and Sonora, and supervised the transshipment of goods and other daily business in Santa Fe,[65] was living in Taos, New Mexico permanently by the late 1830s.

In recognition of this fact, in December of 1837 a deed was drafted between Louis, François, Antoine, and Pierre-Isidore Robidoux and their wives in Missouri, relinquishing all title to lands of their father's estate in St. Louis. The document indicated that the brothers were "residing at present at Santa Fe in Mexico."[66] Shortly thereafter, Julie Desjarlais Robidoux took the unusual step of filing for divorce from Pierre-Isidore Robidoux.[67] Apparently she had had enough of the role of faithful fur-trade wife.[68]

So why did Julie Robidoux, and countless other fur trade wives put up with the long absences and the numerous infidelities? The most likely explanation is that Julie Robidoux – and her male relatives – had come to depend on the wealth, influence, and commercial opportunity that flowed from her marriage to a member of the Robidoux family. It is almost certain that men in the Desjarlais family got employment with the Robidoux brothers. A persistent legend in the Desjarlais family makes reference to one young man having been kidnapped by Comanches. Louis Guyon, the storyteller, describes how his maternal great-uncle, a Desjarlais, escaped to a nearby mission after being freed by a Comanche woman. A fellow captive, who was not so fortunate, was burned at the stake.[69]

Conclusion

After little more than one hundred years of its existence in Canada,[70] members of several branches of the Desjarlais family had already left their home parish of Rivière-du-Loup to re-establish themselves elsewhere. However, they would soon discover that family life in St. Louis was far more complex than that of the St. Lawrence Valley. The communities in Missouri were far more heterogynous, ethnically and racially, than those of Canada. African-American and Indian slaves were integrated into the extended households of ethnic French families, who were themselves fragmented into cliques of French-*Canadiens*, French-Creoles from New Orleans or Illinois, or expatriates from France itself. The relationships and loyalties were taken into the *pays d'en haut* where they became even more convoluted as traders established marriages *à la façon du pays* with Indian women and fathered métis children, often while maintaining, simultaneously, a creole family life in St. Louis.

This situation was a far cry from that experienced by *Canadien engagés* farther north in the Athabasca country, who were able to form fur trade unions thousands of miles away from the prying eyes of priests, parents – and wives. Generally, the *engagés* and clerks in the Montreal-based fur trade were unmarried when they established unions *à la façon du pays* in the fur country. When their time in the *pays d'en haut* was concluded, some of these men chose to formalize their country unions with Native women in a church ceremony. Others separated from their country wives, leaving them in the fur country in order to contract a formalized, church-sanctioned union with a *Canadienne* once they had returned to Quebec. The prevailing marital pattern of the Montreal fur trade, one which can be best described as "serial monogamy," generally enforced a level of separateness between a trader's aboriginal family and his *Canadien* family. Should he decide to move his Native wife and/or children back home to Quebec, he would be expected to have them formally baptized, and then he would be expected to marry the mother of his métis children, who would then enjoy the full rights and privileges that other *Canadiens* enjoyed.

Because the St. Louis-based traders were already involved in family relationships before initiating unions *à la façon du pays*, there was no acceptable way to integrate their country wives into St. Louis society without being branded as bigamists by the Roman Catholic church. Although it was possible to bring their métis children back to St. Louis, they would never experience the same level of respectability or legitimacy that their creole half-sisters and brothers enjoyed. Many St. Louis traders, like Auguste Chouteau and Honoré Picotte, made special efforts to have their métis children educated and otherwise provided for through their estates, but their largesse did not and could not extend to integrating them into their St. Louis families or social circles. The Euro-American families of fur traders already residing in communities such as St. Louis were the families considered legitimate by both the church and the state, regardless of the families these traders had established in Indian communities.

The early and rapid influx of Anglo-American settlers into the Missouri River region after the American Revolution and the War of 1812, solidified the permanent estrangement of the mixed-blood children of the Missouri traders from white society, particularly the male métis children of American fur traders, who generally remained in the Indian country, taking other métis or Indian women as wives. The policies of the U.S. government did not recognize the existence of a distinct and separate Métis culture apart from Indian society. They did, however, make provisions for mixed-bloods by settling them on "half-breed tracts" set aside on Indian reservations, where they experienced an often-uncomfortable coexistence with their Indian kin.[71] For fur traders and their métis sons, particularly those of ethnic

French and Catholic heritage, the half-breed tracts may have appeared to be safer havens than the countryside of the American Midwest, which, by the mid-nineteenth century, had become increasingly hostile to those who were not Anglo-American, Protestant, and white.

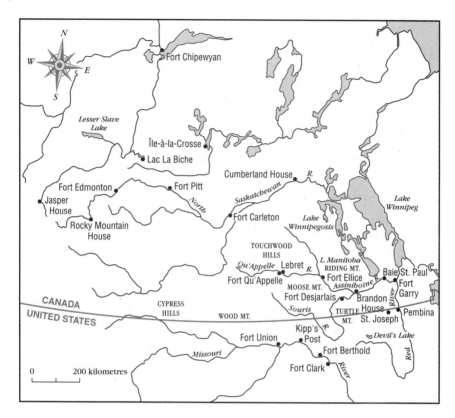

4.1 Rupert's Land and Missouri River area, nineteenth century

4

....

The Emergence of Freemen in Rupert's Land

From the mid-eighteenth century to the end of the nineteenth, at least ten male members of the Desjarlais family of Rivière-du-Loup, Quebec[1] found work as *engagés* on the Great Lakes, in the territories along the Mississippi and Missouri Rivers, and in the Hudson Bay watershed. Only a few *engagés*, however, established separate lives for themselves outside the direct employ of the fur-trade companies. These were the traders living as freemen in loosely knit bands in the western subarctic regions of Rupert's Land. The activities of these freemen have been well documented in the post journals of the Hudson's Bay and North West companies. What are less well-known are the social and familial origins of these traders, their motives for operating independently, and the nature and extent of their relationships with aboriginal hunting bands in the *pays d'en haut*.

This chapter focuses on the activities of various *Canadien* and métis members of the Desjarlais family between 1785 and 1825, tracing their evolution from *engagés* to freemen. The eventual dispersion of branches of the Desjarlais family from the Lesser Slave Lake region laid the groundwork for some members of the family to pursue different economic and political goals, and in doing so move towards a Métis corporate identity.[2]

The Desjarlais in Rupert's Land

Although the British conquest of Québec removed the French elite from key positions in the trade, it offered opportunities for expansion to middle-class entrepreneurs. The *Canadien* outfitters who comprised what remained of the French fur trade carried on as before, relying on the patronage of the few remaining French community leaders with wealth to lend them the working capital needed to trade and the political influence needed to obtain that increasingly-rare jewel; a trading license.

Certainly this appears to be the initial strategy employed by at least one member of the Desjarlais family after the Seven Years' War. In 1783, after a gap of approximately twenty-five years when no Desjarlais names appear in the notarial records of the fur trade, a trading pass was granted to Joseph Desjarlais and Baptiste Plante. The two men were permitted to take one canoe with "five men, 60 gallons of rum, 4 fusils, 70 pounds gunpowder, one cwt. shot, etc. valued at £100" to Grand Portage.[3]

Joseph Desjarlais (b. 3 September 1754 at Contrecoeur, Québec) was the first son of Joseph Desjarlais and Marie-Marguerite Hervieux of Rivière-du-Loup,[4] and the first member of the second generation of Desjarlais family members to enter the fur trade. Joseph Desjarlais' initial foray into the fur trade is noteworthy in itself; of equal interest is how he managed to enter as an independent rather than as an *engagé*. Desjarlais and Plante were the only *Canadien* traders issued licences for the interior that year. The remaining licences were issued to British merchants – Benjamin and Joseph Frobisher, five canoes; Simon McTavish, six canoes; and Holmes and Grant, three canoes. All of the British partnerships were part of the initial incarnation of the North West Company in 1783–84.[5]

The presence of these two *Canadien* independents in this group is an anomaly for another reason. Neither the Desjarlais nor the Plante family numbered among the prominent outfitters of Montreal, unlike Charles Chaboillez, Nicholas Montour, Maurice Blondeau, Jean-Baptiste Adhémar, Venant St.-Germain, and other *Canadiens* whose names appear in the licencing records between 1768 and 1783.[6] The question therefore arises; given the somewhat peripheral status of both of their families in the *Canadien* trading hierarchy, how did Joseph Desjarlais and Baptiste Plante manage to raise enough capital to be granted, or even be considered for, a trading licence in 1783? Entering the Northwest trade was an expensive and complex undertaking, especially during the American Revolution. The flow of trade goods was cut off from the American colonies, and certain trade items, such as powder and blankets, were diverted for the use of troops. Traders loyal to the British crown were forced to relocate to Montreal, and buy their goods in Montreal rather than New York and Albany. Private navigation on the Great Lakes was prohibited, and trade goods were transported on the king's vessels. The number of trading passes was restricted.[7]

Because the average trade canoe carried approximately one-third provisions and two-thirds trade goods, the inland traders were compelled to barter for additional food from Indian groups in the course of the journey, which could be a hazardous enterprise in itself. These pressures encouraged many of the smaller trading concerns to amalgamate their activities under shared licences.[8] This enabled the companies to share the cost of hiring *engagés* and establishing provisioning depots between Grand Portage and the Saskatchewan country, both of which required substantial amounts of money. As a result, participation in the Northwest fur trade tended to be limited to those with solid lines of credit.

The explanation for Desjarlais and Plante's receipt of a trading licence lies in the estate inventory of Luc de La Corne, Sieur de Chaptes, an influential military officer, merchant, diplomat, and politician who died in Montreal in October of 1784. Luc de La Corne was the son of a prominent military family, who parlayed the military appointments of its various members into lucrative fur trade careers as financial backers, as merchant-outfitters, and as commandant-traders at inland posts. La Corne married three times to women of Montreal merchant families and, after the British conquest, maintained his family's social stature by marrying two of his daughters to British officials, one an army officer and the other a member of the British Indian Department responsible for administering the fur trade in British territory. At his death in 1784, Luc de La Corne was one of the richest *Canadiens*, with a fortune estimated at 1,200,000 *livres*. His estate inventory also revealed that his local debtors owed him more than 152,000 *livres* at his death.[9]

Among his debtors were listed Joseph Desjarlais and Ambroise Plante. In the inventory of Sieur de la Corne's estate of 6 December 1784, in the section entitled "Ensuivent les Dettes Actives," it is noted that Joseph Desjarlais and Ambroise Plante, "par Obligation & par Compte" were indebted "au fo. 123 Quatre Mille Six cent Quatre Vingt dix Chelins onze Sols (4690.11)" to Sieur de La Corne prior to his death.[10] This suggests that Joseph Desjarlais and Joseph Plante, the men who received the trading licence, acquired the needed capital by going into debt.[11]

What is interesting about the activities of this generation of Desjarlais men is that Joseph appears to have been the only one who made an attempt to operate as an independent trader. We will never really know what prompted Joseph Desjarlais Jr. to make the decision to ignore the personal and financial risks and enter the cutthroat trade of the interior in partnership with Baptiste Plante, nor can we know for certain why a shrewd businessman like Luc de La Corne was willing to sponsor their (risky) undertaking.

Establishing a line of credit and securing a trading pass did not automatically ensure success. *Canadien* independents had to fight for the right to do business in the *pays d'en haut*. Many small operators, even those affiliated with the prominent Montreal outfitting families, were gradually forced out of business by ruthless competition and mounting debt.[12]

So how did Joseph Desjarlais manage to establish himself permanently as an independent operator in the Athabasca country when individuals with far better financial prospects and commercial connections had failed? Again, the answer lies in family connections – those that Joseph Desjarlais had established in Quebec prior to 1783, and those that he established in the *pays d'en haut* after 1783.

One possible explanation for Joseph Desjarlais' survival as an independent in Athabasca is his kin relationship to a powerful *négociant* already in the interior – in this case, to the trader Toussaint Lesieur of Yamachiche, Quebec. Lesieur, who was Peter Pond's clerk at Lac La Ronge in 1781–82, had already earned a notorious reputation for himself by the time Joseph Desjarlais reached Athabasca. Lesieur had been implicated in the shooting of Swiss trader Jean-Etienne Waddens in 1782, who died in Athabasca under mysterious circumstances, in the presence of both Lesieur and his bourgeois, Peter Pond. Pond was arrested for the crime upon his return to Canada. However, Lesieur was back in the English River region by 1785, under contract to Benjamin and Joseph Frobisher, and apparently free from further prosecution. Peter Pond was notoriously jealous of any trader who might trespass on what he considered his personal territory, and was not averse to taking whatever action he deemed necessary to protect his profits. However, Joseph Desjarlais shared kin with Toussaint Lesieur, his sister and cousin having married members of the Gélinas dit Lacourse family of Yamachiche, who, in turn, were heavily intermarried with the Lesieur family over several generations.[13] No doubt this connection provided him with some insulation from the violence of Pond and other traders, as well as the possibility of largesse in the form of provisions and other necessities from Lesieur.[14]

However, if Joseph Desjarlais wanted to remain permanently as an independent trader in the *pays d'en haut*, it was essential that he establish cordial relations with an aboriginal hunting band, which generally involved contracting a country union *à la façon du pays* with a woman from the group. Genealogical records in St. Boniface suggest that Joseph Desjarlais Jr. contracted such an alliance with an Ojibwa woman named Okimaskwew within two years of his receipt of his trading pass to Grand Portage in 1783.[15] Only fragmentary information survives concerning Okimaskwew. It is not known where she first encountered Joseph Desjarlais. What is known, is that at the time she had at least one known child, her Ojibwa son Tullibee,[16] when she established her union *à la façon du pays* with Joseph Desjarlais. It is possible that she was widowed by the great smallpox epidemic of 1780–83, which is believed to have wiped out between half and three-quarters of the Ojibwa populations living west and north of Grand Portage. Father Picton, the well-known Manitoba clergyman and genealogist, translated her name as meaning "Chief's (okimaw) woman (skwew). However, an alternative translation, in the Northern Alberta Cree (Neheyawak) dialect is "Boss-Lady."[17]

If Okimaskwew was, in fact, known as "boss-lady," it can be assumed that she assumed a role within her family that was unusual for most Ojibwa women. The growth of a powerful personality, according to Ruth Landes, was not deemed necessary for the typical Ojibwa woman, while it was considered essential for men because it was considered indicative of spiritual power. "To women are allotted the quiet, sedentary, and domestic occupations that are not considered dependent upon supernatural gifts."[18] Landes notes, however, that there were always Ojibwa women who took up men's roles and responsibilities due to extenuating circumstances or due to personal inclination. When such women behave in this manner, other women "regard them as 'extraordinary' or 'queer.' Men regard them rather in the light of the occupation they follow; to them a girl who qualifies as a warrior is considered as a warrior, not as a queer girl."[19]

So what does this suggest about the personality of "Boss-Lady"? It suggests that she may have been acting in the role of *okimaw*, or head of the family, when Joseph Desjarlais first encountered her in Rupert's Land sometime after 1783. As indicated earlier, the smallpox epidemic that concluded immediately prior to Joseph Desjarlais' arrival in the west was the kind of devastating event that may have forced Okimaskwew to assume roles normally reserved for men – hunting, warfare, and leadership. Had Okimaskwew been acting in a leadership capacity at the time of her meeting with Joseph Desjarlais, it would have been natural for him, as an independent fur trader, to attempt to establish a commercial alliance with the leader of an Ojibwa family. That the *okimaw*, in this case, was a widowed woman with children, possibly looking for another husband, would have been fortuitous indeed.

Joseph Desjarlais' entry into the fur trade as an independent was the exception rather than the rule. After 1783, most *Canadiens* entered the employ of British trading companies as *engagés* where they had little hope of advancement without literacy skills. *Canadiens* who engaged in the service of British traders did so for their own reasons; i.e., an engagement was a means to an end rather than an end in itself. For the seasonal *engagé* – the "porkeater" going to Grand Portage – the engagement provided an extra source of income to supplement a primary occupation elsewhere. For the winterer committing himself to a three-year contract "au Nord" the occupation of *engagé* was viewed as a temporary, albeit unpleasant apprenticeship under the British until the French gained ascendance in North America[20] once again, or until he could eventually become free in the *pays d'en haut*.

Contract employment was the path that Joseph Desjarlais' brother, Antoine (b. ca. 1760 at Contrecoeur) chose for entering the fur trade. In early 1792 he engaged with David and Peter Grant, who themselves chose to break away from the North

West Company in 1793 and operate as independents.[21] Antoine spent the next several years working for the Grants and for other firms affiliated with the North West Company. Antoine also contracted a country union with an Ojibwa woman, and became a freeman in 1805 after the coalition of the NW and XY Companies, trapping and trading in the vicinity of Red River.[22] In 1792 another Desjarlais from Rivière-du-Loup, François, had entered the service of McTavish, Frobisher, and Company to go to the Northwest.[23] By the early 1800s, Joseph, Antoine, and François Desjarlais were living as freemen along the eastern slopes of the Rocky Mountains and on the shores of Lesser Slave Lake and Lac La Biche.

Hudson's Bay Company clerk John Lee Lewes provided a succinct pre-1821 understanding of the term "freeman" as understood by the traders of the Athabasca region:

> The freemen are Canadians and Iroquois of Lower Canada and their descendants the Canadians are all the old servants of the NWCo who have Indian women and children by them and of this get completely attached to the Country and Indian way of living and are all like them constantly moving about living in leathern tents made of the skins of the Moose or Buffaloe. The half-breeds their descendants are excellent hunters and will generally procure at Slave Lake from 150 to 200 skins in a winter. They are very active in all they undertake and far exceed the generality of Indians in success at hunting. They are fond of finery in dress and this of the finest quality. They possess a large share of pride and vanity and their ignorance is deplorable and indeed it cannot be otherwise as all of the hired servants of both Companies and freemen @ this place there is only one Iroquois that can read or write. But the freemen are much courted by the Traders of the Respective Cos for the sake of the interests of their employers. Their pride and vanity is flattered their faults winked at and in fact honored in every respect. They are fond of spirituous liquors and on coming to the fort seldom fail to indulge in their favorite Beverage.[24]

By 1810 the *Canadien* Desjarlais and their mixed-blood offspring were enjoying regular employment and success as fur suppliers, as hunters, as fishermen, as interpreters, and as guides with the North West and later the Hudson's Bay Company in the Athabasca region. To the chagrin of the North West Company *bourgeois* and clerks compelled by necessity to woo the Desjarlais and other freemen families[25] wintering in the Athabasca hinterland, the success of these *hivernants* in hunting, trading, and forging alliances with local native groups gave the freemen the leverage over the British traders needed to extract trade goods, temporary employment, and other benefits from the competing trading firms as needed.

Because the freemen were not *engagés*, the Nor'Westers were prevented from employing the usual methods of physical coercion that could be applied to recalcitrant servants in their employ. Instead, they were compelled to use persuasion, deception, and bribery to manipulate the behaviour of the freemen.

In July of 1810, for example, Alexander Henry the Younger noted that members of the Desjarlais family and their hunting companions had come to White Earth House to borrow horses for transporting their families from Lac La Biche. It was their intention to go to the Rocky Mountains and then to the Columbia, "where they hoped to find beaver as numerous as blades of grass on the plains." Henry attempted to thwart their plans, commenting, "I took much trouble in trying to make a division among those freemen, to prevent them from crossing the mountains, where they will be even a greater nuisance to us than they are here." A few days later, a frustrated Henry reported "Troubled with those mongrel freemen and Indians all day. No dependence is to be placed upon them; they have neither principles, nor honor, nor honesty, nor a wish to do well; their aim is all folly, extravagance, and caprice: they make worse mischief that the most savage Blackfeet in the Plains."[26] Although Henry did manage to discourage some from travel, by 3 September Joseph Desjarlais Sr. (a.k.a. Old Joseph) and his stepson Tullibee[27] had arrived at White Earth House to borrow horses for the overland trip to the Columbia. Henry noted that:

> ... they propose to go toward the Rocky Mountains for the winter, and thence to the Columbia. These Freemen have

formed extravagant ideas of the numbers of beaver to be found on the W side of the mountains. I fain would prevent them from going there, but in vain; they are bent on the undertaking, and no persuasion will change their minds.[28]

Prior to 1815, the activities of the freemen in the Lesser Slave Lake region appeared untouched by the struggle for control of the Athabasca fur trade. There was occasional social intercourse between employees of both posts, and freemen appeared able to move freely between the two companies' establishments. However, this was to change, as the HBC, under the direction of ex-Nor'Wester Colin Robertson, spearheaded a push into Athabasca territory to establish for the first time a tangible company presence in the form of outposts manned by personnel ready and able to battle the NWCo. on its own terms.

The isolated skirmishes that had heretofore characterized the competition escalated as the companies destroyed their competitors' buildings, stole their furs and trade goods, scared away the game needed for food, and threatened employees. Although the freemen ostensibly benefited from aspects of this competition, the fight for control of the trade also threatened to destroy their livelihood.[29]

Prior to 1815 the NWCo. accounts, such as those of Alexander Henry the Younger, indicate that the family of Old Joseph Desjarlais was affiliated primarily with that concern, though his brother Antoine Desjarlais (a.k.a. Old Antoine) had begun to trade with the HBC by 1810.[30] However, by 1815, Antoine Desjarlais (son of Old Joseph Desjarlais and Okimaskwew) had engaged with the HBC at Lesser Slave Lake. The abrupt switch in loyalty implies that the presence of two competing companies in the area made it possible for freemen to negotiate, for the first time, the best possible financial and labour arrangements for themselves, and also suggests that any affinity held by *Canadien engagés* and freemen for the Montreal-based NWCo. was, in all likelihood, a union of convenience broken when the opportunity presented itself.

In the Lesser Slave Lake Post Journals of 1817–1818 the comings and goings of two generations of Desjarlais family members are recorded frequently by clerk John Lee Lewes. The elder generation consisted of *Canadien*-born brothers Old Joseph Desjarlais, whose home base was the east end of Lesser Slave Lake, and Old Antoine Desjarlais, who was settled at Lac La Biche. The second generation, most of whom appear to be Joseph's and Okimaskwew's sons, were also camped at the east end of Lesser Slave Lake. They include Tullibee, the eldest (step) son of Old Joseph (b. ca. 1784); Joseph Desjarlais Jr.; Baptiste (b. ca. 1790); Martial (a.k.a. Marcel); and Thomas. Only one brother, Antoine (b. ca 1792) lived apart from the family; his position of fort interpreter required him to reside at the HBC post, but he appeared to have spent some time wintering with his family as well.

Antoine's employment as fort interpreter at Lesser Slave Lake benefited both Lewes and *Les Desjarlais* in several ways. Lewes was able to employ the versatile Antoine as interpreter at the post and as an *en derouine* trader, sent to secure the furs of Plains Indian bands before the NWCo. could reach them. Through Antoine, Lewes was also able to monitor the activities of Antoine's brothers and other relations, and use Antoine's influence to keep them away from NWCo. advances.[31]

John Lewes's journal entries for the period indicate that he was required to send Antoine and other men to the Desjarlais lodges to secure their furs and bring them to the posts safely. Whether these steps were taken to prevent the family from being robbed by the NWCo. on the way to the post, or because Lewes was unsure of their willingness to direct their hunts to him, is not clear. However, by mid-February of 1819 Lewes had taken steps to bring the Desjarlais family securely within the HBC sphere of influence.

> 17th Feb.... This afternoon François and Rochleau returned from the Tulibiis tent by whom I Rec'd the following Furs sixteen Beaver, eighty Martin, two Otters two Foxes One Pound Castoreum. François informed me that he had left Baptiste Desjarlais in the Lake and that he wished People to be sent to meet him with Dogs to assist him to the House as he was obliged to have a Sledge himself. The cause of this young

man's coming here is on account that I sent for him to engage to the HBCo. This step I have taken upon myself providing that it will meet with the approbation of the Governor when he is informed that it is out of mere necessity which obliges me to do so.

Feb. 23. Sent off Antoine the Interpreter and François to meet Bapt. Desjarlais they returned in the Evening with the whole Family....

Feb. 25.... I this day had Baptiste Desjarlais engaged at the sum of two Thousand Livres pr Annum. This salary I make no Doubt will appear Enormous to the Eyes of the Governor in Chief and Committee but it was out of mere necessity which makes me take it upon myself to engage him for we are so unfortunately situated that unless we have him to hunt this Post as well as the Lives of the Companys Servants will be inevitably in danger, the Former of being abandoned and the Latter of Starvation.[32]

For the remainder of the winter of 1819 Baptiste was employed as fort hunter, while his brother Antoine acted as interpreter and traded *en derouine* with Iroquois freemen and local aboriginal groups. Baptiste also appears to have acted as fort interpreter in his brother's absence. The post remained in constant communication with Desjarlais family members, who visited the post throughout the winter to trade furs and provisions, but also to report on their living conditions. Food shortages – a by-product of the overhunting engendered by trade competition – were common, and Lewes sent off provisions and ammunition to Lesser Slave Lake to ease the starvation of the families of Joseph Desjarlais Jr. and Tullibee.[33]

Lewes's patronage of Desjarlais family members extended beyond provisions of employment and goods, as he appears to have designated Joseph Desjarlais' step-son Tullibee the Lesser Slave Lake trading chief by the spring of 1819. To wit:

Sun. May 2 – Men sent off with Bapt. they had met with Tolibee & Band coming to the House. I received by these two men Tolibii's Spring hunt consisting of 35 Beaver skins, and 7 lbs. of Castoreum ... they soon arrived. I had the Tolibee

Saluted with several discharges of Fowling Pieces as he is the
Chief Trader of this Place & a man most interested for the
Interest of the Company. I gave him a Chief's Equipt with a
View to intice the Crees of this Place to put confidence in his
greatness and to Listen to his Orations with more zeal in our
Cause the Natives of this Place are all except three waiting his
return at the East End of the Lake.

The Lesser Slave Lake District Report provides this description
of Tullibee, who appeared to have absorbed some of the cultural
influences of his *Canadien* kin:

> The name of the HBCo chief is Tulibii a Soteux by birth and
> of 34 years of age in Nature 5 feet 11 inches. His countenance
> denotes good nature and intelligence. He speaks French like a
> Canadian and dresses the same as the white people. In spring
> and fall he receives a full suit of the finest articles of clothing
> brought up (and a Keg of Indian Rum).[34]

The importance of the trading ceremony in cementing the
leadership status of a band chief should not be underestimated.
Although the presentation of a suit of European clothes might
ostensibly mark the recipient as someone of importance in
European eyes, the apparel had important spiritual implications
as well. One of the spirit helpers in Ojibwa mythology is a
character called the Sun. When the Sun appeared to a person
in a dream, "he was dressed like a Gentleman, i.e. a short coat,
waist coat, short breeches, stockings, boots a hat and a beautiful
feather in it. He speaks English...." A chief "rigged" in these
clothes might also be viewed as having received additional
spiritual power.[35] An Ojibwa such as Tullibee could enhance his
stature and extend his influence amongst the regional hunting
population simply by acquiring and manipulating these symbols
of supernatural power.

In the fall of 1819, a few days prior to receiving his annual
"rigging" and gifts as trading chief, the *Lesser Slave Lake Post
Journal* recorded that "Tolibii the chief and the Indians have
been all the day employed in a Medicine house. They are all
dressed in their gayest apparel."[36]

Over time John Lewes developed a firm friendship with Tullibee, and tented with him and his family outside of the fort. In 1820, Tullibee acknowledged his personal debt to John Lewes in a trading speech:

> ... I will always remain attached to you as I find myself well off – I am extremely proud that my conduct has been represented in so flattering a manner to the Company and approved of – I intend this year if success attends my hunting to go below to see the New Govr. I had thought before I entered here to receive your bounty of immediately returning it as none of my relations are now with me but upon further consideration I take them as the NW might make a scandal of it to ridicule me to relations and the Indians. I am ashamed to take the Presents as none of my relations are here to share it with me. But in spring I expect that many of them shall be here and then I shall use all my influence to prevent them going to war. – I heartily thank the Company for what they now give me and particularly you their Representative. I love you as I love myself for all your past kindnesses. I have served many traders but none like you.[37]

Tullibee's growing influence with John Lewes aided and abetted the ambitions of his younger half-brother Baptiste, who had already demonstrated prowess as a hunter and talent as an interpreter.

> ... all the Evening they Deverted themselves drinking. Bapt the Interpreter also Joined them, as the Tolibii is his Brother by the Mother's side. Late at night they all went over to the NW Fort where they all got fighting & Baptiste being intoxicated came off but second best.[38]

Journal entries for the following days describe Baptiste's subsequent dealings with the Nor'Westers:

> Mon. May 3.... Several Iroquois arrived this day at the NW Fort. One of this tribe sent over a challenge to Fight Bapt. but he was stopped from going to accept it as they are all intoxicated.

> Tues May 4.... Bapt. accordingly went over to the NW
> Fort to see if the Iroquois was in readiness to put his threats
> in execution he accordingly fought Bapt but could not keep
> his Ground as he was too weak. Bapt afterwards went into
> one of the Men's Houses when one of the NW men rushed
> into the House & struck Bapt who immediately returned the
> Compliment & knocked Him Down several others ran in &
> Held Bapt. while the others struck him McDonnell & Henry
> whe were Present Encouraging their People to this unequal
> Contest. But Bapt soon put an end to this unequal Contest by
> a compleat Victory over them all.[39]

The next day Lewes sent Baptiste to join his family at the east
end of the lake, presumably to avoid further battles.

It is not clear whether Lewes allowed Baptiste to fight with
the Iroquois as an indulgence, or whether it was done as a
calculated move to establish Baptiste's influence over Natives
who might possibly be persuaded to join the HBC cause. In any
case, Baptiste's stature in the eyes of both the Iroquois freemen
and the Hudson's Bay British seems to have grown. By June of
1819 Baptiste Desjarlais was identified as the fort Interpreter,
and was trading *en derouine* with Iroquois freemen on behalf of
the post.[40]

In the post journal of 7 August 1819, kept by a clerk named
William Smith, it is recorded that Baptiste Desjarlais traded goods
to an Iroquois *already* indebted to the Company, implying that
Desjarlais should have extracted the skins without payment and
applied them to the Iroquois' outstanding debt. An exasperated
Smith wrote that he hoped Mr. Lewis would "impinge" upon
Baptiste to "understand better not to do it again."

Smith's frustration suggests that he was not in total agreement
with John Lewes's management of the freemen under his employ,
hinting that Baptiste had overstepped his bounds in negotiating
deals with the Iroquois. The Lesser Slave Lake District Report
provides an interesting perspective on Baptiste's rise to power.

> The Master of this District [John Lee Lewes] was under the
> disagreeable necessity of making (Nishecabo) Bapt. Desjarlais
> a half brother of Tulibiis a chief of the same consequence as

the NWCo had made great offers to him to be their Chief – he is a very powerful man and of a daring ambitious disposition and on these accounts much feared by the Indians if he had not been made chief by Mr. Lewes he would have accepted the NWCo offers and left the HBCo with all his brothers and relations and by his influence among the Indians have put the HBCo to double the expense. These people know well how to take advantage of the times but it is to be hoped that a time will very soon come when these fellows will be more kept under by the power of a single trader.... [41]

Although Baptiste Desjarlais' hunting abilities and physical strength impressed the HBC men, it is unlikely that his status among the traders would have been sufficient to establish him outside the post as a man of power in the eyes of the Indians. The possibility that Baptiste took steps to impress upon the Natives of the region that his power was of supernatural origin should not be discounted.[42] It is only *after* Baptiste's exploits of 1819–20 – when he assumes the mantle of trading chief – that he is identified by the name Nishecabo in the trade records. The use of his aboriginal name in the records after the autumn of 1819 suggests that he began using this name publicly after he became a trading chief – hence its appearance in the post journals. Why would Baptiste begin using his aboriginal name, Nishecabo? One possible explanation is that he wished to impress upon others his spiritual links with his "spirit helpers."[43]

Although some of Joseph Desjarlais' sons were establishing themselves as chiefs in the aboriginal tradition, others, such as Antoine Desjarlais the interpreter, chose to identify with their *Canadien* ancestry rather than their aboriginal heritage. This process was probably facilitated by the elder generation of Desjarlais men, who had maintained contact with their relatives in Quebec. Old Antoine Desjarlais, Master of the Post at Red Deer's Lake (Lac La Biche), was receiving letters from family members resident in Varennes.[44] Other documentation suggests that Old Joseph Desjarlais travelled to Quebec for at least one visit. In the *Lesser Slave Lake Post Journal of 1820*, accountant Robert Kennedy recorded the following entry:

... Old [Joseph] Desjarlais who came up from Montreal with the NW canoes, he is the father of our interpreter and of several halfbreeds attached to the HBCo, he returned to the house with me to remain here for his family.... [45]

The occupational preferences exhibited by Antoine Desjarlais[46] – in sharp contrast to his brothers – appears to have caused observers such as Robert Kennedy to draw a distinction between Joseph Desjarlais' offspring. Antoine's behaviours also suggest that at least some of the first generation of "proto Métis" continued to identify with Euro-*Canadien* values and attitudes, a choice no doubt facilitated by their fathers' maintenance of family ties to Quebec. As long as mutual relations with kin and community were maintained, the mixed-race children of *Canadiens* were considered part of the much larger kinship network originating in the French settlements on the St. Lawrence and the outposts along the Mississippi and Missouri, a tradition which was well-established by over two hundred years of frontier exploration and diplomacy. From an "ethnogenesis" standpoint, mixed-race children were not a separate people – not yet.

For the Desjarlais family, maintaining Euro-Canadian links in the trading post via bicultural siblings was an important survival mechanism as well as a matter of personal preference for young Antoine. During times of hardship, having a relative in the post ensured that pressure could be brought to bear to release ammunition, medicines, and other necessary provisions if needed.

Employment in a trading post also served to socialize the children of freemen to Euro-Canadian values, attitudes, and behaviours, enhancing their ability to move freely between both cultures. Biracial *engagés*, and their sisters who had married Euro-Canadian traders, were able to exert a further socializing influence on their siblings and cousins living away from the post. Over time, these prolonged and intimate exposures to *both* cultural milieus served to distinguish métis wintering families from Indian wintering groups, despite the hunting and gathering lifestyle that they both shared.

Conversely, the continued intermarriage of family members with Indians in aboriginal bands[47] also maintained and strengthened the social ties needed to maintain the access of freemen to the furs of aboriginal trappers. Kin ties also permitted freemen themselves to hunt and trap, free from molestation by local aboriginal groups protecting their hunting territories from outsiders.[48]

The Dispersion of the Desjarlais Freeman Band

As was noted earlier, the competition for control of the Athabasca fur trade in the years prior to the 1821 merger caused animal populations to plummet. The HBC employees and freemen suffered constant harassment from the North West Company. In addition to the threat of physical violence, disease took its toll on the Indians. During the fall and winter of 1819–20, a measles epidemic raced through the Native population of Athabasca, killing thirty-nine men, women, and children, including five of Lewes's best hunters. Predictably, the supply of pelts from the winter's trade was small, and Lewes blamed the North West Company, whom he suspected of deliberately introducing the disease into Athabasca to punish the natives for trading with the HBC.[49] This placed added stress on the freemen, and particularly the trading chiefs, who were compelled by both pride and outstanding debt to produce pelts and provisions regardless of their own privations.

The Desjarlais family did not remain untouched by this epidemic. On 2 November 1819, the Lac La Biche post journal noted that "The whole Fort is a hospital." Antoine Desjarlais, the métis interpreter at Lac La Biche, his wife Suzanne Allary, and his children were all sick. Antoine's half-brother, the Ojibwa trading chief Tullibee, accompanied by his brothers Thomas and Marcel Desjarlais, had arrived at the post with their sick mother Okimaskwew. By the following day, both Thomas and Marcel were also ill. Soon Tullibee caught the measles, and was sick for the entire month of December.[50] During the winter of 1820–21, misfortune continued to dog both the HBC traders and the freemen. Reports of starvation and disease from isolated Indian and freeman bands wintering away from the post were not encouraging. Many of the hunters had contracted debts prior to the winter in anticipation of a successful winter's hunt. Their misfortunes over the winter resulted in a reduction of pelts and an outstanding debt in the spring that could not be paid off. The Desjarlais family fared no better.

The measles epidemic had hit the family hard. Thomas Desjarlais, the son of Joseph Desjarlais and Okimaskwew, had suffered a relapse after his bout with the measles. Having lost the power of movement in one arm and along his side, he remained at the post in the company of his mother who was waiting for his recovery. By mid-February of 1820, however, the clerk in charge had had enough of their presence, noting that Thomas was "unable to do anything towards paying his credit." As a result both Okimaskwew and her disabled son were summarily "pitched from the House."[51]

Later, accountant Robert Kennedy observed in the annual *District Report*:

> Nishecabo who was made chief last fall for the seasons then mentioned – Rec'd his usual presents at Red Deer Lake – and gave as a present in return 25 beavers – the Hunt of himself and his Band was not so much as was expected he himself gave 50 Beaver Skins but was unable to exert himself as he had promised as he had the venerial disease. – He with his Brothers and relations have since gone to L.S. Lake where they will remain.[52]

By the early spring of 1821 the Hudson's Bay and North West companies were officially amalgamated, ending the vicious competition that had characterized the Athabasca trade. John Lewes was appointed to the position of chief trader and transferred to the Columbia Department, while William Conolly became chief trader at Lesser Slave Lake, a post he assumed in August of 1821.[53]

Under the direction of Governor George Simpson, the traders began the task of systematizing and regularizing the day-to-day operations of the company, with an eye to cutting staff and reducing expenses that had ballooned out of control during the years of competition. Simpson had had his eyes on the activities of the freemen for some time. As early as 1820 he had discouraged his traders from giving in to the freemen's demands for provisions, and had in fact encouraged his staff to avoid doing business with the freemen altogether.[54]

A number of Hudson's Bay Company personnel had grown to resent the largesse given the freemen and those of their relatives employed with the company, who often enjoyed privileges not accorded to other company workers. As Colin Robertson observed in the *Fort St. Mary's Journal,*

> ... Had some difficulty with a half Gentleman, an Interpreter, named Dejarlais. The fellow wanted to be put on the same footing as St. Germain: sit idle on the Canoes, and have his allowance of tea and sugar; had it not been for Mr. McDonald I would have left him here. I shall certainly purge the Athabasca Department of these *rubbish!*[55]

The new chief trader at Lesser Slave Lake, William Conolly, began the task of scaling-back privileges to freemen at the semi-annual trading ceremony of October 1821.

> Three of Desjarlais Sons, his son-in-law, Cardinal's son ... the Old Tondre and 2 sons arrived with colors flying, firing.... As these freemen took every advantage of the times & was completely spoilt during the opposition I thought it best to let them feel ... that times had altered by receiving them rather coolly & presenting them with nothing more than each a foot of tobacco per man. In fact they got goods [at such a] cheap rate that its impossible to afford them anything greater. this of course they will not like.... Most of the freemen in this quarter are greatly indebted to either, and some of them to both, the companies.[56]

By 10 December 1821 William Conolly had met Tullibee, the Hudson's Bay Company trading chief, for the first time, noting sourly:

> ... This Tolibee was in immense debt which is absolutely impossible he will ever pay, he was one of Mr. Lewes *chiefs*

The People Who Own Themselves

& has been more spoilt than I believe any other. *He will of course feel* the changes that have taken place more severely than others.[57]

Over the winter of 1821–22 the various groups of aboriginal and *Canadien* freemen managed to improve their hunts, but not enough to alter Conolly's treatment of them.

> March 18, 1822.... Their hunts are not great but Suffice to pay their Debts of this year. This Tullibii was one of Mr. Lewes chiefs and appears greatly disappointed at not meeting with his [former] treatment. Be this as it may he must endeavor to content himself with what he can get.[58]

Conolly appears to have dispensed with the spring and fall trading ceremonies shortly thereafter, as they do not appear in the records for 1821–22. The Desjarlais' fall from grace was not only rapid, but must have been humiliating as well. As Conolly notes in his District Report of 1821–22:

> ... the People who go under the Dinomination of Free Men ... were, during the late opposition, accustomed to get goods to any amount they pleased, and at very reduced prices. Besides this, several of those who traded with Mr. Lewes were Cloathed as Chiefs, received Large Kegs of strong Liquor as presents. And Many other things. – Moreover their Brains were stuffed with So many promises that their disappointment at not finding their expectations realized is scarcely to be described.[59]

In his report Conolly also made specific reference to Antoine Desjarlais, commenting that Desjarlais "... is a man of good abilities as an Interpreter, but being also a very good Hunter, the Company will reap more benefits from his labors as such than in a capacity in which his services are not now required."[60]

One can only imagine how the Desjarlais family must have reacted to the rapid collapse of their collective fortunes. In two short years, Tullibee and his half-brother Baptiste Desjarlais, formerly the region's most influential trading chiefs, had been stricken with starvation and disease and publicly humiliated, stripped of the honours to which they had become accustomed.

Joseph Desjarlais' son Antoine, who had chosen to pursue a life in the Euro-Canadian trading sphere, found his options for advancement within the HBC reduced, if not completely eliminated by his arbitrary demotion to hunter from interpreter by William Conolly.[61]

Antoine's reaction to the curtailment of his opportunities was swift. In the *District Report* of 1821–22, William Conolly reported:

> Antoine Desjarlais and Primeau have both come out. The object of the former's trip is, I believe, to determine what encouragement the Red River holds out to people of his description, and if it answers his expectations, himself, his Brothers & and Brother-in-Law would retire thither, an act which would deprive Slave Lake of Six or Seven good hunters.[62]

It is not clear whether Antoine's fact-finding mission was an immediate success. Over the years that followed, the family began trapping with renewed zeal and, according to Conolly, "were determined to exert themselves to pay their debts."[63] The winter of 1823, however, brought with it the same bad fortune that had plagued the family in the previous winters.

> Friday Feb. 25. About 11:00 a.m. Bte Desjarlais arrived half dead with hunger, he left his brother Joseph & their families yesterday morning in so weak a state that they were unable to move. The object of his trip is to beg a supply of provisions.... Starvation is not the only misfortune they have ... having lost 100 skins 80 of which were from Beaver, that were destroyed by Wolverines ... year after year Caches are destroyed by wood animals, yet will these stupid Free Men, & particularly the Iroquois, continue to expose their furs in this foolish way.... [64]

On 14 March 1823, Conolly reported on the Desjarlais family's declining fortunes further:

> ... They saw old [Joseph] Desjarlais & family at the East end of the lake almost dead with hunger & begging for God's Sake

that I should send him some assistance without which they must surely perish.[65]

Conolly advanced the family some provisions and ammunition to relieve their distress. Despite the evidence of their continued hardship, Conolly persisted in his belief that the minuscule returns were the result of their laziness.

> ... the rascals might have done much better had they been inclined to work.... I attempted this spring to punish some for their laziness by refusing them a supply of ammunition for the Summer. This I am confident would have had a good effect were there no other place from whence they could obtain that article.[66]

By spring the Desjarlais families had moved to Lac La Biche, in search of better hunting opportunities. Tullibee and his half-brother Antoine Desjarlais chose other pursuits:

> Monday June 9 Reached Lac La Biche at 2 p.m. and the Big Island at 6 where we found Old [Joseph] Desjarlais, his son Martial and Pembrook. They informed me that Tolibii, with Antoine Desjarlais and Antoine Allarie had joined a party of Crees ... on a war expedition.... [67]

The participation of Tullibee and Antoine Desjarlais in a Cree war expedition suggests that the members of the Desjarlais family were seeking to re-establish their status with their Native neighbours. It also suggests that they may have been attempting, along with the Cree, to expand their hunting territories by forcibly removing rival bands out of hunting areas they coveted for themselves.

As far as William Conolly was concerned however, the actions of the freemen were yet another example of their irresponsibility.

> ... The Coalition has had a good effect with regard to the Indians who saw the necessity of staying Industrious.... But the Freemen are incorrigible. They are addicted to all kinds of vices. I have tried fair means with them in vain and I fear that nothing but the severest of measures will bring them to

their senses. They are now anxiously expecting an American opposition,[68] and endeavor to instill the same notions into the minds of the Indians. As such stories tend to nourish that spirit of independence which was excited by the late Opposition, they must of course be injurious, and the propogation of them ought to be punished.[69]

By the fall of 1824 the same group of freemen was preparing to make war again, this time in the Columbia region, an area where, fourteen years earlier, they had gone in search of beaver "as numerous as the grass on the plains." In George Simpson's journal entry of 21 September 1824, he reported on his visit to

> ... the Banks of Lake la Biche, where we found old [Antoine] Dejoilais the Freeman and his Family likewise Cardinals Family and a posse of Freeman and their followers. These people with a few Cutonais and Soteux were preparing to go on a War Expedition against a poor helpless inoffensive tribe of Indians "Shewhoppes" natives of the North branch of the Thompsons River knowing them to be weak and unprovided with the means of defense and solely with a view to plunder and gain renown as Warriors by taking a few Scalps without incurring danger. On these poor wretches they made a War a few Years ago and treacherously massacred a whole camp in the Mountain on their way to the Fort.[70]

However, Simpson would not tolerate such incursions because it interfered with his own plans to encourage the Shuswaps to cross the mountains to visit Rocky Mountain House in Athabasca Pass. Indeed, Simpson and his associates had finally recognized, to their dismay, that the freemen had become a serious threat to the long-term survival of the Company. Over time, trading relations with aboriginal groups had evolved to the point that *Canadien* and Iroquois *engagés*, speaking aboriginal languages and living *en derouine* with their Native relatives, were exercising control over the critical aspects of the trade. It was *Canadien* and Iroquois *engagés* who were agitating for improved working conditions and creating labour unrest in the firm. And it was *Canadien* and Iroquois freemen – mobile, skilled, and disloyal

– who were encouraging desertion and inviting competition from the Americans to the south.[71] It was clear that something had to be done to neutralize the influence of the freemen and re-establish Company control over their activities. In the meantime, Simpson dealt with his most immediate problem – the Desjarlais family and their plans to make war in the Rocky Mountains.

> ... I therefore spoke my Mind very plainly to those freemen, told them we meant to protect the Shewhoppes and if they did not instantly abandon their cruel intentions they should not this winter have even a particle of ammunition at any of our Establishments and that next Season they should be bundled down to Canada where starvation & misery would follow them. This lecture had the desired effect and they promised that they would no longer entertain hostile feelings towards those people.[72]

During the July 1825 meeting of the governing council of the HBC's Northern Department, the following resolution was introduced into the Minutes:

> 89. That all Freemen Half breed or Iroquois Trappers having no other means of paying (for) their supplies than with their Hunts to be treated on the footing of Indians, unless where otherwise specially provided for by Council and that Freemen not coming under that description having Funds in the Companys hands and unable to pay their supplies with Furs, be charged 200 p. Cent on the District Inventory prices and that no money in payment of furs or other articles be allowed either class without directions from Council.[73]

It is probable that the punitive 1825 operating policies targeting freemen, combined with Simpson's prior ban on their raiding activities, marked the end of the Desjarlais family influence in the Lesser Slave Lake region. Their lack of outstanding fur returns had diminished their stature in the eyes of the new regime of traders, who were not prepared to continue the patronage relationship they had enjoyed in the past with John Lewes. The result was the loss of trading chief status by Tullibee and Nishecabo, and with it the favours and trade goods needed to maintain status among their followers. Their public diminishment by the traders, compounded by their lack of sustained hunting success, their loss of already-harvested pelts through destruction of caches compounded by their bouts with starvation and serious illness, may have convinced their Indian allies and relations that Tullibee and Nishecabo had lost their spiritual power.

As A. Irving Hallowell has noted, there was no formalized mechanism for meting out punishment to individuals in Ojibwa society. The "spirit helpers" in Ojibwa religion did not act to punish. Instead, the Ojibwa believed that a spirit helper would withhold assistance from individuals who had morally transgressed. If a hunter committed a moral offense, it was believed that the hunter's spirit helpers would not allow animals to be caught. There were also sanctions against cruelty to animals in Ojibwa culture. Unnecessary killing of animals, or causing them unnecessary suffering, was subject to sanction by spirit helpers, who would withdraw assistance to hunters guilty of this offense.[74]

The effect of Nishecabo's bout with venereal disease on his stature as a trading chief and shaman should not be discounted. In Ojibwa culture, it was believed that sickness was a punishment for bad conduct on the part of an individual. In particular, any serious illness of unknown origin that proved resistant to treatment was believed to be the result of immoral or unethical dealings, or the violation of taboos. His contemporaries would have assumed that he was being punished for misconduct as a hunter, or for abusing his powers as a shaman, or for not exhibiting the qualities of generosity expected of a band leader.[75]

Governor Simpson's ban on warring against rival groups effectively prevented *Les Desjarlais* from renewing their status as leaders or gaining access to new hunting territories where they might experience renewed hunting success. As a result, the family was denied the only mechanism remaining which would have enabled them to retain their followers and maintain their cohesion in that region. Roger McDonnell has concluded:

... bands were political units that assembled around the promise of benefits associated with the abilities of particular individuals. These abilities were understood to be a manifestation of spiritual powers that were employed for the benefit of others. If such benefits diminished – so, too, might the band: if they increased – so might the number of would-be beneficiaries.[76]

Simpson's threat that the Desjarlais would "be bundled down to Canada where starvation & misery would follow them" was strangely prescient. In 1825 Marguerite Desjarlais Langevin[77] (b. 1766) the sister of Old Joseph and Old Antoine Desjarlais, had applied for curatorship[78] over her siblings' landholdings in the parish of Varennes, stating that her male relatives had no intentions of returning to Lower Canada to live. By the 1820s the seigneuries had become overcrowded and the soil overworked. Land was at a premium, and those who could not obtain new farmland were forced to migrate elsewhere.[79] Had the now-elderly Desjarlais brothers attempted to return to Lower Canada with their Native wives and children, they would have found themselves disinherited. Their choices had run out.

For the Desjarlais family, the opportunities for bettering themselves and their families had ended in the Lesser Slave Lake area, and in Lower Canada as well. Over the next few years the names of Desjarlais family members disappeared from the Lesser Slave Lake post records, suggesting that their regional political influence had diminished and that the bands headed by the two former Desjarlais trading chiefs had disintegrated. By April of 1827 a new HBC trading chief, Le Maigre, was rigged in chief's clothes and given rum.[80]

The Social Dynamics of Boreal Forest Hunting Bands

Most *Canadien* freemen were former *engagés* who had managed to establish a measure of commercial autonomy for themselves apart from the established trading companies. In doing so, they were heirs to the entrepreneurial *ethos* fostered in the early days of New France, where only those who were daring, ambitious, and skilled could achieve the reputation and wealth needed to become "men of consequence" in *Canadien* society. Becoming a freeman was one of the few avenues for social and economic mobility that remained for *Canadiens* in a fur trade dominated by the British. The emergence of freemen in the Athabasca country is interesting not only because it testifies to the persistence of social and economic strategizing among *Canadien* traders, but also because the emergence of *Canadien* freemen was essential for the process of Métis ethnogenesis to take place.

As John Foster indicated in his research on wintering and Métis ethnogenesis, an *engagé* could not become free unless he established an influential relationship with an aboriginal hunting band. However, this was not always an easy process. Not only did the *engagé* have to earn the respect of the band members to be accepted, but he had to alter his values, attitudes, and behaviours to conform to the *mores* of the aboriginal group he wished to join. In the case of the *Canadiens* of the Desjarlais family, the forest/parkland hunting groups which they joined were primarily Ojibwa, and later, Cree.

A typical Ojibwa hunting band was fluid, with its membership expanding or contracting in direct relationship to the seasonal subsistence cycle. In summertime, groups of several extended families would establish adjoining clusters of lodges adjacent to an abundant fishing site. In late fall, the large summer band would break up into smaller winter hunting groups, comprised of an extended family group consisting of two to three families, about sixteen people in all. There would be at least two married couples in each group with their children. The ratio of hunters to non-hunters would be about one to three. In about half of the Ojibwa hunting bands surveyed by A. I. Hallowell, the males would consist of a father and his married sons, or a father and his sons-in-law. This group would move to an isolated area to carry out their hunting and trapping activities until early spring.[81]

Another characteristic of the winter hunting band was its association with a delimited tract of land – a hunting territory – which could range anywhere from thirteen to over two hundred square miles. The size of a hunting territory was fluid, and was determined upon the numbers of active hunters, the abundance of game, and the topography. Prior to the arrival of the fur trade, rights to a hunting territory were based on usufruct (i.e., customary use of the bounty of land). After the fur trade was introduced, however, individual hunters had specific debts contracted with trading houses which they were expected to pay back with pelts. A state of indebtedness required a steady supply of furs, which in turn encouraged the hunter and his kinsmen to discourage interlopers by maintaining a regular pattern of seasonal use.[82]

How a hunting band established dominance or possession over a hunting territory is a matter of some debate.[83] The instances of inter-group warfare recorded during the historic period were instigated, in several instances, in order to prevent enemies from gaining access to trade goods, particularly firearms. For the Cree and Assiniboine, preventing access to trade enabled them to maintain their lucrative role as middlemen in the fur trade, at least until 1821. Possession of firearms made it possible to move aggressively into new hunting areas, and to defend existing hunting territory. Both the Blackfoot and Cree made war on the Kootenay and Shuswap to keep them on the west side of the Rocky Mountains, away from the plains where they could hunt bison, and away from Euro-Canadian traders who could supply them with firearms.[84]

Another factor influencing the establishment and maintenance of hunting territories was the assumption of regional power and influence by a specific hunting band. This regional authority would be determined in part by the manifestation of charismatic and spiritual power by the male members and headmen of these bands. According to Roger McDonnell,[85] band formation and disintegration were both a function and a direct result of the following events:

* the acquisition and manifestation of personal "power" by an individual;

* the attraction of other individuals to follow a leader with power, who used that power to benefit the group;

* the evidence of diminished power of a leader, which in turn results in dissolution of the band.

In Ojibwa society, religion, dreams, and visions provided both the explanations and direction needed to combat the stresses of life in the northern forests; illness, accidents, uncertain food resources, and lack of information.[86] In the world-view of the Ojibwa, everyday events were imbued with personal significance, and were believed to be directly linked "... to the actions of one's spirit guardian, the intervention of other human beings through sorcery or 'medicine,' the pleasure or displeasure of animal spirits at their treatment by hunters, and so on."[87] Individuals sought after an ideal state of being known as *pimådäziwin*, characterized by longevity, health, and freedom from misfortune. In order to achieve this goal, a person's individual talents and efforts were supplemented and enhanced by the help of human and "other-than-human" beings.[88] For this reason, hunting bands evolved around those males who were perceived to possess supernatural power which could be used to benefit the entire group, whether they were blood relatives or not.

In woodland hunting societies, success in hunting was viewed as both a function and a result of an individual's possession of supernatural power, "in being able to anticipate where animals will be when there is little or no evidence to indicate this with certainty." McDonnell notes that while all members of a band would have a general knowledge of hunting and be able to support their families, "there are always some who, on the basis of similar or identical knowledge or equipment or – even better – less information and poorer equipment, consistently produce more impressive results."[89] It is these individuals who are believed to be blessed with power.

Individuals with power were not only able to find animals, but also to prevent other bands from encroaching on their hunting territories by bewitching rival hunters.[90] Both of these goals were facilitated by ceremonial practices such as the "shaking tent" – what Euro-Canadian observers often described as "conjuring." In Hallowell's study of conjuring in Saulteaux society, he determined that approximately 20 per cent of the male members of a band would have practised conjuring at one time or another, based on the presence of known conjurers in contemporary Ojibwa hunting bands. Because success in hunting was believed to be derived from the active intervention of conjurers, as well as spiritual power received through dreams, Hallowell concluded that all hunting bands would have required the presence of at least one conjurer.[91]

The possession of conjuring power by an individual did not automatically result in leader status. A variety of qualities had to be exhibited before band members would consider him as leader. As the Chief Trader at York Factory, Andrew Graham once noted with reference to the Cree,

> When several tents or families meet to go to war, or to the Factories to trade, they choose a leader; but it is only a voluntary obedience. Everyone is at liberty to leave him when he pleases; and the notion of a commander is quite obliterated when the journey or voyage is over. Merit alone gives the title to distinction; and the possession of qualities that are held in esteem, is the only method of obtaining affection and respect out of his own house. Thus a person who is an expert hunter, one who knows the communications between lakes and rivers, can make long harangues, is a conjurer and has a family of his own; such a man will not fail of being followed by several Indians when they assemble in large parties.... They follow him down to trade at the settlements, and style him Uckimow, that is a great man, chief or leader; but he is obliged to secure their attendance by promises and regards, as the regard paid to his abilities is of too weak a nature to purchase subjection.[92]

Leadership, according to McDonnell, depended not only on the capabilities of the individual but "how they deployed the results of their achievements."[93] He goes on to state that:

> ... the person with "power" who was for this reason understood to be outside of society, was required to show that s/he was *for* society and the only way s/he could do this was to show that s/he wielded his (or her) abilities to benefit others. The horses for which a man took such trouble to go

to raiding parties, the meat that he acquired in the hunt, even the advantages he might develop with European traders, were thus translated into social standing and status *only to the extent that others benefited*. His standing was a product not of restricting the access of others to food, transport and other necessary goods and services, but rather of making it available to others. He would quite literally give the stuff away – and in the process draw towards himself an assemblage of those who had come to recognize his "powers" as powers *for* them. To be a recipient of such benefits was, critically, to be a beneficiary of specific powers as these were recognized to be deployed for the benefit of others.[94]

Band leadership was fluid, and a leader's authority was based on the consent of his followers. As Andrew Graham observed,

> They have no manner of government or subordination amongst them. The father or head of a family owns no superior, obeys no command. He gives his advice and opinion of things, but has no authority to enforce obedience. The youth of his family obey his directions; but it is rather filial affection and reverence than in consequence of a duty exacted by a superior.[95]

This brief overview of the dynamics of aboriginal hunting band formation suggests that bands depended on the assumption of leadership by one or more male group members who possessed the combination of personal and spiritual attributes needed for group survival. It also suggests that an outsider, such as a *Canadien* male, would be required to demonstrate that he had personal qualities complementary to, but not supplanting, those already possessed by existing male members of a band before he would be permitted to marry one of their women *à la façon du pays*.[96]

For most Euro-Canadians, their most attractive personal qualities would have been their access to trade goods, and later, their language skills and familiarity with Euro-Canadian practices which would be useful in a broker capacity when dealing with other Euro-Canadian traders in the future. Once admitted as a member of the band via union with a female band member, the *engagé* could assume a position of autonomy outside the trading post sphere. His acquisition of aboriginal relatives and kinship status provided him with protection from hostile Natives and also insulated him from the violence of other Euro-Canadian traders who might wish to coerce him back into direct service. His membership in an aboriginal hunting band would also provide him with the assistance he needed to survive in the wilderness until he was capable of establishing and maintaining a family independently from his aboriginal kinsmen.

Until the freeman was able to establish himself independently, however, he had to ingratiate himself with his Indian wife's relatives. To do this successfully he had to contribute to the band's survival, which meant maintaining its dominance of hunting territories within a geographical region. These obligations required the freeman and his mixed-blood children to cultivate the cultural and spiritual attributes most admired and feared by other Native people.

Once a freeman had established himself, his country wife, and his métis children in a group apart from the aboriginal parent band, they continued to cultivate aboriginal values, attitudes, and modes of behaviour. These "proto-Metis" family groups were compelled to operate as aboriginal hunting bands, not only to maintain solidarity with their Indian relations but also to establish dominance over their own hunting territories.

As was indicated earlier, the boundaries of band hunting territories became less fluid and more defined as hunting pressures engendered by the fur trade compelled hunters to supply specific numbers of pelts based on externally-determined exchange values for furs and not on the carrying capacity of the land. This in turn forced the newly developed "proto-Metis" hunting bands to aggressively define and protect their hunting territories by establishing and maintaining a dominant regional presence. This influence was maintained by its members demonstrating spiritual power through the practice of sorcery, physical dominance through warfare and individual tests of strength, and usufruct dominance of territory by maintaining continued hunting success. Their position of strength was reinforced and enhanced by the European traders, who designated successful hunters – of all ethnic stripes – as trading chiefs and bestowed upon them the symbols of dominance in the European context.[97]

Conclusion

The freeman's role of cultural broker in the hinterland provided prestige, wealth (by wilderness standards), independence, and a surprising degree of power over the lives of both Europeans and Natives. As a result, the freeman directed his efforts towards maintaining his personal autonomy while at the same time devising ways and means to extract the maximum benefits from the fur trading companies without jeopardizing the business relationship.

In order for freemen to maintain their independence, enhance their status, and ensure the physical and social well-being of their families, it was necessary for them to establish their dominance over the fur trade in the areas where they lived. Freemen bands functioned best when they could maintain familial relations with adjacent Indian bands and with personnel at Euro-Canadian trading companies *simultaneously*, a task best accomplished when individual family members contracted marriages *à la façon du pays*, secured employment in trading posts, and wintered with Indian bands. Having family members in both environments facilitated the free flow of goods back and forth, enabling individual freemen to profit from their role as fur brokers between their Indian kin and Euro-Canadian traders, while ensuring a steady and generous supply of the desired European trade goods through their relatives employed in the posts.

Should real or fictive kin relations not enable freemen to achieve the economic goals of themselves or their relatives, their strategies would be adjusted accordingly. In choosing alternative methods, they selected from either the aboriginal or Euro-Canadian cultural repertoire, as individual inclination, talent, or immediate circumstances dictated. One or two family members might seek power and influence among local Indian bands as shamans, hunters, or warriors, forcibly moving into hunting territories through the threat of physical violence, sorcery, or hunting skill. Other family members, in the meantime, would apply pressure to the trading companies by threatening to work for opposing firms, by withdrawing their service as *engagés*, interpreters, and hunters, or by pressuring other *engagés* to desert. They would use their mobility to avoid Euro-Canadian trade sanctions, and manipulate their kin connections to foment discontent among the local natives.

These techniques, however, only worked in an environment where freemen's services were deemed to be essential and irreplaceable, or where the freemen could gain access to alternative, competing markets or employment. Unfortunately for the Desjarlais and other families like them, the ability to manipulate working conditions in their favour began to disappear as the Hudson's Bay Company and the American Fur Company took the place of Montreal-based companies, and as the national boundaries of Canada and the United States shifted to annex and subjugate wilderness areas.

The temporary decline of the Desjarlais family fortunes was, in large part, due to new policies implemented by the Hudson's Bay Company after 1821 to "systematize and regularize" its business practices, and consolidate its trade monopoly in Rupert's Land. To achieve this objective, the company needed to control the activities of individuals both inside and outside of the direct employ of the firm. A key element of its strategy was the development of policies targeted at individuals and groups identified as "freemen," "half-breed," or "Indian," intended to undermine their power, influence, and autonomy by restricting access to essential goods and services. In doing so, the Hudson's Bay Company inaugurated a lengthy tradition of corporate and government ascription of aboriginal identity, and indigenous resistance to same.

The period of 1821–30 was a time of economic and social transition for the Desjarlais family and other freemen in Rupert's Land. Despite the initial hardships brought about by the Hudson's Bay Company monopoly, however, the unique skills of the freeman remained indispensable. The continued trade in pemmican and buffalo robes, so essential to the survival of the Hudson's Bay Company, soon brought a degree of economic prosperity to those freemen who chose to remain in Rupert's Land with their Native wives and children. As time and distance slowly eroded their kin relations with their families in Lower Canada *and* their tribal kin in Rupert's Land, stronger kinship bonds were established with other freemen families. In one or two generations, thriving new communities whose cultural, political, and economic *ethos* embodied the nexus of European and aboriginal values, attitudes, and behaviours would become well established.

5

Migration and Retrenchment: 1821–1869

The 1821 coalition of the Hudson's Bay and North West companies brought with it several changes which negatively affected the labouring classes of the fur trade. The restructuring of the transportation system reduced the need for skilled canoemen, an occupation that had been dominated by *Canadiens* since the Conquest. Those *Canadiens* who were permitted to stay on with the Hudson's Bay Company were those who had useful skills (e.g., facility in Native languages, ability to manufacture canoes) and, more importantly, were prepared to alter their behaviour to conform to the Company's standards of conduct, as embodied in a set of procedures known as the "Retrenching System."[1]

The new standards of conduct were intended to return a sense of obedience and industry to a workforce that had grown far too independent for the Company's liking. During the period of competition between the Hudson's Bay and North West trading firms, the intense rivalry had placed the balance of power in the hands of the employees and freemen. *Engagés* demanded higher wages before they would sign a contract. Freemen demanded, and received, larger advances of provisions, ammunition, and gifts to secure their labour and loyalty in the field.

However, the largesse ended when the Hudson's Bay Company secured its trading monopoly over Rupert's Land. Several *Canadien* freemen and their métis families, Desjarlais among them, chose to leave the Athabasca region and migrate eastward, where they settled in the parishes of the Red River Settlement and engaged in small-scale agriculture, semi-annual buffalo hunts, freighting, and trading, both legal and extra-legal. Other migrants chose to pursue a lifestyle similar to that of their aboriginal and métis relatives left behind in Athabasca; a seasonal round of hunting, trapping, fishing, freighting, and sporadic work for the Hudson's Bay Company.

Chapter 5 details how the involvement of the Desjarlais in regional kinship alliances with aboriginal groups, and the diverse migration patterns of Desjarlais siblings, influenced the ethnic identification of their descendants. It compares and contrasts the development of aboriginal identities in Red River with those of Athabasca between 1821 and 1869, explaining how ecological and religious factors dictated the diverse economic, social, and political choices of Desjarlais family members.

The Establishment of Missions at Red River

Prior to 1821, the increased distribution of gifts, particularly liquor, to secure the loyalties of Native bands and *Canadien* freemen contributed to an overall escalation of violence in Rupert's Land. Eventually the conflict culminated in the death of twenty-one of Lord Selkirk's settlers at the hands of Métis and *Canadien engagés* and clerks affiliated with the North West Company on 19 June 1816. The savagery of the killings at Seven Oaks, which took place at the junction of the Red and Assiniboine Rivers in the heart of the Red River Settlement, shocked officials in both the Hudson's Bay and North West companies, as well as the Roman Catholic clergy in Lower Canada.

With the assistance of influential Roman Catholic traders and clergy, Lord Selkirk began to petition the British government to permit the establishment of a Roman Catholic Mission at Red River, ostensibly to "civilize and Christianize" the métis children of the *Canadiens*, and regulate the behaviour of the *Canadiens* themselves. Selkirk's motivations in this regard were quite clear. As the North West Company partners were unable (and unwilling) to control the actions of the *engagés* and freemen against his colonists, he hoped that the moral suasion of the priests would restore law and order to the area. The presence of a mission would also help to establish the permanence of his colony, by attracting agriculturalists from Europe and the Canadas to settle there. The Roman Catholic officials in Quebec had additional motives for supporting Selkirk's efforts. Besides being alarmed by events in the Northwest, they also saw an opportunity to promote the goals of the Roman Catholic Church in Canada, which had lost considerable political influence since the British takeover of Quebec.[2]

Earlier French penetration of the interior of North America south of the Great Lakes had followed a distinct pattern which the Church now hoped to continue; the establishment of trading and diplomatic relationships with aboriginal groups, followed by the residency of traders and missionary priests in Native communities. These relationships were reinforced by the establishment of permanent military posts, whose commanders also regulated the fur trade in the regions under their control. Because Roman Catholic priests were present in most of these posts from their inception, they were in a position to control the relationships between French traders, soldiers, and Native women. They developed and enforced regulations that compelled Frenchmen cohabiting with Native women within their jurisdiction to marry, or face imprisonment and the loss of their trading privileges. The presence of priests also facilitated the baptism of métis children brought into the posts by their *Canadien* fathers living *en derouine* with aboriginal bands. The result was a level of stability and permanence that attracted migrants from the settlements of the St. Lawrence, particularly farmers and tradespeople related by blood or marriage to the soldiers and *engagés* already living in the area. Within one or two generations most fur trading outposts in old Louisiana had become bona fide agricultural settlements with all of the cultural, religious, and municipal accoutrements of more established *Canadien* communities elsewhere.

But the British conquest of Quebec abruptly altered this pattern of exploration, commerce, and agricultural settlement. The Anglo-British traders who relocated to Montreal after the Conquest were hostile to the presence of priests or agricultural settlers of any ethnic stripe in the fur country, believing them to be detrimental to their business. Furthermore, much of Rupert's Land, particularly the region of Athabasca, was not amenable to agriculture due to its harsh climate, long winters, and swampy, wooded terrain. The great distance between Montreal and Athabasca, traversed by narrow, swift-flowing rivers navigable only by canoe, discouraged even the more intrepid *Canadiens* from visiting their relatives in the far-flung posts. As a result, the establishment of permanent *Canadien* settlements in what is now Western Canada had not taken place as it had in the Illinois country south of the Great Lakes, and in the region west of the Mississippi.

In 1818, Bishop Joseph-Octave Plessis sent two priests to Red River to establish a mission in Rupert's Land. The two priests, J. N. Provencher and J. N. S. Dumoulin, were given detailed instructions for accomplishing their two primary goals; the Christianization and "civilization" of the Native population, and the return of delinquent Christians to the teachings of the Church.[3]

Once they were established at Red River, the priests reported how complex, even chaotic, many unions *à la façon du pays* had become without a regulating influence. Their repeated references to the liquor trade, and to the habitual drunkenness of *Canadien engagés*, suggest that alcohol contributed to the relative lack of social controls in the fur trade community, making the regularization of "country" marriages and the conversion of Indians and métis to Christianity difficult.[4] The priests were reluctant to marry *Canadiens* who were involved in the liquor trade, as they considered this traffic immoral. But as virtually all of the *engagés* were involved in transporting and trading alcohol under the orders of their *bourgeois*, it was unclear to the priests whether the *engagés* could be held morally responsible or not.[5]

The inflexibility of the Roman Catholic Church regarding family relationships also created difficulties for the priests who wanted to perform baptisms and marriages but were prevented from doing so by church doctrine. The priests were uncertain whether to baptize the métis children of Protestant men, whether present or absent, and whether to baptize Native women or children who did not demonstrate a clear understanding of Roman Catholic teachings, especially when the priests did not speak Native languages. Of particular concern was the risk of legitimizing relationships that contravened Church doctrines regarding consanguinity.[6] Bishop Provencher provided a

summary of his more contentious cases for Bishop Plessis'
information:

> I am writing as these things come to my mind. Here are some
> cases that have come up since my arrival here:
>
> A métis, still an infidel, has been married for several years
> to a métis woman, who is also an infidel; some time ago he
> left this wife in the hope of finding another. He has taken her
> in the manner of the country, without much ceremony. For
> the Canadians at least are content to ask a girl or her father if
> she wishes to go with them; once the consent is given the mar-
> riage is accomplished. This man, being the son of a Canadian,
> doubtless did likewise. The woman is quite willing to be
> converted and remain with him; it is he who no longer wants
> her. There are children.... An Indian reared by the French and
> speaking French was married to a squaw who spoke only her
> own language. This man was ill for a long time, and desired
> and requested baptism; his wife had not received the proper
> instruction for baptism and marriage, nor, scarcely, had the
> man himself, though he was easily capable of receiving in-
> struction. Would it be possible to baptize him and leave him
> with his wife still an infidel, especially in the supposition that
> the man, already ill, would not live very long? ...
>
> A believer has an infidel for a wife. The woman wishes to
> become Christian in order to marry the man. The son of this
> man, born of another mother, declares in confession that he
> has had sexual relations with this woman, who will become
> his stepmother by marrying his father ...
>
> Here is Mr. Dumoulin sending me some letters for your
> Lordship, for his mother, and for Mr. Tabeau. At the same
> time he proposes two cases to me, which I am going to submit
> to you. It is again a question of the marriage of infidels.
>
> 1. An infidel woman has formerly had an infidel husband,
> whom she left in order to go to a Christian whom she would
> like to marry now, becoming herself a Christian. Her first hus-
> band is not in these parts. Is it possible to marry her? ...
>
> 2. A man has an infidel wife, with whose first cousin he has
> had illicit intercourse; he is thus related in the second degree.

Mr. Dumoulin asks whether it is possible for me to grant the dispensation at Pembina. I cannot, neither there nor here; my extraordinary faculties extend to the second degree only when the marriage has already been contracted. However, could one call this illicit union a contracted marriage? ...

Case:– An infidel woman has been living for several years with a Protestant, who is unwilling to become Catholic, but who does not object to the woman's doing so. May she be baptized after she has received instruction, in order that she may afterward be married to the very Protestant that she already has as husband? If we do not baptize her, a Protestant minister will do so; in this case ought he to be made to abjure, for she wishes to be a Catholic? The case has not yet presented itself, but it will, for women especially who have Catholic fathers will hardly be willing to become Protestants.... Your Lordship sees by this letter that this country furnishes subject for writing, especially concerning some perplexing cases, which are never met with in Canada. Thus it is not necessary to ask if they worry me; I have enough trouble getting out of ordinary difficulties, and it is much worse in the exceptional ones.... [7]

The desire to harvest souls for the Roman Catholic Church, in the face of incursions from Protestant missionaries newly arrived to Red River, inevitably relaxed the dogmatic approaches of the priests.[8] By 1824, eight hundred adults and children had been baptized, 120 marriages had been conducted, 150 persons had taken their first Communion, and several Protestants had been converted to Roman Catholicism at Red River.[9]

However, the missionaries were only partially successful in achieving their stated goals between 1818 and 1833. Although one of their initial aims was to "Christianize and civilize" the aboriginal population, their lack of facility in Native languages prevented the clergy from ministering to the Indians effectively. Instead, the priests concentrated on proselytizing to the Canadian residents and their métis children, who could communicate in French and had a nominal prior exposure to Christianity.[10]

This was to change with the arrival of Father Georges-Antoine Belcourt to the mission at Pembina. Belcourt was a native of

Saint-Antoine-de-la-Baie-du-Febvre, Yamaska County, Lower Canada, and descended from a well-known seigneurial and commercial family, the Trottier des Ruisseaux.[11] Belcourt's immediate family were farmers of modest means. Georges-Antoine showed academic aptitude early, and by the age of thirteen he entered the seminary to train for the priesthood. Belcourt was ordained in 1827, shortly before his twenty-fourth birthday. He spent the early years of his career as an assistant priest, serving in one parish after another until his appointment to the parish of St. Martine, Chateauguay County, in 1831, where he assumed full responsibility as parish priest.[12]

Shortly into Belcourt's tenure at St. Martine, Monsigneur Bernard Claude Panet approached him on behalf of Father Provencher, Bishop of Juliopolis at St. Boniface in the Red River Settlement, to persuade the young man to move to Red River. Bishop Provencher was in desperate need of priests to work among the Native people of Red River, a group which had been neglected due to the failure of previous clergy to master their languages. Because Belcourt had once asked to be sent to Red River but was refused, he was approached by his superiors to consider the idea once again. This time, Belcourt asked to be excused, citing his lack of experience. His objections were overruled, however, and by the end of February 1831, Father Belcourt was sent to the Sulpician mission at Oka for intensive study in Algonquin, a language closely related to Saulteaux, the predominant Native language at Red River. By the end of April, Belcourt had departed with Bishop Provencher to Red River.[13]

Belcourt was a gifted linguist, and by 1832 was sufficiently confident in his mastery of Saulteaux to begin planning for his missionary work. He chose a site on the Assiniboine River, west of the Métis mission of St. François-Xavier, to establish his Saulteaux mission. In the spring of 1833 he began construction of a log chapel, but a Gros Ventre attack shortly thereafter prompted him to relocate the mission farther east, closer to St. François-Xavier. This new location, later known as Baie-St.-Paul, was to become Father Belcourt's primary residence during his years at Red River.

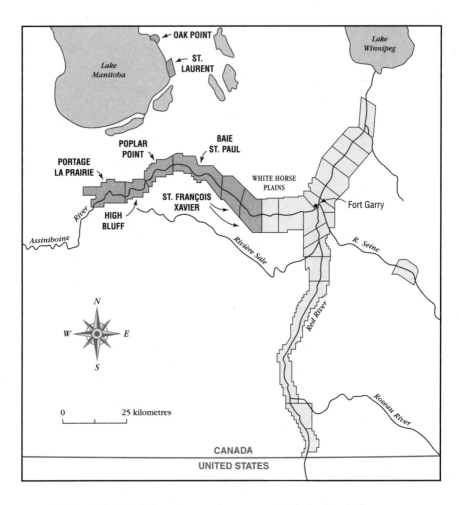

5.1 Red River Parishes, nineteenth century. (Dark shading indicates parishes where most Desjarlais families settled.)

It was during this period that branches of the Desjarlais family came to settle in the vicinity of Baie Ste Paul. Individual members of the family visited the Red River region at least a decade earlier; Antoine Desjarlais, son of Joseph Desjarlais and Okimaskwew, for example, had left the Lesser Slave Lake region for Red River in 1821 to investigate the prospects for "people of his description." However, despite the references to the marriages and baptisms of various family members at St. Boniface between 1818 and 1831, the Desjarlais family does not appear to have established itself permanently in the area until the 1830s.[14] Instead, the family migration eastward took place gradually, over a period of several years.

Some Desjarlais family members remained in the Athabasca region. Joseph Desjarlais Jr., the son of Old Joseph Desjarlais and Okimaskwew, remained in the vicinity of Lac La Biche, where he had established a country union with Josephte Cardinal, the daughter of the *Canadien* freeman Joseph Cardinal and his *métis* wife Louise Frobisher. Antoine Desjarlais, Old Joseph Desjarlais' *Canadien* brother, appears to have left the Athabasca region for parts unknown.[15] Another Desjarlais relative, Antoine Desjarlais dit Moral (b. ca. 1795)[16] continued his employment as a guide, and later as a steersman, at Portage La Loche.[17] While at Fort Alexander, he was hired by Lieutenant James Back as a replacement guide for the Second Arctic Land Expedition,[18] to lead the party westward to Fort Chipewyan in July of 1825, around the same time that many of his *Canadien* relatives in Rupert's Land were turning their attentions eastward.

After 1823, the family of the old *Canadien* freeman Joseph Desjarlais, his Ojibwa wife Okimaskwew, her Ojibwa son Tullibee, their sons Baptiste and Marcel, Joseph's *Canadien* relative François Desjarlais, and their wives and children, left the Lesser Slave Lake region. By 1827, they were trapping along the Carrot River and trading at Cumberland House, in an area of east-central Saskatchewan that was easily accessible to both Lake Winnipeg and the Athabasca country of Alberta via the Saskatchewan River system. The following year the group trapped in the region between Nipawin and Swan River. By 1829 the family had apparently separated into two hunting groups. One group, led by Okimaskwew's son Tullibee, remained in the region of Carlton House, in what is now central Saskatchewan. Another family group accompanied Baptiste "Nishecabo" Desjarlais to the vicinity of Fort Pelly, southwest of Swan River, where he was "clothed" as trading chief in the fall of 1830, and once again in 1832. By the winter of 1833–34 the same group was living at the Fishing Lakes along the Qu'Appelle River, southwest of Fort Pelly.[19]

The increased scarcity of large game animals, and the collapse in the population of fur-bearing animals, particularly muskrats, gradually prompted Ojibwa/métis/Cree hunting bands with kinship ties to plains Cree and Red River Métis to leave the boreal forests of Athabasca and the Saskatchewan country and adopt a subsistence lifestyle that combined hunting and gathering in winter, bison hunting in summer and fall, and fishing all year round.[20]

The region lying between Swan River to the north, the Turtle Mountains to the south, the Qu'Appelle Lakes to the west, and the edge of Lake Winnipeg to the east became the favoured hunting and trapping territory for not only the Desjarlais family, but several other families of freemen,[21] whose nominal home bases were the parishes of St. François-Xavier and Baie-St. Paul. They shared this area, particularly the Moose Mountains, with several aboriginal hunting bands, some comprised of distant relatives from the Athabasca and Saskatchewan regions.

One of the aboriginal bands with whom the Desjarlais shared kinship ties was of Cree, Saulteaux, and *Canadien* origin. Its patriarch was the métis freeman Michel Cardinal who was born in the Bow River region of the Rocky Mountain foothills, and who migrated eastward towards Red River after 1822 to occupy territory whose nexus now comprises Riding Mountain Provincial Park. Michel Cardinal, known as Okanase, or "little bone," had country wives, both Indian and métis, who in turn bore sons who would eventually establish separate hunting bands on their own. Like other kinship groups established by the earliest generations of *Canadien* and métis freemen, the Okanase band had evolved, culturally, into an Aboriginal hunting band in the absence of Euro-Canadian institutions which might have provided an alternative cultural influence.[22]

On 22 October 1833 Joseph Desjarlais, the old *Canadien* freeman, died at Swan River (in what is now west-central Manitoba) at ninety years of age. After his death his body was taken to Red River. His burial, the first in the cemetery of the mission at St. François-Xavier, took place on 11 January 1834, and was presided over by Father Belcourt. An Antoine Desjarlais, assumed to be his son, was present at his interment.[23]

The new permanent mission at Baie St. Paul, founded in 1833, was designed specifically for ministering to the Saulteaux and Métis. Only one older member of the Desjarlais family, however, settled there to pursue agriculture on a full-time basis. This was the *Canadien* freeman François Desjarlais, who moved with his métis wife Madeleine Roy and their children to Baie St. Paul, around the time of Old Joseph Desjarlais' death. It is not entirely clear why François Desjarlais and the majority of his descendants chose to put down roots at Red River, while his relatives chose to follow a more mobile existence as seasonal hunters, fishers, and itinerant labourers.[24] Perhaps, as the only *Canadien* Desjarlais of his generation left in Rupert's Land, he wanted to live out his retirement as a simple *habitant* – even if his commitments to his métis family prevented a return to Quebec.

Many elderly *Canadien engagés* and freemen found Red River to be a satisfactory place to raise their families and end their days. The presence of missions close by must have been a comfort to these old men, if only for the knowledge that they could get the last rites from the priest after being only nominal Christians for most of their lives in the *pays d'en haut*.[25]

Because Father Belcourt believed that the only way to truly Christianize was to "civilize," the development of an agricultural settlement was integral to his missionary efforts. As part of that plan, settlers from Quebec parishes were encouraged to come to the Roman Catholic parishes of Red River, a pattern consistent with *Canadien* chain migration and frontier settlement as practised during the French régime. Several *habitant* families from the St. Lawrence Valley eventually settled along the banks of the Red and Assiniboine Rivers, often in the same communities as their *Canadien* and métis relatives. Among the Desjarlais relatives who settled at Red River were Louis Lamirande, who settled in the parish of Ste. Agathe; and Bazil Plante and Genevieve Lacourse, who settled in the parish of St. François-Xavier.[26]

The Emergence of Métis Populations in the Athabasca Region

By the late 1830s a large métis population lived in the region of Lac La Biche, hunting, trapping, and fishing alongside their Indian cousins. Their social environment was a boreal forest hunter-gatherer culture, dominated by aboriginal spiritual beliefs and customs. Métis children raised in this environment did not necessarily see themselves as culturally separate from their Cree, Saulteaux, or Chipewyan cousins. With few distinctive European cultural markers such as religion and education to differentiate them from Native groups, their cultural separateness was based largely on the strength of the Euro-Canadian cultural influences established by their *Canadien* fathers and grandfathers. If the father was absent, and there was no dominant cultural influence present from another Euro-Canadian person or institution, the child became Indian culturally. The continued intermarriage of métis children into local aboriginal bands further attenuated these already weak links.

Although many of the *Canadien* progenitors of the métis living in Athabasca had long since died or returned to their ancestral homes in Canada, a few elderly *Canadien* freemen still remained in Rupert's Land with their Native families. One of these men was Joseph Cardinal,[27] a North West Company *engagé* turned freeman who had established a union *à la façon du pays* with Louise Frobisher, the country daughter of Nor'Wester partner Joseph Frobisher, in the 1790s.

Over the years, the early death or departure of other *Canadien* freemen from the area resulted in Joseph Cardinal Sr. becoming the *de facto* patriarch of the growing métis population in the region, most of whom were his direct descendants through his daughter Josephte who had given birth to sixteen children, five with the *Canadien* freeman Joseph Ladouceur and eleven with the métis freeman Joseph Desjarlais Jr.[28]

Joseph Cardinal was not happy with the fact that most of his large extended family had yet to be baptized. For several years the aging Cardinal tried to persuade the Roman Catholic priests to establish a mission at Lac La Biche, to no avail. Chief Factor

John Rowand of Fort Edmonton had requested the services of a priest twice, in 1838 and later in 1841. Finally, the Reverend J.N. Provencher, Bishop of Juliopolis at St. Boniface, sent a lay priest, Abbé J. B. Thibault westward to investigate the situation in 1842. Father Thibault returned almost immediately to Red River, but returned in 1844 to establish a mission at a lake he named Lac Ste. Anne, located about forty-five miles northwest of Fort Edmonton. That year Joseph Cardinal persuaded Father Thibault to come to Lac La Biche, where he performed fifty-eight baptisms and eight marriages for local families in the area bearing the surnames Auger, Beaudoin, Berland, Cardinal, Décoigne, Desjarlais, Gladu, Ladouceur, Mondion, Nepissingue, and Quintal.[29]

Between 1844 and 1852 the presence of Father Thibault at Lac Ste. Anne attracted numerous métis who took the opportunity to formally marry their country wives, baptize their children, and learn the rudiments of agriculture. One of these converts was Antoine Desjarlais dit Wabumun (b. 1820 at Lesser Slave Lake), the product of a temporary union between the métis Hudson's Bay Company interpreter and hunter Antoine Desjarlais and a Cree woman named Napitch.[30] Antoine Desjarlais dit Wabumun remained in Athabasca with his Cree mother after Antoine Desjarlais made the decision to migrate eastward with his country wife Suzanne Allary, and other members of the Desjarlais family after 1821.[31] By 1850 Antoine Desjarlais dit Wabamun had married a Native woman named Marie Kaketa at Lac Ste. Anne.[32]

In 1852 a new Roman Catholic mission, named Notre Dame des Victoires by Father Albert Lacombe, was founded at Lac La Biche, and the missionary work began in earnest. The mission and farm were established on the south-central shore of Lac La Biche, at a site now known as Mission Bay.[33] The Desjarlais and Cardinal families, already baptized Catholics, settled near the mission on the shore of Lac La Biche to farm, trap, and trade.

One member of the Cardinal family became a fervent, even fanatical Catholic. Alexis Cardinal was a famous hunter and dog-runner in the Lac La Biche region before he agreed to become

Father Lacombe's guide, a task he performed faithfully for many years until 1872.[34] Although dependable and trustworthy, he was, nonetheless, eccentric. It was, in all probability, Alexis Cardinal whom Methodist missionary John McDougall encountered late in 1863, "a noted character who went by the name 'Who-Talks-Past-All-Things.' He had French blood, was a Roman Catholic, and spent most of his time around the Roman Catholic missions. He sometimes imagined himself to be the Pope, and very often officiated among the Indians as priest. He had come out this time from the Roman Catholic mission at Big Lake for a load of fresh meat, and was now returning."[35]

The establishment of a permanent mission at Lac La Biche by 1852 was no doubt prompted by the incursions of Methodist missionaries such as Benjamin Sinclair, a Swampy-Cree mixed-blood lay preacher from Norway House who moved to Lac La Biche in 1853. By 1855 an Ojibwa Methodist preacher, Rev. Henry Bird Steinhauer, had arrived in the area, and, with Benjamin Sinclair as his assistant, established a mission and agricultural settlement at Whitefish Lake, the first permanent aboriginal agricultural settlement in the West.[36]

In 1860 Rev. George Millward McDougall was appointed chairman of the North-Western District of the Wesleyan Methodist Church, and was sent to Rupert's Land to minister to the Indians and Métis in the Saskatchewan River region. In 1862 he established a mission at a site thirty miles south of the North Saskatchewan River in what is now east-central Alberta. The community was named Victoria, after the reigning British monarch at the time. From this site George McDougall and his son John worked among the local Native groups, teaching agricultural skills, establishing a school, and promoting peace between warring bands of Cree, Blackfoot, and Assiniboine.

Initially the McDougalls, like other clergy in the region, experienced setbacks when trying to convert the Natives to Christianity. Although Protestant and Roman Catholic missionaries had been proselytizing in the region since the 1830s, their interfaith rivalries created skepticism amongst prospective

5.2 Rev. John McDougall – Glenbow NA 589-2

converts such as Cree Chief Maskepetoon (a.k.a. Broken Arm). In 1848, painter Paul Kane expressed Maskepetoon's perspective:

> Mr. Rundell [Robert Rundle, Methodist] had told him that what he preached was the only true road to heaven, and Mr. Hunter [James Hunter, Anglican] told him the same thing, and so did Mr. Thebo [Father J.B. Thibault, Catholic], and as he did not know which was right, he thought they ought to call

a council among themselves, and then he would go with them all three; but that until they agreed he would wait.[37]

Eventually, however, the clergy prevailed, possibly because they arrived in the region at a time when the one doctrine they all shared – a commitment to peace – became increasingly attractive to Native peoples weary of the inter-tribal warfare in the region. There was also a recognition that the escalating violence was directly attributable to the dwindling supply of bison. The more far-sighted leaders realized that they would have to prepare their communities for the eventual disappearance of the buffalo.[38]

One of the close friends and supporters of the McDougalls was Frederick "Keh-kek" (Hawk) Desjarlais, the métis son of Baptiste "Nishecabo" Desjarlais and Marie Cardinal.[39] Although Frederick Desjarlais was, in all probability, at least a nominal Catholic when he first met the McDougalls in 1862, he developed a close friendship with the Protestant clergymen.[40] John McDougall's numerous descriptions of "Keh-Kek" Desjarlais (which survive in his published works) also suggest that he had become fully integrated into the plains Cree way of life by the time he had reached adulthood.

John McDougall first encountered Keh-Kek shortly after his arrival in the Northwest. In 1862, John McDougall and his father George enjoyed the hospitality of Keh-Kek's family in a Cree camp on the shores of Saddle Lake, enroute to Whitefish Lake. They stayed for lunch with "Mrs. Hawke" who loaned McDougall a fresh horse for the journey. They were accompanied on their return to Saddle Lake by Keh-Kek and the beginning of a long friendship was forged.

> We left Whitefish Lake Friday evening, having with us for the first few miles "Ka-kake," or "the Hawk," and some of his people, who were returning to Saddle Lake. "Ka-Kake" was far more than an ordinary personality. His very appearance denoted this. The elasticity of his step, the flash of his eye, the ring of his voice – you *had* to notice him. To me he was a new type. He filled my ideal as a hunter and warrior.
>
> From Peter [Erasmus] I learned that he was brave and kind, and full of resource, tact, strategy and pluck; these were

5.3 Frederick "Keh-Kek" Desjarlais riding a buffalo – frontispiece from John McDougall's book *Forest, Lake and Prairie* (1895)

the striking traits of this man, by whose side I loved to ride, and later on, in whose skin-lodge I delighted to camp.

He had figured in many battles and been the chief actor in many hunting fields. He had surpassed other famous buffalo hunters, inasmuch as he had ridden one buffalo to kill another.

To do this, it is related that he and others were chasing buffalo on foot, and coming to an ice-covered lake, the surface of which was in spots like glass, some of the buffalo fell, and Ka-Kake, with the impetus of his run, went sliding on to one of them, and catching hold of the long, shaggy hair of its shoulders, seated himself astride of its back. Then the buffalo made an extra effort and got to its feet and dashed after the herd, and Ka-Kake kept his seat. In vain the animal, after reaching the ground, bucked and jumped and rushed about. Ka-Kake was there to stay – for a while, at any rate. Then the buffalo settled down to run and soon overtook the herd, which spurted on afresh, because of this strange-looking thing on the back of one of themselves. Now, thought Ka-Kake, is my chance. So he pulled his bow from his back, and springing it and taking an arrow from his quiver, he picked his animal, and sent the arrow up to the feather in its side, which soon brought his victim to a stop. Then, he took his knife and drove it down into his wild steed, just below his seat, and feeling that the buffalo was going to fall, he jumped off to one side, and thus had accomplished something unique in the hunting field.[41]

McDougall had the opportunity to renew his acquaintance with Keh-Kek in the lodge of Chief "Child" (Mistawasis)[42] in January of 1863, where he was also introduced to a young Cree warrior recuperating from a wound sustained during a war expedition.

The young man, whom McDougall identified as being (in later years) the "head-man of Saddle Lake," was probably the Cree chief Pakan. At the time of their initial meeting, Pakan was not yet converted to Christianity. Within five years, however, Pakan had renounced the warpath and become a Christian.[43] He adopted a European name, James Seenum, and conscientiously applied himself to learning the ways of the newcomers, particularly agriculture. He supported the missionaries in their work, and they in turn advised Pakan in his dealings with government officials. Pakan's followers, by and large, became firm Methodists.

Although Frederick "Keh-Kek" Desjarlais was culturally Cree, and permanently settled in the region encompassing Whitefish and Saddle Lakes, he was very conscious of his kin living elsewhere. Like that of most métis people in the region, his kinship network stretched far beyond the boundaries of the Saskatchewan River. In April of 1864, Frederick Desjarlais accompanied John McDougall on a trip to Fort Garry, at the heart of the Red River Settlement. During the trip, they encountered some of Keh-Kek's relatives on the shores of Jackfish Lake – "Saulteaux" (Ojibwa) belonging to the band of Mistihai'muskwa (Big Bear).

> We passed Fort Pitt, and continuing down the north side came to Jackfish Lake, where we found the camp of Salteaux that frequented this lake feasting on the carcases of a great herd of buffalo that had been drowned in the lake the previous winter. Too many had got together in some stampede across the ice and had broken through and were drowned; and now that the ice was off the lake, the carcases were drifting ashore.

These improvident people were glad to get the meat. They offered us some, and though Ka-kake took it out of deference to their kindness, he watched his opportunity and threw it away. Some of the younger men came to our camp that night, *and as Ka-kake was a sort of kinsmen of theirs,* [my emphasis] he undertook to show them the folly of their course in some lawless acts which they were charged with perpetrating (for these fellows had a hard name). One of them, after listening to Ka-kake's talk, began to speak quite excitedly, and said: "You seem to make much ado about our taking some plunder and demanding tribute of parties passing through our country. What will you think when we really do something, for we are disposed to organize and take these Hudson's Bay forts, and drive all the white men out of this country; then you will have something to talk about!"[44]

Later in the journey, they passed the Qu'Appelle lakes and detoured towards Fort Ellice, rejoining their travelling companions at Bird Tail Creek, camping at a spot located near the present community of Birtle, Manitoba.

This was Saturday night, and during that Sunday camp on the bank of Bird Tail Creek I had my first and only difference with Ka-kake. Some hunters on the way out by Fort Ellice camped beside us, and from these Ka-Kake learned that friends of his were camped about twenty miles farther on. About the middle of the afternoon, he and the two Indians from Whitefish Lake began to catch their horses, and make as if they were going to start. I asked what they meant, and Ka-kake told me that they were going on, and would wait for us in the morning. I said he might go on if he chose, but I would not consent to his taking the horses belonging to Mr. Steinhauer, as these were in my charge, and I did not intend to have them travel on Sunday. He was firm, but I was firmer; and finally Ka-kake turned the horses loose and gave it up.[45]

In retrospect, it is not surprising that Frederick Desjarlais was unusually stubborn in his desire to visit friends in the vicinity of Bird Tail Creek. Unbeknownst to John McDougall, Keh-Kek had not only friends, but several relatives who hunted in the region on a regular basis. Twenty miles east of Fort Ellice, at Riding Mountain, lay the camp of Okanase, or "Little Bone," a band of mixed-blood Saulteaux descended from the Cardinal family, a group that also contained members of the Desjarlais family.[46]

Indeed, many of Keh-Kek's Desjarlais relatives, including the family of his father, Nishecabo (Baptiste) Desjarlais were living in the vicinity of Fort Ellice, the Moose Mountains, and Fort Qu'Appelle by the mid-1860s.

The Struggle for Free Trade

The proximity of the Red River Settlement to easily accessible markets in American territory prompted many Métis entrepreneurs to bypass the Hudson's Bay Company trading posts and negotiate better trading terms elsewhere. Old Joseph Desjarlais' son, Antoine Desjarlais, became an active free trader in the Souris River basin, the Moose Mountains, and in the vicinity of Shoal Lake and Riding Mountain. He established two independent trading posts in the Souris River region, in defiance of the Hudson's Bay Company monopoly. The first was a large stockade called Fort Desjarlais on the Souris River near present-day Lauder, Manitoba. This post, which he operated with his son Baptiste, his sons-in-law, Charles DeMontigny, Eusebe Ledoux, and Simon Blondeau, and over seventy other inhabitants, was constructed in 1836 and was in operation through much of the 1840s, and possibly into the 1850s.[47] Antoine also built a small post on the Souris River near present-day Minot, North Dakota, where the Native groups of the Turtle Mountain area knew him as Mitche Cote, or "Hairy Legs."[48]

One of the more intriguing aspects of Fort Desjarlais concerns its very survival as an independent trading post, in a region notorious for raiding activity by the Dakota (i.e., Sioux). During the 1840s and into the 1850s, when operations at Fort Desjarlais were presumably at their peak, the Red River Métis and their Saulteaux kin were engaged in long-term, low-level warfare with at least two groups of Dakota, the Yanktonais and the Sissetons.

In fact, the northern limit of Yanktonai hunting territory during the early- to mid-nineteenth century was the headwaters of the Pembina River, home to the Turtle Mountain Métis. The Yanktonais were noted for their hostility to traders of all stripes, which could only be placated by liberal payments of trade goods to their head chief.[49]

According to Gary Clayton Anderson, kinship ties were necessary to ensure the safety of trading brigades dealing with the Dakota. However, affinal or more permanent kin relations only provided access to Dakota society. Continuous gift-giving was required to maintain these relationships.[50]

A possible explanation for Fort Desjarlais' apparent immunity to Dakota harassment lies in the kin relationship of Antoine Desjarlais and his second cousin, Honoré Picotte, trader in the Upper Missouri Outfit of the American Fur Company, and Antoine's second cousin.[51] In the 1820s, Picotte married a sister of the principal chief of the Yankton tribe, Struck-by-the-Ree. The couple had a son, Charles Felix Picotte, on 20 August 1830.[52] During the 1830s, Honoré Picotte spent most of his time trading with the Yanktonais at the mouth of the Apple River, near present-day Bismarck, North Dakota, and made regular trips to Fort Union, the American Fur Company post closest to the Souris River. By 1835, Picotte was made a shareholder in the Upper Missouri Outfit, and directed operations primarily from Fort Union.[53]

It is possible that Picotte used his kin relations with the Yanktonais to facilitate Antoine Desjarlais' operations at Fort Desjarlais and in Dakota territory. Certainly it was in Picotte's commercial interest to help Antoine because he would be able to secure furs and robes for the American Fur Company as far north as the Moose Mountains, at the expense of the Hudson's Bay Company, which held the monopoly in that region. That Antoine Desjarlais was able to trade in the Lower Souris basin during a period when the Red River Métis were ostensibly in a state of war with the Dakota, suggests that Desjarlais was insulated from the harassment which plagued other Métis in the area. Sharing kin relations with Honoré Picotte, a trader whose own success was based on his family ties with at least three different Dakota groups,[54] may have provided the protection that Desjarlais needed to operate in the region unmolested.

During this period, Antoine Desjarlais, his younger brother Marcel (also known by his Saulteaux name of Qwewezance, or Gwiwisens – "boy"),[55] and their relatives did their best to stay one step ahead of the Hudson's Bay Company authorities, particularly the Warden of the Plains, Cuthbert Grant, who was a resident of the neighbouring Red River parish, St. François-Xavier. Marketing furs, robes, and provisions to any buyer other than the Hudson's Bay Company was strictly illegal in Rupert's Land. The free traders chafed under these restrictions, and sought remedies for the situation. In August of 1845, Antoine Desjarlais was one of several signatories to a letter, addressed to Governor Alexander Christie, concerning the rights of Free Traders at Red River:

Sir,

Having at this present moment a strong belief, that we as natives of this country, and as half-Breeds, have the right, to hunt furs in the Hudson's Bay Company's Territories, wherever we think proper, and, again, sell those furs to the highest bidder, likewise having a doubt, that, natives of this Country can be prevented from trading and trafficking with one another.- We would wish to have your opinion on the subject, lest we should commit ourselves, by doing any thing in opposition either to the Laws of England or the Hudson's Bay Company's privileges, and therefore lay before you, as, governor of Red River Settlement, a few queries which we beg you will answer in course, and address your answer to Mr. James Sinclair. –

No 1st   Has a Halfbreed, a Settler, the right to hunt furs in this Country?

" 2nd   Has a native of this Country/not an Indian/ a right to hunt furs?

" 3rd   If a Halfbreed has the right to hunt furs, can he hire other half Breeds for the purpose of hunting furs?

" 4th   Can a halfbreed sell his furs to any person he pleases?

" 5th   Is a halfbreed obliged to sell his furs to the Hudson's Bay Company at whatever price the Company think proper to give him?

" 6th   Can a Halfbreed receive any furs as a present; from an Indian, a relation of his?

" 7th   Can a Halfbreed hire any of his Indian relations, to hunt furs for him?

" 8th   Can one HalfBreed trade furs from another Half-Breed in, or out of the Settlements?

" 9th   Can a halfBreed trade furs from an Indian in or out of the Settlements?

" 10th   With regard to trading or hunting furs have the HalfBreeds, or natives of European origin, any rights or privileges over Europeans?

" 11th   A Settler, having purchased Lands from Lord Selkirk, or even from the Hudson's Bay Company, without conditions attached to them, or without having signed any bond, deed or instrument whereby he might have willed away his right to trade furs, can he be prevented from trading furs in the Settlement with Settlers or even out of the Settlement?

" 12th   Are the limits of the Settlement defined by the municipal law, Selkirk grant, or Indian Sale?

" 13th   If a person cannot trade furs either in, or out of the Settlement, can he purchase them for his own or family use and in what quantity?

" 14th   Having never seen any official statements nor Known but one report that the Hudson's Bay company has peculiar privileges over the British subjects, natives and half-Breeds resident in the Settlement, we would wish to Know, what these privileges are and the penalties attached the infringement of the same?

We remain your most obedt. Servants.

"signed"

James Sinclair	Edward Harmon
Bapt Larocque	John Dease
Thomas Logan	Henry Cook
Pierre Laverdure	Willm. Bird
Joseph Monkman	John Vincent
Bapt. Wilkie	Peter Garriock
Bapti. Fanian	Jack Spence
Alexis Goulait	Jack Anderson
Antoine Morin	James Monkman
Willm. McMillan	Antoine Desjarlois, Sen.
Louis Le Tendre	Thomas McDermot
Robert Montour[56]	

Unfortunately, the Hudson's Bay Company remained harsh in its dealings with illegal traders. As free trader and fellow petitioner Peter Garrioch observed in his journal in January of 1847,

> ... On my way home, I should have stated, I was informed that Mr. Grant had seized the goods and fur of several of the traders (private Individual traders). Among those plundered were Quewezazse, Antoine Dezerelais' brother, Shigerma's son and one of Shatra's sons. Them are certainly strange and overbearing proceedings. The HBC appear determined at all hazards to establish their points.[57]

Despite these minor victories, the Hudson's Bay Company was unable to fully enforce their monopoly. Without an adequate military force in place to protect Company interests, the Hudson's Bay Company was reluctant to confront the Métis.[58] After 1845, the free traders escalated their activities in open defiance of the Company. In 1849, four Métis, including Guillaume Sayer from the parish of St.-François-Xavier, were arrested and charged with trading furs illegally. The first defendant, Sayer, proceeded to go on trial, but not before prominent free trader James Sinclair was permitted to represent him. Although the jury found him guilty of the offense, they recommended mercy. Moreover, they recommended that charges be dropped against the three other defendants. Their verdict, based ostensibly on the argument that Guillaume Sayer thought he had permission to trade, was actually made to placate a large, well-armed, and increasingly hostile mob of Métis hunters gathered outside the court house. The response to the verdict – a virtual acquittal of the defendants with no penalty – was immediate. The Hudson's Bay Company monopoly was irretrievably compromised, and would never be successfully enforced in the region again.[59]

Although the free traders at Red River succeeded in permanently undermining the Hudson's Bay Company's monopoly with Guillaume Sayer's 1849 acquittal, it was probably too late to take any commercial advantage of their hard-won victory. The decline in big game populations had forced woodland peoples out onto the plains to hunt buffalo; soon it was evident that the bison population was disappearing as well.

Fort Desjarlais was burnt to the ground in about 1856, a few years after Honoré Picotte, the American Fur Company agent for the Upper Missouri Outfit, retired to St. Louis, Missouri. Antoine Desjarlais, by now advancing in age, took work with the Hudson's Bay Company as an *en derouine* trader with the Assiniboine, wintering in the Moose Mountains to acquire provisions for Fort Ellice. By 1859 his contract with the Hudson's Bay Company was concluded, and Antoine was a free man, once again.[60]

On 4 November 1865 Bishop Taché arrived at Fort Ellice from the Qu'Appelle Lakes, where he was establishing a mission to serve the Native peoples of the region. Perhaps his visit led Old Antoine Desjarlais to move to the mission at Lebret (then called St. Florent), situated on the shore of Lac Qu'Appelle, with his wife, Suzanne Allary, and two of their children. His brother Baptiste "Nishecabo" Desjarlais appears to have arrived at Qu'Appelle around the same time. Antoine and Baptiste Desjarlais, accompanied by their children and grandchildren, joined other Métis who had migrated from the Red River parishes of Baie St. Paul and St. François-Xavier. They were joined by Métis from Turtle Mountain, North Dakota, a group with whom they shared close kinship ties.

One of their Desjarlais kinsmen who had migrated to United States territory was Antoine Desjarlais dit Moral, the steersman with the La Loche Brigade, who retired from the Hudson's Bay Company in 1846. After a brief period in St. Boniface, he moved to Pembina, North Dakota. Some of his descendants eventually took treaty as members of the Turtle Mountain Chippewa tribe. Other descendants moved westward to Montana, where they settled with other Turtle Mountain migrants in the vicinity of Lewistown, Montana. Three children moved to Canada. One daughter, Elise, moved to the Qu'Appelle Valley with her husband, Andre Klyne. Another daughter, Caroline, emigrated north to Canada after marrying a bison hunter, Antoine Salois, from the Métis *hivernant* community of Buffalo Lake, in 1873. A son, Charles, migrated to a location east of Fort Qu'Appelle.[61]

The pre-1870 movement of Métis was primarily an economic migration.[62] As the bison populations disappeared, those Red River Métis who had made only an indifferent commitment to agriculture while living in the vicinity of Red River moved westward in pursuit of the waning herds. They settled on the shores of lakes where they could supplement their diet of large game animals with fish and fowl. The Qu'Appelle region was still relatively free of Euro-Canadian settlers, and the Métis could establish their homes on the shores of lakes and rivers with impunity.

According to former Hudson's Bay Company clerk Isaac Cowie,

> As a very aged man [Antoine Desjarlais] became attached to the Rev. Father Decorby's mission at Qu'Appelle Lakes (now Lebret), "doing chores." He was burned to death, when faithful to the end, he attempted to save something from the mission building which was gutted by fire in the winter of either 1870/1 or 1871/2.[63]

His brother Baptiste "Nishecabo" Desjarlais had already passed away prior to this tragedy, under far different spiritual circumstances. Despite having settled in more-or-less Christianized surroundings after leaving Lesser Slave Lake in the 1820s, Nishecabo Desjarlais evidently continued to practise aboriginal spirituality as an elderly man in Saskatchewan. Former HBC clerk Isaac Cowie provides this poignant description of Nishecabo's last days at Fort Qu'Appelle, during the winter of 1871:

> Among the freemen wintering about the lake was one of the wide-spread Disgarlais families, but decidedly more Saulteau than French in tongue and tone. The father, named Wah-ween-shee-cap-po, was a giant in size and ancient in days and devilment. When one of his grandchildren had died during the previous summer, in his grief and rage old Disgarlais, arming himself with his long flintlock, with powder-horn and ball-pouch slung over his shoulders, commenced blazing away at the sun, challenging the power up there to "come down and fight him like a man instead of killing innocent children." As a professor of Indian medicine and black art in general he was dreaded, and he appeared to have the faculty of either hypnotizing or putting himself in a trance, lying so long in that state that during that winter his sons twice thought he was really dead and came to the post for material to bury him. On both these occasions he came to life again after two or three days, during which he said he had visited spirit-land, of which he related his experiences to his fascinated and awestruck family and audience. By the time he fell into the third trance, or actually died that winter, his sons had no occasion to come to the post for winding sheet or coffin nails. The grave had also been dug ready; so, when he once more became apparently dead, his sons lost no time in nailing him down in the coffin and sinking him in a deep grave and covering him with earth. Then they poured water thereon so as to freeze him down in case he should come to life once more to terrorize his panic-stricken and superstitious descendants.[64]

In reading this passage, it is apparent that Nishecabo Desjarlais had continued to cling to an aboriginal *persona* throughout his life, and had remained Ojibwa in his soul despite the fact that most branches of the Desjarlais family, including most of the members of his immediate family, would eventually be legally designated as Métis.[65]

For Nishecabo Desjarlais, the practice of shamanism was a natural response to an environment where options for personal well-being were expanded or diminished by factors outside one's control. The lure of shamanism (or what may have seemed like the "dark side" to his Christianized kinsmen) offered an opportunity to overcome obstacles and become a person of power, a "man of consequence." It was believed that powerful shamans could not be killed because they had control over life and death, and were greatly feared because of it.[66] Nishecabo appeared to enjoy this reputation among his own kin, as demonstrated by his sons' reaction to his repeated "resurrections" after extended, death-like trances.

In exchange for possessing such powerful "medicine," shamans such as Nishecabo were compelled by Ojibwa beliefs to exercise their power judiciously. Should a shaman violate spiritual taboos, the consequence was the loss of spiritual power, and negative consequences for the shaman's family. That Baptiste believed this himself is suggested by his reaction to the passing of his grandchild – a death that he was apparently unable to prevent. Why else would he vent his anger by shooting at the Sun – the Ojibwa "spirit-helper" most associated with European traders?[67]

Conclusion

Although biracial populations developed wherever aboriginal and European people met, the métis populations in northern Rupert's Land did not develop as an identifiable and separate "community," as they had in Red River, until the mid- to late-nineteenth century. There are two explanations for this delay. The first is environmental.

The ecological region encompassing what is now east-central and northern Alberta is what is known as a parkland-boreal forest transition zone. All individuals living outside of the large trading centres, such as Fort Edmonton, lived a nomadic life dictated by the vagaries of the seasonal subsistence round. They lived in small groups and moved frequently in pursuit of game.

Their social organization was fluid, to enable the groups to adjust their size to suit environmental conditions, and to incorporate outsiders who demonstrated the potential to bring benefits to all. The constant movement of these extended family groups, the relative isolation of hunting bands for large portions of the year, and their continued intermarriage with aboriginal populations acted against the development of a shared "Métis" consciousness among métis people in the Athabasca region. What this lifestyle *did* perpetuate was a strong loyalty and attachment to one's extended family. The relationships of Frederick "Keh-kek" Desjarlais are a case in point. "Keh-kek" Desjarlais recognized and fostered kin ties with members of Cree, Ojibwa, and Métis groups hundreds of miles apart, despite living in a primarily Cree cultural context.

The second, and perhaps more significant, explanation for the delay in the emergence of a distinct Métis community in the northern portions of the North-West Territories was the delay in establishing a Roman Catholic mission in the region. At Red River, Roman Catholic priests had been active since 1818, "regularizing" the country marriages of *engagés* and freemen, and establishing permanent missions which served as a locus for the development of communities separate and distinct from those of the plains Indian bands that surrounded them. The existence of a permanent settlement encouraged Métis people to choose Christian mates from their own community, or Christianized natives who were integrated into the Métis parish, as did the children of the *Canadien* François Desjarlais and his métis wife Madeleine Roy in the parish of Baie St. Paul.

However, there was no permanent Euro-Canadian religious presence in what is now north-central Alberta until the 1840s, at least twenty-five years, or one generation, after both Roman Catholic and Protestant clergymen had established missions at Red River. The only Christianizing influences came from elderly *Canadien* and Iroquois freemen who practised the Catholic rituals of their childhood in isolation, or from the occasional baptism, marriage, or mass conducted by clergymen travelling through the region. This only changed with the permanent presence of Roman Catholic priests in 1844, and Protestant clergy by 1853.

A key difference between the Christianization process which took place in Athabasca, and that of Red River, was that in Athabasca the conversion of métis and Indian people took place simultaneously. Because of the continued intermarriage *à la façon du pays* between aboriginal and métis groups living in the remote forests and parkland of Athabasca, the Native population outside of the large settlements was more or less homogenous culturally. And that culture was aboriginal. When the missionaries eventually succeeded in Christianizing the hunting bands of Athabasca, their enterprise did not facilitate the development of distinctive and separate ethnic communities identifiable as Indian and Métis. What Christianization *did* accomplish in the region was the fragmentation of the rural aboriginal population into separate religious factions, either Protestant or Roman Catholic. The arbitrary ascription, and subsequent separation, of these same groups into "Indian" or "Métis" would not take place until the negotiation of treaties in the 1870s.

6

....

Treaties and Rebellion

After acquiring Rupert's Land in 1869–70, the Canadian government moved swiftly to negotiate treaties with the Native residents. Because of the resistance of the Manitoba Métis to settlement without recognition and protection of their rights, the Canadian government was determined to avoid the same difficulties in opening up the remainder of the Northwest to settlement. Within the next decade, a series of numbered Treaties (One to Seven) were negotiated with Indian bands in different regions of the West. The treaties guaranteed each signatory band a tract of land, schools, agricultural training, implements, and livestock; medical services, annuity payments, protection, and relief in times of famine or hardship, in return for the surrender of their indigenous title to the land to the Canadian government.[1]

Doug Owram has argued that one of the factors contributing to the Red River Resistance of 1869–70 was the Canadians' comparative ignorance about Red River and its society.[2] Alexander Morris, the newly-appointed lieutenant-governor of Manitoba, was determined not to compound earlier government errors when extinguishing Indian and Métis aboriginal title in the West. He adopted a liberal approach to ethnic identification for the purposes of awarding treaty or scrip.

The enumeration process accompanying the allocation of Manitoba scrip and the negotiation of Treaties One to Seven seemed relatively simple and straightforward. The government had considered the treaty negotiations a formality, thinking that the Natives would simply sign whatever was presented to them. This of course, turned out not to be the case. The negotiations for each numbered treaty, starting with the Stone Fort Treaty in 1871, proved to be difficult, even acrimonious. The aboriginal negotiators did not intend to give their lands away; moreover, they were not prepared to abandon their Métis cousins.[3]

PRENANT LE RECENSEMENT À MANITOBA CHEZ LES "CRIS"

6.1 Census Enumeration of Cree People in Manitoba – Glenbow NA 1406-91

Despite the cultural differences that existed between Indians and Métis in Manitoba, the First Nations' representatives stressed their ties to the Métis, and requested repeatedly that government authorities consider the needs of their mixed-blood kin in negotiations.[4] Having gone through a series of increasingly difficult treaty negotiations, Alexander Morris soon learned that meeting the needs of different aboriginal populations in the west – particularly those of the Métis – would be far more complicated than the government first envisioned. Based on his travels throughout the west and his consultations with local informants, Alexander Morris observed in 1880:

> The Half-Breeds in the territories are of three classes – 1st, those who, as at St. Laurent, near Prince Albert, the Qu'Appelle Lakes and Edmonton, have their farms and homes; 2nd, those who are entirely identified with the Indians, living with them, and speaking their language; 3rd, those who do not farm, but live after the habits of the Indians, by the pursuit of the buffalo and the chase.[5]

Morris recognized that the diverse lifestyles of the Métis had to be reflected in any agreement to extinguish their claims:

> As to the first class, the question is an easy one. They will, of course, be recognized as possessors of the soil, and confirmed by the government in their holdings, and will continue to make their living by farming and trading.

The second class have been recognized as Indians, and have passed into the bands among whom they reside.

The position of the third class is more difficult. The loss of the means of livelihood by the destruction of the buffalo presses upon them, as upon our Indian tribes; and with regard to them I reported in 1876, and I have seen no reason to change my view, as follows:

There is another class of the population in the North-West whose position I desire to bring under the notice of the privy Council. I refer to the wandering Half-breeds of the plains, who are chiefly of French descent and live the life of the Indians. There are a few who are identified with the Indians, but there is a large class of Métis who live by the hunt of the buffalo, and have no settled homes. I think that a census of the numbers of these should be procured, and while I would not be disposed to recommend their being brought under the treaties, I would suggest that land should be assigned to them, and that on their settling down, if after an examination into their circumstances, it should be found necessary and expedient, some assistance should be given them to enable them to enter upon agricultural operations."[6]

The delays in awarding scrip after 1870, compounded with the disappearance of the buffalo and economic reverses in the Red River Settlement, contributed to an exodus of mostly French-speaking Métis from Manitoba westward to Saskatchewan and Athabasca, and southward into North Dakota and Montana. Some of these Métis established permanent residence in areas where missions had been established or where they had previously fished or wintered. Others continued to pursue the dwindling herds of remaining bison on the plains, or migrated northward into the boreal forest to hunt and trap in the places where many of their ancestors had originally worked as *engagés* for the fur companies. There they reunited with both Indian and métis cousins once- or twice-removed.

Because no separate enumeration of Métis communities had been undertaken west of Manitoba, a number of métis had chosen to "take treaty" under the terms of Treaties Four, Five, and Six. Most of these métis were individuals whom Alexander Morris had previously described as the "second category of Half-Breed" – those who were part of Indian bands, spoke Indian languages, and lived the life of an Indian. However, a small but significant portion of the Métis signatories to treaty were those whom Morris described under "Category Three" – nomadic hunters – *hivernants* – who were culturally Métis but chose to follow the buffalo and had no fixed abode, living apart from Indian bands in their own mobile brigades. Although most of these Métis were indigenous to Saskatchewan or Northern Alberta, others had migrated from Manitoba or elsewhere, or had been born since 1870, the "cut-off" point for eligibility for Manitoba scrip. These delays in negotiating scrip resulted in large mixed-race populations taking treaty that may or may not have considered themselves culturally "Indian," but required the benefits of treaty for their survival nonetheless.[7]

Despite the fact that the Canadian government had promised scrip to Manitoba Métis to extinguish their claims, no such provision was made for biracial people living in the North West Territories. Instead of enumerating and negotiating separately with the Métis population west of Manitoba, the government in the mid-1870s chose not to make any provision for scrip at all. Instead, they permitted mixed-bloods in the region to take treaty as Indians, if they so chose. Treaty Four was an agreement negotiated with the Cree and Saulteaux of the North-West Territories. Treaty Six, signed in 1876, was an agreement negotiated with the Cree, Chipewyan, and Assiniboine Indians living in what is now west-central Saskatchewan and east-central Alberta. Because no separate agreement was negotiated with Métis in the region at the time of the treaty, several groups of métis who hunted and trapped for their livelihood, and/or had extensive kin connections with specific bands of Indians, chose to enter Treaties Four, Five, and Six.[8]

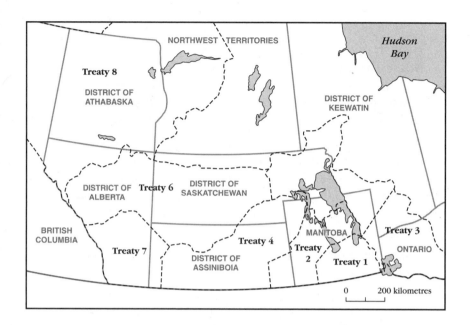

6.2 Treaty Areas in the North West Territories, ca. 1885

The experiences of various branches of the Desjarlais family exemplified the cultural variations existing within the mixed population of Rupert's Land, and their influence over individual and collective decisions to take treaty or scrip between 1875 and 1885. As was noted earlier, two of Old Joseph Desjarlais' sons, Antoine Desjarlais and Baptiste "Nishecabo" Desjarlais had migrated to the Qu'Appelle Lakes region after 1865. Although both men had passed away by 1872, the cultural identification preferred by their respective children is evident in the decisions they made in 1874, when Treaty Four was signed at Battleford. That Nishecabo's family were, as Isaac Cowie said, "decidedly more Saulteau than French in tongue and tone" is illustrated by their decision to become signatories to Treaty Four as members of Muscowequan's band of Saulteaux, located near Fort Qu'Appelle.[9] While two daughters of Antoine Desjarlais had taken treaty with their husbands, his sons and grandsons were homesteading in the same area, and did not take treaty.[10]

In east-central and northern Alberta, where the remaining children of Old Joseph Desjarlais had settled, several members of the Desjarlais families became treaty Indians under Treaty Six, signed in 1876 and administered through the Edmonton Agency of the federal Indian Department. In 1883 the Edmonton Agency of the Indian Department controlled eighteen Indian bands, numbering over two thousand six hundred people. The Agency was divided into three divisions; the Northern Division, consisting of reserves north of the North Saskatchewan River; the Southern Division, covering Indian bands south of the North Saskatchewan, and the Eastern Division, comprising the reserves to the east of Edmonton.[11] The Eastern Division consisted of seven Indian bands – six Cree and one Chipewyan. Of the seven treaty bands located in the Eastern Division, at least one – the Peaysis band at Lac La Biche – was primarily comprised of métis, while other bands, such as Little Hunter's and Pakan's, had one or two métis families in positions of influence.

The band of the Cree chief Ohimnahos – "Little Hunter" – was located mainly at Saddle Lake, although two smaller groups, led by Mus-ke-ga-wa-tik and Blue Quill, were also considered part of the band. The Mus-ke-ga-wa-tik (Wah-sat-now) band was located on Wah-sat-now Creek, about twenty miles from Victoria Settlement. The Blue Quill band of Cree was located at Egg Lake. Ohimnahos was originally considered to be one of the most influential Cree chiefs in the area, but his importance declined in the latter part of the 1870s, possibly due to illness; he died in 1882. One of his sons-in-law was Frederick Desjarlais,[12] known by his Native name "Keh-Kek" (Hawk). Keh-Kek was one of Little Hunter's four councillors, or "headmen," all of whom were married to daughters of Little Hunter.[13] When Little Hunter died in 1882, Keh-Kek took over temporary leadership of the band.[14]

The members of Pakan's Cree band lived on the shores of three lakes: White Fish Lake, Goodfish Lake, and Moving Stone Lake, comprising the largest of the Cree bands in the Eastern District. Unlike the majority of the Christianized Indians in the district, the majority of Pakan's band members were firm Methodists, as was Pakan himself. Although the majority of Pakan's band was Methodist, two mixed-race families of his reserve were known to be Roman Catholic.[15] One was the Cardinal family, specifically that of Gabriel Cardinal dit Labatoche,[16] who was one of Pakan's headmen.[17] Another family of Cardinal relatives, known by the surname of Desjarlais dit Okanase,[18] was also resident on the reserve.

Three bands were located in the boreal forest region north of Victoria Settlement. Antoine's Chipewyan band was located on Heart Lake, northeast of Lac La Biche. Ka-qua-num's Cree band was located on Beaver Lake, adjacent to Lac La Biche. Peaysis' Cree band was situated on Lac La Biche itself on the eastern side of the lake known as "the big bag." The Peaysis band of Lac La Biche was, like most bands, named after its chief, Peaysis (meaning "bird"). Peaysis (a.k.a. François Desjarlais) was the eldest son of Joseph Desjarlais Jr. and Josephte Cardinal. The membership of the band consisted almost entirely of Peaysis' large extended family.[19]

Not all of the Desjarlais and Cardinals, however, had chosen to enter into treaty. The remaining members of these large, extended families were living on the south shore of Lac La Biche in close proximity to both the Roman Catholic mission and the Hudson's Bay Company post. They were faithful Catholics and active trappers, traders, and tripmen.

Around the time of Treaty Six, the Cardinal family lost its most devout Catholic, Alexis, the servant of Father Lacombe. During his twenty years of service to Father Lacombe, Alexis had considered himself as much of a priest as Father Lacombe, even to the point of wearing a priest's cassock. Despite Alexis's pleas to be ordained as an Oblate, Father Lacombe refused to consider the request because he was growing increasingly concerned over Cardinal's mental state.[20] Father Lacombe eventually went to Winnipeg to live, while Alexis remained behind. Cardinal served other priests in Alberta until he decided to go to Winnipeg in search of Father Lacombe. Later, it was reported that Alexis had gone mad, believing himself to be some sort of divine messenger. He travelled from camp to camp across the prairie, until he was found dead on the trail near the mission of Cold Lake in 1876.[21]

The Onset of the Rebellion of 1885

The negotiation of Treaty Six in 1876 required the resolution of several thorny issues. Band leaders wanted to ensure that they would be provided enough resources for their bands to survive the enormous social and economic changes being thrust upon them. Acquiring suitable land for reserves, in locations amenable for both hunting and growing, was preferred. Chiefs Big Bear and Pakan wanted a single large reserve set aside for the Cree that would cover an estimated one thousand square miles of hunting territory and farming land. This they did not receive, although Pakan was convinced that this had been promised to him. He travelled to Regina in 1884, accompanied by Métis interpreter Peter Erasmus, to meet with the Indian commissioner to discuss the matter. Both Pakan and Big Bear refused to settle permanently on reserves until a better deal was offered.[22]

In the years following the signing of Treaty Six, the bands that had not yet taken treaty had ample opportunity to observe how their fellow Natives fared under the government system. They were not impressed by what they saw. Native people throughout the region were angered and disillusioned by what they considered to be dishonesty and neglect by government officials. The disappearance of the buffalo, combined with insufficient supplies of ammunition and netting for hunting and fishing, and less-than-generous provision of relief assistance, left many bands on the brink of starvation.[23]

By January of 1883 the Cree and Stoney (Assiniboine) Indian bands of the Southern District of the Edmonton Department were sufficiently moved to write an open letter to the Minister of the Interior, Sir John A. Macdonald, who was also Canada's prime minister at the time.

To the Minister of the Interior:

Honorable sir. – We, the undersigned chiefs and representatives of the different Indian bands in the district of Edmonton, treaty No. 6, humbly beg you to submit the following statements to your earnest and immediate consideration, and we hold that our very existence is involved in the promptitude with which a remedy shall be applied to the grievances we here undertake to expose to you.

Nothing but our dire poverty, our utter destitution during this severe winter, when ourselves, our wives and our children are smarting under the pangs of cold and hunger with little or no help, and apparently less sympathy from those placed to watch over us, could have induced us to make this final attempt to have redress directly from headquarters. We say final, because, if no attention is paid to our case now we shall conclude that the treaty made with us six years ago was a meaningless matter of form and that the white man has indirectly doomed us to annihilation little by little. But the motto of the Indian is "If we must die by violence let us do it quickly." We say redress because we have many grievances some of which we shall state in this letter, and all of which we are prepared to prove to any honest man sent by government to investigate our cause and in proof of which we can call upon every uninterested white man in the country acquainted with our affairs.

When the government representatives came to make a treaty with us, they said it was in the name of the great mother. The white man had it all his own way. He made the conditions both for himself and for us. We were treated as so many children, unable to judge for ourselves, although we claim a certain amount of the faculty of reasoning in our own interest, and especially where there is a question of the very first law, of nature, self-preservation. The conditions were mutually agreed to. We understood them to be inviolable and in presence of the Great Spirit reciprocally binding; that neither party could be guilty of a breach with impunity. But alas! How simple we were! We have found to our cost that the binding exists all on one side, and the impunity all on the other. For instance a condition on our part is to respect all property belonging to white men. If any of our tribes pushed by hunger, kill an animal belonging to a white man, they are taken and punished according to law.

A condition on the part of the government is to furnish us with a number of farming implements and cattle proportioned to the number of families of each band. Now during six years that we have been in the treaty, the officers acting for the government have robbed us of more than one-half of these things on which we were to depend for a living, and they are not punished according to law. They can break their engagements on behalf of the great mother with impunity.

Now, honourable sir, this is our great complaint. We have never yet been supplied with one-half of what was promised in the treaty. We who send you this letter, represent seven different bands. One article promised to us was one plow to every three families. Three of the bands have received only one-half the number each – the others less than one-half, and in one case, none at all. Harrows, the same way. Axes, hoes, and all other instruments promised have been denied us in the same ratio. Some of us have received all their cattle, some only a portion, and some none at all. Of course, those who have received only a portion or none at all, will loose the increase for so many years. We were promised, during four years, all the seed we could put in the ground, and although many of us have been forced to break the ground with hoes, yet we have on no occasion received more than one-half what we could plant.

Now, we consider this treatment an outrageous breach of good faith, but of course we are Indians. Why does not the head man of the Indians ever appear amongst us, he whom we call in our language the "white beard" and by the whites called Dewdney? He took a rapid run once through our country; some of us had the good or bad luck to catch a flying glimpse of him. He made us all kinds of fine promises, but in disappearing he seems to have tied the hands of the agents so that none of them can fulfil these promises. This is the cause of our dire want now. We are reduced to the lowest stage of

6.3 Chiefs Ermineskin, Samson, and Charles Rabbit – Glenbow NA 1223-21

poverty. We were once a proud and independent people and now we are mendicants at the door of every white man in the country; and were it not for the charity of the white settlers who are not bound by treaty to help us, we should all die on government fare. Our widows and old people are getting the barest pittance, just enough to keep body and soul together, and there have been cases in which body and soul have refused to stay together on such allowance. Our young women are reduced by starvation to become prostitutes to the white man for a living, a thing unheard of before amongst ourselves and always punishable by Indian law. What then are we to do? Shall we not be listened to? Our neighbors, the Blackfeet, are well fed on a pound of flour and a pound of beef a day, men, women, and children, because they are bold, ready to fight and kill cattle if allowed to go hungry, and we, because we are quiet – may be the government think we are cowardly – can get neither food nor clothing, nor the means necessary to make a living for ourselves. We have been calling during several years for the means allowed us by treaty to work for ourselves and we can get no satisfaction. Shall we still be refused, and be compelled to adhere to the conclusion spoken of in the beginning of this letter, that the treaty is a farce enacted to kill us quietly, and if so, let us die at once? Even last year some of those entitled to back pay were refused on authority from Ottawa. The government then can break every article of the treaty in detail or in globo and we have no redress.

We hope, sir, you will pay quick attention to this letter. One great complaint we have is that the government interpreters of this country, with few exceptions, will scarcely or never tell our exact words to the agents, when they fear that the agent, who is very often a man of peevish disposition, would be offended, and so we seldom can say what we desire. But in this letter we have given you in plain talk a short sketch of our position, which we beg you to attend to at once, and we conclude by saying that the half is not told yet.

Your humble servants,

	his	
CHIEF BOB TAIL,	x	
	mark.	
CHIEF SAMSON,	"	
CHIEF ERMINE SKIN,	"	
CHIEF WOODPECKER,	"	
MAMINONATAN,	"	
AGOWASTIN,	"	
SIWIYAWIGES,	"	
IRON HEAD	"	Stoney.
WILLIAM	"	Stoney.[24]

Big Bear, the Plains Cree chief who had refused to sign Treaty Six and settle on a reserve, had attracted a large following of militant Cree to his temporary camp in the vicinity of Frog Lake and Fort Pitt. After unsuccessful negotiations with Big Bear at Fort Pitt in 1883, the deputy minister of Indian Affairs, Lawrence Vankoughnet, threatened to cut the rations of Big Bear's camp if he did not settle on a reserve by November of that year.[25] He

6.4 Native communities in the
North-West, ca. 1885

refused, and his band spent a long, cold winter without rations. Over the winter, Big Bear accepted work freighting goods from Fort Pitt to Edmonton. On the way back, he met with Pakan, the chief of the Cree at Whitefish Lake, whose band had also been refused rations for not settling permanently in one place. By spring of 1884, Big Bear had decided to bring together members of the different bands to discuss their common concerns, and made the decision to host a Thirst Dance that summer at Poundmaker's Reserve near Battleford. He sent messages to other Cree bands inviting their members to attend. Unfortunately, a minor incident at the beginning of the Thirst Dance, involving an assault on a white farming instructor by some young men, escalated into a major confrontation with the North West Mounted Police, who were surrounded and threatened by some of the Cree while apprehending the culprits. Although trouble was avoided, temporarily, the incident was indicative of Big Bear's declining influence over the younger men in his band. They saw him as ineffectual because of his inability to negotiate successfully with the Canadian government. Gradually the young militants, led by Big Bear's own son Imasees, began to assume control of the band.[26]

By the autumn of 1884, Louis Riel, who had been asked to return to Canada to negotiate with the Canadian government on behalf of the Saskatchewan Métis, prepared and circulated a petition of grievances for Métis, English half-breeds, and white settlers to sign. Despite direct appeals from Indians and Métis, and editorials and articles in local newspapers repeatedly warning the federal government of impending trouble,[27] the government did not change its policies, even after a visit by Indian Commissioner Edgar Dewdney in October of 1884 to distribute annuities to the Plains Cree bands of the Southern District, where he listened to their grievances in person.[28] Predictably, the winter of 1884–85 was also bitterly cold, and Big Bear's band, which was still without a reserve and camped adjacent to Frog Lake to be near the government ration house, was hungry, restless, and angry at what they considered to be ineffectual leadership on the part of Big Bear.

By spring of 1885 the inevitable happened. After years of broken promises, various groups of disaffected Native peoples, both Indians and Métis, decided to take matters into their own hands. In March of 1885 Louis Riel and his followers prepared a document called a "Revolutionary Bill of Rights" which asserted their ownership of the land. On 18 and 19 March the Métis established a provisional government, with Louis Riel as its president, Gabriel Dumont as its military leader, and their armed followers as its army. After occupying the community of Duck Lake, between Batoche and Fort Carleton, the Métis clashed with a force of North West Mounted Police officers and citizen volunteers outside of Duck Lake. The skirmish ended with the retreat of the police and volunteers after thirteen of their men were killed.[29]

News of the Métis victory travelled quickly, and the dissident warriors in Big Bear's camp, led by Wandering Spirit, raided the

Indian Agency at Frog Lake and took the residents prisoner on 2 April 1885. During the looting of the stores, Wandering Spirit and his men broke into supplies of liquor and medicine, becoming intoxicated and belligerent. Big Bear, who had now completely lost control of his warriors, sent a messenger to Kehewin's band at Frog Lake, in the hopes that the arrival of this band would prevent more excesses from occurring.

But Big Bear's strategy was too little too late. A decision was made by the warriors to move the prisoners to the Indian camp. When Subagent Thomas Quinn refused to move, Wandering Spirit shot him dead. Despite the pleas of Big Bear to stop the killing, a massacre followed. When it was over, nine people were dead.[30]

Not all of the Cree in Big Bear's camp approved of, or participated in, the murders at Frog Lake. Cut Arm, Chief of the Onion Lake Woods Cree, criticized Wandering Spirit, the war chief then in charge of the camp, for the massacre. The Woods Cree band of Kehewin, who had come to Frog Lake at the request of Big Bear in an effort to prevent violence, moved their lodges closer to those of the other Woods Cree. The response of Wandering Spirit was to encircle the Woods Cree lodges with those of his Plains Cree supporters, in effect, putting the Woods Cree under a form of "house arrest."[31]

Big Bear, who was virtually powerless, sent emissaries westward to other Cree and Métis settlements in the hopes that he might persuade them to join his camp – for their own safety. He knew that raiding parties would eventually turn their attention westward, and they would attack any Native group that did not join their cause. He sent two letters to Chief Pakan at White Fish Lake urging him to come to Frog Lake, but Pakan refused.[32]

The previous October, Pakan had finally concluded an agreement with the government to survey his reserve. Although it was not the size he had originally requested, it was larger than the other reserves, and they had also received agricultural implements and other presents from the Indian Department.[33]

6.5 L-R: Reverend John McDougall; Samson, Cree; Pakan, or James
Seenum, Cree; Reverend R.B. Steinhauer; James Goodstoney, Stoney
– Glenbow NA 4216-33

He was not prepared to jeopardize the hard-won security of
the band, and, despite the Métis victory at Duck Lake, called
an assembly of his people, advising them not to take part in the
uprising, no matter what happened.[34]

Shortly thereafter, rebels appeared in the region, stealing horses, robbing stores, and attempting to persuade or coerce uncommitted Indians and Métis to join their cause. François "Peaysis" Desjarlais, chief of the Peaysis band at Lac La Biche, had already joined the rebel cause.[35] After receiving emissaries from Big Bear's band in early April, Peaysis travelled to the Battle River to meet with the Indians and Métis in that place, presumably to persuade them to revolt. On 17 April Pakan travelled to Lac La Biche to meet with the local authorities, and also with Roman Catholic Bishop Henri Faraud to warn him of the danger. He was accompanied by Rev. Egerton Ryerson Steinhauer of Victoria Settlement; Peter Erasmus, the interpreter and teacher then living at Victoria; Alexandre "Azure" Hamelin, a Métis trader in Lac La Biche; and Harrison Young, the clerk of the local Hudson's Bay Company at Lac La Biche. It was Pakan's intention to encourage the local Indians to resist the rebels and counsel peace. However, on arriving in Lac La Biche, he found that Peaysis was absent, having already gone to Battle River.[36]

Pakan returned to Whitefish Lake to await future events. When rebels attempted to pillage a Métis trader named Adam Howse on 23 April,[37] midway between Whitefish and Goodfish lakes, Pakan's response was to order his band to move camp.

> The camp was then moved, on Chief James Seenum's orders, to a point on Whitefish Lake. This place, being heavily wooded on one side and having the lake with a steep bank on the other, provided a good protection from the rebels if they happened to come around looking for trouble. The bank would be a good place for the women and children to hide and also afforded a vantage point from which to shoot at the enemy. As the people who were not on Riel's side were in danger from the other Indians, great precautions were taken constantly.[38]

However, not all of Pakan's band was ready to obey his orders.

> Some of the other Indians who had come to live at Whitefish Lake with the rest of us *but who were not relations* [emphasis added] joined the rebels and took Mr. Yeoman's horses, one

buckskin and one bay mare. They intended to use these horses when they went east to join the other hostile bands.[39]

The horse thieves were none other than Gabriel Cardinal, Pakan's headman at Whitefish Lake, and his sons. Their Desjarlais relatives, William and Pierre Okanase also joined them.[40] Also known to have gone east was Louison "Wechokwan" Cardinal, who was married to Peaysis Desjarlais' sister Judith.[41]

In contrast, Joseph Cardinal, another son of Gabriel Cardinal dit Labatoche of Whitefish Lake, was, according to one observer, not a rebel at all. Sam Bull, a Whitefish Lake Elder, claimed that Cardinal was away on a beaver hunting trip when the troubles broke out.

> This man [Joseph Cardinal] on arrival from a beaver hunting trip, came home to his camp and upon finding the rest of the people gone, went to Whitefish Lake where they were. While he was there, in the home of Peter Erasmus (who, I believe, was absent at the time), he was sitting on a home-made stool. The chief was talking to him and advising him not to interfere or have anything to do with those rebels. Besides a number of men, there were also several women. In fact, the cellar door was open while some of the women folks were getting potatoes. A man entered and without any warning drew a gun from under a blanket which covered him and shot the man sitting on the stool, flooring and killing him almost instantly. The man gave one expressive word, rubbed his chest and died. The mad killer then fled.
>
> Everybody there was so surprised that they had no time to do anything, although everyone was armed. The chief gave an exclamatory word, such as it is used in the Cree language when one is sorry or when anything serious happens. Then the majority of the people left the scene of the murder, except Baptiste Rose. The Chief sent word to all his people, who happened not to have been there with him. News of the murder went forth.[42]

According to the account of interpreter Peter Erasmus however, Joseph Cardinal *was* a rebel, sent by Wandering Spirit to persuade

6.6 Peter Erasmus – Glenbow NA 3148-1

Pakan's band to join them at Frog Lake. When Cardinal reached Erasmus's house, he found chief Pakan and some of the band members gathered. He requested permission to speak to the gathering, which Pakan granted. Cardinal then proceeded to encourage people to join the rebellion. An argument broke out between Cardinal and Peter Shirt, and Cardinal demanded that Hudson's Bay Company goods that were in the house be handed over. It was at this point that band member William Stamp shot Joseph Cardinal.[43]

Chief Pakan was immediately and painfully aware of the crisis that had suddenly been created by the murder of Joseph Cardinal. It was bad enough that a band member had been killed in cold blood by another band member, for simply speaking his mind. But it was *who* Joseph Cardinal was, or rather, whom he was *related to*, that turned a tense situation into one that was truly dangerous for the entire band. Not only was Joseph Cardinal the son of one of his headmen, Gabriel Cardinal, but Joseph Cardinal was also married to Eliza Desjarlais, the daughter of François "Peaysis" Desjarlais, chief of the Peaysis band and a supporter of the rebels himself.

Besides Pakan's, Peaysis', and Little Hunter's bands, there were Cardinals – and Cardinal relations – in most of the other Cree bands in the area, including those of Chiefs Bobtail and Ermineskin at Bear's Hill south of Edmonton[44]; Kah-qua-num's band on Beaver Lake near Lac La Biche; Kehewin's band near Frog Lake;[45] and the Mistawasis[46] band near Carleton, to name but a few. Many of these bands had already joined the rebels, or were thinking of doing so. From Pakan's perspective, the killing of Joseph Cardinal could well be the one factor that would incite these groups to revolt. Of even more concern was the possibility that Wandering Spirit's followers, who were already threatening to kill anyone who did not support the rebellion, would attack the members of the band once it was discovered that one of them had murdered one of their emissaries.

Because of these possibilities, Pakan acted quickly to cast the murderer out of the band, because the man's continued presence threatened the lives of those around him. Sam Bull recalled,

I saw the murderer lying on the ground when Chief Pakan came along. He walked straight toward him and hollered at him, telling him to get right off that place and "make it quick." The Chief told him again to go and to make it snappy, saying, "Didn't you know how much trouble you have caused?" The man knew it had been murder in cold blood as the victim was innocent and a very good-natured, friendly man who had never caused anyone any trouble.[47]

Chief Pakan's next task was to calm Joseph Cardinal's relatives and make immediate reparations for the murder, to forestall any further revenge killings or lootings.

> On hearing this, Thomas Hunter, a brave warrior in his young days, c ame to assist Chief Pakan in quieting the bereaved relatives of the murdered man for they were ready for revenge. While this was being discussed, Egerton Ryerson Steinhauer (a son of the late Reverend Steinhauer) who had returned home from college in Ontario the preceding fall, and another man, acted as undertakers, making a coffin and burying the murdered man. There were only two of them present.[48]

Thomas Hunter, who was also a member of Pakan's band at Whitefish Lake, was the son of the deceased Cree chief Little Hunter, and a brother-in-law to Frederick "Keh-Kek" Desjarlais. As he was the closest available person with kin ties to the Cardinals, it was natural for Pakan to call on his old friend's brother-in-law to assist him in dealing with the relatives.

> This murder caused an uprising amongst the people which it was feared would end in a fight amongst the relatives. The father of the murdered man was given five cayuses and several cattle – I don't know the exact number. Nobody was allowed to see the corpse or attend the funeral as this might cause someone to seek revenge since the bereaved relatives had intended to settle at Whitefish Lake with the rest of the Band. This happening, however, quickly changed their minds and instead they went east, wishing to leave while they still had their tempers under control as it was unbearable to stay where their friend had been killed.[49]

Seenum's final move was to relocate his band farther westward, deeper into the bush. The entire band was soon on the move, on foot and on horseback, in canoes and in carts, herding their cattle and oxen with them through the slush and ice of the early spring. They survived by catching fish and butchering their cattle for food along the way. They moved camp a total of five times until reaching safety at Victoria Settlement, where soldiers and militia were stationed. There the band remained until July of 1885, when the rebellion was declared officially over, and it was safe to return to their homes.[50]

While the killing of Joseph Cardinal was unfolding at Whitefish Lake, Big Bear's representatives had reached Lac La Biche in the middle of the night on 26 April 1885. They arrived on the shores of Beaver Lake, where they coerced some local Cree camped on the lakeshore to accompany them to the Hudson's Bay Company post at Lac La Biche, which was then looted. After raiding the HBC store, it was the rebels' intention to loot the Roman Catholic mission. Upon hearing this news, members of the Cardinal family took steps to protect the priests and the mission. Bishop Henri Faraud recounted,

> The night of the arrival of Big Bear's emissaries the old mother of our good and loyal servant, Julien Cardinal, had hurriedly come across forest and swamp to warn us of the danger. She arrived at six thirty in the morning. Her son Julien, the first warned, having given the alarm, left on horseback to warn the residents of the west end of the lake, the most numerous and civilized, that the moment of danger had arrived, and that all those of stout hearts should prove it by leaving immediately for the defense of the mission.[51]

While Lac La Biche residents armed themselves and proceeded to the mission, Big Bear's emissaries went to the home of Alexandre "Azure" Hamelin. According to Bishop Henri Faraud, Hamelin was considered by Big Bear to be "the leader of the movement at Lac La Biche." Therefore, the rebels were under orders to "come to an understanding with him" about their intention to loot the mission. To their surprise, Azure Hamelin was completely opposed to their plans.[52]

Why Big Bear's emissaries expected Azure Hamelin to support them is not evident unless one is aware of the family relationships linking Azure Hamelin to Big Bear's band. Azure Hamelin was married to Peaysis' sister, Marie Desjarlais. Prior to their marriage, Marie Desjarlais had been married to a man named Antoine Blondion, a half-brother of Big Bear, by whom she had several children.[53] Marie Desjarlais' prior marriage to Antoine Blondion, as well as the other kin relationships that the Desjarlais and Cardinal families shared with Saulteaux and Cree bands in the region, partially explains why Big Bear's messengers expected Azure Hamelin to assist them.

As the Rev. John McDougall had noted in his memoirs, his good friend Frederick "Keh-Kek" Desjarlais was related to a band of Saulteaux living east of Fort Pitt on the shores of Jackfish Lake.[54] This particular group was actually a mixed band of Cree and Ojibwa who had been occupying the shores of Jackfish Lake for at least sixty years. Their original leader at this site was an Ojibwa named Black Powder. As one of only sixty lodges of mixed Ojibwa and Cree trading in the entire Upper Saskatchewan region in 1825,[55] it is not surprising that they would have been related in some way to the Desjarlais family of Lac La Biche, and to Keh-Kek's father, Baptiste "Nishecabo" Desjarlais, a respected and feared warrior, trading chief, and shaman whose mother was Ojibwa.[56]

Black Powder (also known as Wabasca Dion, Blondion, Powder, or LaPoudre) had several wives with whom he fathered children. One of Black Powder's sons, Mistamhimaskwa, or Big Bear, was born on the shores of Jackfish Lake in 1825. As noted earlier, another son of Black Powder, Antoine Blondion, has married Marie Desjarlais, the daughter of Joseph Desjarlais and Josephte Cardinal, on 19 May 1846, immediately after her baptism as an adult.[57]

Because Black Powder spent most of his adulthood crisscrossing the Athabasca region trading and trapping, he and his children were tied by loyalty, blood, and marriage to many of the prominent aboriginal chiefs and hunters of the region, such as Maskepetoon, Mistawasis, Ohimnahos (Little Hunter),

Ermineskin, Peyesiwop (a.k.a. Petit Couteau, or Little Knife), Le Grand Bâtard, and the Grand Nipissing. They, in turn, were related to (or descended from) many of the *Canadien* freemen and their children who had been operating in the Saskatchewan River watershed, from the foothills of the Rockies eastward into Manitoba, since the late 1700s.[58]

By 1885, at the outbreak of the North-West Rebellion, all of these families had been intermarrying for at least three, perhaps four, generations. Their kin ties, and their loyalties, were so intertwined that for any Desjarlais and Cardinal in treaty *not* to have considered joining their relatives on a war expedition would have lowered their status considerably amongst their aboriginal relations. As far as Big Bear's representatives were concerned, Marie Desjarlais Blondion Hamelin, like her Desjarlais and Cardinal relatives, was kin to Big Bear, and the kin ties were still recognized.

Other than their shared kinship with Big Bear, there was no compelling explanation as to why the treaty Indian Cardinals and Desjarlais chose to join the Rebellion, when the vast majority of their non-treaty Métis relations in the Lac La Biche area did not.[59] One possible explanation is that, like most of the other members of boreal forest hunting bands, they suffered the most from privation when the government failed to provide sufficient provisions and ammunition.

However, the Desjarlais and Cardinals, like most of the rebel supporters in the Lac La Biche region, soon lost their stomach for the revolt, particularly after the looting of the HBC post at Lac La Biche. The local rebel sympathizers who had ransacked the post were ashamed of what they had done. Moreover, they were horrified at the thought of attacking the Roman Catholic mission.

> Thus when it was proposed [by Big Bear's emissaries] that they loot the mission they replied with a single voice and with their chief as speaker: "We have followed you as far as the Fort but we will not loot the mission. We love our priests who do well by us. The big Priest (the Bishop) particularly loves us. He has saved the lives of several of us with his medicines. His words

are good; they give the heart solace and banish sorrow. Were we resolved to do evil, his look alone would make us retreat. We will not follow you. Go alone if you want to."[60]

And what happened to Gabriel Cardinal and his family, after leaving Whitefish Lake? According to various oral accounts, Gabriel Cardinal, his family, and his Okanase relations from Whitefish Lake travelled eastward, where they encountered Big Bear's warriors shortly after they had captured the Hudson's Bay Company post at Fort Pitt and taken the Factor, W. J. McLean, and his family prisoners. Fortunately for McLean and his family, Gabriel Cardinal and his Okanase relatives were old acquaintances of McLean.

> We remained in the vicinity of Frog Lake for over two weeks. At one point Mr. James K. Simpson became my confidential interpreter and was always camped near my tents with his family, as were a number of Indians and half-breeds who were compelled to join the rebellious camp by some of Big Bear's followers.
>
> Among them were three or four very intelligent and influential Indians from the Riding Mountains in the Swan River District. They were well known to me during the ten years I was stationed in the district, which at that time included Fort Qu'Appelle. I sounded them out as to their sentiment and found that they were loyal.[61]

Over subsequent days Chief Factor McLean negotiated with the Woods Crees through St. Paul "Menoomin" Cardinal,[62] and William and Pierre Desjarlais dit Okanase, who were originally from Keeseekoowenin's reserve at Riding Mountain. The Saulteaux from Riding Mountain arranged to protect McLean and his family, particularly his two daughters, with the help of the Woods Cree in camp. One of the leaders of the Woods Cree, Louison Mongrain, took responsibility for protecting the McLean family.

> This Louison [Mongrain] was proving to be our friend indeed. He was a man to whom the Wood Crees naturally turned for advice and guidance, for he seemed to understand their

situation better than any other. And now we too were turning to him in our anxiety. That night he brought a rifle and cartridges to my father.

"You might need them," he said, "but I shall try to prevent that. I shall stand guard at night in front of your tent, and Manoomin will stand at the back." Manoomin was one of the friendly Indians from Riding Mountain.

Naturally we were all very quiet within our tent, wondering what the morrow would bring forth. As I lay there, trying to sleep, I found myself shivering, probably more with apprehension than with cold. I asked my father if our dog Carlo might come and lie at my feet to warm them. I remember wondering if Manoomin were really standing guard at the back at the tent as arranged. As the moon rose, I saw the shadow of his head and shoulder gradually come into view. He was leaning on his rifle, perfectly still. I felt so relieved and grateful that we had such a faithful friend. Then I wondered if Louison were still standing at the front. When the moon was at its height it was as bright as day. Then, as it gradually went down, I saw the full silhouette of Louison, a silent sentinel and a trusted friend.[63]

Later, the Woods Cree, led by Kehewin and Louison Mongrain managed to slip away from the Plains Cree. They carried with them the prisoners, among them Chief Factor McLean and his family. McLean had written a letter to the military authorities on behalf of the Woods Cree who had protected him and his family, recommending that they receive clemency from the Canadian government for their heroic actions on behalf of himself, his family, and the other prisoners.[64]

Conclusion

The extinguishment of aboriginal title by treaty was a necessary precursor to settlement of the Canadian West by Euro-Canadians. In almost every treaty negotiation undertaken between the Government of Canada and the First Nations, however, the disposition of métis peoples was raised by the tribal groups involved, because they recognized them as blood kin who shared similar, if not identical, aboriginal rights.

The government representatives were eager to avoid another round of conflicts like those experienced with the Red River Métis in Manitoba, and prepared to settle the Métis claims in the North-West Territories separately from, though contiguously with, those of Indians. However, the negotiators soon discovered that being biracial and being Métis were not necessarily the same thing. As indicated earlier, the cultural differences which eventually emerged between aboriginal populations in the Athabasca region were not racial divisions per se, but were based on tribal affiliations acquired through kinship; different subsistence patterns which necessitated mobility or settlement; and opposing Christian practices. In Athabasca, the cultural practices most closely associated with "civilization," i.e., Christianization and the practice of agriculture, were introduced to, and adopted by, both métis and Indian residents at approximately the same time; a conversion facilitated by the rapid disappearance of buffalo and other large game animals.

The cultural divide that developed between Plains Indians and Red River Métis upon the arrival of Christianity did not manifest itself in the region now encompassing north-central Alberta and Saskatchewan. Therefore, the enumeration of the aboriginal population of the North-West Territories for the purposes of awarding treaty and scrip was much more problematic. Government officials chose not to grapple with the inherent shortcomings of their aboriginal land claims strategy, which failed to take into consideration the differing lifestyles of aboriginal communities, or the more inclusive concepts of community that many "Indians" and "Métis" shared. Had they done so, they might have discovered how closely bonded the aboriginal communities of the North-West Territories had actually become by 1885.

Instead, the government assumed that Indian groups and Métis groups would eventually separate into two clearly identifiable and separate entities, like oil from water. Of course this separation did not take place. Rather, the Native peoples of the

North-West Territories fractured along lines of kinship, personal loyalty, religious affiliation, and lifestyle that did not correspond to race.

The Cree and Métis of Lac La Biche refused to attack the Roman Catholic Mission because they loved their priests. Conversely, however, they did not hesitate to join in the looting of the local Hudson's Bay store, which was run by a chief factor who was universally disliked by the Natives in the community. But as the relationship between Factor W. J. McLean and the Saulteaux of Riding Mountain illustrates so eloquently, personal loyalties could transcend the corporate barriers of the Hudson's Bay Company. Chief Factor McLean and his daughters had developed bonds of trust and friendship with the Saulteaux/Cree mixed-bloods of the Swan River District long before 1885.

Gabriel Cardinal, St. Paul Cardinal (a.k.a. Manoomin) and their Okanase relatives, in turn, shared close ties of kinship and friendship with Mistawasis and the other Woods Cree bands because of their residence at Whitefish Lake. As a result, Mistawasis and his followers were prepared to take the considerable risk of separating from Wandering Spirit and his followers and taking the White prisoners with them – because they trusted the words of Gabriel Cardinal, Pakan's headman, who in turn trusted his old friend from Swan River, William McLean.

The events of the Northwest Rebellion, particularly the death of Joseph Cardinal, bring into sharp relief the intricate network of relationships that bound Indians, Métis, and Whites together in the Northwest. Traditionally, aboriginal hunting bands were fluid in their membership. But Euro-Canadian religious, economic, and political policies would soon rupture Native communities in ways that would create permanent, even irreparable, divisions between their people.

7

·····················

Some Difficult Choices: The Desjarlais
after 1885

After the Canadian government successfully put down the
Northwest Rebellion of 1885, it implemented policies designed
to subdue and pacify Western Canada's aboriginal population.
One of the effects of its policy was the removal of métis people
from Indian bands, and the institutionalized partition of "Métis"
and "Indian" into separate ethnic entities, a process later reinforced, and refined, by the simultaneous negotiation and signing
of Treaty Eight and the issuance of Métis scrip in 1899–1900. In
Northern Alberta, Indian Department regulations and judicial
practices placed pressure on treaty Indians of mixed descent,
inducing them to withdraw from treaty voluntarily and accept
scrip. As a consequence, several members of the Desjarlais family
withdrew from Treaty Six after 1885, and subsequently migrated
westward and northward into the Peace River country to continue trapping and to pursue agriculture.

The Aftermath of the Rebellion

After the final defeat of Louis Riel's forces at Batoche, the
government moved swiftly to reassert control over the
aboriginal population by punishing those responsible for the
uprising and implementing new management policies intended
to prevent further revolts. In 1885 Hayter Reed, assistant
Indian Commissioner, prepared a memorandum recommending
sweeping changes to the management of treaty Indians.[1] It
was a startling document, so punitive in tone that even Reed's
colleagues recognized quickly that some recommendations were
simply unenforceable without depriving their Indian charges of
all sense of free will and identity.

However, Hayter Reed was concerned with matters besides
punishing rebellious Indians. Lack of sufficient financial

resources was always a problem when managing the Indian Department. Using the rebellion as an excuse for cutting rations, withholding annuities, and forcing Indians in treaty to labour for their benefits enabled the Canadian government to persist with underfunding Indian Affairs without attracting criticism from the public. Since the government had no desire to extend treaty rights and privileges to any more people than was absolutely necessary, it sought to encourage those métis who had taken treaty to withdraw from treaty and accept scrip instead.

The government was also intent on neutralizing the treaty Indians politically. A key element of this strategy was to remove dissident elements from the reserves and subvert, or remove entirely, the traditional leadership within the bands. The individuals considered most influential, and therefore most dangerous, on reserves, were the métis or "half-breeds" who had taken treaty in 1876 when the opportunity presented itself. The government recognized that several métis in treaty had assumed prominent and influential positions as chiefs and headmen. The traditional fur trade roles of the métis as cultural brokers, advisors, and intermediaries, however, were no longer welcomed by or useful to the Canadian government, which found it easier to impose its wishes on an Indian population less familiar with its motives and practices. For this reason, the policies implemented after the rebellion were sufficiently unpleasant that they compelled many métis in treaty to renounce their treaty rights and accept scrip.

Of the recommendations listed in Hayter Reed's memorandum, the following policy changes were to have the most significant impact on members of the Desjarlais family:

4. That the tribal system should be abolished in so far as is compatible with the treaty, i.e. in all cases in which the treaty has been broken by rebel tribes; by doing away with the chiefs and councillors, depriving them of medals and other appurtenances of their offices. Our instructors and employees will not then be hampered by Indian consultations and interferences, but will administer direct orders and instructions to individuals; besides by this action and careful repression of those that become

prominent amongst them by counselling, medicine dances, and so on, a further obstacle will be thrown in the way of future united rebellious movements.

5. No annuity money should now be paid any bands that rebelled, or any individuals that left well disposed bands and joined the insurgents. As the Treaty expressly stipulated for peace and good will, as well as an observance of law and order, it has been entirely abrogated by the rebellion. Besides this fact, such suggestion is made because in the past the annuity money which should have been expended wholly in necessaries has to a great extent been wasted upon articles more or less useless and in purchasing necessaries at exorbitant prices, entailing upon the Department a greater expenditure in providing articles of clothing, food, and implements, not called for by the terms of the Treaty, than need have been entailed if the whole of the annuity money had been well and economically applied to the purchase of such necessaries. All future grants should be regarded as concessions of favour, *not of right*, and the rebel Indians be made to understand that they have forfeited every claim as "matter of right."

6. Disarm all rebels, but to those rebel Indians north of the North Saskatchewan who have heretofore mainly existed by hunting, return shotguns (retaining the rifles) branding them as I.D. property and keeping lists of those to whom arms are lent. Those to whom arms are thus supplied if left to their own resources – under careful supervision – would suffer great hardship and doubtlessly be benefitted by experiencing the fact that they cannot live after their old methods. They would soon incline to settlement and be less likely to again risk losing the chance of settling down.

11. All halfbreeds, members of rebel bands. Although not shewn to have taken any active part in the rebellion, should have their names erased from the paysheets, and if this suggestion is not approved of, by directing that all belonging to any bands should reside on the reserves.

Most of these halfbreeds would desire to be released
from the terms of the treaty. It is desirable however that
communication between such people and the Indians be
entirely severed as it is never productive of aught but bad
results.[2]

Depending on their place of residence and their degree of involvement in the 1885 Rebellion, the branches of the Desjarlais family
scattered across Western Canada would experience a variety of
consequences from the new government policies, impacts which
would shape the corporate identities of their descendants.

Conditions in Assiniboia and Saskatchewan

By 1885, several different families of Desjarlais were living in
the districts of Assiniboia and Saskatchewan. Some of these
families were headed by individuals who had signed Treaties
Four and Six, only to withdraw from treaty and accept Métis
scrip after the Northwest Rebellion. They included Desjarlais
family members living on the Ketawayhew Reserve at Muskeg
Lake near Prince Albert, in the Saskatchewan district,[3] and
Desjarlais family members resident on Muscowequan's Reserve
north of Fort Qu'Appelle in Assiniboia.[4] Other Desjarlais
relatives, who identified themselves as Métis and had migrated
to the Qu'Appelle Valley in the 1860s, were farming near the
Roman Catholic Mission of Lebret. Additional Métis relatives
who migrated westward after disposing of their Manitoba scrip
in the 1870s later joined them.

The transition to a settler lifestyle was eased by the activities of the Roman Catholic Mission, which established an
Industrial School for treaty Indian pupils at Lebret. Because the
local treaty Indians were reluctant to send their children away
to live at the school, the Roman Catholic authorities who administered the school had difficulty in attracting and retaining
pupils. Technically, non-treaty pupils were not eligible to attend
this school, which was intended to meet the educational needs
of Indian pupils from the numerous reserves in the area. One

7.1 Father Hugonard and Pupils at Lebret Industrial School, 1880s
– Saskatchewan Archives Board R-A448

family of Desjarlais found a way to circumvent this restriction, however.

Thomas Desjarlais, the son of Baptiste "Penawich" Desjarlais and Marie Martin, had claimed land in Manitoba in exchange for scrip. After Thomas sold his land, he moved to Lebret, Saskatchewan,[5] where a brother, François, and a sister, Madeleine, were living nearby as members of the Muscowequan Reserve.[6] Thomas later married Madeleine Klyne, a *Métisse* from St. Joseph, Dakota Territory, at Lebret on 24 June 1879.[7]

By 1885 Thomas and Madeleine Desjarlais had three children, two girls and a boy. In order to have their eldest daughter, Rosine, admitted to the Industrial School, they arranged for her maternal aunt, Marie Klyne and her husband, Joseph Bellegarde, to informally adopt her into their family. The Bellegardes were signatories to Treaty Four, and lived at the File Hills Agency north of Fort Qu'Appelle near Balcarres, Saskatchewan. The File Hills Agency consisted of four reserves: Little Black Bear, Starblanket, Okanase, and Peepeekeesis. As treaty Indians the Bellegardes had access to the Industrial School for their children. Although her younger sister Justine disliked the Industrial School, and "was always trying to run away from there," Rosine Desjarlais was

7.2 The Thomas Desjarlais family, Lebret, 1890s – Saskatchewan Archives Board R-A8825

"happy and contented" there. Because the Industrial School was home to Native students of several linguistic and cultural backgrounds, the pupils taught each other several Native languages despite the official proscriptions against them. Rosine could speak Saulteaux, Cree, Sioux, Metchif, French, and English. According to her descendants,

> Rosine did know how to speak several languages but I know she was ashamed of her Métis connections. She certainly would not speak the Indian languages in too many places.

Also, it was understood that children were supposed to be briefly seen and not heard from, especially when company was present. This gave them [Rosine's children] little opportunity to pick up any languages. Also the sentiment over Métis ancestry would discourage them from trying to speak or even learn these languages.[8]

Northern Alberta After 1885

One of the more unpalatable consequences of the rebellion was the restriction on the use of rifles by treaty Indians in the North West Territories. Although it was believed, initially, that most of the rebels had surrendered their firearms to Canadian authorities, word that rifles still remained in the hands of some Indians prompted the government to take action to neutralize what they believed was a continued military threat.[9] An August 1885 amendment to the Indian Act which prohibited the sale, gift, or disposal of "fixed ammunition or ball cartridge" to Indians in the Northwest Territories upon the pain of fine and/or imprisonment was enacted, which was designed to render any rifles in Indian hands useless.[10]

For treaty Indians in boreal forest regions, this restriction would compound their difficulties during the winter of 1885. Virtually all of the bands in the Victoria Agency (with the exception of the Pakan and Blue Quill bands) had been deemed "disloyal" by Hayter Reed.[11] These bands were situated in the boreal forest, on land that was primarily muskeg and unsuitable for agriculture. They were hunters and gatherers by necessity, and were having trouble acquiring sufficient firearms and ammunition *before* the rebellion. If they remained as "Indian," they could only hope to have access to shotguns using birdshot, which were good for fowl but not big game. Although the northern hunters were adept at using snares and deadfalls for hunting, these traps were generally for smaller animals, not the large ungulates preferred. To make things even more uncomfortable, prices of some basic foodstuffs had risen substantially in the northern areas since the rebellion, where people could afford it the least.[12]

7.3 James Seenum (Pakan) and Wife – Glenbow NA-1668-2

If eligible métis in treaty refused to withdraw, other means were available to force them off the reserves. One of them was to place pressure on their chiefs. Sam Bull at Whitefish Lake recalled,

> Chief Seenum told me later that Commissioner Reid had told him to release those rebels from the Band and let them go back to Frog Lake where they belonged. The Chief refused. The Commissioner then told him, "Pakan, you will be sorry in the future. Those people are going to cause lots of trouble. If you will not let them go, at least never elect any of them as leaders for the Reserve." From this I gathered the idea that Commissioner Reid came for two reasons – to help the people since they had no crops to live on during the coming winter, and to assure himself of the Band's loyalty to the Government.[13]

Indian agents were instructed to identify individuals and bands that participated in the uprising or otherwise broke the law during the troubles. Then the Department instructed the Indian agents on how to handle these people's relief assistance and annuity payments.[14] Although individuals and bands guilty of minor misdemeanors had been granted amnesty by the government, treatment of "rebels" and bands deemed "disloyal" was harsh, well in keeping with Hayter Reed's recommendations. Dissident bands were refused rations, or had their annuity payments held back. When visiting the reserves in his district in the fall of 1885, a police escort accompanied Indian Agent John Mitchell of the Saddle Lake Agency. Prior to distributing annuity payments, he would make arrests of insurgents.[15] As the *Edmonton Bulletin* stated,

> Reports from Lac La Biche say that the Indians there are in a very bad state – hungry and discontented. A very large number received no treaty money on account of their participation in the rebellion, and none of them receive any rations. Those who drew out of the treaty on the promise of receiving scrip are very impatient at it not having yet been issued, while the half-breeds entitled to it are not in a much more pleasant frame of mind. The local food supply is even more scanty than usual as almost nothing was raised in the way of crop owing to the excitement of last spring which prevented farming operations, or at least was made the pretext for neglecting them. At the same time the loyal Indians of Whitefish Lake find themselves in the same condition, except that they received their treaty money. To improve the matter no provision has been made for the families of the prisoners taken by the police at the time of the treaty payments, and this gives to the arrests an appearance of especial hardship which is by no means conciliatory in its effect. While it is no doubt right and proper to arrest the men it is anything but right to leave the families unprovided for.[16]

However, many of the local leaders of the rebellion had long since fled. François "Peaysis" Desjarlais, chief of the Cree at Lac La Biche, had gone south, as had many of the dissidents from Big Bear's band. Like many others who had participated in the uprising, Peaysis was suspicious of any amnesty that was offered by the government, particularly after the execution of Louis Riel. When he applied for and received scrip years later, he filed his affidavit in Calgary, over three hundred miles south of Lac La Biche.[17] He never returned to live in Northern Alberta, but moved east to Battleford instead, where he died in 1899.[18]

Most of the métis who were eligible to withdraw from treaty took steps to do so as quickly as possible. In order to speed up the government action in this regard, Indian Agent J. A. Mitchell sent a letter to his superiors, outlining the considerable economic benefits of issuing scrip to mixed-race members of northern bands without delay. He noted that of the 150 people of the Peaysis band paid annuities in 1884, "fully one hundred and twenty are halfbreeds, the majority of these being women, the wives of non-Treaty men."[19] In later correspondence, Agent Mitchell adjusted these figures, claiming as many 134 people were eligible to be discharged from treaty.[20]

Not surprisingly, the authorities responded swiftly to these optimistic projections and the substantial cost savings they implied. Virtually the entire Peaysis band of Lac La Biche withdrew from treaty, as did the eligible members of Ka-qua-num band at Beaver Lake. With their leaders under arrest or absent as fugitives from the law, the communities soon disintegrated. The remaining members became attached to other reserves, and by 1900, these reserves had ceased to exist.

The few remaining bands deemed "loyal" by the government, such as Pakan's, were treated generously. Sam Bull remembered,

> After the haying was finished that fall, Commissioner Reid came. As the people had fled the previous spring nobody had taken time to put in their crops. There was no grain or potatoes, just a few stacks of grain left from the preceding autumn but these were spoiled owing to heavy rains. Rations were issued by the Band; we got so many rations that there was always a surplus from the preceding month. I recall when in our family we got 300 lbs. of flour and a side of bacon every month.[21]

Although amnesty had been granted to the rebels, and despite Pakan's determination not to force métis members of his reserve out of treaty, Gabriel Cardinal chose to withdraw from treaty with his family. As Acting Indian Agent John Mitchell reported,

Sir;

> I beg to report the arrival, from Moose Lake on the boundary of the Ft. Pitt and Victoria Districts, of Gabriel Cardinal (Menomiw) and five of his sons, who took part in the rebellion of last Spring under Big Bear.
>
> They have wintered at Moose and Mosquito Lake with Spo-kaw, Headman of the Moose Lake rebel Stragglers, but inform me that they are now desirous of Settling down to farming.
>
> They tell me that having once broken the Treaty they now desire to be released from its obligations and request that they be granted Scrip as Halfbreeds.
>
> As they certainly are Halfbreeds and there are objections to their reentering the Treaty and Remaining on the Reserves, I would recommend that they be discharged from Treaty and receive Scrip at an early date.
>
> Though undoubtedly rebels, there remains one point in their favour, that they were the leaders of the party of Wood Crees who to save the McLean family and other prisoners, Separated from Big Bear at Loon Lake and carried the prisoners with them.... [22]

The Transition to Settlement in Northern Alberta

In the next two decades, the métis who withdrew from Treaty Six attempted to settle on a more-or-less permanent basis. They included the métis members of Desjarlais families who, despite having no involvement in the hostilities, also chose to withdraw from treaty after the 1885 rebellion. Antoine Desjarlais dit Wabumun, the son of Antoine Desjarlais and the Cree woman Napitch, was a member of the Michel Reserve (considered by the Indian Department to be a "loyal" reserve) when he withdrew from Treaty Six with his family in June of 1885.[23] Why he withdrew is not known, though it was rumoured that several treaty Indians in the Edmonton area, including members of Michel's Band, withdrew to collect scrip in the mistaken belief that remaining members of their immediate family could continue to collect annuities every year.[24]

Frederick "Keh-Kek" Desjarlais was another métis who chose to withdraw from treaty, despite his long-standing cultural identification as Cree. The reasons for his choice are unclear; his home was Whitefish Lake, and most of his extended family were members of Little Hunter's and Pakan's reserves. Nonetheless, he and his family withdrew from treaty in 1886, and collected scrip from the government. In later years, Keh-Kek petitioned the Department of the Interior to obtain scrip on behalf of two of his deceased children, Thaddeus and Sarah. Despite repeated written entreaties by the Reverend John McDougall on behalf of his friend, Keh-Kek's claims were disallowed, because of the argument that his children's claims had been extinguished when their parents withdrew from treaty.[25] Keh-Kek and his family continued to remain in the vicinity of Whitefish Lake, and he was recorded in the local history of Andrew, Alberta as the first settler in the area. He settled on N.W. 28-56-16-4, living there with his family until his death shortly after the turn of the century.[26]

Métis who had been squatting on river lots adjacent to the Roman Catholic Mission at Lac La Biche soon got the opportunity to consolidate their land holdings. Surveyors working for the Department of the Interior had reached Lac La Biche a few years after the rebellion, and proceeded to subdivide the Lac La Biche Settlement in 1889. The settlement was surveyed into eighty river lots, extending over forty miles along the lakeshore. At the time of the survey, the government's intent was to encourage agriculture. The government surveyor, P. R. A. Belanger, noted, however, that the inhabitants relied heavily on fishing. He concluded that the easy access to fish from the lake was an impediment to farming.

> With regard to the agricultural capacities of the land in that settlement I may say that they are very good. The soil is either clay or sandy loam, and will produce all kinds of cereal or root crops. The only apparent objection to this district for

7.4 St. Augustine Mission, Shaftesbury Trail, 1900 – Provincial Archives of Alberta, A-4582

> settlers is the labour involved in clearing a forest country.... I
> am inclined to believe that as long as there are fish in the lake
> the settlement is bound to remain at a standstill.[27]

Although several members of the Cardinal family settled on lots at Lac La Biche, only three Desjarlais families did so.[28] Where did the Desjarlais families from Lac La Biche go? Some kinsmen of François "Peaysis" Desjarlais, went farther west into the Peace River region of northwestern Alberta to join relatives already settled there. François Desjarlais' brother, Jean-Marie Desjarlais, had left Lac La Biche in 1869, moving to Lesser Slave Lake with his family where they lived until 1873. They relocated to Peace River Landing (now the community of Peace River, Alberta) in 1874.[29]

By 1899 several métis families were living along Shaftesbury Trail, a road which ran down the western bank of the Peace River near St. Augustine's Roman Catholic Mission, which had been established in 1888. According to one observer, the métis settlers along the trail were "more hunters than farmers and the most worthless gang on whole length of Peace River."[30] This was not a fair assessment. The fur trade was still a profitable activity, while large scale farming was in its infancy. Like most of the Native

7.5 Unidentified Residents, Shaftesbury Trail, 1895 – Provincial Archives of Alberta, B-3041

people living in the vicinity of Peace River Crossing, the residents of Shaftesbury combined trapping and trading with small-scale farming and gardening – to great advantage, in some cases.

Guillaume Desjarlais, the son of Jean Marie Desjarlais and Rosalie Batoche, was one such individual.[31] A successful free-trader, he had arrived in the Peace River district from Edmonton along with several other free traders. He owned trading stores at

Fort St. John in 1898, and at Lesser Slave Lake. He also established a store at Peace River Crossing located on the downstream corner of the Heart and Peace River junctions. Because Desjarlais was a "half-breed from the prairies" and could not speak English, he was assisted by Akenum Shaw and William Whitford in the operation of the business. Unfortunately, Guillaume Desjarlais' success ran out. His Peace River store was eventually destroyed when the river ice went out one spring, knocking the timbers out.[32] In later years, according to old-timer W. F. Bredin,

> He went broke. Went bugs. He chased a priest with an axe, which was a dreadful thing to do. I was a J.P. at the time and committed him to Edmonton to be examined to see if he was crazy or not. He went out on the lake one time in a small dugout canoe, going three or four miles. Any but a crazy man would have drowned.[33]

St. Paul des Métis

In 1895 Father Albert Lacombe approached the federal government with proposals to establish a farming colony for the Métis. The proposal was intended not only to provide education and agricultural training, but also to maintain a Roman Catholic presence in the region, which was threatened by the influx of Protestant settlers. St. Paul des Métis was established east of the Saddle Lake Indian Reserve, near the present site of St. Paul, Alberta, in 1896. A board of management was formed, consisting of Roman Catholic clergymen, federal politicians, and a priest who was also the colony's manager. Four townships were leased, plus two sections of land for the Oblate Mission and school. A sum of two thousand dollars was set aside for seed grain and agricultural tools. Only destitute Métis were permitted to apply for residence on the colony, and the land was administered solely by the Oblates. Thirty Métis families moved to the colony in its first year, and fifty families were there by the second year. Each family was granted an eighty-acre plot, though title was retained by the government. Among the families granted land were those of Pierre Desjarlais dit Okanase, Simon Desjarlais dit Sekirac, and Gabriel Cardinal.[34]

Unfortunately, the colony was beset by problems from the outset. Since the Oblates were not trained to provide instruction to the Métis to become farmers, they tried to recruit members of agriculturally-oriented Roman Catholic religious orders, such as the Salesians and the Trappists, to handle the agricultural training for the colony. When this effort failed, the goals of the colony abruptly shifted. Now, instead of focusing on agriculture, the priests concentrated on supplying religious instruction and schooling for the colony's children. Most of the limited financial resources were spent on the construction of a large boarding school, church, and presbytery. The families received no agricultural equipment or livestock. Not surprisingly, the agricultural colony was soon a failure.

There is some debate over whether the colony was a "planned" failure or not. Some evidence suggests that the first priest and manager of the colony, Father Therien, was not only skeptical from the outset about the prospects for success, but was actually more committed to creating a community of French-Canadians in the St. Paul area. After the destruction of the boarding school by fire in January 1905 (reputed to be arson by Métis students), Therien devoted his efforts to encouraging French-Canadians to settle at St. Paul des Métis. He encouraged young Métis to take up homesteads outside of the colony, while quietly encouraging French-Canadian settlers to move in. In 1908 the board of management for the colony informed the government that it wanted to terminate its land leases. In 1909, when the colony was terminated, approximately two hundred and fifty French-Canadian claims were registered on the former Métis leases. This was allowed to occur despite evidence that the government was aware of Métis discontent over the plan. Many of these French-Canadians had been squatting on leases prior to the colony's official termination, with the full knowledge of Therien. Some Métis continued to remain on leases and farm, but within a few years most of the remaining Métis had left the area, migrating to Lesser Slave Lake and also to Fishing Lake.

7.6 Deome 'Dieudonne' Desjarlais and wife Isabel, Grouard – Glenbow
NA-1830-4

Discrimination against the Métis by the French was cited as one factor, as well as the preferential treatment that the French received from local lenders.[35]

Treaty Number Eight

By the late 1880s deteriorating economic conditions in northern areas prompted non-status Indians to begin petitioning the government for formal recognition under treaty. The sharp decline of fur prices in the 1870s and 1880s, and the increased unwillingness of the Hudson's Bay Company to provide relief to indigent Natives, prompted the Canadian government to provide modest amounts of aid to local missionaries and fur traders to distribute to needy Natives. However, these payments were discretionary and Natives in the Athabasca, Mackenzie, and Peace River districts felt disadvantaged compared to those Natives already protected under Treaties Six and Seven. In early 1890, after a New Year's Day meeting to discuss the matter, Cree Chief Kinosayoo approached local trader Dieudonne Desjarlais[36] to contact the government on behalf of the Natives of the region.[37]

Dieudonne Desjarlais, who was illiterate, dictated a letter to Edgar Dewdney, Minister of the Interior, in the office of Frank J. Oliver in Edmonton.[38] Desjarlais made his "mark" on the letter, and it was sent. The letter informed Dewdney that

> I have been requested by Chief Kinosayo, of the Crees at Slave Lake to inform you that a meeting of the Indians of Lesser Slave Lake was held at the Roman Catholic Mission, Lesser Slave lake, on New Years day, 1890, to consider the matter of applying for a treaty with the government. A very few of those present were against the treaty, but a very large majority were in favor of it. After it was over many letters written in Cree characters were received from Indians who were unable to attend, but who wished to have the treaty. The Indians of the Upper part of Peace River are also anxious to have the treaty. There are about 177 families of indians at [Lesser] Slave lake and about 100 in Peace River, not including Vermillion.

The fur in the country is getting scarcer each year and the Indians poorer. Those in Peace River are starving every winter, and need assistance very much. The traders and missionaries assist them as much as they can, but they cannot afford to do it all the time. The government should begin to do something.[39]

However, Lawrence Vankoughnet, the Deputy Superintendent-General of Indian Affairs, recommended that such negotiations be delayed, on the belief that conditions were improving in the Lesser Slave Lake area.[40]

Negotiations for Treaty Eight, which were initiated by the Canadian government in 1899, were not in response to hardship among northern Native people, but in reaction to the huge influx of miners passing through the region on their way to the Yukon gold fields in 1898. As the goldseekers passed through Northern Alberta, stories of clashes between the transients and the local Natives drifted back to Ottawa. Realizing that widespread settlement of the region could not be far behind, the government took steps to extinguish aboriginal rights through treaty and scrip before settlers moved in.[41]

Despite the experiences of Treaty Six, the government appeared to have made little attempt to craft a land claims settlement that would take into account the subsistence patterns of local Native communities in the Athabasca region, or reflect the fact that the aboriginal people in the area did not necessarily live in separate and distinct enclaves. Pioneer businessman James K. Cornwall, who witnessed the treaty negotiations at Lesser Slave Lake, made the following points in a signed affidavit of his recollections of Treaty Eight:

1. I was present when Treaty 8 was made at Lesser Slave Lake and Peace River Crossing.

2. The treaty, as presented by the Commissioners to the Indians for their approval and signatures, was apparently prepared elsewhere, as it did not contain many things that they held to be of vital importance to their future existence as hunters and trappers and fishermen, free

7.7 'Peace River' Jim Cornwall – Glenbow NA-2760-1

from the competition of white men. They refused to sign the treaty as read to them by the Commissioner.

3. Long discussions took place between the Commissioners and the Indian Chiefs and headmen, with many prominent men of the various bands taking part. The discussion went on for days, the Commissioners had unfavorably

The People Who Own Themselves

impressed the Indians, due to their lack of knowledge of the Bush Indians' mode of life, by quoting Indian conditions on the Prairie. Chief Moostoos (The Buffalo) disposed of the argument by telling the Chief Commissioner that "a Plains Indian turned loose in the bush would get lost and starve to death."[42]

Given the opposition of the Indians to the government proposals, the treaty commissioners promised, on behalf of the Crown, to recognize the demands of the Indians regarding their hunting and fishing rights, which had *not* been addressed in the treaty document presented to them.[43]

The Lesser Slave Lake Métis had other concerns. They did not like the fact that the scrip being offered was non-transferable, i.e., not redeemable for cash. Father Lacombe, who had initially opposed transferable scrip, changed his position after a meeting with those affected.

> Referring to the meeting of the Half-Breeds today at which I acted as intermediary and advisor, after careful consideration of what was urged as to the form of scrip, I have come to the conclusion that very much trouble will arise if the parents be not able to make use of their children's scrip for their benefit during their minority. As you have no doubt observed, the Half-Breeds here have evinced more intelligence and industry than did the Half-Breeds to whom scrip was issued in 1870 and 1885, and although I came here strongly impressed with the desirability of doing everything possible to prevent the parents from using the scrip of their children and from freely disposing of their own, the conditions here have led me to the conclusion that action in that direction will not result in any benefit to the Half-Breeds here but to their disadvantage, for they are determined to make prompt use of their scrip and that of their children. I find that the Half-Breeds here, when they heard that scrip was to be issued, counted upon turning it into money for investment in cattle for themselves and their children. Very, very few if any of them will take land scrip, and I am convinced that none of those who take money scrip will use it in direct payment for land, and the result

7.8 J. A. Coté, of the Scrip Commission and Father Lacombe, Treaty
Commission, Athabasca Landing, Alberta, 1899 – Glenbow NA-949-91

of the impediment to free disposition will therefore be the
depreciation of the scrip. They are bound to dispose of it and
it is in their interest that they should be in a position to get the
best return possible for it. The dissatisfaction with the form
of certificate is so great and so widespread that I fear if the
Commissioners have to persist in using it the dissatisfaction
will spread in advance of the Indian Commission and make
it very difficult if not impossible to further extend the treaty
which I am so anxious to have all of the Indians enter into.
In the interest of the Half-Breeds and in the public interest,
I would therefore advise that if it be in the power of the
Commissioners, they should take upon themselves to amend
the scrips as to meet the wishes of the Half-Breeds.[44]

When the Treaty Commission arrived at Peace River Landing
in July of 1899, the Desjarlais family members living along

Shaftesbury Trail were understandably ambivalent about the prospect of taking treaty, having experienced the negative consequences of treaty in the past. Jean Marie Desjarlais, the brother of François "Peaysis" Desjarlais, reluctantly took treaty as "number two" of Duncan Tustawit's Cree Band. His son James was listed as "number three" on the paylist. It is clear, in retrospect, that this was not necessarily their preferred choice. Jean Marie Desjarlais had already applied for scrip in 1895, only to be turned down because no mechanism existed at that time to issue scrip to Métis in Athabasca.[45] He applied for scrip a second time in 1900 – even refusing his treaty annuities for that year – only to be refused once again.[46]

Louison "Wetchokwan" Cardinal, the husband of Jean-Marie Desjarlais' sister Judith, was also a member of Duncan's Band. When requesting a farm allotment as part of his treaty entitlement, Cardinal asked for, and received, 160 acres of land on the northeast side of Bear Lake, approximately sixteen miles west of Peace River – a considerable distance away from the remainder of the land held by members of Duncan's Band.[47] Alex McKenzie, a well-known local resident, protested the land grant because some of the land allotted to Cardinal he had intended to claim for himself. In his letter of protest to the Department of Indian Affairs, McKenzie noted that he had been settled adjacent to the land in question since 1895. He also observed that Cardinal, who, although a treaty Indian, was "really a halfbreed from Lac La Biche," and had rented the land, subsequently, to a third party.[48]

The Promised Land

One small group of five or six Saulteaux families, who were related to the Cardinal and Desjarlais families in the Saddle Lake and Whitefish Lake areas, had been present at Frog Lake during the 1885 Rebellion. They were with the Woods Cree bands that had freed the white prisoners and fled from Big Bear's warriors in the dying days of the rebellion.[49] From a variety of oral accounts provided by their descendants, it is possible to piece together the history of this group from the time of the rebellion to the signing of the adhesion to Treaty Eight in 1914.

> Mrs. John Dokkie was Kathleen Courtoreille before she married and her father was the son of Mrs. Harry Garbitt, whose parents came from Saskatchewan. Her father was a Desjarlais, and ran away from the Riel Rebellion. These were Saulteaux. Kathleen says her grandmother, Mrs. Harry Garbitt, would sit for hours and hours and tell stories of early days and ways of life. She tells a story from the Rebellion when after the massacre of Police Officers, the Indian people were trying to hide. After praying a long time [they] were told by the medicine man to go west to the white peaks and they'd find food and peace, but they must go quietly. At one time they could hear the police and men coming after them and when they started to pray a white fog completely surrounded them and cut off all view. They stayed absolutely quiet and prayed. Not even a dog barked or baby cried, and they were saved. They endured terrible hardships and privations on their journey, as they dared not show at any place for food. A few stayed behind at Athabasca Landing, some at Grouard, and along the way by Sturgeon Lake and the last of the band got as far as the "Saulteau Encampment" near Sukunka, spoken of so often in other stories. Their descendants have eventually signed treaty and were moved onto the Moberly Lake Reserve.[50]

Another account, by Moberly Lake old-timer Harry Garbitt, states that the tiny band of refugees had been tracked by a "force of half-breeds" and promised amnesty if the white prisoners were released.[51] The Saulteaux, not trusting in the promised pardon, moved westward. They were led by their leader Gwillim Desjarlais, who originally came from Saddle Lake, Saskatchewan.[52]

"Old Gwillim" as the chief was called, led his band west and north, stopping at lakes along the way so they could fish – at Sturgeon Lake, at Lac Ste. Anne,[53] and at Flyingshot Lake near the present city of Grande Prairie, Alberta. However, Old Gwillim had seen a special lake in a dream, a lake that would be the site of their "promised land." The lake in his dream was a long lake, running east to west. At the far end of the lake there were two mountains resembling a woman's breasts. Here would be the promised land.[54] Finally the little party wandered to the Sukunka Valley, and then to Moberly Lake. There, Chief Gwillim saw the lake that had been in his dreams.

The band of refugees settled at the east end of Moberly Lake. Up to the end of his life, Old Gwillim Desjarlais refused to sign or "take" treaty.[55] When he died, his family moved onto the Moberly Lake Reserve where his descendants live today.[56]

Conclusion

Most members of the Desjarlais family who had taken treaty in 1876 wanted to put behind them the experience of being "Indian." When offered a set of alternatives after 1885, almost all the different members of the family made choices designed to give them the flexibility to adapt to changing economic circumstances, and the freedom to govern themselves.

Staying in treaty did not provide the flexibility they required. The restrictions placed on "disloyal" treaty Indians after 1885, particularly the restrictions on guns and ammunition, made acceptance of money scrip the most logical and palatable alternative. Although modern observers of the scrip process have tended to view its subsequent sale by the northern Métis as nothing short of disastrous (and rightly so), one must examine the sale of scrip within the context of immediate needs.

The northern métis were faced with a "Hobson's choice" when it came to accepting and selling their money scrip. For the métis in treaty, particularly those members of the Peaysis and Ka-Qua-Num bands near Lac La Biche, the acceptance and sale of scrip were necessary in order to avoid starvation during the winter of 1885. As has been noted, the policies of the Indian Department were particularly harsh towards what were termed "dissident bands." The events of the rebellion had prevented most of the spring and summer subsistence activities that would normally have been undertaken to prepare for the winter. As a consequence, hunting and fishing were essential for their immediate survival.

For them to stay in treaty was to be denied the use of a rifle, a necessity for big game hunters in the boreal forest, and to forego the money needed to purchase netting, trapping supplies, and other necessities. For most of these "rebel" métis, particularly those responsible for looting the Hudson's Bay Company store in Lac La Biche, the possibility of receiving goods on credit was non-existent.

It is also clear that fear of reprisal was one of the driving forces behind the decision to take scrip. The rebellion destroyed any trust that the métis under treaty might have had for government officials responsible for their welfare. They did not believe in the promises of amnesty, and chose to remove themselves from east-central Alberta, moving as far away as they could from the scenes of the rebellion and the possibility of future arrest and imprisonment.

The only logical alternative was to take money scrip, sell it, and use the money to get the "grubstake" necessary to establish themselves elsewhere, which is precisely what many of them did. While most of the non-treaty Métis, who had been settled on land for some time, gained title to their lots in Lac La Biche, their cousins leaving treaty exchanged their scrip certificates for money, which they used to relocate where they could continue to hunt and trap. The destination of choice was the Peace River country to the west, where it was still possible to hunt, trap, and engage in commercial activity without overt government interference.

However, this economic strategy was only effective for the short term. Not only would Treaty Eight and the 1900 scrip commission force northern Native peoples to make identity decisions once again, but the old lifestyle of hunting, trapping, trading, and freighting was coming to an end. It was time to settle in one place, if only to prepare one's children for the uncertain future ahead.

That was easier said than done, however. By the 1930s the living conditions of the Northern Alberta Métis had deteriorated seriously.

> Conceptually, treaty had been intended only for the Indians of the region, and scrip for the Métis. However, it was decided to offer scrip in place of treaty to any northern resident with elements of indigenous ancestry, *for so many did not know whether or not they had any traces of European blood* [my emphasis]. Onthe eve of settlement, it was estimated that about two-thirds of the people at Lesser Slave Lake would opt for scrip.[57]

In the end, 1,195 money scrips for $240.00 were distributed, and forty-eight land scrips for 240 acres were issued in the region of Treaty Eight.[58] Making Métis land scrip transferable did not preserve its value, unfortunately. The scrip speculators who followed in the wake of the 1899 Half-Breed Commission paid only a fraction of the face value of the scrip. According to the *Edmonton Bulletin*,

> The highest price paid for scrip was at the Landing [Peace River Landing]. There the competition was very keen and up to $130.00 was paid for a $240.00 scrip. The lowest price was at Vermilion and Wolverine Point, on Peace River. There the price was as low as $70. C. Alloway of Winnipeg followed the Commission throughout, buying scrip. R. Secord also bought on Upper Peace River, the Athabasca and Wapiscow. But on the Lower Peace Alloway had the market to himself.[59]

As a result of the sale of Métis scrip to speculators after Treaty Eight, most of the Métis in the northern regions did not have actual title to their own land. Instead they subsisted as squatters. Crown land, which the Northern Métis relied upon for hunting, fishing, and gathering was about to be opened for homesteading after the federal government transferred responsibility for the management of natural resources to provincial governments in 1930.[60]

8

·················

The People Who Own Themselves

The ancestors of the freemen who fathered Métis populations existed in a world of considerable turmoil. The people who emigrated to New France were searching for improved opportunities for themselves and their families. Often they were single people leaving situations so untenable that the prospect of life in a faraway wilderness colony was an improvement in their prospects. Unmarried women from poor families, orphans, religious dissidents, landless *petits bourgeois*, and transient career soldiers like Jean-Jacques De Gerlaise all found their way to New France to begin new lives.

Once in New France, they found a society in the process of creating itself. Because the most influential social institutions – the government and the church – were not yet fully rooted and operational in the country, the most important institution governing life in New France during its first century became, by default, the family unit.

The instability of life in New France, particularly in the face of constant threat from environmental and human enemies, enhanced the importance of finding oneself a family. As a result, the consanguinal, affinal, and patronage linkages the immigrants established in North America rapidly supplanted any tenuous kinship links still existing with people in Europe. Newly ramifying colonial bonds now permeated most aspects of daily life. They influenced with whom one would work, whom one would marry, and, ultimately, one's social and economic status – as Jean-Jacques De Gerlaise soon discovered when he found himself in a marriage arranged by his commanding officer and a local resident!

Because fur trading was the only viable and consistent source of income in the colony, most people had some connection to the fur trade, if only peripherally. A habitant might farm all his life, but his sons might spend a year or two as voyageurs in the *pays d'en haut* before acquiring land of their own to farm. His daughters, like the daughters and granddaughters of Jean-Jacques De Gerlaise, were likely to acquire husbands who had spent time in the wilderness, trading furs, soldiering in militia units, or providing goods and services to the fur trade or the military. Certain families became fur trade professionals, as importer-exporters, as outfitters, and as shopkeepers and tradespeople servicing the business. Kinship was the "glue" that tied these disparate groups together.

One's occupational status in the fur trade was a function of one's family relationships. *Engagés* – boatmen, itinerant labourers, and tradespeople – were recruited from various seigneuries and settlements by the outfitters, who exploited their kin relationships to fill these positions. Those *engagés* with some literacy, business acumen, and a relative as sponsor might eventually become outfitters as well. Those who did not often acquired enough working capital to marry and establish a separate home in the countryside or town, engaging in agriculture or a skilled trade.

However, this pattern was irrevocably altered as a result of the Seven Years' War. The conquest of Quebec by the British disrupted the kin-based economic networks established during the French régime. The importer-exporters, at the top of the economic hierarchy, owed much of their prosperity to their patronage relationships with government and church officials. The elimination of these preferential relationships as a by-product of the Conquest not only separated the importer-exporters from their traditional (European) sources of goods, but pushed them to the margins of a new economic order dominated and directed by Anglo-Scots. The importer-exporters who did not migrate back to France assumed lesser positions in the newly-created province of Lower Canada, retiring to their seigneuries, entering local government, or maintaining their involvement in the fur trade as outfitters or financial backers to the various small companies that emerged in Montreal to assume control of the North West fur trade. However, with few exceptions, the remaining French participants were not in influential positions.

As the influence of *Canadiens* waned in the Montreal fur trade, the business ceased to be an attractive long-term option for those individuals who might have considered the fur trade as a profession. The kin-based relationships with the bourgeoisie that made employment as a lowly *engagé* palatable, and which offered the opportunity for professional advancement to the ranks of the outfitters and the skilled trades, virtually ceased under the British. Those individuals of ethnic French extraction who managed to remain as participants in the fur trade did so as *engagés* – common labourers – or, more rarely, as independent entrepreneurs – *négociants* – in the upper country.

Who were these individuals? More often than not, they were members of families with a history of involvement in the fur trade, the sons and grandsons of military officers, outfitters, and prosperous habitants with the skills, tenacity, working capital, and commercial connections needed to compete against the British. Like other *Canadiens* in the Anglo-North American fur trade, most started their careers as *engagés* – canoemen or labourers working on contract for fixed periods of time. What differentiated the neophyte independent traders from the other *habitant-voyageurs*, however, was their overall intent.

For the habitant-voyageur involved in the Montreal-based fur trade after 1763, the fur trade was a seasonal occupation, intended to supplement a primary occupation of agriculture or skilled trade. It was also a badly-needed source of additional income. Increased population pressure, combined with over-worked agricultural land and antiquated farming practices, had created an agricultural crisis in Lower Canada. Unoccupied farm land was virtually non-existent; virtually all of the arable land was in production, and had been subdivided to the point where the individual plots awarded to habitants were too small to adequately support a family. The response of many *habitants* was to migrate southward to the long-established French villages located in the fertile bottomlands of the Mississippi and Missouri ivers. There they could establish new farms or participate in the St. Louis-based fur trade, then still dominated by ethnic French trading companies.

For a brief period the *Canadien emigrés* succeeded in recreating the Laurentian society they had left behind – or so they thought. They soon discovered, however, that St. Louis was not Montreal. The close proximity of the Indian territory to St. Louis fostered tensions between the Christianized, monogamous social environment of the settlements and the kinship requirements of the fur trade. Instead of serial monogamy, the men of the St. Louis fur trade found themselves in country unions with aboriginal women while maintaining, simultaneously, households of *creole* wives and children in St. Louis. As St. Louis made the transition from a French *creole* settlement to an Anglo-American frontier metropolis, it became more and more difficult to reconcile the maintenance of separate familial ties. The mixed-race children of *Canadien* fur traders – like those of Antoine Desjarlais and Honoré Picotte of the American Fur Company – remained with the tribes of their mothers. Others settled on "half-breed tracts" where they were estranged, physically and culturally, from their Euro-*Canadien* siblings. And, as increased numbers of Anglo-American settlers flooded into St. Louis and other *creole* settlements, the *Canadiens* themselves became marginalized, and their culture eventually extinguished.

For those *Canadiens* who remained in Canada, there were still limited opportunities to become "men of consequence" in the Montreal-based fur trade. In order to acquire the skills and personal contacts needed to become permanent, rather than seasonal, labourers, a longer commitment was required. In the past, all that was required were family connections and a solid line of credit to establish oneself as an independent in the Montreal fur trade. But as competition between Montreal trading firms grew, and companies consolidated, *Canadien* independents were gradually forced out of the trade. A new strategy was required. Ambitious young men took three-year contracts as winterers in the distant northern posts of the Athabasca country, adjacent to the Rocky Mountains.

During those three years, the wintering *engagés* mastered the hunting, trapping, and other skills needed to survive in the parkland, plains, and boreal forests of Western North America.

During this time they often established kin relations with an aboriginal hunting band, as the *Canadien* Joseph Desjarlais did when he married the Ojibwa woman Okimaskwew *à la façon du pays*. The winterers who were successful in maintaining good relations with their aboriginal kin were better able to remain outside the direct employment of a trading company and establish themselves as independent traders in the *pays d'en haut*. These *hivernants* – men such as Joseph Desjarlais – became known as freemen.

Between 1763 and 1821 a sizeable number of freemen and their mixed-race families had established themselves in the Hudson Bay watershed, usually on the shores of large lakes and at the junctions of river systems for ease of travel and access to food resources. Loosely organized into family bands comprised of one or two related groups, they subsisted on hunting and gathering in a seasonally-based subsistence round that varied little from that of their aboriginal relations – except for the intermediary role of *en derouine* fur broker that they assumed in the fur trade.

Freemen like Joseph Desjarlais, his sons Antoine, Marcel, and Baptiste, and their Ojibwa half-brother Tullibee, functioned best in a competitive economic milieu. Such an environment existed in Rupert's Land between the period between 1800 and 1821, when two firms vied for control of the Athabasca fur trade. Because the freemen had mastered aboriginal languages and skills, wintered outside of the posts with Native bands, and established the kin connections essential for commerce and diplomacy, they wielded considerable economic and political power, to the dismay of the Anglo-Canadian traders forced to accede to their various demands.

Both the Hudson's Bay and North West companies tried to gain control over the activities of the freemen, to neutralize their influence over the Natives, to contain their power, and to channel their activities to the benefit of the trading companies. As long as more than one company existed in Rupert's Land, however, it was impossible to eliminate the generous gifts of trade goods and other indulgences, particularly the traffic in liquor which contributed to the escalating level of violence in the Athabasca region.

As an interim measure, the Hudson's Bay Company and the North West Company, at the urging of Lord Selkirk and Roman Catholic clergy in Quebec, permitted the Roman Catholic Church to establish missions in Red River in 1818. Their role was to re-establish some form of spiritual influence over the freemen and their families, regularizing the unions *à la façon du pays* between freemen and their Native wives, baptizing their children, and providing continued spiritual leadership to their communities. This process began with the creation of a mission at Pembina, where a large concentration of freemen was settled, and at St. Boniface in the heart of the newly created Selkirk Settlement at the forks of the Red and Assiniboine Rivers.

The missions served not only to regularize family relations in the Northwest, but also to create a geographic base from which freeman family groups could stage their semi-annual buffalo hunts and practice seasonal, small-scale agriculture. In doing so the freemen and their mixed-race children established a cultural space in Red River that was separate from that of their Cree and Saulteaux relations. The regulatory influence of the church reinforced the separateness of the freemen families, who shifted naturally into the endogamous, parish-based marital patterns of their *Canadien* forefathers. Those freemen who continued to marry Indian women generally did so within the context of the established parishes at Red River and Pembina, thereby main-taining the Euro-Canadian spiritual and cultural influences over their mixed-race children. It was the establishment of a separate geographical, economic, and cultural space, rather than bio-logical *métissage* itself, which led to the creation of a distinctive ethnic consciousness that came to be identified as Métis.

In 1821 the North West and Hudson's Bay companies amalgamated, ending the ruinous competition and creating a corporate monopoly over most of the Rupert's Land fur trade. Sir George Simpson, the overseas governor of the new concern who had viewed the power of the freemen with considerable alarm, now had the ability to curtail those activities that moral suasion or bribery had been unable to control. As a monopoly, the Hudson's Bay Company controlled access to the ammunition and other trade goods essential to the continued survival and independence of the freemen in Rupert's Land. Simpson employed these levers to his advantage. He coerced the freemen into line by enacting punitive trade policies targeting freemen and Indians; by restricting access to essential trade goods, particularly ammunition; and by charging higher percentages for goods. The curtailing of patronage relations with "trading post bands" such as the Desjarlais families at Lesser Slave Lake effectively undermined the power of the freemen associated with these groups. No longer could the freemen play one trading company off against the other, or demand an excess of goods and other favours to keep their loyalty. The dismissal of excess labourers from the company, swelling the ranks of freemen already in the region, further undermined their economic position.

For the freemen, the period between 1821 and 1830 was a time of retrenchment. Two alternative courses of action were open to the *Canadiens* who found themselves "underemployed" in the Northwest; return to Lower Canada, or migrate to areas where they could continue to make a living by hunting and trading. For most *Canadien* freemen such as Joseph Desjarlais, a return to Quebec was out of the question. Agricultural land was at a premium, and making a new start in Lower Canada at middle age, with a Native wife and several métis children unaccustomed to a sedentary existence, was an unlikely prospect. Those *Canadiens*, like the freeman François Desjarlais who opted to remain in Rupert's Land, chose what was for them the most palatable alternative; establish themselves on a semi-permanent basis in the Roman Catholic parishes at Red River, within reach of the plains where their children could hunt bison. Because the Roman Catholics had established a permanent presence at Red River as early as 1818, followed by clergy of other denominations, the Red River Settlement became the focus of the cultural, spiritual, and political activities of the métis hunters and their families. With some exceptions, even for those métis that chose to winter on the plains rather than return to the settlements, their cultural orientation was toward the tiny parishes and their extended families that maintained residence there. As their numbers increased, they ceased to look outside their communities for European or aboriginal partners. Instead, they sought mates within their own parishes, reinforcing a nascent ethnic solidarity.

The proximity of the Red River communities to American markets to the south also provided a strong economic incentive to free traders wishing to relocate. The settlement of Pembina, one of the earliest freeman communities, had access via the Red River to the trading establishments of St. Paul, Minnesota. The Souris River, which flowed into the Assiniboine River west of the French Métis settlement of Baie St. Paul, was an ancillary trade route providing access to both the bison grounds and the trading forts. The Souris River had long been a popular site for the establishment of trading posts, because of its connection to the Moose Mountains and the Qu'Appelle River to the west, and to the Missouri River system to the south. Besides access to bison, it was also a transport link to an alternative market for furs and hides: the American Fur Company posts at Fort Union and Fort Clark. All in all, migration eastward to the Red River and its tributaries offered considerable potential for economic activity, the Hudson's Bay Company monopoly claims notwithstanding. Illegal Red River free traders, such as Antoine "Mitche Cote" Desjarlais and his brother Marcel "Gwiwisens" Desjarlais, eventually prevailed. By 1849 the Hudson's Bay Company had failed to curtail the illegal commercial activity in the region, and the Company's authority was permanently undermined.

The métis who chose to remain in the Athabasca region of Rupert's Land, such as Joseph Desjarlais Jr., Frederick "Keh-Kek" Desjarlais and Antoine Desjarlais dit Wabamun, occupied a somewhat different ecological and cultural niche than that occupied by the Métis of Red River. The boreal forest and parkland regions of what is now north-central Alberta, northern Saskatchewan, and northern Manitoba were heavily forested, swampy, and generally unfit for agriculture due to their forbidding terrain and long, harsh winters. Far from the major forts, and geographically isolated for much of the year, the métis bands in the boreal forest lived as they had lived since their *Canadien* grandfathers had first become freemen – as hunters and gatherers, living in small family groups, hunting moose and other game in winter, fishing in summer, and migrating southward into the parkland for the spring and fall bison hunts.

Another important difference characterizing the lives of the métis in the boreal forest and parkland was the absence of a significant, consistent, Euro-Canadian religious influence. With the exception of one or two isolated visits by Roman Catholic priests, no permanent mission was established in the Athabasca region until the arrival of the Sulpicians and Oblates in the 1840s, a full twenty-five years after a permanent religious presence had been established at Red River.

Living in isolated camps in the bush, virtually cut off from the expanding settlements, the boreal forest métis differed little culturally from their Indian kin. Removed from the Euro-Canadian influences of clergy and settlement, they continued to choose mates from Indian bands. As a result, the aboriginal cultural influences on the boreal forest métis remained strong, undiluted by the cultural influence and proximity of Euro-Canadian settlement, and the economic and religious influences which served to coalesce the Red River Métis into a population culturally distinct from adjacent Indian groups.

As a result, when Father Thibault arrived in Lac La Biche in 1845 at the urging of the aged *Canadien* freeman Joseph Cardinal, he found a largely nomadic, Cree and Chipewyan–speaking population, in which Indians and métis were largely indistinguishable, culturally or racially, from one another. Years of intermarriage and cultural interaction in the fur trade milieu had blurred the boundaries between Indians and métis, creating a homogenous population sharing most of the diagnostic ethnic characteristics used to differentiate between Indian and Métis populations elsewhere. This apparent homogeneity was to create problems for northern aboriginal people and the Euro-Canadians who administered Rupert's Land when it came time to negotiate treaties.

After the troubles at Red River in 1869–70, the Canadian authorities who had assumed control over Rupert's Land realized that they would be compelled to negotiate separate agreements with Cree, Assiniboine, and Saulteaux Indians, and the Red River Métis who shared entitlement to the land, but who exhibited vastly different cultural characteristics. The first step in this process was the enumeration of these separate populations, in order to negotiate collective land agreements in the form of treaties with the Indian bands, and to award title to individual plots of land to the Métis population in the form of scrip.

For Treaties One to Five, the task of enumerating the distinct Indian and Métis populations was fairly straightforward, or so the authorities assumed. The Métis populations at Red River and in Saskatchewan were, on the whole, cultural entities which had evolved separately from the plains tribes for well over fifty years. The disappearance of the buffalo as a primary source of livelihood hastened the transition to a sedentary, largely agricultural lifestyle in the Métis communities along the Red and Assiniboine Rivers, in the Qu'Appelle Valley, and along the Saskatchewan rivers. Those métis who lived with aboriginal bands, spoke aboriginal languages, and who generally viewed themselves as "Indian" were permitted to "take treaty" if they wished to do so.

However, when Treaty Six was negotiated and signed in 1876 with the woodland and Plains Cree bands of the North-West Territories (now comprising Saskatchewan and Alberta), no provision was made to differentiate between the Indian and Métis populations, and, therefore, no provision for extinguishing Métis land title in the form of giving scrip was made. Despite the large numbers of Métis living in the larger settlements, the only option available to them was to take treaty as part of an Indian band. As a result, it was the métis living in the boreal forest and parkland, living in autonomous hunting bands with only sporadic contact with the settlements, who entered treaty along with their Indian cousins. Consequently, several of the Indian bands that took treaty in 1876 incorporated as "Indians" many people of mixed descent, particularly those in the area around Lac La Biche and Saddle Lake.

But the failure of the government to live up to its treaty commitments created discontent amongst the Cree bands, particularly those who felt they were being starved while the Blackfoot of Treaty Seven were being appeased. Resentment over the failure of the government to negotiate scrip for Métis communities in the North-West Territories also grew. The métis members of Treaty Six bands (who continued to share and acknowledge their kinship links and obligations with Métis communities elsewhere) agitated to join the Northwest Rebellion, particularly after their Ojibwa/Cree relatives in Big Bear's band attacked Frog Lake and Fort Pitt in the spring of 1885.

The varying responses of the different Cree bands towards participation in the Northwest Rebellion reflected the religious, cultural, and racial diversity of this so-called "Indian" group. Treaty Six bands identified by local government authorities as "rebel" bands were generally those with large populations of people who were of mixed descent but were culturally Ojibwa, Cree, Chipewyan or a combination of all three. The Peayasis band of Lac La Biche, comprised almost entirely of the extended family of François "Peayasis" Desjarlais, fit this description. One rebel band that was ethnically Cree, Big Bear's band, was linked to the Lac La Biche Métis through their shared Ojibwa kinship links, as were the members of several other Cree bands in the region.

After the suppression of the rebellion, the government authorities were determined to prevent further Native uprisings. In doing so, they developed policies intended to remove dissident elements from Indian bands – dissidents who were invariably identified as "half-breeds." Steps were immediately taken to identify métis members of Indian bands and induce them to accept scrip, thereby removing them from the rolls of the Indian bands. Most métis gladly seized upon this opportunity, as the restrictions of treaty were viewed as onerous and the offer of scrip provided badly needed money. As a result of the scrip offerings in Northern Alberta, some Treaty Six bands, such as the group led by François "Peaysis" Desjarlais at Lac La Biche, literally disappeared as corporate entities by 1900, their members scattered in several directions.

By 1899 and 1900, when negotiations for Treaty Eight were initiated, the government had already determined to separate the northern Indian and Métis populations, offering treaty to the Indians first, and scrip after. Scrip would not be issued to the Métis until the Indians had identified the members of their communities, negotiated, and signed the treaty.

While the Indians had no alternative but to take the treaty, they were, in the long term, better off than their Métis cousins who opted to take scrip. Unlike treaty Indians, whose hunting and fishing rights were ostensibly protected by treaty, the Métis did not have such protection with scrip. By taking scrip they undermined their future access to hunting and fishing, and abrogated their rights to the annuities, education, and health benefits which they would have been promised under treaty.

The result was that the northern Métis who took scrip in 1899 saw very little benefit. Many chose to sell their scrip for a fraction of its value, in the belief that the money was of more value than agricultural land in Northern Alberta, which was of marginal quality. In the end, many of the signatories for scrip in 1900 were left indigent, forced to live on the margins of Indian reserves or deep in the bush, where they suffered from poverty and disease.

Ethnic identification, at its most elemental, is rooted in ties of kinship, which are strengthened by geographical proximity and shared religious beliefs, cultural practices, values, and history. By nature ethnicity is fluid, reflecting the responses of human groups to the vagaries of the ecological, economic, political, and cultural environments in which they function.

The Canadian government, in its desire to exert political and economic control over aboriginal populations, implemented policies intended to pacify these groups and make them easier and cheaper to manage. Because their bicultural heritage and ongoing kin relationships with Native groups permitted some métis people to maintain both their residency and their political influence in Indian communities, they were key participants in the negotiation and signing of Treaties Three to Six. But after the conflicts of 1885, métis members of Indian bands were considered disruptive influences – disruptive, that is, to the Euro-Canadians who may not have viewed the Métis as a separate aboriginal people to begin with.

Integrating ethnic ascription as part and parcel of negotiating aboriginal rights became a mechanism for undermining the cohesion of aboriginal communities. This "divide and conquer" strategy, first introduced by the Hudson's Bay Company monopoly after 1821, and further refined by the Canadian authorities in the later nineteenth century, served to blunt the ability of Native people to effectively defend their collectively-held aboriginal rights, and resulted in the economic marginalization and cultural extinction of many Métis communities by the beginning of the twentieth century.

Despite the negative impact of many government policies on aboriginal families and communities, the tools needed for reformulating ethnic identity and revitalizing communities exist. Today thousands of people of mixed ancestry are using the vast accumulation of corporate, government, and religious records to document their origins and reclaim their Native heritage. In archives and libraries, at genealogical workshops and family reunions, on Internet newsgroups, and at aboriginal festivals and conferences, they exchange their family histories, meet their distant cousins, and discuss their shared experience of being Métis-in-diaspora.[1]

From a scholarly perspective, the use of genealogical reconstruction as demonstrated in this study can provide the basis for reassessing the behaviours and decision-making strategies of aboriginal groups in the past. Kinship is the "glue" that bound aboriginal societies together, and served as the basis for establishing relationships with outsiders. As the story of the Desjarlais family demonstrates, viewing the values, attitudes, and behaviours of aboriginal families through a kinship "lens" can serve as the basis for compelling reappraisals of pivotal events in Western Canadian Native history.

Appendix 1

A Note on Sources

Numerous primary and secondary sources contain genealogical information on the earliest generations of mixed-race people in Canada. Generally, it is preferable to work with primary sources (i.e., parish records, scrip affidavits, etc.) and then extract genealogical data from them, rather than to rely solely on secondary genealogical sources, such as prepared family histories.

Even the most trustworthy secondary sources may have genealogical errors. Wherever possible, secondary genealogical records should be critiqued by qualified genealogists to determine whether they were produced according to sound genealogical principles.

In the vast majority of cases, however, there is no documentation on the methodology employed by researchers to compile genealogical data. In the genealogical community, horror stories abound of people who have either concocted totally fictitious genealogies, or have inadvertently incorporated faulty genealogical data into otherwise accurate material. It is particularly frustrating when such errors occur in publications considered reputable, such as the Hudson's Bay Record Society or the Champlain Society publications. Because these scholarly series have a well-deserved reputation for accuracy, the occasional genealogical errors that appear in some of the earlier volumes are rarely challenged.[1] Instead, they are cited by other scholars, and the errors are entrenched in the literature.

It is ironic that the genealogies of the labouring classes of the fur trade may actually be more accurate than those of the officer class, because of the abundance of primary data available to researchers. Also, the fact that the labouring classes have been ignored in the literature may be a blessing in disguise. Because there is little published genealogical data on labourers to begin with, there is a reduced possibility of contaminating one's work with inaccurate secondary data. When secondary genealogical sources are used, it is important to utilize sources where the methodology for generating the records is provided in the documents, and the primary sources are cited for individual pieces of genealogical information.

The most trustworthy source of information is primary documentation which is generated as near to the actual genealogical event (i.e., birth, marriage, or death) as possible. What follows is a discussion of the primary sources used to compile genealogical data in this study.

Parish Records

The Roman Catholic parish records pertaining to Alberta which are cited in this study include "Fort des Prairies, Registre de Baptêmes, Mariages, Sépultures 1842–1851," and "Registre de Baptêmes, Mariages, Sépultures de Notre-Dame des Victoires du Lac La Biche, 1853–1885," which comprise a portion of the *Archives of the Oblates of Mary Immaculate* (hereinafter referred to as OA), housed as Record Groups MI 11 and MI 12 at the Provincial Archives of Alberta (hereinafter PAA).[2] Saskatchewan parish records cited in this study include *Registre de la Mission St. Florent au Lac Qu'Appelle*, Vol. 1 (1868–1881) and Vol. 2 (1881–1887) (photocopies of original parish records, Geoff Burtonshaw Genealogical Collection, Calgary, Alberta). Miscellaneous baptisms, marriages, and deaths were recorded by priests travelling through the region which now comprises Oregon, Washington, British Columbia, Alberta, and Saskatchewan. These records can be found in Harriet Duncan Munnick, ed. *Catholic Church Records of the Pacific Northwest – Vancouver – Vols. 1 and 2 and Stellamaris Mission* (St. Paul, OR: French Prairie Press, 1972).

Extracts and photocopies of Manitoba Roman Catholic parish records cited in this study include Joanne J. Hughes, trans. "Nommes des hommes que ent marié par les Missionaires Catholiques depuis l'etablessement de la Mission de la Rivière Rouge en 1818 jusqu' en 15 Fevrier 1831." Transcribed from the *Red River Collection*, Add. MSS. 345, British Columbia

Provincial Archives, Victoria, British Columbia (photocopy courtesy of Dr. Mary Black-Rogers, Edmonton, Alberta); *Anciens Registres de St. Boniface 1825–1834* (transcription/summary of entries from St. Boniface Parish Register – photocopy); *Register of Baptisms, Marriages and Deaths – St. Francis Xavier Church – Manitoba, Canada – 1834–1851* (Extracted from photocopy of original records. Portland, OR: Genealogical Forum, n.d.); *Register of Baptisms, Marriages and Deaths – St. Francis Xavier Church – Manitoba, Canada – 1836–1863.* Photocopy of Original Records. Access to photocopies courtesy of Geoff Burtonshaw Genealogical Collection, Calgary, Alberta.

Most, if not all, of the Roman Catholic marriage registers for Quebec are available on microfilm, either through the National Archives of Canada (NAC), or through the Mormon Church, more properly known as The Church of Jesus Christ of Latter Day Saints (hereinafter LDS). The Mormon Church maintains the world's largest and most sophisticated genealogical library, in Salt Lake City, Utah. Its resources have been thoroughly indexed and the catalogue has been made available to researchers on-line at http://www.familysearch.org/. Microfilmed records can be ordered from the Mormon Family History Library and studied at local Family History Centres, which are housed in local LDS churches in most towns and cities. Microfilmed parish records can also be ordered from the National Archives of Canada (hereinafter NAC). See Patricia Birkett, ed. *Checklist of Parish Registers 1986* (Ottawa: Manuscript Division, Public Archives of Canada 1987) for NAC microfilm reel numbers of specific parish records (NOTE: this material has not been indexed electronically, so the *Checklist of Parish Registers 1986* cannot be accessed on-line via the NAC website). The extracts from, and microfilmed copies of Quebec parish records cited in this study include *Quebec-Verchères – Ste-Trinité de Contrecoeur – Vol. 4 (1744–1774), Vol. 5 (1775–1795) and Vol. 6 (1796–1819).* Latter Day Saints (hereinafter LDS) microfilm reel #1290059); *Quebec – St. François du Lac, Yamaska, Canada – Index to Parish Registers 1687–1876 – Vols. 1–14* (LDS microfilm reel #103749); *Paroisse de Sainte-François-du-Lac, Quebec – Parish*

Register 1687–1749, NAC Manuscript Group 8, Series G30, Vols. 1 and 2, Microfilm reel #C-3024; *Quebec – Sainte-Maurice – Trois-Rivières: Église Catholique – Immaculée Conception Trois-Rivières BMD 1693–1800* (also contains BMD records for Repentigny (1726), Verchères (1773), Lanoraie (1761–1762), St.-Ours (1758), Longe Pointe (1776–1785), Laprairie (1682), St. Antoine de Lavaltrie (1752–1786), Longueuil (1699–1795), and Varennes (1697–1803), NAC microfilm reel # M-866; *Loiselle Marriage Index* – David, F.-Delisle, E. (LDS microfilm reel #0543695), Deschamps, A.–Desjarlais, A. (LDS microfilm reel #0543698, and Desjarlais – Desrocher (LDS microfilm reel #0543699).

Genealogical compendiums of Quebec families consulted for this study include Cyprien Tanguay, *Dictionnaire généalogique des familles canadiennes depuis la fondation de la colonie jusqu'à nos jours* (7 vols.) (Montréal: 1871–79); and René Jetté, *Dictionnaire généalogique des familles du Québec: des origines à 1730* (Montréal: University of Montreal Press, 1983).

In 1966 the *Programme de Recherche en Démographie Historique* (PRDH) (Research Program in Historical Demography) at the University of Montreal began the process of compiling a massive register of the Quebec population from its origins in the seventeenth century to the present day. In 1999, the PRDH made its computerized population register available, by subscription, to researchers on the Internet. The database contains the vital statistics of all individuals in the Quebec population recorded in parish registers and civil archives during the seventeenth and eighteenth centuries. The existence of this database has made it possible to validate the records contained in existing genealogical compendiums, as well as uncover hitherto-unknown relationships between individual and family groups. For more information: http://www.genealogy.umontreal.ca/en/main.htm.

The following indexed marriage records for Missouri were cited in this study: Edna M. Olson, comp. *Index to the St. Charles County, Missouri Marriages, 1792–1863. Recorded in the Saint Charles Borromeo Catholic Church of St. Charles and in the Saint Francis Catholic Church of Portage Des Sioux.* Reprint

Edition (St. Charles: Author, 1969), and St. Louis Genealogical Society, *Catholic Marriages, St. Louis Missouri – 1774–1840* (St. Louis: Author, n.d.). The following microfilmed Missouri parish records were also cited in this study: *Catholic Church – St. Ferdinand (Florissant, Missouri) 1790–1993* (LDS microfilm #s 1902787, 1902788). Extracted parish records for Oregon used in this study are cited from Harriet Duncan Munnick, comp. *Catholic Church Records of the Pacific Northwest: St. Paul, Oregon 1839–1898* (Vols. 1, 2, and 3 (Portland, OR: Binford & Mort, 1979), and Harriet Duncan Munnick, comp. *Catholic Church Records of the Pacific Northwest: St. Louis Register, Vol. 1 (1845–1868); St. Louis Register, Vol. 2 (1869–1900): Gervais Register (1875–1893); Brooks Register (1893–1901)* (Portland, OR: Binfort & Mort, 1982). For isolated references to Desjarlais baptisms in Mendota, Minnesota, see "Early Baptisms at St. Peter's Church, Mendota, Mn." In *Lost in Canada?* 3, no. 1 (January 1977): 41–42.

For this study, the principal source for births, marriages, and deaths at the French outposts in the Great Lakes-Illinois country is Marthe Faribault-Beauregard, *La Population des Forts Français d'Amérique – XVIII siècle* (Montréal: Editions Bergeron, 1984).

Several issues of *Rapport de l'archiviste de la Province de Québec* (hereinafter RAPQ) contain extracts of contracts signed by various *Canadien engagés* during the French and British régimes. These extracts, compiled by archivist A.-Z. Massicotte from Quebec notarial records, span a period from about 1680 to after 1820. See issues of *RAPQ* for the years 1922–23; 1929–30; 1930–31; 1942–43; 1943–44.

Scrip

Eligible Métis people were issued certificates (i.e., "scrip") which could be redeemed for a land grant or a cash settlement in recognition – and extinguishment – of their aboriginal rights. Scrip was distributed at different times in different places; during the 1870 Manitoba Scrip Commission, the North West

Commission of 1885, the Athabasca Half-Breed Commission of 1899, and the adhesions to these commissions. In order to collect scrip, Métis people were required to file a legal declaration, or affidavit, to collect their scrip allotment. Each Métis family head would apply for scrip on behalf of his or her children, and, in some cases, for deceased relatives who were still entitled to receive scrip as descendants of original European settlers. Scrip affidavits are a valuable source of information on Métis families, and provide the "documented historical proof of Métis ancestry" required by the Métis National Council for identification and enumeration as Métis. Information they contain includes the claimant's parish of residence, the claimant's parents, and the claimant's date and place of birth. Some affidavits may also contain written declarations by claimants, which may include additional information not required on standard affidavits. All Métis scrip affidavits (Record Group 15 – Department of the Interior) are housed in the National Archives of Canada in Ottawa and are indexed alphabetically by surname. These affidavits, which are recorded on microfilm and available through interlibrary loan, contain information on all applicants for scrip – including those whose applications were denied. Documents on Métis scrip are included in the records of the Department of the Interior – Record Group (RG) 15, housed in the National Archives of Canada. Within these records, RG15, Series D II 8a consists of scrip applications (1885); Series D II 8c also consists of scrip applications (1886–1906); series D II 8d comprises scrip applications for the Mackienzie River district. Scrip applications which were subject to further evaluation were placed in case files, which can be found in the corresponding registries of the Dominion Lands Branch, specifically correspondence Headquarters, Series RG15 D II1; Manitoba Act files, Series RG15 D II 2; and Half-Breed Files, Series RG15 D II 3.[3]

Indian Affairs Documents

A large volume of correspondence and other information exists in the federal government records pertaining to Indian

Affairs administration. The records dealing specifically with administration of Indian Affairs in Western Canada comprises Record Group 10, also known as the "Black Series." Indian agents were required to keep lists of enrolled members of the different Indian bands that signed the numbered treaties, in order to keep track of membership, and annuities and other benefits distributed. Treaty paylists can provide information on family relationships, and can also identify when individuals "took treaty" or withdrew from treaty. These paylists are of particular interest to researchers investigating Métis family history in Northern Alberta, as many Métis families were originally part of Indian bands that signed treaties prior to the availability of Métis scrip. Within the Black Series, records for Indian bands in Saskatchewan and Alberta are housed in a number of different file series; the General Administration Records of the Manitoba Superintendency, 1879-83 (Vols. 9176-9176A); the General Administration Records of the Northwest Territories Superintendency, 1887–1909 (Vols. 1144, 1303-1304, 1681); the General Administration Files of the Office of the Indian commissioner, Regina, 1883-1901 (Vol. 1026). Other relevant information about individuals can be found in the correspondence and journal files of specific Indian agencies. In this study, the records of the Saddle Lake Agency, Alberta, 1885-1912 were consulted, specifically the Agent's Letterbooks, 1885–1912 (Vols. 1569–1582); and the Agent's Journals, 1887-1910 (Vols. 1567–1568).[4]

The Desjarlais Family in the Records

A limited amount of genealogical data on the European roots of the Desjarlais family exists. Men of the family sat as *bourgue-metres* (mayors, councillors, or officials) for the city of Liège as early as the fourteenth century, where the patronym is known variously as Gerlays, Gerlaise, De Gerlaise, and Gerloisse. A nobleman named Jean Gerlais, who possessed a coat of arms, was present in the court of the Duke of Lorraine in France in 1500. There is also a record of at least one De Gerlaise who was knighted while in the service of the king of Spain. Unfortunately, genealogists have been unable to locate a birth record for Jean de Gerlaise or a marriage record for his parents, possibly a result of the destruction of churches and archives during the two World Wars.[5]

The process of carrying out the genealogical reconstruction of various branches of the Desjarlais family became, in some cases, genealogical revisionism. Secondary genealogical records, particularly those without thorough documentation of the research methodology and primary sources employed, must be viewed skeptically, if used at all. This is especially true when utilizing secondary genealogical data generated prior to 1950, when standards of documentation were often uneven, and researchers had limited access to microfilm, microfiche, and electronic databases containing primary source information.

Even conscientious genealogists of the Métis, such as Father Pierre Picton of Winnipeg, were forced to depend upon secondary sources when access to primary information was impeded by time, distance, and unfortunate circumstances, such as the destruction of the parish records of St. Boniface when the original cathedral burnt down in the mid-nineteenth century. Fortunately, his private correspondence, which documents some of his research activity on the Desjarlais family, has been preserved at the St. Boniface Historical Society in Winnipeg. In one memorandum to himself, Picton documented the many "difficultés extraordinaires" he faced when attempting to research the genealogical records of the Desjarlais family. They included: the lack of essential documents relating to the first generations of the family; the frequent and inexplicable alteration of given names and surnames of one or both parents; and sometimes the use of names of another person. Why, Picton asked plaintively, do the entries not give the habitually-used names, surnames, and residences of these people?[6] To his credit, Father Picton did his best to solve genealogical puzzles before generating family tree charts. In the case of the Quebec origins of the Desjarlais family, Picton consulted a Montreal genealogist, Madame Louis-J. Doucet, who sent him genealogical information on the family.[7]

A1.1 Father Pierre Picton (right), Francis Falcon and unidentified priest – St. Boniface Historical Society, SHSB0635

The accuracy of Madame Doucet's family charts on the Desjarlais family were never formally challenged until the early 1970s, when Anton Pregaldin of Missouri identified inaccuracies in the genealogical information pertaining to the Missouri branches of the Desjarlais family, which he later shared in print.[8] The introduction of the PRDH database of Quebec parish records has also resulted in the identification of genealogical errors heretofore undetected. The PRDH electronic database is a comprehensive compilation of primary data from the earliest years of New France to 1799. Its program extracts and compiles information previously collected from parish records, civil documents and other miscellaneous sources, enabling the user to produce family group lists that are far more accurate and complete than previous genealogical charts. Because of the advent of the PRDH database, it may be necessary to review and revise the vast number of family trees that currently exist in various archives, and have often been reproduced on the Internet.

The earliest genealogical documentation of the Desjarlais families of Red River is sketchy, at best. The first parish records from that region (pre-1824), that document specific acts performed by the priests, have not survived. However, one undated transcription, listing men married by priests at Red River between 1818 and February 1831, makes references to the following Desjarlais marriages: Antoine Desjarlais (1821); François Desjarlais (1822); Antoine Desjarlais fils (1824), and Louis Desjarlais (1827).[9]

Symbols next to names on the list indicate individuals who left the country (/) or died in the country (X), implying that these individuals were *Canadien* by birth, as opposed to "country-born" residents of Rupert's Land. The names of Antoine Desjarlais (1821) and François Desjarlais (1822) are followed by an "X," indicating that both men died in Rupert's Land. The Antoine Desjarlais (1821) who is recorded as having died in Rupert's Land is possibly the *Canadien* Antoine Desjarlais, brother of Joseph Desjarlais, who was a clerk at Pembina ca. 1804 and later operated the post at Lac La Biche prior to 1821. The last recorded reference to the *Canadien* freeman Antoine Desjarlais Sr. (brother of Joseph Desjarlais) in the records is Sir George Simpson's reference to "Old Dejoilais" of Lac La Biche preparing to make war on the Shuswaps and Kootenai in 1824.[10] It has been noted by genealogists such as Father Picton that references to Antoine Desjarlais, and his children, do not appear in parish records or scrip records, unlike the descendants of Joseph and François Desjarlais.[11]

The François Desjarlais mentioned in this early Red River document is likely the *Canadien* François Desjarlais who is recorded as the husband of Madeleine Roy, and remained in Rupert's Land until his death. He was a relative of Antoine and Joseph Desjarlais, probably a first cousin. Although genealogists such as Father Picton and Louis-Joseph Doucet have suggested that François is a brother to Antoine and Joseph (b. to Joseph Desjarlais and Marie-Marguerite Hervieux at Contrecoeur the 7 August 1771), it should also be noted that the PRDH has record of a burial for one François Desjarlais, aged twelve, of Rivière-du-Loup, on 27 February 1784. Present at the burial was the father of the deceased, Joseph Desjarlais. Despite the one-year discrepancy in age between the date of birth and the child's recorded age at death (a not uncommon occurrence during this period), the existence of the burial record suggests that Joseph and Antoine's younger brother died during childhood. Therefore the *engagé*-turned-freeman named François Desjarlais is probably not the sibling of Joseph and Antoine, but is a relative, likely a first cousin.[12]

The person listed as Antoine Desjarlais *fils* is possibly the métis son of Joseph Desjarlais and Okimaskwew, b. ca. 1796. He is known to have visited Red River in 1821.[13] On 13 July 1825 Antoine Desjarlais, "homme libre" and Suzanne Allary had two children baptized by Father Destroimaisons at St. Boniface – Louise (b. 12 November 1823) and François (b. 2 January 1820).[14]

The parentage of the Louis Desjarlais mentioned here is not known, though it is possible that he is a descendant of Louis Desjarlais (b. 2 July 1761), the son of Louis Desjarlais and Catherine Banhiac dit Lamontangue of Rivière-du-Loup, Quebec. The Louis Desjarlais mentioned here may be the same person as the Louis Desjarlais and his wife Françoise, who had four children baptized at St. Peter's Church, Mendota, Minnesota (near Red Lake and Leech Lake, Minnesota) on 28 June 1839 by Bishop Loras of Dubuque. The children baptized included: Peter (b. 20 September 1832); Rosyle (b. 17 September 1834); David (b. 11 May 1836?); and Josette (b. 2 February 1836?).[15]

Parish records and scrip affidavits from Northern Alberta provide indirect documentation of the unions *à la façon du pays* which took place between the first generation métis sons and daughters of various *Canadien* freemen and their hunting and trapping partners, both aboriginal and non-aboriginal. Although the earliest unions *à la façon du pays* were rarely "regularized" by Christian ceremonies, the subsequent baptisms and marriages of the adult children arising from these initial unions *have* been recorded. In many cases, the parents of these children have been identified in the marriage register, providing the evidence that certain unions did take place. This is how some of the earliest Desjarlais country marriages have been determined. One Desjarlais daughter, for example, established a union with Ignace Nipissing, a Native hunter who frequented Lesser Slave Lake and Lac La Biche. The evidence of this early union is identified in the Fort des Prairies marriage register, where it is noted that on 14 November 1844 Joseph Nipissing, the son of ____ Desjarlais and Ignace Nipissing, married Suzanne Desjarlais, daughter of Joseph Desjarlais Jr. and Josephte Cardinal, at Lac La Biche, immediately after their baptism by Father Thibault. Three days earlier Josephte Desjarlais, thirty-year-old daughter of the *Canadien* freeman Joseph Desjarlais, formalized her union with Pierre-François Decoigne, the thirty-nine-year-old métis son of the North West Company clerk François Decoigne and Louise Allary, herself the métis daughter of a *Canadien* freeman.[16]

Conclusion

Although there is an abundance of primary and secondary source data for generating genealogical records, this material must be selected and interpreted with care. Despite the advantages the Internet provides in conducting genealogical research, family historians are encouraged to investigate closely the validity of the electronic sources that they access on-line. As the managers of the PRDH database note:

> The database of the PRDH contains hundreds of thousands of entries of various nature. We are aware that errors may exist, in spite of all our precautions.[17]

Even award-winning databases, run by professional demographers, may have errors from time to time. The important thing to remember is that genealogy not only requires accuracy, but a certain degree of skepticism and flexibility. Do not be afraid to revise family records when new documentation makes it necessary to do so!

Appendix 2 which follows deals with the unique characteristics of names and naming as encountered during this study, and offers approaches to interpreting this material.

Appendix 2

Naming Practices

Appendix 2 is a detailed discussion of naming practices, based on the premise that Métis naming practices are an amalgam of Euro-Canadien and First Nations approaches to naming. It is important to elucidate clearly the steps involved in accurately determining the identity of various Desjarlais in the historical record who share identical given names and surnames. This process is necessary, because the generalizations and conclusions arrived at in the course of this study are based, in part, on inferences made about the activities of various individuals. This discussion begins by detailing the characteristics of French Canadian given names and surnames, particularly the usage of "dit" to differentiate between descendant branches of families. This is followed by a summary of aboriginal naming practices, focusing, in particular, on the practices of the Cree and Ojibwa, and their cultural and spiritual significance. The overview of naming practices is followed by a discussion of names as they appear in primary and secondary sources, and of approaches I have used to distinguish between particular individuals sharing identical given names and surnames in the same period.

Name Variation: Spelling and the Problem with "dit"

One common difficulty researchers encounter is variations in given names and surnames. Many of these difficulties arise from the use of multiple and hyphenated first names, and the use of surname aliases – what are sometimes referred to as "dit" names.

The choice of first names, or "given names" in New France and Lower Canada was dictated by Roman Catholic decree.

> Among Catholics, choice of first name wasn't left to chance or parents' imagination. On the contrary, the church liked to control the attribution of first names to ensure that on the

day they were baptised, children received the name of a saint who would guide them throughout their life. In the *Rituel du Diocèse de Québec*, which laid out the rules to follow for writing baptismal, marriage, and burial certificates in Quebec, Monsignor de Saint-Vallier stipulated, "The Church forbids Priests from allowing profane or ridiculous names to be given to the child, such as Apollon, Diane, etc. But it commands that the child be given the name of a male or female Saint, depending on its sex, so that it can imitate the virtues and feel the effects of God's protection." A list of accepted names – 1,251 for boys and 373 for girls – was published in an appendix to the *Rituel*. As well as a strong religious flavour, these rules resulted in a high concentration of relatively few first names in New France.[1]

As well as the custom of naming children after saints, parents in New France and Lower Canada also liked to use hyphenated double-first names (e.g., Jean-Baptiste; Marie-Madeleine) and might also choose to name all the boys (or girls) in the family with identical first names, using the second given names in the hyphenated double-first name as a means of differentiation (e.g., Jean-Baptiste, Jean-Paul, Jean-François; Marie-Marguerite, Marie-Charlotte, Marie-Madeleine). Confusion results when documents use only one-half of a hyphenated double-first name in a document (e.g., either Jean or Baptiste rather than Jean-Baptiste); or when a given name and a middle name are mistaken for a hyphenated double-first name.[2] Difficulties are compounded when parents reuse a given name for a newborn child after an older sibling with the same name dies. Moreover, families in Quebec and Lower Canada were partial to using the same given names over and over, christening children after their grandparents or godparents (who were often aunts or uncles). As a result, it is not uncommon to find several individuals of similar age, living in the same community or parish, bearing identical given names and surnames.

The term "dit" was used by the French as a means of differentiating between non-related families sharing identical surnames, or to differentiate between descendent branches of the same family. A family would have their primary surname, and then a secondary surname would be attached by the word "dit" to differentiate the specific branch of the family from other branches. This was a necessary strategy, given that there might be several branches of a family living in one area, and that many of the adults and children from different branches could have identical given names.

In medieval and early modern times, the use of the family surname was restricted to the eldest son and unmarried daughters of landowning families. Younger sons were required to use surname aliases – the names of their communities or the names of their estates (assuming they were fortunate enough to inherit land of their own). "Dit" names were also derived from words describing a person's physical features, his temperament, or his line of work. Similar naming practices were also adopted by the peasantry.[3]

Like most social customs, the practice of using "dit" crossed the Atlantic with the early French colonists. Initially the sparse population and the lack of kinship ties between migrants made differentiation between families a simple task. However, the extensive intermarriage of families in New France, combined with the lack of new migrants, ensured the development of large, extended families – most employing "dit" names to differentiate between their various descendant branches.

The problem for researchers arises when surnames and the "dit" aliases are used interchangeably in censuses, contracts, and other primary source documents. For example, the surname "Trottier" has the following "dit" aliases associated with it: Desruisseaux; Desaulniers; LaBissionnière; Bellecourt; Belcour; Pombert; Valcourt; Duvernay; Desrivières.[4] It should also be noted that the use of certain aliases is not confined to a single family; other families may also employ the same "dit" names. For example, the "dit" surname Desruisseaux is also used as an alias for the surnames Houde, Lusseau, and Mailloux, as well as Trottier.[5] Fortunately, the patterns of usage for "dit" names have been well documented by Francophone genealogists.[6] However, in order to match "dit" names correctly with the proper surname, it is important to be able to trace families and individuals geographically and identify kinship networks to cross-reference the use of these names.

It is possible to sort through the confusion of names with some leading clues, an understanding of naming practices, and access to a comprehensive database. Ascertaining the ancestry of the *Canadien* freeman Joseph Cardinal is a case in point.

The surname Cardinal is of particular interest to researchers tracing the roots of Northern Alberta communities, because of the thousands of aboriginal people who bear this name. Joseph Cardinal (and several relatives of the same patronym) were members of a Montreal-based family of outfitters whose commercial activities in the fur trade date back to the 1680s. While some branches of the Cardinal family chose to establish themselves in Detroit and in the French settlements of eighteenth-century Louisiana, Joseph and his relatives Jacques, Jeremie, and Joachim were among the earliest *Canadien engagés* identified in the Athabasca fur trade of the 1780s. Their activities took them from the lakes of Northern Manitoba to the foothills of the Rocky Mountains. There they intermarried with Indian women or métis women raised in an aboriginal social environment.[7]

Joseph Cardinal's daughter Josephte had fourteen children – four by her first husband, the *Canadien engagé* Joseph Ladouceur, and ten by her second country husband, Joseph Desjarlais Jr. These children, in turn, intermarried with other Indians and Métis resident in the region around Lac La Biche, beginning a tradition of endogamy so pronounced that by 1880 most of the three hundred Métis making up the population of Lac La Biche could trace their ancestry back to Joseph Cardinal and Joseph Desjarlais.[8]

Father Jean-Louis Quemeneur, O.M.I., who served in the Grouard-McLennan Roman Catholic diocese from 1924 to 1965, was perhaps the first person to compile genealogical records on the Cardinal families in Northern Alberta. Father Quemeneur's notes identified Joseph Cardinal's birthplace as being the parish of St.-Laurent, at Montreal, and stated that he was born ca. 1756 (based on his estimated birthdate of 98 years in November of 1854). His parents were identified as Joseph Cardinal and Amable Thibault, and his maternal grandparents as Guillaume Thibault and Marguerite Gastinon.

Because the Programme de Recherche en Démographie Historique (PRDH) electronic database at the University of Montreal contains all of the vital statistics records for Quebec from the 1600s to 1799, it is now possible to validate these genealogical notes. First of all, a preliminary search was made for all of the references to people named Joseph Cardinal appearing in the vital records between 1740 and 1799. Out of 111 references, seven of these references referred to a Joseph Cardinal born between 1740 and 1766. There were no references from the 1750s. Of the seven references, only one Joseph Cardinal was born in the parish of St. Laurent. This was the record that was checked first.

The birth record in question was for one Joseph Amable Cardinal, born in the parish of St. Laurent on 23 April 1766. His parents were listed as being Joseph Cardinal and Amable Imbaut Matha. The father's name (Joseph Cardinal) conformed to the information provided by Father Quemeneur, but Amable Imbaut Matha made no sense whatsoever. There were a couple of other baptisms of Cardinals listed for St. Laurent in the same time period. A baptismal entry was found for a Marie Amable Cardinal (b. 5 March 1763) whose parents were Joseph Cardinal and Marie Josephe Imbaux. The godparents were Pierre Cardinal and Genevieve Gatignon. There was reference to another baptism, of Marie Josephe Cardinal (b. 16 December 1764), whose parents were listed as Joseph Cardinal and Amable Matha. Other baptisms of children, born to the same couple, were located; Jacques Cardinal (b. 6 April 1769 at St. Laurent); Antoine Cardinal (b. 12 August 1771); and Pierre Cardinal (b. 23 May 1778).

The next step was to locate a marriage for Joseph Cardinal and Amable Thibault. There were no marriage records for a Joseph Cardinal married to a person named Amable Thibault, but there was a marriage record for a couple named Joseph Cardinal and a Marie Amable Imbots which took place on 20

May 1762, in the parish of St. Laurent. The parents of the groom were listed as François Cardinal and Marie Josephe Meloche, and the parents of the bride were listed as Guillaume Imbots and Marie Catherine Gatignon.

An additional search was conducted in the same database, this time using a search feature called "Couple" which extracts data on an identified couple and their entire family. This step was attempted in order to get additional information on the couple most likely to be Joseph Cardinal the freeman's parents, Joseph Cardinal and Marie Amable Imbaut. The data stated that Joseph Cardinal and Marie Amable Imbeault were married on 10 May 1762. The parents of Joseph Cardinal Sr. were listed as François Marie Cardinal and Marie Josephe Meloche. The parents of Marie Amable Imbeault were listed as Guillaume Imbeault Masta and Marie Marguerite Gatignon Duchesne.

Father Quemeneur had listed Joseph Cardinal's parents as Joseph Cardinal and Amable Thibault. The baptismal records compiled in the PRDH database listed the parents of Joseph Cardinal as Joseph Cardinal and Amable Imbaut Matha. Because the surname variations Imbot, Imbeau, Imbeault, Imbaut, Matha, and Masta had been listed as surnames for Joseph Cardinal's mother, a search for the names was carried out using René Jetté's Dictionnaire Généalogique des Familles du Québec.

According to Jetté, a family known by the surname IMBAUT dit MATHA, was based at Montreal prior to 1730. There was also a family known as GATIGNON dit DUCHESNE based in Montreal.[9] Father Quemeneur had listed Joseph Cardinal the freeman's maternal grandparents as being Guillaume Thibault and Marguerite Gastinon. Based on the documentation in the Quebec records, the "Guillaume Thibault" identified by Father Quemeneur was probably Guillaume IMBAUT, and the Marguerite Gastinon identified as Joseph Cardinal's maternal grandmother was actually Marie Marguerite GATIGNON.

The ability to validate genealogical data based on oral information gathered from relatives is now possible, if the example of Joseph Cardinal's ancestry is any indication. Joseph Cardinal the freeman was born on 23 April 1766, in the parish of Saint Laurent in Montreal. His parents were Joseph Cardinal and Marie-Amable Imbaut dit Matha. His paternal grandparents were François Marie Cardinal and Marie Josephe Meloche. His maternal grandparents were Guillaume Imbault dit Matha and Marie Marguerite Gatignon dit Duchesne. Despite the ten-year discrepancy between Joseph Cardinal's birthdate (as reported by Cardinal relatives in Northern Alberta at his death in 1854) and the 1766 birthdate recorded for Joseph Cardinal in St. Laurent, it is probable that these two men are one and the same. There is no record of a Joseph Cardinal being born in the 1750s in any Quebec parish. Any birthdate for a Joseph Cardinal later than 1766 is probably too late to be seriously considered, given that Joseph Cardinal fathered children in Rupert's Land as early as 1785.[10] In any case, the parental profiles above are the only ones that even remotely approximate the information gathered by Father Quemeneur, which has been proven to be at least partially accurate. Joseph Cardinal was born at St. Laurent; his father was Joseph Cardinal; his mother was named Amable, and his maternal grandparents were Guillaume, and Marguerite Gatignon (mistaken for Gastinon). The resemblance between the surname Imbaut, and the more common Quebec surname Thibault could also account for the misidentification of ancestry by relatives. The investigation of Joseph Cardinal's ancestry not only illustrates the great potential for reconstructing the Quebec origins of Métis families, but also reinforces the importance of understanding French-Canadian naming practices when validating genealogical records.

Aboriginal Naming Practices

When *engagés* travelled into the interior of North America, they brought their naming customs with them. When they formed marital unions with Native women, the children's names that resulted were an amalgam of European and aboriginal practice.[11]

In Northern Algonquian cultures, the naming of children had spiritual significance. In Ojibwa and Cree communities, the parents would host a feast approximately one year after the birth of a child for the purpose of naming the infant. Grandfathers, or a person of the grandfathers' generation, were considered to have great spiritual power would be invited, and they would be formally requested to name the child after receiving ceremonial offerings of cloth and tobacco. The grandfather would smoke a pipeful of tobacco and pray to the Creator and his personal "spirit helpers" for guidance, after which he would sing one of his "power songs." The grandfather would take the child in his arms, and name the child after a character from one of his visions, a vision provided by his "spirit helper." After asking his "spirit helper" to protect the child, the baby would be passed from one guest to another, who would say the child's name and extend wishes for its future life. Then the feast would be conducted, and the ceremony would be concluded. The naming ceremony embodied the transfer of spiritual power to the infant from the grandfather, who in turn had received these powers from "other-than-human persons." For this reason, personal names received in formal ceremonies were rarely used in everyday life. Instead, nicknames which described a person's appearance, gender, or personality were used.[12] Euro-Canadians having regular dealings with Native peoples also acquired aboriginal nicknames as a matter of course.

The multiplicity of names for a single person can cause difficulty for researchers trying to identify an individual in a historical document, and/or track the migrations and other activities of that person. This is particularly true when studying people of mixed ancestry who may be identified by their European name, their European "dit" name, their aboriginal nickname, their aboriginal nickname as expressed in English or French, or diminutive (shortened) versions of any of these names.

A search for these surnames and their aliases was conducted in the electronic database of Métis Scrip records compiled from the RG15 (Department of the Interior) documents housed in the National Archives of Canada. Several different surnames were encountered which had aboriginal, French, and English aliases. Of equal interest was the discovery of hitherto-unknown kin connections among aboriginal families in Northern Alberta, both Indian and Métis, spanning several generations.

These kinship connections date back to the arrival of the earliest Europeans in Athabasca, when the initial contacts were being made between local Cree, Assiniboine, Ojibwa, Iroquois, and Beaver Indians with *Canadien* and other Montreal-based freemen and clerks in the Rocky Mountain foothills.

It is impossible to know precisely when the earliest union *à la façon du pays* took place in the Athabasca region. Some *métis* surnames, like Finlay, can be traced directly to one man, the Montreal "pedlar" James Finlay, the first English trader from Canada known to have reached the Saskatchewan River in 1768.[13] However, many country unions are known to have taken place where European surnames have not survived.[14]

For example, Duncan McGillivray noted the October 1794 arrival of two Cree chiefs to Fort George on the Saskatchewan River with the following comment:

> The Grand Soteau and French Bastard with about 20 men arrived – these being Cheifs [*sic*] of considerable influence were presented after the usual ceremonies were over with 2 large kegs of rum and the night therefore was devoted to intoxication and tumult.[15]

The name "French Bastard" makes an inference about the ancestry of the trading chief bearing this name. First of all, it suggests that he was of mixed French and Native parentage, but probably born as the result of a temporary meeting rather than as part of a more permanent relationship *à la façon du pays*, and that the French father of this person did not remain with the mother – certainly not long enough to complete the bride service and other kin obligations characteristics of country unions among both the Plains Cree and Ojibwa[16] – hence the appellation "Bastard."[17]

The term "bastard" also suggests that the individual thus named may not possess the necessary kinship connections to be considered a legitimate member of the residential hunting band. Marriage partners were generally chosen from within the band itself rather than from the ranks of outsiders; the product of a union with an outsider might not have the same membership status as one born under more conventional circumstances.

One of the most important Ojibwa cultural markers is its kinship system, which is based on membership in patrilineal clans, or *doodimag*. Although a union between a European man and an Ojibwa woman would not violate any kinship taboos, her children would be denied membership in an Ojibwa clan because their European father was not part of the Ojibwa clan structure, except perhaps in a fictive sense.[18] The only way the child of such a union could acquire clan membership for his descendants would be for his daughter to marry an Ojibwa man, and for a son to marry an Ojibwa woman and ensure that their children, in turn, married people possessing clan *dodems*.[19]

Despite their quasi-outsider status, the métis children of these early unions did not seem to have encountered difficulty assuming the status of trading chief or headman later in life. No doubt their dual ancestry could be used to the band's benefit in terms of initiating and maintaining ongoing relationships with Europeans.

The preponderance of métis ancestry among Cree bands who make up the House People is a case in point. The House People, *wasahikanwiyiniwak*, acquired their name from their long association with the Hudson's Bay Company trading forts.[20] The Plains Cree chief Mistawasis, whose band was one of those comprising the House People, was of métis extraction, being the offspring of a *Canadien* or métis with the surname Belanger and a Cree woman.[21]

The métis daughter of Mistawasis, Jane Belanger, married the Plains Cree chief Ermineskin, whose name may reflect his métis parentage.[22] Ermineskin (whose Cree name was Sehkosowayanew) was also known by the French-métis name of Baptiste Piche.[23] To further complicate matters, the Plains Cree chief Poundmaker was the brother-in-law of Ermineskin,[24] suggesting that Jane Belanger dit Mistawasis was Poundmaker's sister or half-sister.[25] Ermineskin's brother, the Plains Cree chief Bob Tail, was known by the Cree name Keskayiwew, in addition to his French/métis name Alexis Piche.[26] Bob Tail's métis wife was Catherine Cardinal dit Mustatip, a.k.a. Catherine Pierre.[27]

Several members of the Piche family intermarried with members of the Cardinal family, as numerous scrip affidavits attest. Louise Piche, "Piyeskaketoot" was married to Suzanne Cardinal, the daughter of Laurent Cardinal and Marie Mondion.[28] Eugene Piche, or "Waweyenam," was married to Elise Cardinal, daughter of Antoine Cardinal and Cecile Boucher.[29] Frederick Ballendine, the son of Ermineskin and Jane Belanger dit Mistawasis, was married to Sophie Cardinal, the daughter of Gabriel Cardinal and Marie Bruneau dit Piwapiskapow of Whitefish Lake, and the sister of Joseph Cardinal. Rosalie Ermineskin, the daughter of Ermineskin and Jane Belanger dit Mistawasis, married Métis trader Adam Howse in 1884.[30]

What might prompt such extensive intermarriage between the Cardinal and Piche families? A clue lies in the roster of Fort Vermilion on the Saskatchewan River in 1809, in which Alexander Henry the Younger conveniently lists the occupants of the various houses and tents of the post. House number two is occupied by the families of Cardinal, Ladouceur, and Ottawa, as well as a single man, Pichette (Piche). Joseph Cardinal (later a freeman) was employed as an interpreter at Fort des Prairies in 1804; Joseph Ladouceur was a voyageur at Fort des Prairies at the same time. An *engagé* named Piche was with Henry at Rocky Mountain House in 1810, where he packed provisions to David Thompson. Joseph Ladouceur married Joseph Cardinal's daughter Josephte. Her second country union was with Joseph Desjarlais Jr., son of the *Canadien* freeman Joseph Desjarlais. All of these men hunted and trapped together. It was not uncommon for *engagés* to marry the widows and daughters of their companions, or become the husbands of country wives who separated from their former partners. It is possible that the "Pichette" listed in the roster is the ancestor of the *métis* Piches who intermarried with the Cardinals. It is also probable that the Cree chiefs Bob-Tail and Ermineskin are descended from this person.[31]

The names of three other aboriginal hunters who appear very early in fur trade texts also have descendants who eventually led aboriginal bands under treaty. The two hunters, Grand Bâtard and Little Knife, also appear in Alexander Henry the Younger's Journal listed among the hunters.[32] In the Métis scrip affidavits, the surname Little Knife appears in the records associated with the following aliases: Piyessiwop, Paspaschase, Ayotchow, Piehsi-moop, Ke-ke-ko-sis-on, and Jackknife.[33] In parish records, Grand Bâtard appears in association with these names: Otaikijik; Nittawikijik.

The French surname Dion/Dionne is a diminutive version of the term "blondion" which, in turn, is an aberration of the French word "blondinet" (masculine) or "blondinette" (feminine) meaning "fair-haired child." The root word of "blondinette" is "blond" (masculine) or "blonde" (feminine) which means "fair-haired" in French.[34] When this surname is found in parish records, fur trade documents, and Métis scrip affidavits, other variations of this name, such as Blondion, Blayonne, Mondion, Moignon appear. The surnames Dion or Blondion are sometimes used simultaneously with the Cree name Wabasca, which also means "white" or "fair." One of the earliest references to this name is in relation to the Ojibwa chief Black Powder (a.k.a. Mukatai, or Powder), who was the leader of a small band of mixed Cree and Ojibwa, who wintered on the shores of Jackfish Lake in west-central Saskatchewan, and hunted bison on the plains in the spring and fall. Black Powder was the friend and sub-chief of Kee-a-kee-ka-sa-coo-way – "The Man Who Gives the War Whoop," the most important Plains Cree chief of the mid-nineteenth century. The son of Black Powder, Antoine Blondion, married a daughter of Joseph Desjarlais and Josephte Cardinal. He is also noteworthy because he is the brother of Mistahimusqua, better known as Big Bear.

Conclusion

As Edward S. Rogers and Mary Black-Rogers discovered in their research into surname adoption among the Weagamow

Ojibwa, it is impossible to rely upon a single source. Because of the proliferation of given names, surnames, and their aboriginal, English, and French aliases, it is prudent to utilize as many sources as possible in order to cross-reference names.[35] Also, in spite of all of the precautions one may take, it is always possible to make an error, despite the most careful research. For this reason, primary sources should be employed wherever possible, or secondary sources that have been proven.

Appendix 3

Genealogical Charts

A number of genealogical charts and related materials were compiled in the course of this study. The information at the following website will be updated as new genealogical and historical data become available: www.uofcpress.com/books/people

Notes

....

Definitions

1 See Helen Hornbeck Tanner, ed., *The Settling of North America: The Atlas of the Great Migrations Into North America from the Ice Age to the Present* (New York: Macmillan, 1995), 48–49, 58–59.

2 See Laura Peers' detailed discussion of the synonymy of the term in Peers, *The Ojibwa of Western Canada* (Winnipeg: University of Manitoba Press, 1994), xv–xviii.

3 See Appendix of this book for a more detailed discussion of scrip.

4 *The Metis Nation* (Ottawa: Metis National Council, fall 1984), 1:6. As quoted in Jacqueline Peterson and Jennifer Brown, "Introduction," in Jacqueline Peterson and Jennifer S.H. Brown, eds., *The New Peoples: Being and Becoming Métis in North America* (Winnipeg: University of Manitoba Press, 1985), 6.

5 Peterson and Brown, "Introduction," in *The New Peoples*, 6.

Acknowledgments

1 See Appendix for a discussion of genealogical errors entrenched in the scholarly literature.

Chapter 1

1 Peterson and Brown, eds., *The New Peoples*, 243–51. For a succinct summary of the scholarly issues arising out of the Metis ethnogenesis debate, see John E. Foster, "Some Questions and Perspectives on the Problem of Métis Roots," 73–91, featured in this anthology.

2 R. K. Thomas, "Afterword," in Peterson and Brown, *The New Peoples*, 245.

3 See Jacqueline Peterson and John Anfinson, "The Indian and the Fur Trade: A Review of Recent Literature," in William R. Swagerty, ed., *Scholars and the Indian Experience: Critical Reviews of Recent Writing in the Social Sciences* (Bloomington: Indiana University Press, 1984), 248.

4 Foster, "Some Questions and Perspectives on the Problem of Métis Roots," in Peterson and Brown, *The New Peoples*, 74.

5 Peterson and Anfinson, "The Indian and the Fur Trade: A Review of Recent Literature," in Swagerty, *Scholars and the Indian Experience*, 241.

6 Grace Lee Nute, *The Voyageur* (St. Paul: Minnesota Historical Society, 1955).

7   Studies that deal with *Canadien* indentured labour in the fur trade in the larger context of colonial history include, for example, W.J. Eccles, *The Canadian Frontier, 1534–1760* (New York: Holt, Rinehart & Winston, 1969); Marcel Trudel, *The Beginnings of New France, 1524–1663* (Toronto: McClelland and Stewart, 1973); Louise Dechêne, *Habitants and Merchants in Seventeenth-Century Montréal* (Kingston and Montreal: McGill-Queen's University Press, 1992); Allan Greer, *Peasant, Lord and Merchant: Rural Society in Three Québec Parishes, 1740–1840* (Toronto: University of Toronto Press, 1985). Published studies which focus on *engagés* include Gratien Allaire, "Officiers et marchands: les sociétés de commerce des fourrures, 1715–1760," *Revue d'histoire de l'Amerique français* (hiver 1987): 409–28; and Gratien Allaire, "Fur Trade Engagés, 1701–1745," in Thomas C. Buckley, ed., *Rendezvous: Selected Papers of the Fourth North American Fur Trade Conference, 1981* (St. Paul: North American Fur Trade Conference, 1981), 15–26.

8   Marginal note to Gov. Buade de Frontenac's memorial on illicit fur traders, 1681, in *Rapport de l'archiviste*, 1926–1927, 123, as quoted by Peter N. Moogk in "Reluctant Exiles: Emigrants from France in Canada before 1760," *William and Mary Quarterly* (3rd series) 46, no. 3 (July 1989): 463–505.

9   Approximately 350 Iroquois from the mission villages of Caughnawaga (Kanawake), St. Regis (Kanesetake), and Lake of Two Mountains appear in the engagement records in the Judicial Archives of Montreal between 1790 and 1815. Because of the incompleteness of these records, it is possible that many more were engaged under private contracts. See Trudy Nicks, "The Iroquois and the Fur Trade in Western Canada," in Carol M. Judd and Arthur J. Ray, eds., *Old Trails and New Directions: Papers of the Third North American Fur Trade Conference* (Toronto: University of Toronto Press, 1980), 86.

10 John E. Foster, "Wintering, the Outsider Adult Male and the Ethnogenesis of the Western Plains Métis," *Prairie Forum* 19, no. 1 (Spring 1994): 1–13.

11 There is extensive ethnohistorical research devoted to the relations between aboriginal groups and outsiders, particularly in regard to kinship, diplomacy, and trade. A few notable examples include Cornelius Jaenen, *The French Relationship with the Native Peoples of New France and Acadia* (Ottawa: Research Branch, Indian and Northern Affairs Canada, 1984); Shepard Krech III, ed., *The Sub-Arctic Fur Trade: Native Social and Economic Adaptation* (Vancouver: University of British Columbia Press, 1984); John McManus, "An Economic Analysis of Indian Behavior in the North American Fur Trade," *Journal of Economic History* 32 (1972): 36–53; Arthur J. Ray, *Indians in the Fur Trade: Their Role as Hunters, Trappers, and Middlemen in the Land Southwest of Hudson's Bay* (Toronto: University of Toronto Press, 1974); Arthur J. Ray and Donald Freeman, *'Give Us Good Measure': An Economic Analysis of Relations Between the Indians and the Hudson's Bay Company Before 1763* (Toronto: University of Toronto Press, 1978); E.E. Rich, "Trade Habits and Economic Motivation Among the Indians of North America,"

Canadian Journal of Economics and Political Science (1960): 35–53; and Abraham Rotstein, "Trade and Politics: An Institutional Approach," *Western Canadian Journal of Anthropology* 3 (1972): 1–28.

12 E.R. Leach, *Pul Eliya: A Village in Ceylon* (Cambridge: Cambridge University Press, 1961), 66, as quoted in Fred Plog and Daniel G. Bates, *Cultural Anthropology* (2d ed.) (New York: Alfred A. Knopf, 1980), 256.

13 See Michael Asch, "Kinship and Dravidianate Logic: Some Implications for Understanding Power, Politics and Social Life in a Northern Dene Community" (unpublished paper, Department of Anthropology, University of Alberta, 1993), 6.

14 Bishop Plessis of Quebec was quite eager to promote the establishment of missions in Rupert's Land, because of his belief that it would facilitate the establishment of a hierarchy which would eventually result in the formal recognition by the British government of the Catholic Church in Canada. Because of the great distance between Quebec and Red River, a bishop based in Quebec would be unable to make the regular confirmations and ordinations necessary to sound administration. The establishment of a Red River Mission would require the British government to provide a bishop at Red River to administer the work of the priests. However, the presence of two bishops in British North America would also require that the British permit the appointment of an archbishop for Canada to oversee the decisions of the bishops. Grace Lee Nute, *Documents Relating to Northwest Missions, 1815–1827* (St. Paul: Minnesota Historical Society, 1942), xii–xiii; and Raymond J. Huel, *Proclaiming the Gospel to the Indians and the Métis* (Edmonton: University of Alberta Press, 1996), 11.

15 Nute, ibid.; Huel, *Proclaiming the Gospel to the Indians and the Métis*, 12.

16 Jean Friesen, "Magnificent Gifts: The Treaties of Canada with the Indians of the Northwest 1869–70," *Transactions of the Royal Society of Canada* (Series 5) 1 (1986): 41–51.

17 See Tamara K. Hareven, "The History of the Family and the Complexity of Social Change," *American Historical Review* 96, no. 1 (February 1991): 95–124.

18 See Joanne Nagel's overview of the "Indians as ethnics" controversy in Joanne Nagel, *American Indian Ethnic Renewal: Red Power and the Resurgence of Identity and Culture* (New York: Oxford University Press, 1996), 7–9.

19 See Roger L. Nichols, "Historians and Indians," in Roger L. Nichols, ed., *American Frontier and Western Issues: A Historiographical Review* (Westport, CT: Greenwood Press, 1986), 168.

20 An innovative, though flawed approach to documenting the formation and dispersal of the Red River Métis communities through a computerized data base of parish records was featured in D.N. Sprague and R.P. Frye, comps., *The Genealogy of the First Métis Nation: The Development and Dispersal of the Red River Settlement, 1820–1900* (Winnipeg: Pemmican Publications, 1983). For a recent work devoted to the culture of *engagés*, see Carolyn Podruchny, *"Sons of the Wilderness": Work, Culture and*

Identity Among Voyageurs in the Montreal Fur Trade, 1780–1821 (unpublished PhD dissertation, University of Toronto, 1999).

21 Thomas Flanagan, "Louis Riel and the Dispersion of the American Metis," *Minnesota History* (spring 1985): 185.

22 Most genealogical manuals provide step-by-step instructions for conducting genealogical research, which differs little, methodologically, from other forms of historical research using primary sources. See Angus Baxter, *In Search of Your Roots: A Guide for Canadians Seeking their Ancestors* (Toronto: Macmillan of Canada, 1978), 1–3, 8–18; and Angus Baxter, *In Search of Your Canadian Roots: Tracing Your Family Tree in Canada* (Toronto: Macmillan of Canada, 1978), 1–24.

23 For more detailed discussion of these references, please refer to "Appendix 1: A Note on Sources," in this study.

24 For detailed information on this software program, see: http:// www.leisterpro.com/Doc/What_is_Reunion.html.

25 Frederic W. Gleach, "Controlled Speculation: Interpreting the Saga of Pocahontas and Captain John Smith," in Jennifer S.H. Brown and Elizabeth Vibert, eds., *Reading Beyond Words: Contexts for Native History* (Peterborough, ON: Broadview Press, 1998), 24.

26 Gleach, ibid., 24–26.

Chapter 2

1 The reference in this heading to 'psychological terrain' is inspired by Chapter 4, "Ethnicity: The Conceptual and Theoretical Terrain," 56–83, in Siân Jones, *The Archaeology of Ethnicity: Constructing Identities in the Past and Present* (London and New York: Routledge, 1997). In this chapter, devoted to explaining various theories of ethnicity, Jones likens the study of ethnicity to unfamiliar and potentially dangerous terrain where the unwary traveller may become lost without a thorough understanding of the environment.

2 André Corvisier, *Armies and Societies in Europe.* Abigail T. Siddall, trans. (Bloomington: Indiana University Press, 1979), 21–25.

3 Jiu-Hwa L. Upshur et al., *World History* (New York: West Publishing, 1998), 191.

4 Ibid., 16–17. See also Brian Fagan, *The Little Ice Age: How Climate Made History 1300–1850* (New York: Basic Books, 2000), 90–96.

5 Ibid., 16.

6 Edward McNall Burns et al., *World Civilizations: Their History and Culture*, vol. 1, 7th ed. (New York: W.W. Norton, 1986), 687–728.

7 André Burguière and François Lebrun, "The One Hundred and One Families of Europe," in André Burguière, Christiane Klapisch-Zuber, Martine Segalen, Françoise Zonabend, eds, *A History of the Family*, vol. 2, *The Impact of Modernity* (Sarah Hanbury Tenison, trans.) (Cambridge, MA: Belknap Press of Harvard University Press, 1996), 11–94.

8 Burguière and Lebrun, "The One Hundred and One Families of Europe," 15.

9 Ibid., 13–15.

10 Jean-Louis Flandrin, *Families in Former Times: Kinship, Household and Sexuality* (London: Cambridge University Press, 1976), 40–43, 145–53.

11 For an extended discussion of state-sanctioned physical punishment in early modern France, see Michel Foucault, *Discipline and Punish: The Birth of the Prison* (2d ed.), Alan Sheridan, trans. Originally published in France as *Surveiller et Punir: Naissance de la prison* [Paris: Editions Gallimard, 1975] (New York: Vintage Books, 1995), 3–69.

12 Jean-Jacques de Gerlaise signed his marriage contract at a time when only a select few in society were literate. Existing genealogical and heraldic records indicate the presence of the Gerlays (a.k.a. Gerlache) family living in the vicinity of Liège and Namur, Belgium since the eleventh century. See John DuLong, *Genealogical Notes*, Berkeley, Michigan (n.d.). See *La noblesse Belge: Annuaire de 1900* (1903), 102–23; see also *Annuaire de la noblesse de Belgique* (1864), 313–16.

13 See Jones, *Archaeology of Ethnicity*, 56–83.

14 Jack Verney, *The Good Regiment: The Carignan-Salières Regiment in Canada, 1665–1668* (Montreal: McGill-Queen's University Press, 1991), ix.

15 André Corvisier, *Armies and Societies in Europe*, 142–48.

16 See Verney, *The Good Regiment*, 7. According to Corvisier, "regiments and companies had become actual property that could be accumulated, inherited, bought, and sold." See Corvisier, *Armies and Societies in Europe*, 43–44.

17 Corvisier, *Armies and Societies in Europe*, 63–64, 72.

18 Verney, *The Good Regiment*, 7–8; 189n18; 190n19.

19 Ibid., 11, 162.

20 Ibid., 12–13.

21 Ibid., 16–18.

22 See Leslie Choquette, "Recruitment of French Emigrants to Canada, 1600–1760," in Ida A. Altman and James Horn, eds., *"To Make America": European Emigration in the Early Modern Period* (Berkeley: University of California Press, 1991), 137.

23 Choquette, "Recruitment of French Emigrants to Canada, 1600–1760," 133–39.

24 See Moogk, "Reluctant Exiles": 463–505; and André Guillemette and Jacques Légaré, "The Influence of Kinship on Seventeenth-Century Immigration to Canada," *Continuity and Change* 4, no. 1 (1989): 82.

25 Guillemette and Légaré, "The Influence of Kinship", 79, 83.

26 Maureen Molloy notes: "as Flandrin (1979: 92) puts it 'the peasants who were in the process of being uprooted from their villages, and the workers and the younger sons of noble houses who migrated to the towns, were condemned to live in someone else's house or alone, or, at best, in small conjugal houses, unable to keep their children.' These people, sundered from property and kin, were those most likely to find that the frozen

New World offered a better life than the Old did." Maureen Molloy, "Considered Affinity: Kinship, Marriage and Social Class in New France, 1640–1729," *Social Science History* 14, no. 1 (Spring 1990): 2.

27 The *"filles du roi"* or "the king's daughters" were seven hundred women sent to Canada between 1663 and 1700 under an immigration scheme sponsored by the king of France. It was his intention to build the sparse population of New France by providing brides for the unattached male colonists, who outnumbered women in the colony as much as twelve to one. Louis XIV's scheme was successful; by 1673 the population doubled annually, reaching a total of about eighty-five hundred people by 1673. See Yves Landry, "Gender Imbalance, Les *Filles Du Roi*, and Choice of Spouse in New France," in Bettina Bradbury, ed., *Canadian Family History: Selected Readings* (Toronto: Copp Clark Pitman, 1992), 14–32.

28 See Verney, *The Good Regiment*, 92–96.

29 Ibid., 102–6, 109–12.

30 Paul-Eugène Trudel, O.F.M., *Généalogie de la famille Trudel(le)* (Montréal: Sourds-Muets, 1955), 51, 75–76.

31 Only sixty-six individuals from the Belgian provinces are recorded as having emigrated to New France and Acadia between 1620 and 1765. See Marcel Fournier, "Belgian Immigration to Canada from its Origins Until 1765," [unofficial translation of an article originally published in *L'Intermediare des Genealogistes*, Brussels, no. 265 (Jan.–Feb. 1990), translated copy provided to author from personal file of Howard K. Thomas, Washington, D.C.].

32 See Appendix 1 for a discussion of the research on the Desjarlais family's Belgian roots.

33 See Moogk, "Reluctant Exiles": 500–1; and Molloy, "Considered Affinity": 3–6.

34 See Burguière and Lebrun, "The One Hundred and One Families of Europe," 11–94.

35 See Molloy, "Considered Affinity": 24.

36 Archives du Séminaire Manuscrits 147(b), "Advice to young man contemplating marriage," fols. 4v-5. As quoted in Cornelius Jaenen, *The Role of the Church in New France* (Toronto: McGraw-Hill Ryerson, 1976), 137.

37 J.F. Bosher, "The Family in New France," in *Business and Religion in the Age of New France – 1600–1760: Twenty-Two Studies* (Toronto: Canadian Scholars' Press, 1994), 99.

38 Bosher, "The Family in New France," 100–101.

39 Natalie Maree Belting, *Kaskaskia Under the French Regime* (Urbana: University of Illinois Press, 1948), 75–76.

40 Raymond Douville and Jacques Casanova, *Daily Life in Early Canada*, Carola Congreve, trans. (London: George Allen and Unwin, 1968), 193–94.

41 Contrat du mariage, Jean De Gerlaise and Jeanne Trudel, *Greffes des notaires du régime français*, C. Aubert, 12 September 1667, Archives

Nationales du Québec as quoted in Paul-Eugène Trudel, *Généalogie de la famille Trudel(le)*, 76–77.

42 For additional biographical information on Charles du Jay, see Germain Lesage, O.M.I., *Manereuil: Fondateur de Louiseville 1665–1672* (Louiseville, Que.: Presbytère de Louiseville, 1966).

43 Joseph Giffard was the son and heir of Robert Giffard (d. 14 October 1668) master surgeon, colonizing seigneur, member of the Communauté des Habitants (a society for trade with the Indians), first doctor of the Hôtel Dieu of Quebec and doctor to the king of France. See Honorius Provost, "Robert Giffard De Moncel," *Dictionary of Canadian Biography* (hereinafter *DCB*), 2:330–31. Joseph Giffard inherited the seigneuries of Beauport and Mille-Vaches from his parents in 1663. See René Jetté, *Dictionnaire généalogique des familles du Québec des origines à 1730* (hereinafter DGFQ) (Montréal: Les Presses de l'Université de Montréal, 1983), 494–95.

44 Jean Juchereau, sieur de Laferté (d. 16 November 1685) was the son of Jean Juchereau de Maur. He was appointed to the Conseil Souverain in 1663, and was also a merchant. He was married to Marie Giffard, the daughter of Robert Giffard, the most prominent colonizing seigneur in the history of New France. See Lucien Campeau, "Jean Juchereau de La Ferté," *DCB*, 2:400; and Jetté, *DGFQ*, 612–13.

45 Nicholas Juchereau de Saint-Denis (d. 4 October 1692) was a seigneur, colonizer, businessman, member of the council of the colony for the fur trade, director of the Tadoussac trade, and a soldier in New France. See Bernard Weilbrenner, "Nicholas Juchereau de Saint-Denis," *DCB*, 2: 401–2.

46 Damoiselle de Carion is tentatively identified as Pétronille Desheures, wife of Philippe de Carion, Sieur de Fresnoy, a lieutenant in the LaMothe Company of the Carignan-Salières Regiment. See Jetté, *DGFQ*, 199.

47 Jeanne Trudel was eleven years, one month, and two days old at the signing of her marriage contract. According to J.F. Bosher, "The average age of women at their first marriage was nearly twenty-two in New France and about twenty-five in Old France. There are, of course some well-known cases of girls being married at twelve, which was the youngest a girl might legally marry in New France." Such early marriages were described by Bosher as 'extreme.' See Bosher, "The Family in New France," 94. See also Paul-Eugène Trudel, *Généalogie de la famille Trudel(le)*, 76; and Germain Lesage, O.M.I., *Histoire de Louiseville, 1665–1960* (Louiseville, Que.: Presbytère de Louiseville, 1961), 20–21.

48 Lesage, *Histoire de Louiseville*, 18–22; R.P. Paul-Eugène Trudel, *Généalogie de la famille Trudel(le)*, 79.

49 The probability that the marriage was *not* consummated immediately is suggested by the gap between the De Gerlaise marriage and the appearance of their first child. Jean-Jacques' and Jeanne De Gerlaise's first child, Catherine, was born in April of 1673, over five and one-half years after their marriage, when Jeanne Trudel De Gerlaise was sixteen years of age. See Jetté, *DGFQ*, 489.

50 During this period Rivière-du-Loup was actually two settlements: Rivière-du-Loup *en haut* and Rivière-du-Loup *en bas*, where the De Gerlaise concession was located. In 1880, Rivière-du-Loup *en haut* was renamed Louiseville, in honour of Princess Louise of Lorne, daughter of Queen Victoria and wife of the Marquis of Lorne, Canada's Governor-General at the time. The old community of Rivière-du-Loup (now Louiseville) should *not* be mistaken for the current Quebec community named Rivière-du-Loup, which exists on the south shore of the St. Lawrence River, on the Gaspé penininsula. See Lesage, *Histoire de Louiseville*, 239–40.

51 Madame Louis-Joseph Doucet, "Généalogie de Gerlaise-Desjarlais," from *Memoires de la Société Généalogique*, vol. 7 (Montréal: Author, 1956), 77–78; Lesage, *Histoire de Louiseville*, 18–22; R.P. Paul-Eugène Trudel, *Généalogie de la famille Trudel(le)*, 75–79; and Roland J. Auger, "Judith Rigaud," *French-Canadian and Acadian Genealogical Review* 9, nos. 1–4 (1981): 21.

52 See Lesage, *Histoire de Louiseville*, 25.

53 In 1681 the local population consisted of nine families, mostly veteran soldiers of the La Fouille company of the Carignan-Salières Regiment. Lesage, *Histoire de Louiseville*, 35–36.

54 See René Chartrand, "Introduction," in E.Z. Massicotte, ed., *Canadian Passports, 1681–1752*. Originally published in Province de Québec, *Rapport de l'archiviste de la province de Québec* (hereinafter *RAPQ*) (1921–23), with a supplement from *Bulletin des Recherches Historiques*, vol. 32, 1926; reprint, New Orleans: Polyanthos, 1975: iv–vi.

55 Chartrand, "Introduction," v.

56 Their policy of 'francisation,' as their colonial assimilation program came to be known, was based on three approaches: intermarriage, education, and sedentarization. Jaenen, *The French Relationship with the Native Peoples of New France and Acadia*, 68–77.

57 Ibid.

58 Despite the integral military and economic function served by Indian interpreters in New France, they were never accorded the level of respect and social prominence that one would assume such a sensitive position would deserve. The social obscurity and penury of the explorer, trader, and diplomat Nicolas Perrot is a case in point. See Claude Perrault, "Nicholas Perrot," *DCB*, 2: 516–19.

59 See W.J. Eccles, *The French in North America, 1500–1783*, rev. ed. (East Lansing: Michigan State University Press, 1998), 56. The intendant of New France, Jean Talon, attempted to force marriage on these men by forbidding the involvement of single men in hunting and trading activities by decree. Unfortunately the regulation was difficult to enforce, and therefore did not have the desired effect. Verney, *The Good Regiment*, 112–13.

60 Eccles, *The French in North America, 1500–1783*, 94.

61 See Douville and Casanova, *Daily Life in Early Canada*, 87–90.

62 Verney, *The Good Regiment*, 112–13.

63 See Auger, "Judith Rigaud," 15–16.

64 Because Judith Rigaud was purportedly of Huguenot origin, it is not
surprising that she would seek business partners in La Rochelle, a port
city whose early commerce was dominated by Huguenot merchants and
mariners, but which later became the principal embarkation point for
overseas colonization and investment. See J.F. Bosher, "La Rochelle's
Primacy in Trade with New France, 1627–1685," in Bosher, *Business and
Religion in the Age of New France*, 120, 141.

65 Auger, "Judith Rigaud," 20–22.

66 Ibid., 23. Eventually the latter two would act as witnesses for the prosecution against Guyon, who was accused of committing a murder on a fur-
trading expedition. Guyon's charges were apparently dropped, as he later
relocated to Quebec City and became a domestic servant. His two accusers
remained in the fur trade. See also Lesage, *Histoire de Louiseville*, 22; and
Jetté *DGFQ*, 547–48.

67 See Auger, "Judith Rigaud," 24.

68 See Archange Godbout, O.F.M., "Jean Daigle dit Lallemand," dans
Mémoires de la Société généalogique canadienne française, t. 4, Janvier
1950, 12. As quoted by Lesage, *Histoire de Louiseville*, 37.

69 See Eccles, *The French in North America, 1500–1783*, 54–56.

70 Lesage, *Histoire de Louiseville*, 35, 44.

71 The ceremony took place in the home of Jean De Gerlaise. See Lesage,
Histoire de Louiseville, 39.

72 See Perrault, "Nicholas Perrot," *DCB*, 2: 516–19.. See also Lesage,
Histoire de Louiseville, 45–48.

73 See Richard White, "Introduction," in Emma Helen Blair, trans., ed. and
ann., *The Indian Tribes of the Upper Mississippi Valley and the Region
of the Great Lakes*. (1911. New Edition: Lincoln and London: University
of Nebraska Press, 1996), 2. See Perrault, "Nicholas Perrot," *DCB*, 2:
516–19.

74 See Lesage, *Histoire de Louiseville*, 47–49.

75 Lesage, *Histoire de Louiseville*, 50–52.

76 Ibid.

77 At least seven children were born between 1688 and 1695, according to
Lesage, *Histoire de Louiseville*, 47–54.

78 The following censitaires contracted to deal in furs between 1684 and
1698: Joachim Germano (1685); Pierre LeMaître, Charles LeMaître-Auger,
and Jean LeMaître-Lalongée (1686); Joachim Germano (1687); Christophe
Gerbaud (1689); Joachim Germano (1692. See Lesage, *Histoire de
Louiseville*, 42–55.

79 The hapless Perrot, who had been forced to spend the previous four years
constructing fortifications and travelling amongst distant Native allies in
pursuit of the hard-won peace, was now obliged to hand over title of the
seigneurie to Le Chasseur. Moreover, he was required to pay interest on
the capital he owed to Le Chasseur during the previous seven years he
held the fief, plus a further 385 livres for other titles sold. To add insult
to injury, Perrot was saddled with the court costs. Lesage, *Histoire de
Louiseville*, 55–56.

80 Pierre Trottier, Sieur Desaulniers (b. 1673) was a fur trade *engageur* (recruiter) between 1718 and 1720, ending his life as a merchant bourgeois and seigneur of Ile aux Hérons. Joseph Trottier, Sieur Desruisseaux (b. ca. 1668) was an *engagé* in 1701 and became a merchant shortly thereafter, purchasing the Ile Perrot seigneury in 1703. Julien Trottier, Sieur Desrivières (b. 1687) became an *engagé* in 1716 and later a merchant. See Jetté, *DGFQ*, 1091–1094.

81 See José Igartua, "The Merchants of Montreal at the Conquest: Socio-Economic Profile," *Histoire Sociale–Social History* 8, no. 16 (November 1975): 275–93.

82 See the following records from the Programme de récherche en démographie historique (PRDH) database, which list the marriage dates and spouses of the De Gerlaise children: "Family Group Sheet for Jean Jarlais St. Amand and Marie Jeanne Trudel" (#4044); "Family Group Sheet for Jean François Jarlais St. Amand and Marie Catherine Aubert" (#13184).

83 Eventually the changing of the family surname De Gerlaise, was adjusted to its current spelling Desjarlais, no doubt to reflect the Canadien pronunciation of the "er" syllable as "ar." Anton Pregaldin, Clayton, Mo., to the author, personal correspondence dated 17 November 2001.

84 See Edmund Robert Murphy, *Henry De Tonty: Fur Trader of the Mississippi* (Baltimore: Johns Hopkins University Press, 1941), 72; and Theodore Calvin Pease and Raymond C. Werner, eds., *The French Foundations: 1680–1693* [(French series, vol. 1, of *Collections of the Illinois State Historical Library*, vol. 23): Springfield: Illinois State Historical Library, 1934]: 299–301.

85 See Jetté, *DGFQ*, 82, for genealogical information on the Benoist dit La Forest family. See also Archange Godbout, "Nos Ancêtres au XVII Siècle," in *RAPQ* (1956–57): 406–408 for his biographical sketch of the family of Gabriel Benoît dit La Forest and *RAPQ* (1929–1930), 202, 204, 209; for records of Pierre Benoist's engagements to Antoine La Mothe, Sieur de Cadillac, François Couturier, and les Messieurs de la Compagnie de la Colonie du Canada respectively.

86 There are various spellings of the Dulignon de Lamirande surname. The earliest version of the surname appears to be Du Lignon de La Mirande. Later generations gradually altered the surname to Dulignon de Lamirande; some branches of the family chose to be known by a single surname Dulignon, or Lamirande. See Jetté, *DGFQ*, 379–80; and Lesage, *Histoire de Louiseville*, 56, 61, 67, and 83 to see spelling variations. There has been a great deal of debate amongst genealogists concerning the relationship of Pierre Dulignon and Jean Dulignon. Formerly it was believed that Pierre du Lignon was Jean du Lignon's son. However, the recent discovery of a Quebec burial record for Pierre du Lignon Lamirande in 1736 identified his age at death as being 80 years of age. Additional research by Pierre Desjardins of PRDH and Denis Beauregard, a wellk-nown Quebec genealogist, has revealed that Pierre and Jean du Lignon were actually brothers. Both men were the sons of Theodore Élie du Lignon, public

prosecutor for the duchy of La Rochefoucauld, and Marthe Pacquet. Their baptismal records have recently been found in France. See discussion on Internet newsgroup soc.genealogy.french (16 December 2000).

87 Since LaSalle reached the mouth of the Mississippi in 1682, the Jean Dulignon referred to in LaSalle's account is clearly Jean Dulignon Sr., husband of Marie Testard. They were married in 1684, shortly after he returned from the Mississippi. See the translated correspondence of La Salle, from B.F. French, ed., *Historical Collections of Louisiana*, Part I (New York: Wiley & Putnam, 1846), 35–36, 45–46, 48–50), reprinted in "Adventures of La Salle and his Associates, 1678–87," in Cary F. Goulson, ed., *Seventeenth Century Canada: Source Studies* (Toronto: Macmillan of Canada, 1970), 344–48.

88 Jean du Lignon married Marie Testard, daughter of Charles Testard and Anne Lamarque, in Montreal in 1684. He died ca. 1689 at Montreal or Pointe-aux-Trembles. See Jetté, *DGFQ*, 379–80, and Archange Godbout, *Généalogie de la famille Testard de Montigny* (Montreal: Beauchemin, n.d.) for further information.

89 See Jetté, *DGFQ*, 172, and Lesage, *Histoire de Louiseville*, 64, 68.

90 Marie-Angelique Pelletier was the daughter of the late François Pelletier dit Antaya and his widow Marguerite Madeleine Morriseau. At least three of her brothers were involved in the Illinois trade; her mother, Marguerite Morrisseau, was issued a trading pass for the Illinois on 1 August 1688, after which she outfitted her sons with trade goods. Members of the family later relocated to Cahokia in the Illinois country. See Jetté, *DGFQ*, 888 and 489–90 for genealogical information on the De Gerlaise and Pelletier marriage; *RAPQ* (1929–30): 197 for record of the trading pass issued to the widow Pelletier; Pease and Werner, *French Foundations*, 162–78 for a detailed account of the Pelletier family's trade accounts for the Illinois; as well as Lesage, *Histoire de Louiseville*, 16.

91 Claude Auber, Marie-Catherine's great-grandfather, had presided over the marriage contract of Jean-Jacques De Gerlaise and Jeanne Trudel in 1667. Claude Auber had a distinguished career in New France. As well as the position of Royal Notary, he was also made deputy judge of the Conseil Souverain, housed in Quebec City, in 1684. See Honorius Provost, "Claude Auber," in *DCB*, 2:72.

92 As one of two surviving sons of Jean-Jacques De Gerlaise, he had preferential access to agricultural land, particularly since his sisters and brothers had married holders of concessions at Rivière-du-Loup. By 1724, Jean-François Desjarlais had two concessions in his name, while his brother Antoine farmed the concession inherited by his wife Marie-Angélique Pelletier, widow of François Banhiac dit Lamontagne. Lesage, *Histoire de Louiseville*, 80–85. See also Doucet, "Généalogie de Gerlaise-Desjarlais," 79.

93 Loosely translated: "I, the undersigned Jean Gerloisse dit Saint-Amant, spouse of Jeanne Trudel, my wife, have received from Jean Trudelle and Marguerite Thomas, our mother and father, all that they promised us in marriage, with which I am content [happy]." See Lesage, *Histoire*

de Louiseville, 51; and Paul-Eugène Trudel, *Généalogie de la famille Trudel(le)*, 79.

94 See Chartrand, "Introduction," iv–vi.

95 E.R. Adair, "The Evolution of Montreal under the French Régime," *Canadian Historical Association Reports, 1942*, 22–26.

96 Perrot was governor of Montreal from 1669 to 1684. Although Governor Perrot was married to the niece of Jean Talon, this did not insulate him from criminal prosecution. He was eventually removed as governor of Montreal and jailed by Frontenac for supporting the activities of illegal *coureurs de bois*, and for violence and sedition. The two men eventually formed an alliance of convenience in order to resume their trading activities. In 1682, Frontenac was dismissed as governor of New France. By 1683, Perrot was stripped of his position as governor of Montreal and threatened with removal to France. He was eventually sent to Acadia, where he became governor in 1684. See W.J. Eccles, "François-Marie Perrot," in *DCB*, 1:540–42.

97 Adair, "The Evolution of Montreal under the French Régime," 29.

98 Adair, 34.

99 W.J. Eccles, *France in America* (Markham: Fitzhenry & Whiteside, 1972), 147.

100 Igartua, "The Merchants of Montreal," 275–93.

101 Ibid., 279–83, 285.

102 See Doucet, "Généalogie de Gerlaise-Desjarlais," 76.

103 Pierre Lamirande, as noted previously, was the brother of Jean Dulignon dit Lamirande, a former associate of La Salle. Jean Dulignon's wife, Marie Testard de Montigny, came from a prominent military and commercial family in Montreal, who were in turn related to the Le Moynes and the Le Bers. One of her cousins, Jacques Testard de Montigny, a prominent military officer and Chevalier of the Order of St. Louis, was appointed commander of Baye des Puants (Green Bay) in 1721 by Governor Rigaud de Vaudreuil, and appointed commander of Michilimackinac by 1730. See Louise Dechêne, "Jacques Testard de Montigny," *DCB*, 2:625–27.

104 See *RAPQ* (1922–23), 212–14, where summaries of these *congés* are recorded.

105 *RAPQ* (1922–23), 212. See also Massicotte, *Canadian Passports, 1681–1752*, 58–60, for a record of the *congés* dated 1–2 June 1745, listing the names of the contractors and *engagés* manning the canoes.

106 See "Répertoire des Engagements pour L'Ouest," *RAPQ* (1930–31), 390.

107 Ibid., 397.

108 See "Répertoire des Engagements pour L'Ouest," *RAPQ* (1922–23), 263.

109 Ibid.

110 The eventual fate of Pierre-François remains unknown, though he appears to have been settled at Rivière-du-Loup. Although the PRDH lists a death certificate for one Pierre Jacquet in Quebec City in 1755, the origin of the deceased is "Honfleur, Normandy," which is not the origin of Pierre-François De Gerlaise, who was born in Canada. Moreover, a man named François Desjarlais, listed as "oncle paternel" to the bride, is listed as

being present at the wedding of Hélène Desjarlais and Jean Baptiste Picotte, held at Rivière-du-Loup, Quebec on 20 October 1775. Hélène Desjarlais was the daughter of Louis Desjarlais (brother of Pierre-François Desjarlais), and Catherine Banliac dit Lamontagne. See PRDH, Record # 361435, marriage of Jean Baptiste Picotte and Hélène Desjarlais. See also PRDH, Record #251586, Sepulture at Quebec – Pierre Jacquet, 1755–08-05.

111 See PRDH, Record #13184, "Family Group Sheet for Jean François Jarlais St. Amand and Marie Catherine Aubert," where Louis Desjarlais' marriage to Marie-Catherine Banhiac Lamontagne is recorded.

112 See *RAPQ* (1931), 390.

113 In seventeenth-century New France, the credentials of anyone claiming noble status were investigated thoroughly. The Du Lignons were the only family at Rivière-du-Loup considered to have legitimate status as nobility. See Lesage, *Histoire de Louiseville*, 56–57.

114 Between 1745 and 1756 a total of twelve separate contracts are recorded for Joseph, Louis, Pierre, and Jean Desjarlais. Although Pierre and Jean Desjarlais are cited as having engaged for one time only, Louis and Joseph Desjarlais had engaged five separate times each. In the 1740s the engagements were to Green Bay and the Illinois country, while in the 1750s the engagements were to Michilimackinac. See "Répertoire des Engagements pour L'Ouest," *RAPQ* (1922–23); *RAPQ* (1931–32); *RAPQ* (1932–33), ibid.

115 Igartua, "The Merchants of Montreal," 279–83, 285.

Chapter 3

1 The 'decapitation thesis' – which asserts that the removal and/or departure of New France's commercial and political elite after the British takeover resulted in the economic marginalization of the *Canadien* population – was rarely challenged in Francophone historiographical circles prior to the mid-twentieth century. For a summary of the various Francophone arguments dealing with this see Dale Miquelon, *Society and Conquest: The Debate on the Bourgeoisie and Social Change in French Canada, 1700–1850* (Vancouver: Copp Clark, 1977), Serge Gagnon, *Quebec and Its Historians: 1840–1920* (Montreal: Laval University Press, 1978), and Michel Brunet, *French Canada and the Early Decades of British Rule 1760–1791* (Ottawa: Canadian Historical Association, 1981). An alternative argument asserting that technological innovation rather than anti-*Canadien* policy contributed to British pre-eminence in the post-Conquest fur trade is convincingly drawn by Fernand Ouellet, "Economic Dualism and Technological Change in Quebec, 1760–1790," in Fernand Ouellet, *Economy, Class and Nation in Quebec: Interpretive Essays*, Jacques A. Barbier, ed. and trans. (Toronto: Copp Clark Pitman, 1991), 161–209. Quebec historian José Igartua suggested that *mentalité* also had an influence over commercial success in post-Conquest Quebec in his essay "A

Change in Climate: The Conquest and the *Marchands* of Montreal," in *Historical Papers*, [Canadian Historical Association, 1974]: 197–214. Igartua argued that most local merchants and small-scale fur traders did not have connections back in France, so most of them chose to stay in business, searching for new suppliers and financing locally. While they may not have enjoyed access to the British corridors of power, they nonetheless had the local advantage, at least initially. Perhaps more difficult was the transition to a much more competitive business environment where old patronage alliances were obsolete.

2 Jacqueline Peterson documents the early history of these settlements as a refuge for illegal traders in "Many Roads to Red River: Métis Ethnogenesis in the Great Lakes Region," in Peterson and Brown, *The New Peoples*, 42–43.

3 See J.M. Carrière, "Life and Customs in the French Villages of the Old Illinois Country (1736–1939)." The Canadian Historical Association, *Historical Reports 1939*: 34–47. See also Tanis Thorne, *The Many Hands of My Relations: French and Indians on the Lower Missouri* (St. Louis: University of Missouri Press, 1996), 66, 72.

4 Louis Houck, *A History of Missouri from the Earliest Explorations and Settlements until the Admission of the State into the Union*, vols. I, II and III (1908; Reprint, New York: Arno Press and the New York Times, 1971), 2:13.

5 See William R. Swagerty, "General Introduction," 5; and Janet Lecompte, "The Chouteaus in the St. Louis Fur Trade," xiii–xiv, in William R. Swagerty, ed., *A Guide to the Microfilm Edition of Research Collections of the American West: Papers of the St Louis Fur Trade* (St. Louis: Missouri Historical Society, 1991).

6 See Lecompte, "The Chouteaus in the St. Louis Fur Trade," xiv.

7 It is possible, through the analysis of the community histories and parish records from Quebec, the Illinois settlements, and Missouri, to trace the migration of various Quebec families southward to Missouri. Like other ethnic groups, the *Canadiens* practised "chain-migration", a term used to describe the gradual movement of family members from one locale to another, characterized by one or two family members, generally male, migrating to a new region and establishing themselves, after which they are joined by other family members, who in turn sponsor other relatives and friends. The process of chain-migration may take anywhere from a few months to several decades. The process of settling the Illinois country through chain-migration is clearly illustrated in Jacques Mathieu et al., "Mobilité et Sédentarité: Stratégies Familiales en Nouvelle-France," *Recherches Sociographiques* 38, nos. 2–3 (1987): 211–27.

8 Greer, *Peasant, Lord and Merchant*, 227. For a detailed discussion of the economic evolution of rural Quebec after the British conquest, see Fernand Ouellet, "Ruralization, Regional Development, and Industrial Growth Before 1850," in Ouellet, *Economy, Class and Nation,"* 124–60.

9 Jacques Mathieu et al., "Mobilité et Sédentarité," 226.

10 Ouellet, "Ruralization," 137–51.

11 Of this large family, only two children did not survive to adulthood. See Family Group Sheet #13184 (Jean-François Jarlais St. Amand and Marie Catherine Aubert), PRDH.

12 See Anton J. Pregaldin, Clayton, Mo., to the author; personal correspondence dated 11 June 1998.

13 See Marthe Faribault-Beauregard, *La population des forts français d'Amérique (XVIII siècle)* (Montreal: Bergeron, 1982–84), 1:142–43 and 2:88.

14 This person was identified by Missouri historian Louis Houck as Jean-Baptiste Lamirande in the genealogical notes to his book, *The Spanish Regime in Missouri*, in 1909. In the lists, the French names were "hispanicized" by the Spanish authorities – hence the Spanish name. See "First Company San Luis de Ilinueses Militia," (Database online) Accessed 8 March 2004. Available from http://www.geocities.com/bourbonstreet/Delta/3843/.

15 Louis Houck records Antoine Desjarlais at this spot in 1790. Houck, *History of Missouri*, 2:68. However, Anton Pregaldin, a descendant of Antoine Desjarlais found him listed in the 1787 Spanish Census, a copy of which resides in the Missouri Historical Society. See Anton J. Pregaldin, Clayton, Mo., to the author; personal correspondence dated 23 March 1998 and 17 November 2001.

16 See Family Group Sheet #37364 for Charles Jarlais St. Amand and Marie Madeleine LaMaître Auger Beaunoyer, showing children married before 1800. PRDH.

17 See "Mottin and St. Cin Families," in *French-Canadian and Acadian Genealogical Review* 3, no. 1 (Spring 1971): 62–63.

18 Three children of Antoine Desjarlais and Thérèse Pelletier were baptized 9 June 1818; Charles Desjarlais (b. January 1814); Cecile (b. 22 March 1813); and Hélène (b. 14 January 1818). These delayed baptisms suggest that the parents were not close to a church where their children could be baptized at birth. *Roman Catholic Church Records – St. Ferdinand de Florissant Missouri 1790–1993* [Latter Day Saints Family History Library, Salt Lake City, Utah (hereinafter *LDS*)] microfilm #1902788.

19 Houck, *History of Missouri*, 2:69.

20 The Gagnés and the Pelletiers were long-established families in the Illinois country. The Dubreuil family was one of the earliest families to receive a land grant in St. Louis.

21 It is not unusual to see such papers in the Chouteau collection, as Auguste Chouteau was "continually requested to execute wills and to supervise the affairs of widows and orphaned children, both of French and mixed-blood." See Thorne, *The Many Hands of My Relations*, 79. See *Papers of the St Louis Fur Trade: Part 1 – The Chouteau Collection, 1752–1925*, (hereinafter called The Chouteau Collection), Missouri Historical Society (hereinafter *MHS*), St. Louis, Missouri. Reel#1: July 1795; Reel #3: 17 February 1801; 28 December 1821.

22 Lecompte, "The Chouteaus and the St. Louis Fur Trade," xiv.

23 Much of this land remains in the hands of various descendants. Anton Pregaldin, Clayton, Mo., to the author; personal correspondence dated 11 June 1998.

24 See "Engagement Contract of Joseph Dejarlay," dated 21 April 1830. In *Papers of the St. Louis Fur Trade: Part 1: The Chouteau Collection, 1752–1925* (Reel 16). Missouri Historical Society, St. Louis.

25 Anton Pregaldin, Clayton, Mo., to the author. Personal correspondence dated 23 March 1998.

26 Anton Pregaldin, ibid. Some of information provided by Mr. Pregaldin is also contained in Harriet Duncan Munnick, comp., *Catholic Church Records of the Pacific Northwest: St. Louis Register*, vol. 1 (1845–1868); *St. Louis Register*, vol. 2 (1869–1900); *Gervais Register* (1875–1893); *Brooks Register* (1893–1901) (Portland, OR: Binfort & Mort, 1982), *St. Louis Register*, 1:6–7.

27 See Kaskaskia marriage records for Jacques Gélinas-Lacourse, to Jeanne Bienvenu (1743); and Charlotte Guillemot dit Lalande dit Canada (1749), and Pierre Gélinas-Lacourse and Elizabeth Bienvenu (1743). Various Gélinas-Lacourse marriages and baptisms follow in the records. See Marthe Faribault-Beauregard, *La population des forts*, 2:90.

28 See "Appendix B – Biographies of Voyageurs and Traders," in Harry W. Duckworth, ed., *The English River Book: A North West Company Journal and Account Book of 1786* (Montreal: McGill-Queen's University Press, 1990), 156–58.

29 See Houck, *History of Missouri*, 2:105–8, 159. Other traders attracted to New Madrid included Antoine Gamelin, son of Ignace Gamelin, a prominent import-export merchant in Montreal. Antoine Gamelin settled in New Madrid in 1791 after trading with the Indians in Indiana and acting as interpreter for General George Rogers Clark in 1778 and 1779. Louis Baby, son of the Montreal outfitter Colonel Louis Baby, became a school-teacher in the settlement. Also see Houck, 2:139, 153, 266.

30 See Houck, *History of Missouri*, 2:159–63. Marie-Josèphe Desjarlais was the daughter of Joseph Desjarlais and Marie-Josephte Hervieux of Contrecoeur, Quebec. Louis Houck refers to Michel Lacourse and his wife Marie-Josephe separately in his notes. It is possible that the couple assumed separate title over parcels of land in different locales in order to acquire more property, hence Houck's notes which suggest that they were individual settlers, rather than a married couple. Another daughter of Joseph Desjarlais and Marie Josephte Hervieux, Marie-Pélagie, also settled in the St. Louis area, as the wife of Jean-Baptiste Bellefeuille. Bellefeuille's estate papers (1802–03) can be found in the *New Madrid Papers*, St. Louis Historical Society Library, St. Louis, Mo. Anton Pregaldin, Clayton, Mo., to the Author; personal correspondence dated 17 November 2001.

31 Thorne, *The Many Hands of My Relations*, 79, 96–97.

32 In the parish records for the Catholic Church of St. Ferdinand de Florissant, Missouri, there are numerous entries recording the baptism of métis children of fur traders. However, notations within the entries suggest that the baptisms did not take place at the church. For example, the entry

for 21 August 1827 records the baptism of the children of at least thirteen different fathers. At the bottom of the entry, however, is the notation "chez M. Liguest Chouteau," indicating that the baptisms took place at the home of Liguest Chouteau. A second mass baptism, taking place on 27 August 1827 is accompanied by the notation "à Hancock Prairie," possibly referring to the farm established by Americans William and Stephen Hancock on the north side of the Missouri River, about fifty miles north of the settlement of St. Charles. See Houck, *History of Missouri*, 2: 91–93.

33 The trader Honoré Picotte, for example, successfully juggled a succession of country marriages with Sioux women while being respectably married in St. Louis. However, he only narrowly avoided an embarrassing confrontation between his St. Louis and Indian wives when he was informed by a colleague that his wife, along with some other St. Louis matrons, had decided to take the steamboat up the Missouri and pay them a visit at their post! See Annie Heloise Abel, *Tabeau's Narrative of Loisel's Expedition to the Upper Missouri* (Norman: University of Oklahoma Press, 1939), 216.

34 The sources on Honoré Picotte cited include: Annie Heloise Abel, *Chardon's Journal at Fort Clark 1834–1839*. Pierre, S.D.: Department of History, State of South Dakota, 1932. John S. Gray, "Honoré Picotte, Fur Trader," *South Dakota History* 6, no. 2 (Spring 1976): 186–202; PRDH; Charles-Arthur Milot, "Un Picotte Aventureux," *Bulletin Société d'Histoire de Louiseville* (5 Mars 1989); Charles-Arthur Milot, "Famille Picotte" (family group sheet, n.d.); Lecompte, "The Chouteaus and the St. Louis Fur Trade"; Thorne, *The Many Hands of My Relations*.

35 Hélène Desjarlais was the daughter of Louis Desjarlais and Catherine Banhiac dit Lamontagne. She married Jean Picotte, an Acadian, at Maskinongé 20 October 1775. Milot, "Famille Picotte." See Baptismal Record #488380 for Honoré Picotte, born 7 November 1796, baptized 9 November 1796, the son of Jean-Baptiste Picotte and Hélène Desjarlais, PRDH.

36 Hélene Desjarlais Picotte's first cousins were the brothers Joseph and Antoine Desjarlais, who eventually became freemen in Athabasca (see Chapter 4). Hélène was also a first cousin to François Desjarlais, an *engagé* who became a freeman in Athabasca as well. Antoine became a clerk in the North West Company in the Lower Red River Department, although he did not do any book-keeping. Honoré Picotte was a cousin once removed to Joseph, Antoine, and François Desjarlais, and a cousin twice removed to their métis children living in Rupert's Land.

37 An elderly Honoré Picotte gave details of his life to Thaddeus A. Culbertson during an 1850 trip up the Missouri, which were later published in Thaddeus A. Culbertson, *Journal of an Expedition to the Mauvaises Terres and the Upper Missouri in 1850*, ed. John Francis McDermott, Smithsonian Institution, Bureau of American Ethnology, Bulletin no. 147 (Washington, D.C., 1952), 101–3.

38 While a member of the House of Assembly, Louis Picotte is known to have demonstrated his virtuosity in several Native languages acquired in the *pays d'en haut*. See Renald Lessard, "Louis Picotte," *DCB*, 6:642.

39 LeRoy Hafen in his biographical series *The Mountain Men and the Fur Trade of the Far West*, refers to these men as former employees of the North West Company. See LeRoy Hafen, *The Mountain Men and the Fur Trade of the Far West*, 10 vols. (1935; reprint, Stanford: Academic Reprints, 1954), 2:217–24, 3:167–73, 2:201–5. As cited by Gray, "Honoré Picotte, Fur Trader," 188.

40 These firms included Joshua Pilcher's Missouri Fur Company, Pierre Chouteau's French Fur Company, and the Western Department of the American Fur Company under Ramsay Crooks. See Gray, "Honoré Picotte," 188–89.

41 Gray, "Honoré Picotte," 189–90. See also Lecompte, "The Chouteaus," xviii.

42 Gray, "Honoré Picotte," 190–91. See also Lecompte, "The Chouteaus," xviii.

43 Gray, "Honoré Picotte," 191–93. See also "Charles F. Picotte," *South Dakota Historical Collections*, vol. 1 (1902), 113–14.

44 Quebec folklorist Ernest Gagnon related a story concerning two young men named Tellier and Desjarlais, who had been funded by their rich uncle, Honoré Picotte, to travel to California. On their way across the plains, they encountered a former resident of Rivière-du-Loup named Boisvert, who had become a chief of the Snake Indians. Ernest Gagnon, *Choses D'autrefois feuilles éparses* (Québec: Typ. Dussault & Proulx, 1905); see also Louis Guyon, *Étude généalogique sur Jean Guyon et ses descendants* (Montreal: Mercantile Printing, 1927), 126–27.

45 Gray, "Honoré Picotte," 202.

46 Eloi Desjarlais (b. 23 May 1770 at Contrecoeur, Lower Canada) was the son of Joseph Desjarlais and Marie-Josephte Hervieux. He was the younger brother of Joseph and Antoine Desjarlais, the freemen who participated in the Athabasca fur trade (see Chapter 4).

47 Information on the Robidoux family has been compiled from the following sources: Orrall Messmore Robidoux, *Memorial to the Robidoux Brothers Who Blazed the Western Trails for Civilization: A History of the Robidouxs in America* (Kansas City, Mo.: Smith-Grieves, 1927); Joseph J. Hill, "Antoine Robidoux, Kingpin in the Colorado River Fur Trade, 1824–1844," *The Colorado Magazine* 7, no. 4 (July 1930): 125–32; William Swilling Wallace, *Antoine Robidoux 1784–1860: A Biography of a Western Venturer* (Los Angeles: Glen Dawson, 1930); Hugh M. Lewis, "Pierre Isadore Robidoux," in *Robidoux Chronicles: French–Indian Ethnoculture in the Trans-Mississippi West* (electronic document copyright Hugh M. Lewis 2002 at http://www.lewismicropublishing.com/Publications/RobidouxFrames.htm); St. Louis Genealogical Society, *Earl Fischer Database of St. Louisans* (electronic database at http://www.rootsweb.com/~mostlogs/efdb/index.htm) (St. Louis: Author, 1999); David J. Weber, *The Taos Trappers: The Fur Trade in the Far Southwest,*

1540–1846 (Norman: University of Oklahoma Press, 1971); Thorne, *The Many Hands of My Relations*; Lecompte, "The Chouteaus," xiii–xxii; David J. Weber, *The Extranjeros: Selected Documents from the Mexican Side of the Santa Fe Trail 1825–1828* (Santa Fe: Stagecoach Press, 1967); Rebecca McDowell Craver, *The Impact of Intimacy: Mexican-Anglo Intermarriage in New Mexico, 1821–1846* (El Paso: University of Texas Press, 1982); Stella M. Drumm, *Down the Santa Fé Trail and into Mexico: The Diary of Susan Shelby Magoffin, 1846–1847* (New Haven: Yale University Press, 1926).

48 Wallace, *Antoine Robidoux 1784–1860*, 1–2.

49 Ibid., 6.

50 See Thorne, *The Many Hands of My Relations*, 125–26.

51 Lecompte, "The Chouteaus," xviii.

52 Ibid., xvi–xvii.

53 By the beginning of the nineteenth century, it was estimated that two-thirds of St. Louis' population were cousins. See Thorne, *The Many Hands of My Relations*, 84, 114. According to Janet Lecompte, "when the widow Chouteau died in 1814, it was said that all the prominent people in St. Louis could legitimately put on mourning for her." See Lecompte, xiii.

54 Joseph Robidoux III married twice, first to Eugénie Bienvenu dit Delisle, and a second time to Angélique Vaudry in 1814 after the death of his first wife. François Robidoux married Thérèse Bienvenu dit Delisle in 1807. Michel Robidoux married Susanne Vaudry of Cahokia, the twin sister of his brother Joseph's second wife Angélique, in 1825. For records of these marriages, including that of Isidore Robidoux and Julia Desjarlais, see Robidoux, *Memorial to the Robidoux Brothers*, 277–84, and St. Louis Genealogical Society, *Catholic Marriages St. Louis, Missouri 1774–1840*: 34.

55 A St. Louis census conducted in the 1830s notes the presence of six slaves in the household, two adult males, one adult female, and three children. Other letters from Joseph Robidoux to Pierre Chouteau and Jean P. Sarpy, requesting permission to draw funds from the company account, make reference to Isidore needing money to purchase farmland. See Lewis, "Pierre Isadore Robidoux," 2.

56 See Thorne, *The Many Hands of My Relations*, 127.

57 Ibid., 155–56.

58 Weber, *The Taos Trappers: The Fur Trade in the Far Southwest, 1540–1846*, 85; William S. Wallace, "Antoine Robidoux," in LeRoy Hafen, ed., *French Fur Traders and Voyageurs in the American West* (Lincoln: University of Nebraska Press, 1997), 270–71; Wallace, *Antoine Robidoux 1784–1860*, 10–11.

59 Craver, *The Impact of Intimacy*, 26–29.

60 Ibid., 29.

61 Ibid., 30–31, 38–39.

62 See Appendix 2, "The Mexican-Anglo Unions Arranged Alphabetically by the Men's Surnames," Craver, *The Impact of Intimacy*, 57.

63 See Weber, *The Taos Trappers: The Fur Trade in the Far Southwest, 1540–1846*, 88.

64 Baptismal records indicate that François Robidoux was fathering children with his creole wife Thérèse Bienvenu Delisle as late as 1830–31. See entry for Genevieve Robidou, christened 27 April 1831 in St. Louis, Missouri (parents: François Robidoux and Thérèse Bienvenu Delisle), St. Louis Genealogical Society, *Earl Fischer Database of St. Louisans*, ibid. It is not clear when François established his common-law relationship with Luisa Romero, though church records indicate that three of her sisters contracted marriages with *extranjeros* in 1826 and 1829, respectively. See Appendix 1"The Mexican-Anglo Unions Arranged Alphabetically by the Women's Surnames," Appendix 2 – "The Mexican-Anglo Unions Arranged Alphabetically by the Men's Surnames," and Appendix III "Church-Sanctioned Mexican-Anglo Marriages Arranged by Year," in Craver, *The Impact of Intimacy*, 49–53, 54–57, 58–60.

65 See Wallace, *Antoine Robidoux 1784–1860*, 13.

66 Collet's Index, Grantors, p., 848: R2 181, St. Louis City Recorder of Deeds, as quoted by Lewis, "Pierre Isidore Robidoux," 3–4.

67 Apparently Pierre-Isidore Robidoux did not remain in Santa Fe. He eventually died in Nebraska on 30 May 1852. His estate was admitted to probate at St. Joseph, Missouri on 6 July 1852. See Louise Barry, *The Beginnings of the West: Annals of the Kansas Gateway to the American West, 1540–1854* (Topeka: Kansas State Historical Society, 1972). Descendant Hugh M. Lewis documents Isadore's activites in Kansas and Nebraska on his website "Pierre Isidore Robidoux,": http://www.lewismicr opublishing.com/Publications/RobidouxPierreIsadore.htm (accessed 1 July 2000; site now discontinued).

68 An electronic document entitled "Some St. Louis Divorces and Separations (1808–1863 accessed August 2000)" (http://genealogyinstlouis.accessge nealogy.com/dldivorces.htm), part of a larger electronic website entitled *Genealogy in St Louis* (http://genealogyinstlouis.accessgenealogy.com), summarizes hundreds of divorces and separations printed in St. Louis newspapers during the time frame indicated. Among them is the following entry: "Robidoux, Julie vs., Isidore-Divorce-date missing. (married about 22 years ago, came to Missouri after that. Has one son age 16. Robidoux left her about 4 years ago and went to Mexico)." Using marriage and birth data, it can be determined that the divorce was filed in 1837–1838, probably after the Robidoux brothers relinquished their St. Louis property to their wives. The divorce action is unusual, given that there are very few French names listed in divorce actions during that period, probably due to Catholic restrictions on divorce and the social disgrace that invariably resulted.

69 Guyon, *Étude généalogique sur Jean Guyon et ses descendants*, 126–27. Guyon's great-uncle was one of the sons of Pierre-Madore Desjarlais and Angelique Saucier of Rivière-du-Loup. In Guyon's telling of the tale, the capture took place in California (then a Spanish possession). However, it is probable that the event actually took place in areas of New Mexico

or East Texas where Comanche territory extended during the nineteenth century. During this period, the fur trade of the American Southwest was largely controlled by the Robidoux brothers and their associates from the Spanish settlement of Santa Fe, within one hundred miles of Comanche territory. For maps of the extent of Comanche territory in the nineteenth century, see Thomas W. Kavanagh, "Comanche," in Raymond J. Demallie, ed., *Handbook of North American Indians*, vol. 13, *Plains* (part 2 of 2) (Washington, D.C.: Smithsonian Institution, 2001), 886–87.

70 The first Desjarlais family in Canada was that of its founder, Jean-Jacques De Gerlaise and hs wife Marie-Jeanne Trudel who married in 1667. Their Lamirande grandsons were living in the Illinois country by 1750, while the Desjarlais great-grandchildren migrated in the mid-1780s, approximately 120 years after their ancestors' marriage.

71 See Thorne, *The Many Hands of My Relations*, 214–18.

Chapter 4

1 This figure is based on information from indexed engagment contracts. There is a possibility that other Desjarlais engagements are simply not on record. As Fernand Ouellet has noted, the *Repertoire des Engagements pour l'Ouest* and the Quebec notarial records are notoriously incomplete. Trading licences and engagements negotiated privately are not included in these records, nor are engagements that were contracted in the interior. See Ouellet, *Economy, Class and Nation*, 194–95.

2 A version of this chapter has been published in Theodore Binnema, Gerhard J. Ens and R. C. Macleod, eds., *From Rupert's Land to Canada: Essays in Honour of John E. Foster* (Edmonton: University of Alberta Press, 2001), 129–58.

3 Gordon Charles Davidson, *The North West Company* (New York: Russell & Russell, 1967), 23. See also Harold A. Innis, *The Fur Trade in Canada* (Toronto: University of Toronto Press, 1956), 198.

4 Joseph Desjarlais Sr. had married Marie-Josephte Hervieux on 23 May 1752. They had eleven children. See Doucet, "Généalogie de Gerlaise-Desjarlais," 80.

5 See Innis, *The Fur Trade in Canada*, 198.

6 Ibid., 188–99.

7 Ibid., 180–81.

8 Ibid., 188–200. See also Davidson, *The North West Company*, 3–31.

9 See Pierre Tousignant and Madeleine Dionne-Tousignant, "Luc de La Corne," *DCB*, 4:425–28.

10 After the British conquest of Canada, their currrency system was introduced into Quebec. After 1777 the "Halifax pound" became the standard of currency, although French units of currency continued to appear in business and in the countryside. According to Allan Greer, one pound in Halifax currency was equal to one *livre*; one *livre* was worth 20 *sols*; 20 *sols* equalled one *chelin*, or shilling. However, Harry Duckworth's research suggests that the North West Company considered a Halifax

pound to be worth approximately 12 *livres* during the 1780s. Based on Duckworth's values, the 4,690 *livre* loan that Desjarlais and Plante contracted would have been worth approximately 390 pounds Halifax currency. If they paid 1,000 livres for a guide, and 800 livres apiece for a *gouvernail* (steersman) and a *devant* (bowsman), and 550 livres apiece for three *milieu* (middlemen), they would have devoted much of the loan to wages. It is probable that Desjarlais and Plante would have needed to forego their own wages as canoemen and use the money for trade goods. See Harry W. Duckworth, "Introduction," in Duckworth, *English River Book*, xi–xxxviii; xxviii–xxix; and 178–79. See also "Appendix 7: Units of Measure and Currency," in Greer, *Peasant, Lord and Merchant*, 250.

11 See "Inventaire des Biens de La Succession de L'Honerable Luc De Chap Ecuyer Sr. De LaCorne," in Quebec Provincial Archives, *Rapport de l'archiviste de la province de Québec pour 1943–44* (Quebec: Redempti Paradis, 1948), 37–63. This document suggests that Joseph Desjarlais and Ambroise Plante contracted a sizeable debt around the same time that Joseph Desjarlais and Baptiste Plante obtained their trading licence and outfitted their canoe for the interior. While it is not clear whether the Joseph Desjarlais identified in the inventory is Joseph Desjarlais Jr. or Sr., it is probable that the Ambroise Plante mentioned is the Ambroise Plante, from the parish of Sorel, who married Joseph Desjarlais' Jr.'s cousin Archange (daughter of Pierre-Amador Desjarlais and Madeleine Duval) at Rivière-du-Loup in 1781. See PRDH, Record #217815 (Marriage record for Ambroise Plante and Archange Jerlais at Rivière-du-Loup, 19 November 1781).

12 See "Appendix," in Arthur S. Morton, ed., *The Journal of Duncan M'Gillivray* (Toronto: Macmillan of Canada, 1929), 18–21. See also Ouellet, "Economic Dualism," where he explains how transportation costs, labour costs, and competition placed pressure on small operators of all ethnic stripes, forcing amalgamation. In Ouellet, *Economy, Class and Nation*, 161–209.

13 The family relationships are (predictably) complex. Marie-Josephe Desjarlais, Joseph Desjarlais' sister, had married Michel Gélinas dit Lacourse, Toussaint Lesieur's second cousin. Madeleine Desjarlais, Joseph Desjarlais' first cousin, was married to Alexis Gélinas dit Lacourse. Her mother-in-law was Marie-Catherine Lesieur Desaulniers, first cousin to Toussaint Lesieur's father Charles. See Jetté, *DGFQ*, 483 for the genealogy of the first generations of the Gelinas family, and 722–23, for the genealogy of the first generations of the Lesieur family. See PRDH, Record #29754 *Family Group Sheet for Joseph Jarlais St. Amand and Marie Joseph Hervieux Lesperance*, where the marriage of their daughter Marie Josephe to Michel Gelinas Lacourse is recorded as having taken place 31 January 1774 at Varennes. See also PRDH, Record #62543, *Family Group Sheet for Alexis Gelinas and Marie Madeleine Jarlais St. Amand*, where their marriage is recorded as having taken place 9 January 1786.

14 See the brief biography of Toussaint Lesieur in Appendix B, "Biographies of Voyageurs and Traders," in Duckworth, *English River Book*, 156–58.

15 See Fr. Pierre Picton to Mr. Coté, Saint-Norbert, Manitoba dated 12 September 1947. Desjarlais Family File, *Pierre Picton Papers*, St. Boniface Historical Society, St. Boniface, Manitoba.

16 In the fur trade documents, several different spellings of the name Tullibee appear, e.g., Tolibee, Tullibii, etc., I have chosen to use a standardized spelling for the name; Tullibee (which translates as "Whitefish").

17 See Father Picton's notations in the Desjarlais Family File, *Pierre Picton Papers*, St. Boniface Historical Society, St. Boniface, Manitoba. When discussing Desjarlais genealogy over the telephone with two *métis* Cree people from the Lesser Slave Lake region of northern Alberta, both individuals responded immediately, and in the identical manner, when I mentioned the name Okimaskwew – "Boss Lady!" My thanks to Doreen Wabasca of Edmonton, Alberta and Gordon Sinclair of Slave Lake, Alberta. Both meanings of the term "okimaskwew" are listed in H.C. Wolfart and Freda Ahenakew, *The Student's Dictionary of Literary Plains Cree* (Winnipeg: Algonquian and Iroquoian Linguistics, 1988). See also Charles Mair's reference to Queen Victoria's Cree appellation, "*Kitche Okemasquay*," which supports the translation of "boss-lady." In Charles Mair, *Through the Mackenzie Basin: An Account of the Signing of Treaty No. 8 and the Scrip Commission, 1899*. Introductions by David W. Leonard and Brian Calliou. (1908; reprint, copublished by: Edmonton and District Historical Society and University of Alberta Press, Edmonton, 1997).

18 Ruth Landes, *The Ojibwa Woman*. (1938; reprint, London and Lincoln: University of Nebraska Press, 1997), 124.

19 Ibid., 136.

20 That at least some *engagés* harboured these sentiments is illustrated by Duncan McGillivray, who noted the following interpretation of "sundogs" in the winter sky by his *engagés*: "Among many constructions put upon this wonderfull phenomenon, a few Canadians who are still attached to their Mother country make it ominous of the present situation of France. – for as the sun has dispersed and outshone these other luminaries, which seemed to rival it in brightness, so in like manner (they fondly presage) will France after a long struggle overcome and triumph over all her enemies." Morton, *Journal of Duncan M'Gillivray*, 68.

21 See "Introduction," p. li, of Morton, *Journal of Duncan M'Gillivray*, regarding David Grant's break with the North West Company. The date of Antoine Desjarlais' engagement with the Grants suggest that they had been planning to leave the North West Company prior to 1793.

22 Harry Duckworth, Winnipeg, Manitoba to the author, re: engagements of Antoine Desjarlais. Letter dated Monday, 30 March 1998. See also *RAPQ* (1942–43), 318, 356. On 3 February 1804 Alexander Henry the Younger visited Antoine Desjarlais and his country wife at their cabin on the east shore of Lake Manitoba, where Antoine was netting whitefish. See Elliott Coues, ed., *The Manuscript Journals of Alexander Henry the Younger and David Thompson 1799–1816*, 2 vols. (Minneapolis: Ross & Haines,

1965), 1:237. See also W. Kaye Lamb, *The Journal of Gabriel Franchère* (Toronto: Champlain Society, 1969), 167–68.

23 See *RAPQ* (1942–43), 313, for the 14 June 1792 engagement of François Desjarlais with McTavish Frobisher to "aller au Nord." The relationship between François Desjarlais and the brothers Joseph and Antoine Desjarlais is not fully understood. See Appendix 1 for a detailed discussion of same.

24 See HBCA 1M779 B/115/E/1, *Lesser Slave Lake Report on District 1819–1820*. This definition was expanded by William Conolly in the Lesser Slave Lake Report on District 1821–22 (HBCA 1M779 B/115/E/3), who stated "... the People who go under the Dinomation of Free Men Consist of Canadians, Halfbreeds, Iroquois, Sauteux, Courteroielles, and Nepisingues who were, during the late opposition, accustomed to get good to any amount they pleased, and at very reduced prices."

25 Population figures are sketchy due to the mobility of *Canadien* and Iroquois freemen, who were encouraged by the fur companies to travel widely after furs. Trudy Nicks identifies five "neighbourhoods" in the Athabasca region frequented by freemen: the Lower Peace River; the Upper Peace River; Smoky River/Jasper House; Upper Athabasca; and Lesser Slave Lake/Lac La Biche. Trudy Nicks states that in the Lesser Slave Lake District alone there were twenty-three freemen, sixteen women, and fifty-eight "subadults" for a total of ninety-seven in 1820. If one assumes that most adult women were married *à la façon du pays* to a freeman, this would amount to at least fifteen nuclear families, living in possibly seven or eight extended family units, based on the average size of boreal forest hunting bands. According to Nicks, the greatest concentration of freemen was in the Lesser Slave Lake/Lac La Biche "neighbourhood." In 1822 the number of freemen hunters outnumbered the local Cree hunters by fifty to thirty men. In 1823 there were fifty freemen recorded as hunters in the Lesser Slave Lake District; the total freeman family population was 184. See Trudy Nicks, *Demographic Anthropology of Native Populations in Western Canada, 1800–1975* (unpublished PhD dissertation, University of Alberta, Edmonton, 1980), 35, 56–57, 59.

26 See Coues, *Manuscript Journals*, 2:609–14, 612–13.

27 According to Hudson's Bay Company records, Tullibee was 34 years of age in 1820, which would place his birthdate approximately 1786. Because these accounts indicate repeatedly that Joseph Desjarlais' sons by this woman were Tullibee's half-brothers, Tullibee would appear to be Joseph's stepson. See HBCA B/115/E/3, *Lesser Slave Lake Report on District 1819–1820*, for a description of Tullibee.

28 See Coues, *Manuscript Journals,*, 2:624. By 26 September 1810, Henry himself was headed towards the mountains, where various members of the Desjarlais family, including Joseph Sr., his son Baptiste (b. ca. 1787) and Joseph's relative François were wintering with David Thompson at Rocky Mountain House and engaged in hunting and trading with the Peigans and Sarcees. See Coues, *Manuscript Journals*, 2:659, 665–66, 675, 691.

29 There are other scholarly monographs that discuss the activities of free-
    men (and the Desjarlais in particular) in the Lesser Slave Lake area. One
    article which focuses exclusively on the effects of trading competition and
    monopoly on freemen bands is Trudy Nicks, "Native Responses to the
    Early Fur Trade at Lesser Slave Lake," in Bruce Trigger, Toby Morantz,
    and Louise Dechêne, eds., 'Le Castor Fait Tout': Selected Papers of the
    Fifth North American Fur Trade Conference (Montreal: Lake St. Louis
    Historical Society, 1987), 278–310. See also D.R. Babcock, Lesser Slave
    Lake: A Regional History (unpublished manuscript on file, Historic Sites
    Service, Historic Sites and Cultural Facilities Division, Alberta Community
    Development); W. P. Baergen, The Fur Trade at Lesser Slave Lake, 1815–
    1831 (unpublished MA thesis, University of Alberta, 1967); and Edward
    J. McCullough and Michael Maccagno, Lac La Biche and the Early Fur
    Traders (Edmonton: Canadian Circumpolar Institute, 1991).

30 See Coues, Manuscript Journals, 2:614.

31 On 9 December 1817, Lewes notes: "This evening Joseph Desjarlais
    arrived from his father's tent." On 11 December, Lewes states "This
    morning Jos. Desjarlais returned to his tent and three NWt. with him. I
    accordingly sent off Antoine and one man after them." See HBCA, Lesser
    Slave Lake Post Journal 1817–1818, B/115/a/1; and Lesser Slave Lake
    Post Journal 1818–1819, B/115/a/2.

32 See entries for 17–25 February 1819 by John Lee Lewes in HBCA, B/115/
    a/1, Lesser Slave Lake Post Journal 1817–1819.

33 See entries for 10 March and 3 April 1819 by John Lee Lewes in HBCA,
    B/115/a/1, Lesser Slave Lake Post Journal 1817–1819.

34 See HBCA, Lesser Slave Lake Report on District 1819–1820, B/115/E/3.

35 As described by trader George Nelson in Jennifer S.H. Brown and Robert
    Brightman, eds., "The Orders of the Dreamed": George Nelson on Cree
    and Northern Ojibwa Religion and Myth, 1823 (Winnipeg: University
    of Manitoba Press, 1988), 50. Brown and Brightman also noted that
    George Nelson was the first person to place "on record the only known
    identification of The Sun with the Euro-Canadian traders, this spirit
    speaks English, wears English clothing, and possesses the power to repair
    firearms." See 113.

36 See entry for 5 October 1819 in HBCA, B/104/a/2, Journal of Lesser Slave
    Lake District – Lac La Biche 1819–20.

37 See entry for 30 October in HBCA, B/115/A/4, Lesser Slave Lake Post
    Journal 1820–1821. In this passage it is clear that Tullibee was well aware
    of his responsibilities as chief and benefactor to his followers, in that he
    expressed regret at not being able to immediately redistribute the wealth
    among them.

38 See entries for 2–4 May 1819 in HBCA, B/115/A/2, Lesser Slave Lake Post
    Journal 1818–1819.

39 Ibid.

40 Where was Antoine Desjarlais, who had acted as Lesser Slave Lake
    interpreter prior to this point? We know that he was travelling inNorthern
    Alberta in the summer of 1819 (see note 273): Another clue to Antoine's

whereabouts is provided by Isaac Cowie, in his "Editorial Notes" for *The Journal of Daily Occurrences at the Hudson's Bay Company's Fort Ellice, Swan River District – From 1st May 1858 to 27th April 1859*, 39. He discusses Antoine Desjarlais in endnote #21: "Antoine Desgarlais [*sic*] was a Metis employee, who in the days of conflict between the H.B. and N.W. Companies had been employed by the H.B.C. to take out letters from Athabasca to Red River during the winter. He had to avoid being taken prisoner by the N.W.C. on his long solitary journey, full of privations, but succeeded eventually."

41 See HBCA, *Lesser Slave Lake Report on District 1819–1820*, B/115/E/3. Robert Kennedy was in charge of the Lesser Slave Lake Post during the latter half of 1820 in the absence of John Lee Lewes, who travelled elsewhere in the district to trade. See McCullough and Maccagno, *Lac La Biche and the Early Fur Traders*, 102–3.

42 Northern Algonquians believed that spirit helpers could take on a variety of human, animal, or other forms in real-life encounters. From a spiritual perspective, the seemingly impossible victory of Baptiste Desjarlais in a trading post brawl over impossible odds is the kind of everyday event which assumes supernatural implications when other corroborating events take place. See Brown and Brightman, "*Orders of the Dreamed*," 120.

43 Ojibwa children were always given names by their grandfathers, or a member of their grandfathers' generation. "The name carries with it a special blessing because it has reference to a dream of the human grandfather in which he obtained power from one or more of the other-than-human grandfathers." See A. Irving Hallowell, "Ojibwa Ontology, Behavior, and World View," in *Contributions to Anthropology: Selected Papers of A. Irving Hallowell*, 360, and further discussion in Appendix 2.

44 See Lamb, *The Journal of Gabriel Franchère*, 167–68 where Franchère encounters Antoine Desjarlais at Lac La Biche, and reads his letters for him, due to his illiteracy. It is possible that Antoine Desjarlais made this request of Franchère due to shared family and community ties. Gabriel Franchère's cousin, Thercille Franchère, married Jean-Baptiste Picotte, son of Jean Picotte and Hélène Desjarlais, in 1806. Hélène Desjarlais, daughter of Louis Desjarlais and Catherine Banliac Lamontagne, was a first cousin to both Antoine and Joseph Desjarlais. See PRDH, Record #361435; Marriage of Jean Baptiste Picot and Hélène Dejarlais, 20 October 1775, Louisville Quebec, and Milot, *Famille Picotte*, for records of their children's marriages.

45 See entry for 10 September 1820 in HBCA, B/115/A/4, *Lesser Slave Lake Post Journal 1820–1821*. Joseph Desjarlais' travels between Montreal and the *pays d'en haut* suggest that he was much more devoted to maintaining his kin relationships in *both* environments than many of the stereotypic depictions of freemen would suggest. As recently as 1968, Frederick Merk described freemen as follows: "They were usually worn-out voyageurs... [who]... chose to remain in the Indian country living among the natives. Shiftless and irresponsible, they found in the Indian country refuge both from the necessity of regular labor and the restraints of civilized life."

See Frederick Merk, *Fur Trade and Empire* (Cambridge, Mass.: Harvard University Press, 1968), 20.

46 See the biographical sketch of Antoine Desjarlais in E.E. Rich, ed., *Journal of Occurrences in the Athabasca Department by George Simpson, 1820 and 1821, and Report* (Toronto: Champlain Society, 1938), 436. In this summary, Antoine is identified as "a Canadian, born in 1792." Because it was HBC practice to ascribe biracial employees of some status with the ethnicity of their Euro-Canadian fathers, this may account for the description of Antoine Desjarlais as "a Canadian." See Jennifer Brown, "Linguistic Solitudes and Changing Social Categories," in Judd and Ray, *Old Trails and New Directions*, 147–59, where she notes that the application of various ethnic identities to individuals was contextually-bound. It was determined by company affiliation, local usage in specific geographical areas, and rather arbitrary labelling based on the social and cultural attributes exhibited by individuals, regardless of the identities these actors might have ascribed to themselves.

47 Although John Foster's essay on the emergence of freemen, and the marital patterns of Red River Métis (e.g., see Sprague and Frye, *The Genealogy of the First Métis Nation: The Development and Dispersal of the Red River Settlement, 1820–1900*) suggest that the marriages of freemen families were primarily endogamous, this was not the case in Northern Alberta. The boreal forest environment, which favoured the proliferation of hunter-gatherer bands, and the lack of permanent Euro-Canadian settlements and religious influences in the first half of the nineteenth century, delayed the development of endogamous marital patterns among the *métis* children of Canadien freemen. See Chapter 5 of this study, where these ideas are developed further.

48 See Appendix 2 for a detailed discussion of these early unions.

49 McCullough and Maccagno, *Lac La Biche and the Early Fur Traders*, 95–102.

50 HBCA, B/104/a2, *Journal of Lesser Slave Lake District – Lac La Biche 1819–20.*

51 The clerk in charge is believed to have been Robert Kennedy. John Lee Lewes left the post frequently on business, and reference is made to Lewes having gone to Rock Depot to apply for advances promised to Antoine Desjarlais in the fall of 1819, but not given. See entries for 17 February 1820 and 1 May 1820. HBCA, B/104/A2, *Journal of Lesser Slave Lake District – Lac La Biche 1819–20.*

52 HBCA, B/115/E/2, *Lesser Slave Lake Report on District 1820–1821.* It is possible that Thomas Desjarlais later died from the effects of his illness, because there is no definitive documentary evidence that he formed any unions *à la façon du pays* in subsequent years, or sired any children.

53 See R. Harvey Fleming, ed., *Minutes of Council Northern Department of Rupert Land, 1821–31* (Toronto: Champlain Society, 1940), 2–7. See also McCullough and Maccagno, *Lac La Biche and the Early Fur Traders*, 103–4.

54 See R. Harvey Fleming, *Journal of Occurrences in the Athabasca Department*, 68.

55 See HBCA, B/190/A/2, *Fort St. Mary Post Journal, 1819–1820*, entry for Tuesday, 24 August 1819.

56 HBCA, B/115/A/5, *Lesser Slave Lake Post Journal 1821–22*.

57 Ibid.

58 Ibid.

59 See HBCA, B/115/E/3, *Lesser Slave Lake Report on District 1821–22*.

60 Ibid.

61 In the post-coalition Hudson's Bay Company, mixed ancestry hampered one's opportunities for advancement. As the uneducated son of a *Canadien* freeman, Antoine would have had no future whatsoever outside of a labouring capacity. See Jennifer Brown, *Strangers in Blood: Fur Trade Company Families in Indian Country* (Vancouver: University of British Columbia Press, 1980) for her discussions of social mobility and mixed-blood populations. See also Merk, *Fur Trade and Empire*, xxxxi–xxxxiii, for a summary of the organizational hierarchy of the Hudson's Bay Company after 1821.

62 B/115/E/3, *Lesser Slave Lake Report on District 1821–22*.

63 B/115/A/6, *Lesser Slave Lake Post Journal 1822–23*.

64 Ibid.

65 Ibid.

66 B/115/E/4, *Lesser Slave Lake Report on District 1822–1823*.

67 Ibid.

68 See HBCA, B/89/A/7, *Ile-à-la-Crosse Post Journals*, where George Keith notes on Sunday, 14 December 1823 that "the Plains Cree of the Saskatchewan acquaint them [the local woodland Cree] that there is an American Party (probably the Scientific & Exploratory Expedn that reached Red River in August last) have reached the skirts of the Rocky Mountain and is selling large Blankets for only 5 Muskrats apiece and other articles in a like proportion! Hence they conclude and were strongly assured by the above informants, that they will soon see an opposition in this Country." A likely source of an "American Party" during this period would be the trapping expeditions funded by William Henry Ashley, c. 1778–1838, a fur trader and politician based in St. Louis. He and his partner, Andrew Henry, advertised widely in the St. Louis newspapers for "free trappers." He sent fur-trading expeditions up the Missouri River to the Yellowstone in 1822 and 1823, and was responsible for organizing the first of the annual Rocky Mountain trappers' "rendezvous." It is obvious that this news was spreading like wildfire amongst the Natives and freemen of Rupert's Land. See also William R. Swagerty and Dick A. Wilson, "Faithful Service Under Different Flags: A Socioeconomic Profile of the Columbia District, Hudson's Bay Company and the Upper Missouri Outfit, American Fur Company, 1825–1835," in Jennifer S.H. Brown, W.J. Eccles, and Donald P. Heldman, eds., *The Fur Trade Revisited: Selected Papers of the Sixth North American Fur Trade Conference, Mackinac*

Island, Michigan, 1991 (East Lansing: Michigan State University Press, 1994), 243–44.

69 B/115/e/4, *Lesser Slave Lake Report on District 1822–1823.*

70 See Merk, *Fur Trade and Empire,* 20.

71 For a regional perspective on these issues, see Swagerty and Wilson, "Faithful Service Under Different Flags," 243–67. See also Edith I. Burley, *Servants of the Honourable Company: Work, Discipline and Conflict in the Hudson's Bay Company, 1770–1879* (Toronto: Oxford University Press, 1997), 85–96; and the Introduction to Fleming, *Minutes of Council Northern Department of Rupert Land, 1821–31,* xi – lxxii which discuss, in some detail, the strategies adopted by the Hudson's Bay Company to manage *Canadien engagés,* curtail costs and neutralize American competition.

72 Merk, *Fur Trade and Empire,* 22.

73 Fleming, *Minutes of Council Northern Department of Rupert Land, 1821–31,* 120.

74 See Chapter 5, "World View and Environment," in A. Irving Hallowell, *Ojibwa of Berens River, Manitoba,* Jennifer S.H. Brown, ed. (New York: Harcourt Brace Jovanovich, 1992), 62.

75 See A. Irving Hallowell, "Ojibwa World View and Disease," in *Contributions to Anthropology* (Chicago: University of Chicago Press, 1976), 418–19.

76 See Roger McDonnell, *Paper on Band Formation Used as Supporting Evidence in the Bill C-31 Litigation* (Unpublished manuscript on file, Department of History and Classics, University of Alberta, n.d., 67–68.)

77 Marguerite Desjarlais (b. at Sorel on 28 February 1766) married Isidore Langevin at Varennes on 9 July 1782. Another sister, Judith (b. at Sorel on 29 August 1758) married her second husband, Louis-Augustin Fontaine dit Bienvenu at Varennes on 7 May 1802. See Doucet, "Généalogie de Gerlaise-Desjarlais," 81–82. One of these sisters was writing to Antoine while he was at Lac La Biche, as Gabriel Franchère noted in June of 1814: "He [Desjarlais] asked me to read two letters that he had in his possession for two years without finding anyone able to read them. They were dated from Varennes and were from one of his sisters." See Coues, *Manuscript Journals,* 1: 237n6. See also Lamb, *The Journal of Gabriel Franchère,* 167–68.

78 See Curatelle #525, dated 21 October 1825. "Tutelles et Curatelles," Archives Nationales du Québec à Montréal (microfilm #s 1800–1841), as quoted in "Absents – Curatelles de Personnes Absentes du District de Montréal du 03-09-1794 – 30-03-1830." (Unpublished manuscript on file, St. Boniface Historical Society, Winnipeg.)

79 The economic crises in Lower Canada, beginning in the 1820s, are believed to have contributed to the Rebellion in Lower Canada in the 1830s. See Fernand Ouellet, *Lower Canada 1791–1840: Social Change and Nationalism* (Toronto: McClelland and Stewart, 1980).

80 B/115/A/8, *Lesser Slave Lake Post Journal 1826–1827.*

81 These numerical estimates of seasonal band populations, and those that follow, are based on the field research of Irving A. Hallowell, who studied the ecological cycles of the Berens River Ojibwa in Manitoba during the 1930s. See Hallowell, "Northern Ojibwa Ecological Adaptation and Social Organization," in *Contributions to Anthropology*, 334–36.

82 Among the northern Ojibwa with whom Hallowell worked, rights to specific hunting territories were recognized, and trespass was resented. Hallowell noted that the Natives were able to identify the approximate boundaries of hunting territories, which Hallowell then recorded on maps. See A. Irving Hallowell, "Northern Ojibwa Ecological Adaptation and Social Organization," 335. See also Chapter 4, "Ecological Adaptation and Social Organization," in Hallowell, *Ojibwa of Berens River, Manitoba*, 44–46.

83 Hallowell found no surviving tradition among the Ojibwa for the allocation of hunting regions through chiefs or headmen. See Hallowell, *Ojibwa of Berens River, Manitoba*, 46.

84 See Eugene Y. Arima, *Blackfeet and Palefaces: The Pikani and Rocky Mountain House* (Ottawa: Golden Dog Press, 1995), 96–98, 138–40; John S. Milloy, *The Plains Cree: Trade, Diplomacy and War, 1790 to 1870* (Winnipeg: University of Manitoba Press, 1988), xv–xvi; 12–23, and Peers, *The Ojibwa of Western Canada*, 6–7.

85 See Roger McDonnell, *Paper on Band Formation*, 23, 37–45, 47–48, 50, 51–54.

86 See Brown and Brightman, "*Orders of the Dreamed*," 145.

87 Ibid., 120.

88 Hallowell, "Ojibwa Ontology, Behavior, and World View," in *Contributions to Anthropology* (Chicago: University of Chicago Press, 1976), 383–85.

89 See McDonnell, *Paper on Band Formation*, 41.

90 George Nelson, a North West and later Hudson's Bay Company clerk, occasionally consulted conjurors to locate missing men, to divine information, and to assist in locating game animals for food. See Brown and Brightman, "*Orders of the Dreamed*," 8–9. He also commented on the use of conjuring to curse rival hunters, to wit (p. 71): "... they succeed in bewitching any one they are averse to, and prevent them from killing such animals as they please. They draw the likeness of the animal or animals they do not chuse the others to kill, part of this medicine (tho' most commonly mixed with some others in this latter case) upon the hearts, and desire that they may become shy and fly off upon any the least appearance or approach of them. Or they will conjure, and desire some one of their *familiars*, one, or several, to *haunt such a one* in all his motions and scare and frighten off, and *render wise* any *such* and *such* animals; and let the distance be hundreds of miles off – their familiars that are spirits residing in the air, and transport themselves in an instant to any place they please and who see all that is going on *below*, keep *all* away accordingly. To evade this is a task but few succeed in."

91 A. Irving Hallowell, *The Role of Conjuring in Saulteaux Society* (Philadelphia: University of Pennsylvania Press, 1942), 27–29.

92 G. Williams, ed., *Andrew Graham's Observations on Hudson's Bay, 1767–91* (London: Hudson's Bay Record Society, 1969), 169–70, as quoted by Ray and Freeman in '*Give Us Good Measure*', 17.

93 See McDonnell, *Paper on Band Formation*, 43.

94 Ibid., 50.

95 Williams, *Andrew Graham's Observations on Hudson's Bay, 1767–91*, 169–70, as quoted by Ray and Freeman in '*Give Us Good Measure': An Economic Analysis of Relations Between the Indians and the Hudson's Bay Company Before 1763*, 15.

96 For a detailed discussion of Euro-Canadian wintering practices and the factors and processes governing Euro-Canadian integration into aboriginal hunting bands, see Foster, "Wintering, the Outsider Adult Male and the Ethnogenesis of the Western Plains Métis," 8–17.

97 Peers, *The Ojibwa of Western Canada*, 12–13, 36–37.

Chapter 5

1 Burley, *Servants of the Honourable Company*, 40.

2 See Grace Lee Nute, "Introduction," in Grace Lee Nute, ed., *Documents Relating to Northwest Missions, 1815–1827* (St. Paul: Minnesota Historical Society, 1942), xiii.

3 See J.O. Plessis, Bishop of Quebec, Quebec City, to Fr. Antoine Tabeau, Montreal, "Instructions for Messrs. J.N. Provencher and J.N.S. Dumoulen, missionaries assigned to the Indian country situated to the north and west of Canada," dated 20 April 1818, in Nute, *Documents Relating to Northwest Missions*, 58–61. See also Huel, *Proclaiming the Gospel to the Indians and the Métis*, 11–12.

4 Fr. Dumoulin, Pembina to J.O. Plessis, Bishop of Quebec, Quebec City dated 5 January 1819; see also Dumoulin, Rainy Lake, to Plessis, Quebec City dated 27 July 1819; and Dumoulin, St. Boniface to Plessis, Quebec City dated 16 August 1821 in Nute, *Documents Relating to Northwest Missions*, ibid., 168–72, 242–47 and 314–27.

5 See Dumoulin, Pembina to Plessis, Quebec City dated 4 January 1819; see also Destroismaisons, St. Boniface to Bishop Plessis, 3 January 1821 in Grace Lee Nute, ed., *Documents Relating to Northwest Missions*, 172–76, 281–83.

6 Provencher, St. Boniface to Plessis, Quebec City dated 31 January 1819; Dumoulin, Pembina to Bishop Panet, Rivière Ouelle, dated 30 January 1820; Dumoulin, St. Boniface, to Plessis, Quebec City dated 3 July 1820; and Plessis, Quebec City to Dumoulin, Red River dated 10 April 1821, in Nute, 198–99, 263–64, 269–71, 291–96.

7 Provencher, St. Boniface to Bishop Plessis, Quebec City, dated 29 November 1822. In Nute, 379–86.

8 The Rev. John West, sponsored by the Church Missionary Society, arrived in Lord Selkirk's colony in 1820, as a chaplain to the Hudson's

Bay Company. The Church Missionary Society made the Red River one of its missionary stations in 1822, and sent out the Rev. David Jones in 1823 and the Rev. and Mrs. William Cochran in 1824. In Nute, 257n13, 437n93. The arrival of Protestant missionaries and their social impact at Red River is also discussed in Frits Pannekoek, *A Snug Little Flock: The Social Origins of the Riel Resistance of 1869–1870* (Winnipeg: Watson & Dwyer, 1991).

9 "Dumoulin's Plea for the Missions at Red River and Sault Ste Marie," dated 10 March 1824. In Nute, 415.

10 Huel, *Proclaiming the Gospel to the Indians and the Métis,* 12–14.

11 Information on Georges-Antoine Belcourt was taken from the following sources: James Michael Reardon, *George Anthony Belcourt: Pioneer Catholic Missionary of the Northwest, 1803–1874: His Life and Times* (St. Paul, Minn.: North Central Publishing, 1955); and "George-Antoine Bellecourt," *DCB,* 10:46–47.

12 Reardon, *George Anthony Belcourt,* 4–7; and and "George-Antoine Bellecourt," 46.

13 Ibid., 17–18.

14 See "Noms des homme qui ont été mariée par les Missionaires Catholiques depuis l'etablissement de la Mission de la Rivière Rouge en 1818 jusqu'an 15 Fevrier 1831." Undated MS, from the *Red River Collection,* Add. MSS 345, British Columbia Provincial Archives, Victoria, B.C., Joanne J. Hughes, transcriber.

15 The fate of Antoine Desjarlais is unknown. The last definitive record of his presence in Athabasca is an 1819 reference to "Old Antoine Desjarlais," in the Lesser Slave Lake post journal, though Frederick Merk also believes that the "Old Dejoilais" that George Simpson encountered in 1824 was Antoine Desjarlais as well. See HBCA, B/115 a1-a3, *Lesser Slave Lake Post Journal 1819,* and Merk, *Fur Trade and Empire,* 20. See Appendix 1 for further discussion of Antoine Desjarlais.

16 Antoine Desjarlais dit Moral is a shadowy figure who is often mistaken in the records for his métis cousin Antoine Desjarlais (the son of the *Canadien* freeman Joseph Desjarlais) or his *Canadien* cousin Antoine Desjarlais (the former postmaster at Lac La Biche, who was the brother of the *Canadien* freeman Old Joseph Desjarlais). His genealogy is not entirely clear; a search of Quebec parish records between 1793 and 1799 provides only one birthdate for an individual named Antoine Desjarlais. This Antoine Desjarlais, born 1 November 1795, is the son of Pierre-Madore Desjarlais and Angelique Saucier. This person married a woman named Marguerite Garceau in 1821, however, which eliminates him as a likely match for Antoine Desjarlais dit Moral. What we do know, is that this person identifies himself clearly, and repeatedly as a *Canadien* in the records available. For example, he identifies his origins as *Canadien* (and not as Red River British) in the Pembina censuses. In the Ile-à-la-Crosse records his origins are listed as Lower Canada.

17 In the "List of Families Supported at the Company's Establishments in the English River District," Antoine Dejarlais, a steersman (country of origin,

Canada) is listed as a "former protector or parent" of one woman and one female child. It further notes that Desjarlais' residence during 1823–24 was Canada, and that his dependents were placed under the care of Gons. Ayotte. See HBCA, B89, A7, *Ile-à-la-Crosse Post Journals, 1823–24*.

18 In a journal entry from July 1825 it notes that "Antoine de Charlait the Guide" was hired at Fort Alexander to lead the expedition as far as Fort Chipewyan. He was paid 1,395 livres in Old Quebec currency. See Richard Clark Davis, ed., *Sir John Franklin's Journals and Correspondence: The Second Arctic Land Expedition, 1825–1827* (Toronto: Champlain Society, 1998), 77–78.

19 References to various members of the Desjarlais family appear in the post journals for Cumberland House (1827–28); Carleton (1828–30), at Fort Pelly (1830–34), and at the Fishing Lakes along the Qu'Appelle River (1833–34). See summary in Peers, *The Ojibwa of Western Canada*, 104–7, 109–14.

20 See Peers, *The Ojibwa of Western Canada*, 112–14.

21 See Nicole J.M. St-Onge, "Variations in Red River: The Traders and Freemen Métis of Saint-Laurent, Manitoba," *Canadian Ethnic Studies* 24, no. 2 (1992): 3.

22 Information on the Okanase band comes from the following sources: Peter Lorenz Neufeld, "The Notable Michael Cardinal Family," *Indian Record* 49, no. 1 (January 1986): 20–21; Peter Lorenz Neufeld, "The Clear Lake Indian Cemetery," The *Minnedosa Tribune* (Minnedosa, Manitoba) Bo. 3, no. 50 (Wednesday, 2 March 1994): 30; Peter Lorenz Neufeld, "Keeseekoowenin," *DCB*, 13 (1901–1910): 537–38; N. Jaye Goosens, "Indians of the Fort Ellice Region." Unpublished manuscript on file, Historic Resources Branch, Province of Manitoba (March 1976), 21–22. See also the various scrip affidavits for members of the Okanase family in NAC, RG1, Dept. of the Interior, Series D-II-8-C, "William Desjarlais or Cardinal or Okanase" for his deceased daughter Marie (vol. 1344); "Caroline Okanase or Okanens or Desjarlais" (vol. 1362); "Pierre Okanase or Okanens or Desjarlais," heir to his deceased children (vol. 1362); "Antoine Bone or Okaness" (vol. 1337).

23 See *Register of Baptisms, Marriages and Deaths – St. Francis Xavier Church – Manitoba, Canada – 1834–1851*. Extracted from photocopy of original records (Portland, Oreg.: Genealogical Forum, n.d.); *Register of Baptisms, Marriages and Deaths – St. Francis Xavier Church – Manitoba, Canada – 1836–1863*. Photocopy of original records. The fate of Old Joseph Desjarlais' country wife, Okimaskwew, is unknown. There is a remote possibility that she is the woman referred to as "Old Wife Dijerlais" who appears in the *Ile-à-la-Crosse Post Journal* for 1861 trading for cloth and ammunition with her two sons, one of whom is named Michel, the other Thomas. See HBCA, B89, a31-a35, *Ile-à-la-Crosse Post Journals*, 1861–1865 (p. 42). The registers of St. Francis Xavier de la Prairie du Cheval Blanc (White Horse Plain), well into the 1840s, record the marriages of Joseph's sons, and the baptisms of their children. In 1869 members of the Desjarlais family were featured in the parish

records of Baie St. Paul, St. Laurent, and Whitemud River. See the file
for the Desjarlais family, and Father Picton's correspondence re: Joseph
Desjarlais and his sons, in the Desjarlais Family File, *Father Picton Papers*,
unpublished manuscript collection on file, St. Boniface Historical Society,
Winnipeg, Manitoba.

24 Of the Desjarlais family branches to settle at Baie St. Paul, the only
families that farmed on a relatively constant basis were the sons and
grandsons of François Desjarlais and Madeleine Roy, who continuously
occupied river lots at Baie St. Paul from the 1830s to the early to mid-
1870s. In 1870, the occupants of the following river lots were recorded:
grandson Antoine Desjarlais and his wife Louise Richard (at or between
Lots 227–219); son Baptiste Desjarlais and wife Marie Martin (Lot
215); grandson Louis Desjarlais and Julie Chartrand (at or between Lots
194–207); grandson Jean-Baptiste Desjarlais and Josephte Fleury (Lot
227); grandson Joseph Desjarlais and Isabelle Lafreniere (at or between
Lots 215–24). The exceptions were son Joseph Desjarlais and wife Marie
Slater, and grandson Antoine Desjarlais and Marie Falcon, who resided at
St. Laurent on the shore of Lake Manitoba. See Tables 4 and 5 of Sprague
and Frye, *The Genealogy of the First Métis Nation*; See also Gerhard Ens,
"Desjarlais Family – Land Holding Red River" (summary of landholdings
in the Parish of Baie St. Paul based on surveyors' notebooks and parish
files from the Provincial Archives of Manitoba, and the Manitoba
Act [scrip] files from the National Archives of Canada). Unpublished
manuscript, n.d., in the collection of the author.

25 In their correspondence to Bishop Plessis, the priests at Red River make
constant reference to the Old Canadiens and métis as "weak Christians,"
citing their numerous sins throughout their letters. See Nute, *Documents
Relating to Northwest Missions*, 283.

26 Louis Lamirande (claimant #375), who is listed as Louis Lamiraude, was
the son of Jacques Lamirande and Marie-Anne Hébert, of St. François
du Lac, district of Trois-Rivières. Bazil Plante and his wife Genevieve
Lacourse (the latter was listed as claimant #426) also appear in the
"Index of Names of Claimants to Share in the grant of Scrip to original
white settlers who came to the Red River country or to the North-West
Territories, between 1813 and 1835, inclusive, and their descendants,
not being Halfbreeds, who were alive on the 26th May, 1874," *Manitoba
Free Press*, 16 January 1911. Numerous other families are listed in this
document, which also includes Scottish settlers from Kildonan.

27 Joseph Amable Cardinal was born on 16 December 1764 in the parish
of St. Laurent in Montreal. His parents were Joseph Cardinal and Marie-
Amable Imbault dit Matha. His paternal grandparents were François
Marie Cardinal and Marie Josephe Meloche. See Appendix 2 for
additional information on Joseph Cardinal's family.

28 Although Joseph Desjarlais had migrated eastward to the Swan River
district in the 1820s, his son and namesake, Joseph Desjarlais Jr. remained.
Joseph Desjarlais had established a country union with Joseph Cardinal's
eldest daughter Josephte, previously the wife of another *engagé* turned

freeman, Joseph Ladouceur. See RG15, vol. 1325–1327, *Métis Scrip Affidavits 1885/1900*. See affidavit of Marguerite Desjarlais filed for the claim of her mother Josephte Cardinal, deceased. In the affidavit all of Josephte Cardinal's children, and their spouses, are listed.

29 From Aristide Phillipot, "Grouard: la Perle des Vicariats Apostoliques de l'Amérique du Nord," Premié rédaction, #3, polycopie, 196; as quoted by Juliette Champagne, *Lac La Biche: Une Communauté Métisse au XIXeme Siècle* (unpublished MA thesis, on file in the Department of History, University of Alberta, Edmonton, fall 1990), 57.

30 A search of Métis scrip affidavits from the National Archives of Canada suggests that Antoine Desjarlais Jr. had at least two liaisons with other women outside of his more permanent relationship with Suzanne Allary. Desjarlais is recorded as having fathered a daughter, Suzanne (b. 1819 in the Northwest Territories) to Pelagie Martin, possibly the daughter, but more likely the sister, of *métis* freeman François Martin Jr. (b. ca. 1790, son of *Canadien* freeman François Martin and Louise Crise). RG15, Dept. of the Interior, Series D-II-8-b, vol. 1327, Reel C-14937, *Scrip Affidavit of Susanna Desjarlais*. François Martin Sr. was a North West Company *engagé* at Fort Vermilion in 1810, where he, his Cree wife Louise, and six children occupied a tent. See "Introduction," lix–ix, in Morton, *Journal of Duncan M'Gillivray*.

31 Suzanne (a.k.a. Catherine) Allary, the country wife of Antoine Desjarlais, was the former country wife of métis freeman François Martin Jr. François Martin Jr. and Suzanne Allary had a daughter, Julie, born 1815 at Fort Pelly. François Martin, Jr. and Suzanne Allary appear to have ended their country union, as Suzanne Allary established a union with Antoine Desjarlais Jr. shortly thereafter. Suzanne and Antoine had their first child, Marie, by April of 1817. François Martin, in turn, formed another country union with Marguerite Racette, the daughter of *Canadien* freeman Charles Racette, by 1819. See baptismal records #79–80 (13 July 1825) for the children of Antoine Desjarlais and Suzanne Allary: François (five years on 2 January 1825); and Louise (age one year, 12 November 1824). Also see baptismal records #97–99 (7 August 1825) for the children of François Martin and Marguerite Racette: Simon (four years); Laurent-Etienne (one year); Marie (six years); and Françoise (three years). From *Ancien Registres de St. Boniface 1825–1834* (transcription/summary of entries from St. Boniface Parish Register; photocopy); RG15, Dept. of the Interior, Series D-II-8-c, vol. 1357, Reel C-14986, *Scrip Affidavit for Julie Martin*.

32 After Marie's death in 1870 Antoine Desjarlais dit Wabumun married a second time, to a Cree woman known only as Genevieve, in 1877. NAC, RG15, Series D II-8-b, vol. 1327, Reel C-14937, *Antoine Desjarlais – Concerning his Claim as a Head of Family*, Claim 688.

33 M.E. Bradford and J.M. Hanson, "Lac La Biche," in Patricia Mitchell and Ellie Prepas, eds., *Atlas of Alberta Lakes* (Edmonton: University of Alberta Press, 1990), 152.

34 Dr. James Hector of the Palliser Expedition made this observation about Alexis: "M. La Combe, the Roman Catholic priest, has frequently been

driven from Lac Ste. Anne to the fort in a dog cariole – 50 miles: after which his man Alexis, one of the best runners in the country, loaded the sled with 400 pounds of meat and returned to the mission before next morning!" Quoted in Katherine Hughes, *Father Lacombe: The Black-Robe Voyageur* (Toronto: McClelland and Stewart, 1920), 74.

35 See John McDougall, *Saddle, Sled and Snowshoe: Pioneering on the Saskatchewan in the Sixties* (Toronto: William Briggs, 1896): 86–87.

36 Peter Melnycky, *A Veritable Canaan: Alberta's Victoria Settlement* (Edmonton: Friends of Fort Victoria Historical Society, 1997), 8–9.

37 See James G. MacGregor, *Father Lacombe* (Edmonton: Hurtig, 1975), 96. Original quotation taken from Paul Kane, *Wanderings of an Artist Among the Indians of North America* (1859; reprint, Edmonton: Hurtig, 1974), 276.

38 Because of the shrinking supply of bison, the Crees and Assiniboines found themselves moving farther west, where they inevitably clashed with Blackfoot and Sioux. As early as the 1850s the Cree were beginning to explore agricultural alternatives to buffalo hunting. The skirmishes between these Blackfoot and Cree did not end, however. Casualties on both sides of the "buffalo wars" continued to escalate, despite the activities of peacemakers such as the Cree chief Maskepetoon, who was murdered by the Blackfoot in 1869 while acting as peace emissary in their camp. See Milloy, *The Plains Cree*, 103–18.

39 Frederick "Keh-Kek" Desjarlais was another *métis* son who remained in the Athabasca region while his father moved elsewhere. According to the scrip affidavit of Frederick (Keh-Kek) "Hawk" Desjarlais, his parents were Neshokpo Desjarlais and Marie Cardinal. In a later claim filed on behalf of his deceased son Thaddeus, Keh-Kek further noted that his father was named Baptiste Desjarlais and his mother was Marie Cardinal. Although Baptiste "Nishecabo" Desjarlais was married to Charlotte Cardinal rather than Marie Cardinal, I believe that Neshopko is Nishecabo. Baptiste Desjarlais left the Lesser Slave Lake/Lac La Biche area in the 1820s and migrated eastward to the Cumberland House area and later to Carleton House and Fort Pelly (1832). However, the scrip affidavit of Marguerite Desjarlais, a daughter of Nishecabo and Charlotte Cardinal, indicates her birthplace as being Fishing Lake, NWT in 1834. This birthplace, Fishing Lake, places Nishecabo in the region adjacent to Frog Lake in east-central Alberta, an area near to the place where Frederick Desjarlais was born, and in approximately the same time period See RG15, Series D-II-8-C, vol. 1344, Reel C-14954, *Métis Scrip Affidavits 1885/1900, Affidavit of Frederick 'Keh-Kek' Desjarlais*.

40 Keh-Kek married the daughter of Chief Ohimnahos, or Little Hunter, of Whitefish Lake. They were married in 1853 at St. Paul des Cris, Father Lacombe's mission. See RG15, Series D-II-8-C, vol. 1344, Reel C-14954 Métis Scrip Affidavits 1885/1900, *Affidavit of Frederick 'Keh-Kek' Desjarlais*.

41 The illustration accompanying this anecdote shows Keh-Kek, in buckskins and feathers, chasing bison with a drawn bow and arrow, while astride

another buffalo. John McDougall, *Forest, Lake and Prairie: Twenty Years of Frontier Life in Western Canada – 1842–62* (Toronto: Ryerson Press, 1895), 154–56.

42 The name "Mistawasis" translates to "Big Child" in English.

43 McDougall, *Saddle, Sled and Snowshoe*, 24.

44 See McDougall, *Saddle, Sled and Snowshoe*, 132–33.

45 Ibid., 138–39.

46 The Desjarlais dit Okanase family, who later took treaty as members of Keeseekoowenin's band at Riding Mountain, resided at Pakan's reserve at Whitefish Lake for several years, where they collected their annuities between 1881 and 1884. See RG15, Dept of the Interior, Series D-II-8-c, vol. 1362, Reel C-14994, *Affidavit for Pierre Desjarlais (dit Okanase)* where Agent J.G. Mackay notes that Pierre Desjarlais dit Okanase, his wife Josephte Marron, and their children were "former members of the Kesikowenin's Band of Indians owning the Reserve situated at Riding Mountain, Manitoba." The family were formally discharged from treaty on 18 September 1886 at Battleford. Pierre Desjarlais dit Okanase received 160.00 in scrip on 20 September 1886 at Battleford.

47 The large number of inhabitants associated with this post suggests that this is the man to whom Marcel Giraud referred when he wrote of "the Métis Antoine Desjarlais, whose following consisted of a hundred persons, over whom he wielded the authority of an Indian chief." Giraud based this information on a report written by HBC governor George Simpson dated 20 June 1853, a few years before Desjarlais' post burnt down. Marcel Giraud, *The Métis in the Canadian West* (2 vols.) George Woodcock, trans. (Edmonton: University of Alberta Press, 1986), 2:329, 621n38.

48 The precise location of Fort Desjarlais is Section 31-5-24 north of Lauder, Manitoba. According to an elderly Métis informant named Filoman Lafontaine, Fort Desjarlais was built ca. 1836 and burnt to the ground twenty years later in 1856, possibly by a prairie fire. Although Mrs. Lafontaine identified Fort Desjarlais as having been built by one Joseph Desjarlais, the men she listed as Joseph Desjarlais' sons-in-law are actually the sons-in-law of his brother *Antoine* Desjarlais, according to genealogical data. Moreover, parish records for Joseph Desjarlais Jr., his wife Josephte Cardinal and their children indicates that Joseph Jr., his wife and children remained in the Lac La Biche area during the period when Fort Desjarlais was in operation (ca. 1836–56). Joseph Desjarlais Jr. died at Lac La Biche in 1854. For genealogical information on Joseph Desjarlais Jr., see family charts for Joseph Desjarlais and Josephte Cardinal (#1156.000); Antoine Desjarlais and Catherine Allary (#1228.000) in the C.D. Denney Papers, Glenbow Archives, Calgary Alberta. See also the *Forts des Prairies, Registre de Baptêmes, Mariages, Sépultures 1842–1851*, which records the marriage of Joseph Desjarlais and Josephte Cardinal, and the subsequent baptism and marriages of their adult children on 4 November 1844 at Lac La Biche (*Fort des Prairies, Registre, 1842–1851*, Acc: 71.220, Item 5214; Oblate Archives, Provincial Archives of Alberta, Edmonton, Alberta). For information on Fort Desjarlais, see G.A.

McMorran, *Souris River Posts and David Thompson's Diary of His Historical Trip Across the Souris Plains to the Mandan Villages in the Winter of 1797–98* (Souris, Manitoba: Souris Plaindealer, 1953), 12–13; and Bruce Wishart, "Archaeology on the Souris River: Fort Desjarlais" (Parts 2 and 3 of a four-part newspaper article, n.d.). Manuscript on file at the Provincial Archives of Manitoba, Winnipeg.

49 The head Chief of the Yanktonais, Wah na ton, instituted this policy prior to his death in 1840. While this "protection" policy did not necessarily guarantee that traders would not be ambushed or pillaged by Yanktonai war parties, it did guarantee that the traders' losses would be reimbursed by Wah na ton. See Edwin Thompson Denig, *Five Indian Tribes of the Upper Missouri: Sioux, Arikaras, Assiniboines, Crees, Crows* (Norman and London: University of Oklahoma Press, 1961), 30–36.

50 See Gary Clayton Anderson, *Kinsmen of Another Kind: Dakota–White Relations in the Upper Mississippi Valley, 1650–1862* (Lincoln and London: University of Nebraska Press, 1984), 51–56, 118.

51 Refer to Chapter 3 for detailed information on the family ties between the Picotte and the Desjarlais families.

52 Charles was sent to St. Louis to be educated by Father Pierre De Smet in the 1840s. By 1854 Charles Picotte had returned to Dakota territory, where he became a trader, treaty counsel, and agency interpreter for his maternal uncle, Struck-By-the-Ree. Gray, "Honoré Picotte," 191–92. It has been noted that of all of the Yanktonai leaders, Struck-By-the-Ree was the friendliest to whites. Doane Robinson, *A History of the Dakota or Sioux Indians* (Minneapolis: Ross & Haines, 1967), 70, 247–49, 456–57. See also "Charles F. Picotte," *South Dakota Historical Collections* (1902), 113–14.

53 See Gray, "Honoré Picotte," 191–94, 202.

54 In 1837 Honoré Picotte's first wife died (possibly in the smallpox epidemic of 1837). Picotte took a second Sioux wife, Wambdi Autopewin (Eagle-Woman-That-All-Look-At) the daughter of Two-Lance, a Hunkpapa chief, and Rosy-Light of-Dawn, a woman of the Two-Kettle band of Sioux. Ibid.

55 During the research, I noted that Marcel "Gwiwizens" Desjarlais bears a name identical to that of a Saulteaux-Cree chief named Cowessees, whose ancestry is unknown, but who signed Treaty Four on behalf of his band, which was located east of Fort Qu'Appelle. Cowessees died in the 1880s. Because direct references to Marcel Desjarlais disappear from the records after 1847, the possibility that Marcel Desjarlais might, in fact, be Cowessees, is compelling. See Kenneth J. Tyler, "Kiwisance (Cowessess, Ka-we-zauce, Little Child)," *DCB*, 11:477–78.

56 HBCA, MG 2 B5-2, 15–17, *Red River Settlement – Red River Correspondence*. Letter to Alexander Christie, Governor, Hudson's Bay Company from Red River Métis traders re: jurisdiction over trade, dated 29 August 1845.

57 The individuals identified besides Antoine and Marcel Desjarlais are St. Germain (Shigerma) and a son of Chartrand (Shatra), men from families based at Baie St. Paul and St. François-Xavier to whom the Desjarlais

were linked by marriage. See HBCA MG 2 C38, *Peter Garrioch Journal, 1843–47*, entry for Tuesday, 6 January 1847.

58 Although the British government had sent different companies of troops into Red River over the years to discourage American expansion northward, they were never intended to be Hudson's Bay Company militia, although the Company would have liked to use them in that capacity. The troops stationed in Red River in the latter half of the 1840s were the Chelsea Pensioners, a group of military retirees, many of whom were disabled. Although they acted as constables in Red River, they were capable of little else. See J.M. Bumsted, *The Red River Rebellion* (Winnipeg: Watson & Dwyer, 1996), 32.

59 The other defendants, besides Guillaume Sayer, were McGillis, Laronde, and Goulet. See the discussion of the Sayer trial in Margaret Arnett Macleod, *Cuthbert Grant of Grantown: Warden of the Plains of Red River* (Toronto: McClelland and Stewart, 1963), 134–37.

60 See HBCA, MG 1 C6 (A) and (B), *Journal of Occurrences at Fort Ellice 1856–1859*.

61 Buffalo Lake is near present-day Stettler, Alberta. All of the children listed are identified as the children of Antoine Desjarlais dit Morel and LaLouise Vallee. See RG15, Dept. of the Interior, Series D-II-8-b, vol. 1327, *Affidavit for Caroline Desjarlais* (b. 15 July 1854 at St. Joe); RG15, Dept. of the Interior, Series D-II-8-b, vol. 1327, *Affidavit for Charles Desjarlais* (b. winter 1850 at Pembina Mountain); and RG15, Interior, Series D-II-8-b, vol. 1329, *Affidavit of Elise (Desjarlais) Klyne*, (b. 10 June 1850 at St. Joe).

62 See Gerhard Ens, "Dispossession or Adaptation? Migration and Persistence of the Red River Métis, 1835–1890," *CAA Historical Papers 1988*, 133–34.

63 See Cowie, "Editorial Notes" (#21) for *The Journal of Daily Occurrences at the Hudson's Bay Company's Fort Ellice, Swan River District – From 1st May 1858 to 27th April 1859*: 39. Unpublished manuscript on file, Provincial Archives of Manitoba, Winnipeg. Antoine Desjarlais' widow, Suzanne Allary, died at Lebret on 17 January 1878, aged "quatre-vingt-dix-ans" (90 years of age). *Registre de la Mission St. Florent au Lac Qu'Appelle*, vol. 1 (1868–1881), 216. Photocopies of original parish records, Geoff Burtonshaw Genealogical Collection, Calgary, Alberta.

64 Isaac Cowie, *The Company of Adventurers* (Toronto: William Briggs, 1913), 416–17.

65 Whether their designation as Metis was voluntary or forced is not known. However, it should be noted that several members of different Desjarlais families, including Nishecabo's son Benjamin Desjarlais (who was struck off the Muscowequan band list) had withdrawn from treaty on 1 June 1888. See *List of Halfbreeds Who Have Withdrawn from Treaty June 1, 1888*. Unpublished manuscript on file in possession of the author. See also RG15, Dept. of the Interior, Series D-II-8-c, vol. 1344, *Affidavit of Baptiste Desjarlais, dec'd* (filed by son Benjamin). This record confirms the birthplace of Baptiste as being Lac La Biche, ca. 1790, and his marriage

to Charlotte Cardinal ca. 1815 at Baie St. Paul (St. Paul-des-Sauteux), and
Baptiste's death in the winter of 1871 at Little Fork, Qu'Appelle Lakes.

66 A. Irving Hallowell observed that shamans had considerable social and
political influence because "they held in their hands the power of life and
death." Ruth Landes notes that among the Ojibwa, it was believed that
"a sorcerer could not be killed." See Hallowell, *Ojibwa of Berens River,
Manitoba*, ibid., 36; and Landes, *The Ojibwa Woman*, ibid., 133.

67 It was believed by the Ojibwa that children's illness or death was a result
of the wrongdoing of their parents or grandparents. See Hallowell,
"Ojibwa World View and Disease," 391–444.

Chapter 6

1 Not all of these (i.e., medical benefits) were available when the first
numbered treaties were negotiated. However, by 1876, a revision to the
Indian Act standardized these benefits so that they would be consistent
across the country. Olive Dickason, *Canada's First Nations: A History
of the Founding Peoples from Earliest Times*, 2d ed. (Don Mills, Ont.:
Oxford University Press, 1997), 252–58.

2 Doug Owram, "'Conspiracy and Treason': The Red River Resistance From
an Expansionist Perspective," in R. Douglas Francis and Howard Palmer,
eds., *The Prairie West: Historical Readings* (Edmonton: Pica Pica Press, a
division of the University of Alberta Press): 167–84.

3 Dickason, *Canada's First Nations*, 253–55.

4 The negotiations for Treaty Three, for example, were salvaged largely
through the efforts of Red River Métis intermediaries, who negotiated
with opposing Ojibwa factions and brokered the agreement. As the chief
of Fort Frances informed Alexander Morris, "I wish you to understand
you owe the treaty much to the Half-breeds." Later, during the Treaty
Four negotiations at Fort Qu'Appelle in 1874, the chiefs asked Morris
to consider the Métis, particularly their hunting rights. Arthur J. Ray,
Jim Miller, and Frank Tough, *Bounty and Benevolence: A History of
Saskatchewan Treaties* (Montreal: McGill-Queen's University Press, 2000),
69, 117–18.

5 Alexander Morris, *The Treaties of Canada with the Indians of Manitoba
and the North-West Territories* (Toronto: Belfords, Clark & Co., 1880.
Reprint ed.: Toronto: Coles, 1971), 294.

6 Ibid., 294–95.

7 See Dickason, *Canada's First Nations*, 245, 269–70.

8 Treaty Six was signed at Fort Carleton on 8 August 1876. Several métis
people are listed on the treaty document itself, in their capacities as
chiefs and headmen of various bands. They include: Pee-nay-sis (Peaysis,
a.k.a. François Desjarlais), chief of the Crees on Lac La Biche; Pierre
"Mitchoominis" Cardinal, listed as Mah-cha-me-wis, an advisor to
Peaysis; Isaac Cardinal (councillor to Chief Kehewin); Charles Cardinal
(councillor to Wee-has-hoo-hee-say-yin); Cake-Cake, a.k.a Frederick "Keh-

Kek" Desjarlais or "Hawk," councillor to Pakan (a.k.a. James Seenum), chief of the Crees at Whitefish and Goodfish Lakes; Mass-an (Massan Cardinal), councillor to Chief Mistawasis, chief of the Crees near Fort Carleton; Pierre Cadien (Pierre Cardinal), councillor to Chief Mistawasis. The identities have been confirmed by identification of, and comparison to, the names on treaty paylists. See NAC, RG10, Indian Affairs, *Treaty Annuity Paylists, 1879–1885* (vols. 9413–9418) for Mistawasis band, Carleton 1880 (vol. 9414); 1884 (vol. 9417); Kehewin band 1885 (vol. 9418) and 1886 (vol. 9419); Kah-Qua-num band, Lac La Biche, 1885 (vol. 9418); Bob Tail band, Bear's Hill, 1885 (vol. 9418); James Seenum band, Whitefish Lake, 1879 (vol. 9413), 1880 (vol. 9414), 1884 (vol. 9415), 1885 (vol. 9416); Little Hunter (Ohimnahos) band, Saddle Lake, 1879 (vol. 9413), 1885 (vol. 9416). See also Morris, *The Treaties of Canada with the Indians of Manitoba and the North-West Territories*, 356–62.

9 On the Muscowequan paylist for 1879 are listed Benjamin Desjarlais, Joseph Desjarlais, Noel Desjarlais, Madeleine Desjarlais, Francis Desjarlais, Isobel Desjarlais, Francis Desjarlais, Julia Desjarlais, Cyrille Desjarlais, as well as Joseph Tate Sr., Joseph Tate Jr., Antoine Rocheblanc and Pierre Rocheblanc (a.k.a. Rocheblave). Joseph Tate was the second husband of Marguerite Desjarlais, daughter of Baptiste "Nishecabo" Desjarlais and Charlotte Cardinal. François Rocheblanc was the husband of Judith Desjarlais, daughter of Baptiste Nishecabo Desjarlais and Charlotte "Lizette" Cardinal. See RG15, Dept. of the Interior, Series D-II-8-c, vol. 1344, Reel C-14964, affidavit of Judith Desjarlais. See also RG15, Dept. of the Interior, Series D-II-8-c, vol. 1365, Reel C-14999, affidavit of Antoine Rocheblanc, husband of Judith Desjarlais. In 1884, immediately prior to the Northwest Rebellion, Antoine Rocheblanc and Benjamin Desjarlais were listed as headmen to Muscowequan. See RG15, Dept. of the Interior, Series D-II-8-c, vol. 1344, Reel C-14963, affidavit of Benjamin Desjarlais on behalf of his deceased father Baptiste Desjarlais, listing surviving heirs Benjamin, Madeleine Marguerite, Josephte, Emmanuel and Charlotte. One of the daughters of Nishecabo's relative Baptiste Desjarlais (son of the *Canadien* freeman François Desjarlais and Madeleine Roy) and his wife Marie Martin, named Madeleine Desjarlais, took treaty at Muscowequan with her husband Alphonse Pelletier and their children. See RG15, Dept. of the Interior, Series D-II-8-c, vol. 1363, Reel C-14996, affidavit of Alphonse Pelletier.

10 The scrip affidavits of Antoine Desjarlais' sons Michel (married to Julie Bonneau) and Baptiste (married to Julie Grant), place them in the Qu'Appelle area, where their sons were homesteading parcels of land at the same time scrip was distributed. Some opted to secure title to the land already homesteaded, and take money scrip. See NAC, RG15, Dept. of the Interior, Series D-II-8-b, vol. 1327, Reel C-14937, *Affidavits of Exupert and Isidore Desjarlais* (sons of Baptiste Desjarlais and Julie Grant).

11 "The Edmonton Agency," *Edmonton Bulletin*, Saturday, 31 March 1883.

12 According to the scrip affidavit of Frederick (Keh-Kek) "Hawk" Desjarlais, his parents were Neshokpo Desjarlais and Marie Cardinal. In a

later claim filed on behalf of his deceased son Thaddeus, Keh-Kek further notes that his father was named Baptiste Desjarlais and his mother was Marie Cardinal. Although Baptiste "Nishecabo" Desjarlais was married to Charlotte Cardinal rather than Marie Cardinal, I believe that Neshopko is Nishecabo. Although Baptiste Desjarlais left the Lesser Slave Lake/Lac La Biche area in the 1820s and migrated eastward to the Cumberland House area and later to Carleton House and Fort Pelly (1832), the scrip affidavit of Marguerite Desjarlais, a daughter of Nishecabo and Charlotte Cardinal, indicates her birthplace as being Fishing Lake, NWT in 1834. This birthplace, Fishing Lake, places Nishecabo in the region adjacent to Frog Lake in east-central Alberta, an area near to the place where Frederick Desjarlais was born, and in approximately the same time period. See NAC, RG15, Dept. of the Interior, vols. 1343–1344, *Affidavit of Frederick Desjarlais*. See also Peers, *The Ojibwa of Western Canada*, 104–6, 112, 114.

13 See NAC, RG10, vol. 9413, *Treaty Annuity Paylist for Little Hunter's Band, 1879*, which notes in the "Remarks" column beside the names of the headmen, that daughters of Chief Little Hunter married the councillors.

14 See NAC, RG10, vol. 9416, *Treaty Annuity Paylist for Little Hunter's Band, 1882*, which notes in the "Remarks" column "Little Hunter dead (ticket issued)." At the top of the paylist, dated 9 September 1882, the heading is "Kake Kake's Followers." The band also included Louis "Wechokwan" Cardinal, who was married to Judith Desjarlais, sister of François "Peaysis" Desjarlais. See RG15, Dept. of the Interior, vols. 1325–1327, *Scrip Affidavit for Judith Desjarlais*. "Wechokwan" Cardinal's son, Henry Cardinal, stated that his father and Little Hunter were sent out on behalf of the band to select land for their reserve. See "Henry Cardinal Sr. Interviewed About the time of the Signing of Treaty 6," in Saddle Lake Indian Reserve, *O-Sak-Do: Treaty No. 6 Centennial Commemorative Tabloid, Saddle Lake Indian Reserve, Alberta Canada – July 1976* (Saddle Lake, Alta.: Author, 1976), 12–13.

15 It is not fully understood why a staunchly Roman Catholic family such as the Cardinals chose to join Pakan's Band. References to the family in oral accounts by Saddle Lake Elders often make mention of the fact that the Cardinals were separate from the other band members because they were Catholic, or not related to them, or that they were from somewhere else. See "Peter Shirt Remembers: Memories of Early Days on the Reserve," 7–10, 30–31; "Henry Cardinal Sr. Interviewed About the time of the Signing of Treaty 6," 12–13; Saddle Lake Indian Reserve, *O-Sak-Do*; see also Sam Bull, *100 Years at Whitefish 1855–1955* (typescript, unpublished). Glenbow Archives, Calgary, Alberta: 4–5.

16 Gabriel Cardinal dit Labatoche, the son of Baptiste Cardinal dit Labatoche and Emmy "Amy" Moignon, was born about 1835. He married Marie Bruneau dit Piwapiskapow on 22 May, 1854, at Lac La Biche. In NAC, *Index to Métis Scrip, 1885/1900*. See also Provincial Archives of Alberta (hereinafter *PAA*), Oblate Archives (hereinafter *OA*) *Notre Dame des*

Victoires, Lac La Biche, BMD 1853–: ACC. 71.220; item 3798, Box 255, Roll 12.

17 See NAC, RG10, vol. 9413, *Treaty Annuity Paylist* for James Seenum's Band, where Gabriel Cardinal is listed as one of Pakan's headmen.

18 This surname was used, on occasion, by certain branches of both the Cardinal and Desjarlais families, usually those associated with the Keeseekoowenin band situated near Riding Mountain, Manitoba.

19 In conducting the genealogical information forming the basis of this paper, the author compiled genealogical data from Lac La Biche Roman Catholic parish records, treaty paylists, and Métis scrip affidavits, supplemented with information from contemporary reminiscences and other documentation. This data was entered into a genealogical computer software program called Reunion® for the Macintosh®. Using this software, family charts were constructed spanning several generations. This software can also generate relationship charts, capable of listing an identified individual's relations by their degree of consanguinity. Such a chart was generated for François "Peaysis" Desjarlais. By comparing this chart to identified individuals on the annuity paylists for the Peaysis Reserve, it was then possible to ascertain precisely the number of relatives related to Peaysis who were members of his band.

20 MacGregor, *Father Lacombe*, 211–12.

21 K. Hughes, *Father Lacombe*, 265–67.

22 Melnycky, *A Veritable Canaan*, 28–29.

23 See "Lac La Biche," in the *Edmonton Bulletin*, Saturday, 9 December 1882.

24 See *Edmonton Bulletin*, Saturday, 3 February 1883. I have been unable to ascertain precisely who wrote this letter on behalf of the chiefs, but it is possible that it was written by the Roman Catholic priest Constantine-Michael Scollen, who was responsible for the mission at Bears Hill (Hobbema) in 1884–85, and had a great deal of influence with local Cree leaders. Brian M. Owens, and Claude M. Roberto, *A Guide to the Archives of the Oblates of Mary Immaculate: Province of Alberta–Saskatchewan* (Edmonton: Missionary Oblates, Grandin Province, 1989), 125. See also Bob Beal and Rod Macleod, *Prairie Fire: The 1885 North-West Rebellion* (Edmonton: Hurtig, 1984), 74–75, 210–12.

25 Hugh A. Dempsey, *Big Bear: The End of Freedom* (Vancouver and Toronto: Douglas & McIntyre, 1984), 120–21.

26 Dempsey, *Big Bear: The End of Freedom*, 120–34.

27 See editorials and articles in the *Edmonton Bulletin*: "Indian Troubles," Saturday, 7 July 1883; Saturday, 4 August 1883; "Indians," Saturday, 14 June 1884; "Halfbreed Lands," Saturday, 9 August 1884; "Bear's Hill," Saturday, 28 March 1885.

28 See *Edmonton Bulletin*, "Bear's Hill," Saturday, 8 November 1884.

29 Beal and Macleod, *Prairie Fire: The 1885 North-West Rebellion*, 135–36, 151–60.

30 Dempsey, *Big Bear: The End of Freedom*, 151–62.

31 Ibid., 164–66.

32 *Edmonton Bulletin*, Saturday, 25 April 1885.

33 *Edmonton Bulletin*, Saturday, 4 October 1884.

34 Bull, *100 Years at Whitefish 1855–1955*, 4–5.

35 A comprehensive summary of events in Lac La Biche during the North West Rebellion can be found in Evelyn Rowand, "The Rebellion at Lac La Biche," *Alberta Historical Review* 21, no. 3 (summer 1973): 1–9.

36 *Edmonton Bulletin*, Saturday, 25 April 1885. See also "Mgr. Henri Faraud, O.M.I., of Lac La Biche to Fr. Joseph Fabre, O.M.I., Superior-General," in Stuart Hughes, ed., *The Frog Lake "Massacre": Personal Perspectives on Ethnic Conflict* (Toronto: McClelland and Stewart, 1976), 328–29.

37 See *Edmonton Bulletin*, Saturday, 9 May 1885, which reported this incident as having taken place on 23 April. The scrip affidavit of Adam Howse indicates that he was married to one Rosalie Ermineskin. A study of Rosalie Ermineskin's scrip affidavit, and reference to her home address of Bear's Hill, indicates that she was the daughter of Cree Chief Ermineskin. Although these relationships are not readily apparent to modern researchers, Pakan would have been aware of these familial relationships, and would have been alarmed that warriors of Big Bear's band had actually attacked Ermineskin's kin. His desire to maintain his neutrality in an increasingly awkward situation would have prompted his quick decision to move the camp.

38 Bull, *100 Years at Whitefish 1855–1955*, 5.

39 Ibid.

40 National Archives of Canada (NAC), RG10, Indian Affairs, vols. 1569–1582, *Indian Agent's Letterbooks, 1885–1912, Saddle Lake Agency, Alberta, 1885–1912*. John Mitchell, Acting Indian Agent, Victoria to Indian Commissioner, Regina, dated 20 July 1885.

41 See *Edmonton Bulletin*, Saturday, 25 April 1885, which states, "Mr. Young brought in the government horse taken by the Indians at Saddle Lake. It had been taken to Frog Lake and brought back again by Louis We-chak-win... the Indian We-chak-win, who brought the Fort Pitt news to Victoria last week, was amongst the Indians and an eye witness of the bloodshed which he told of. See also RG15, Dept. of the Interior, Series D-II-8-c, vol. 1340, *Affidavits of Judith (Desjarlais) Cardinal* and *Louison "Wechokwan" Cardinal*.

42 Bull, *100 Years at Whitefish 1855–1955*, ibid.

43 Peter Erasmus, *Buffalo Days and Nights: as told to Henry Thompson*, reprint ed. (Calgary: Glenbow Institute, 1999), 281–82.

44 Chiefs Bobtail and Ermineskin were brothers of mixed ancestry themselves. Bobtail's European name was Alexis Piché. His wife was Catherine Cardinal, daughter of Pierre Cardinal dit Eia-io-wew and Marie Cardinal, and granddaughter of Joseph Cardinal and Louise Frobisher. His sister Bethsey Piche was married to Jacques Cardinal, his wife's brother. See NAC, *Index to Métis Scrip, 1885/1900*, entries for Alexis Piché (HB Claim #179); Catherine Piché (HB Claim #171). Ermineskin was also known by the French-*métis* name of Baptiste Piche. See RG15, Dept. of the

Interior, Series D-II-8-c, vol. 1334, Reel C-14946. *Scrip claim of Frederick Ballendine* (b. 1860), son of Ermine Skin (adopted son of Peter Ballendine) and Jane Belanger (Métis).

45 An individual named Napasis is listed in the Kehewin Reserve Treaty Annuity Paylist as a headman. This man is possibly Joseph "Nahpasis" Desjarlais, son of François "Peaysis" Desjarlais and Euphrosine Auger. Although his scrip affidavit lists him as #1 in the Peaysis band, his name does not appear on any of the treaty paylists for the Peaysis band. There is, however, a Napasis listed clearly on the Paysheets for Kehewin's band. See NAC, RG10, *Indian Affairs – Treaty Annuity Paylists, 1879–1885* (vols. 9413–9418) for Kehewin band 1885 (vol. 9418) and 1886 (vol. 9419); NAC, RG15, Dept. of the Interior, Métis Scrip Affidavits, 1885/1900, *Claim of Joseph Desjarlais*.

46 See NAC, RG10, *Indian Affairs – Treaty Annuity Paylists, 1979–1885* (vols. 9413–9418) for Mistawasis Band, Carleton 1880 (vol. 9414); 1884 (vol. 9417), where Mass-an Cardinal and Pierre Cardinal are listed as #s 2 and 3 respectively on the paylist, as headmen, William "Oosawanatin" Cardinal is listed as #15, and Harry "Achusk" Cardinal is listed as #72.

47 Bull, *100 Years at Whitefish 1855–1955*, 5.

48 Ibid., 5–6.

49 Ibid., 6.

50 Ibid., 6–8.

51 See "Mgr. Henri Faraud, O.M.I., of Lac La Biche to Fr. Joseph Fabre, O.M.I., Superior-General," in S. Hughes, *The Frog Lake "Massacre"*, 332. See RG15, Dept. of the Interior, Series D-II-8-c, vol. 1340, *Affidavit of Julien Cardinal*, who was the son of Laurent Cardinal and Marie Moignon of Lac La Biche.

52 See "Mgr. Henri Faraud, O.M.I., of Lac La Biche to Fr. Joseph Fabre, O.M.I., Superior-General," 328–36, 332.

53 RG15, Dept. of the Interior Series D-II-8-b, vol. 1328, scrip affidavits of *Augustin "Azure" Hamelin* and *Marie [Desjarlais] Hamelin*.

54 McDougall, *Saddle, Sled and Snowshoe*, 132–33.

55 Dempsey, *Big Bear: The End of Freedom*, 11–13.

56 Laura Peers notes Nishecabo was a trading chief at Carleton House by 1832, living in the same region as the Black Powder band. See Peers, *The Ojibwa of Western Canada*, 104–6, 112, 114.

57 Antoine Blondion's mother was Marguerite Piyesiwop, most likely the daughter of Piyesiwop, or Petit Couteau (Little Knife). Antoine Blondion's first country wife was Catherine Berland, believed to be the daughter of Pierre Duboishue dit Berland, a well-known *Canadien* freeman operating in the Rocky Mountains in the first three decades of the nineteenth century. See entry for B16 (baptism of Marie Desjarlais) and M16 (marriage of Antoine Dionne and Marie Desjarlais), 19 May 1846, Father Jos. Bourassa, ptr., *Fort des Prairies, Registre de Baptêmes, Mariages, Sepultures 1842–1851*. Acc. 71.220 Oblate Archives, PAA.

58 A cursory study of the scrip affidavits of métis descendants clearly indicates the links between some aboriginal leaders and *Canadien* freemen.

Many of the métis bearing early birthdates have parents known by aboriginal surnames, French surnames, or both in tandem. For example, many *métis* bearing the surname Belanger are also known as Mistawasis; individuals bearing the surname Piche are associated with both Ermineskin and Bobtail; the name "Nehwatam" is associated with the French surname Amiotte, and so on. See appendix 2 for a more detailed discussion of the origin of such aliases.

59 The only Métis Desjarlais known definitively to have participated in the 1885 North-West Rebellion was Michel Desjarlais (whom I believe to be the son of Michel Desjarlais and Julie Bonneau of Lebret, Saskatchewan) who died of head injuries sustained at Fish Creek. See G. F. G. Stanley, "Gabriel Dumont's Account of the North-West Rebellion," in Antoine S. Lussier and D. Bruce Sealey, eds., *The Other Natives: The/Les Métis* (Winnipeg: Manitoba Métis Federation Press, 1978), 165, 167.

60 See "Mgr. Henri Faraud, O.M.I., of Lac La Biche to Fr. Joseph Fabre, O.M.I., Superior-General," 333.

61 See p. 251, W. J. McLean, "Tragic Events at Frog Lake and Fort Pitt During the North West Rebellion," Parts 1 to 5. From S. Hughes, *The Frog Lake "Massacre"*, 251.

62 St. Paul Cardinal was the son of Laurent Cardinal and Marie Mondion, and the brother of Julien Cardinal, the servant at the Roman Catholic Mission. Although he was born at Moose Lake in 1851 and married Marguerite Tremblay at Lac La Biche in 1875, he appears to have lived at Riding Mountain as well hence his acquaintance with the McLean family. RG15, Dept. of the Interior, Series D-II-8-c, vol. 1340, Reel C-14957, *Affidavit of St. Paul Cardinal*. Adrian Hope states the following, "Father Lacombe called the infant settlement 'St. Paul des Metis.' The appellation commemorates an early pre-Rebellion settler St. Paul (Menoomin) Cardinal, who in 1884 erected a cabin on the site occupied by the old Roman Catholic cemeteery. Cardinal later served as a government scout in the Riel Rebellion and received a Middleton grant for his services." Adrian Hope, "Into the Great Lone Land: The History of the St. Paul Half Breed Reserve," in Saddle Lake Indian Reserve, *O-Sak-Do*, 25.

63 Elizabeth M. McLean, "The Siege of Fort Pitt," "Prisoners of the Indians," "Our Captivity Ended." From S. Hughes, *The Frog Lake "Massacre"*, 290. That the Woods Cree guard is Louison Mongrain is confirmed in W. J. McLean, "Tragic Events at Frog Lake and Fort Pitt During the North West Rebellion," 244–71, where he makes reference to guarding McLean and his daughters. In S. Hughes, *The Frog Lake "Massacre"*, 258–59. Ironically, Louison Mongrain would later be hanged for his murder of Corporal David Cowan of the NWMP at Fort Pitt. See Beal and Macleod, *Prairie Fire: The 1885 North-West Rebellion*, 217, 332.

64 W. J. McLean, "Tragic Events at Frog Lake and Fort Pitt During the North West Rebellion," 264; see also Elizabeth M. McLean, "The Siege of Fort Pitt," "Prisoners of the Indians," "Our Captivity Ended."

Chapter 7

1 Glenbow Archives [hereinafter GA], Edgar Dewdney Papers, box 4, f. 66, 1414–20, as quoted in "Appendix Three, "Hayter Reed on the Future Management of Indians,"" in Blair Stonechild and Bill Waiser, *Loyal till Death: Indians and the North-West Rebellion* (Calgary: Fifth House, 1997), ibid., 250–53.

2 Points 4, 5, 6, and 11 taken from "Hayter Reed on the Future Management of Indians," in Stonechild and Waiser, ibid.

3 See RG15, Dept. of the Interior, Series D-II-8-c, vol. 1344, *Affidavit of LaLouise Desjarlais Whitford* (daughter of Baptiste 'Nishecabo' Desjarlais and Charlotte Cardinal); and Series D-II-8-c, vol. 1344, *Affidavit of Louise Desjarlais Ledoux* (daughter of Antoine Desjarlais and Suzanne Allary). Their brother Benjamin Desjarlais is also known to have been a former member of the Muscowequan Band; see NAC, RG10, Series B-8-M, vol. 10038, *List of Halfbreeds Who Have Withdrawn from Treaty, June 1, 1888.*

4 See RG15, Dept. of the Interior, Series D-II-8-c, vol. 1344, *Affidavit of Judith Desjarlais Rocheblave*; and Series D-II-3, vol. 200, *Affidavit of Marguerite Desjarlais Tate* (daughters of Baptiste 'Nishecabo' Desjarlais and Charlotte Cardinal). Descendants of the *Canadien* freeman François Desjarlais also took treaty at Muscowequan; see RG15, Dept. of the Interior, Series D-II-8-c, vol. 1363, *Affidavit of Josephte Pelletier Desjarlais* for her absent husband François Desjarlais (son of Baptiste Desjarlais and Marie Martin); vol. 1344, Reel C-14964 Affidavit of *Joseph Henri Louis Desjarlais* (son of François Desjarlais and Josephte Pelletier); and vol. 1363, *Affidavit of Alphonse Pelletier* (husband of Madeleine Desjarlais, daughter of Baptiste Desjarlais and Marie Martin).

5 Thomas Desjarlais' grandfather was the *Canadien* freeman François Desjarlais, who settled at Baie St. Paul in the early 1830s with his wife Madeleine Roy (see chapter 5). RG15, Dept. of the Interior, Series D-II-8-a, vol. 1320, Reel C-14927, *Affidavit of Baptiste Desjarlais*. See NAC, RG15, Dept. of the Interior, vol. 154, File 4377, which notes that Lot 215, Baie St. Paul Parish was claimed by Thomas Desjarlais, who sold the land to George Fisher on 8 March 1876 for $150. See "Desjarlais Family – Land Holding Red River," Record of Lot 15, Baie St. Paul. Information courtesy of Dr. Gerhard Ens, Edmonton, Alberta.

6 See RG15, Dept. of the Interior, Series D-II-8-c, vol. 1363, *Affidavit of Josephte Pelletier Desjarlais* for her absent husband François Desjarlais (son of Baptiste Desjarlais and Marie Martin); and vol. 1344, Reel C-14964, *Affidavit of Joseph Henri Louis Desjarlais* (son of François Desjarlais and Josephte Pelletier). Thomas Desjarlais' sister, Madeleine Desjarlais Pelletier, was also resident at Muscowequan with her husband, Alphonse Pelletier and their children when they withdrew from treaty.

7 See RG15, Dept. of the Interior, Series D-II-8-b, vol. 1329, *Affidavit of Madeleine Klyne*; and Series D-II-8-c, vol. 1344, *Affidavit of Rosine Desjarlais.*

8 Art Fisher, Regina to the Author, Calgary. Letter dated 24 April 2001.

9 See *Edmonton Bulletin*, Saturday, 15 August 1885, for the following:
   "... Some of the Indians who took part in the outbreak at Saddle Lake
   and afterwards joined Big Bear, have returned. They are not in favor with
   those of the band who remained at home. They say they were sent to their
   reserve by the military authorities at Pitt, but have no documents to show
   in proof. They tell how the troops at Pitt were humbugged in the matter
   of disarmament. Many of the best weapons were not brought in, but were
   cached safely in the woods. Of those brought in many were taken to pieces
   before hand, and as their pieces shown were no use they were allowed to
   keep them. Afterwards the pieces were put together and the guns were as
   good as new."

10 See *Edmonton Bulletin*, Saturday, 10 October 1885 where the official
   government advertisement (dated 19 August 1885) denoting the change to
   the Indian Act is printed. The swift amendment of the Indian Act suggests
   that the government acted quickly when word leaked out in early August
   that the troops were tricked when confiscating firearms.

11 See appendix 4, "Hayter Reed's List of Band Behavior During Rebellion,"
   in Stonechild and Waiser, *Loyal till Death*, 259.

12 In the 19 December 1885 edition of the *Edmonton Bulletin*, it states:
   "Strong Baker's flour is $10 at Victoria and $15 at Lac La Biche."

13 The "rebels" to whom Commissioner Reid was referring would have
   included the members of Cardinal and Desjarlais dit Okanase family who
   had joined Big Bear's rebels. In particular, Reid was probably concerned
   that Gabriel Cardinal, one of Chief Pakan's headmen, would remain on
   the band council if pardoned. Bull, *100 Years at Whitefish 1855–1955*, 8.

14 See NAC, RG10, Indian Affairs, vol. 1570, *Indian Agent's Letterbook
   – Saddle Lake Agency*, 1885, J. A. Mitchell, Victoria to Asst. Indian
   Commissioner, Regina, 20 July 1885.

15 See NAC, RG10, Indian Affairs, vol. 1570, *Indian Agent's Letterbook
   – Saddle Lake Agency*, 1885, J. A. Mitchell, Victoria to Asst. Indian
   Commissioner, Regina, 28 November 1885.

16 *Edmonton Bulletin*, 16 January 1886.

17 See RG15, Dept. of the Interior, Series D-II-8-c, vol. 1344, *Affidavit of
   François Desjarlais*.

18 See RG15, Dept. of the Interior, Series D-II-8-c, vol. 1344, *Affidavit of
   Joseph Desjarlais*, son of François Desjarlais and Euphrosine Auger, for his
   deceased sister Delphine.

19 See NAC, RG10, Indian Affairs, vol. 1570, *Indian Agent's Letterbook
   – Saddle Lake Agency*, 1885, J. A. Mitchell, Victoria to Asst. Indian
   Commissioner, Regina, 6 August 1885.

20 See NAC, RG10, Indian Affairs, vol. 1570, *Indian Agent's Letterbook
   – Saddle Lake Agency*, 1885, J. A. Mitchell, Victoria to Asst. Indian
   Commissioner, Regina 27 November 1885.

21 Bull, *100 Years at Whitefish 1855–1955*, 5.

22 See NAC, RG10, Indian Affairs, vol. 1571, *Indian Agent's Letterbook
   – Saddle Lake Agency*, 1886, J. A. Mitchell, Victoria to Indian

Commissioner, Regina, 13 May 1886. Note that Mitchell refers to Gabriel Cardinal by the name "Menomiw" in his letter, a variation of Menoomin, the Indian name of St. Paul Cardinal (see chapter 6, note 62). Is it possible that the man named Menoomin in the McLean family accounts is actually Gabriel Cardinal?

23 RG15, Dept. of the Interior, Series D-II-8-b, vol. 1327, affidavit of Antoine Desjarlais dit Wabamun. He withdrew from treaty at St. Albert on 12 June 1885.

24 See Elizabeth Macpherson, *The Sun Traveller: The Story of the Callihoos in Alberta* (St. Albert, Alta.: Musée Heritage Museum, 1988), 58–59.

25 Frederick's children, Thaddeus and Sarah, were born, and had died, prior to their parents taking treaty. See RG15, Dept. of the Interior, Series D-II-8-c, vol. 1344, affidavit of Frederick Desjarlais.

26 Two Métis named Philip and Andrew Whitford, who served as guides for the Canadian authorities during the Riel Rebellion, received military homesteads in 1893 adjacent to Keh-Kek's land. Andrew Whitford held the SE and SW quarters of Sec. 28-56-16-4, the SE quarter of which became the site of the Village of Andrew. See Andrew Historical Society, *Dreams and Destinies: Andrew and District* (Andrew, Alta.: Author, 1980), 3–4.

27 See P. R. A. Belanger, "Field Notes of the Survey of the Settlement of Lac La Biche Northwest Territories," [PAA 1889], as quoted in McCullough and Maccagno, *Lac La Biche and the Early Fur Traders* (Edmonton: Canadian Circumpolar Institute, 1991), 160.

28 According to Belanger's field notes, the following river lots were issued to Cardinal and Desjarlais families: #8 Joseph Cardinal; #14 François Cardinal; #29 Joseph Cardinal; #30 Leon Desjarlais; #44 Julien Cardinal; #45 Louis Cardinal; #56 widow St. Luc (Cardinal); #58 Joseph Cardinal; #59 Paul Cardinal; #60 Unoccupied, claimed by Alexis Cardinal; #73 Philomene Cardinal, wife of Jules Desjarlais; #74 Antoine Desjarlais; #76 Jerome Cardinal; #77 Dominique Cardinal, and #79 Hypolite Desjarlais. P. R. A. Belanger, "Field Notes of the Survey of the Settlement of Lac La Biche Northwest Territories" [PAA 1889], as quoted in McCullough and Maccagno, *Lac La Biche and the Early Fur Traders* (Edmonton: Canadian Circumpolar Institute, 1991), 163.

29 RG15, Dept. of the Interior, Series D-II-8-c, vol. 1344, affidavits of Emile Desjarlais and François Desjarlais, sons of Jean Marie Desjarlais.

30 Warburton Pike, a friend of John Gough Brick, the local Anglican missionary at Peace River. As quoted in David Leonard, *Delayed Frontier: The Peace River Country to 1909* (Calgary: Detselig, 1995), 190–91.

31 RG15, Dept. of the Interior, vol. 1485, *Affidavit of Guillaume Desjarlais.* As cited by Patricia Bartko, "Desjarlais Information" (23 March 2001). Unpublished research document on file, Aboriginal Land Claims, Alberta Aboriginal Affairs and Northern Development, Edmonton Alberta.

32 See "Interview with Mr. Barney Maurice, High Prairie Alberta July 1956," Interview by Isabel Loggie, Fairview, Alberta, *Peace River Country Research Project 1837–1956 (Isabel and Margaret Loggie Papers),*

hereinafter cited as *Peace River Country Research Project 1837–1956*: M 4560 Glenbow Archives, Calgary, Alberta. Having grown up in Peace River and witnessed at least one major flood (in 1972), I am aware that subsequent businesses located in the identical spot of Guillaume Desjarlais's store have also been destroyed by flooding!

33 "Miscellaneous and Personal Notes of Old Timers – Interview with W.F. Bredin, on June 12, 1933 by W.D. Albright," *The Peace River Country Research Project: 1837–1956*.

34 See appendix 5, schedule A, "St. Paul des Métis: List of Half-Breed Claims Allowed and Entries Granted," in Joe Sawchuk et al., *Métis Land Rights in Alberta: A Political History* (Edmonton: Métis Association of Alberta, 1981), 255–56.

35 Much of the evidence of Therien's personal attitudes towards managing the colony and the Métis are recorded in Therien's own memoirs. For further reading, see "St. Paul des Métis," in Sawchuk et al., *Métis Land Rights in Alberta*, 159–85.

36 An extensive search of Métis scrip records, treaty paylists, trading post journals, and census records by the research staff of Alberta Aboriginal Affairs and Northern Development – and myself – has failed to yield any records of a Dieudonne Desjarlais. See Patricia Bartko, Aboriginal Land Claims, Alberta Aboriginal Affairs and Northern Development, Edmonton, to the author. Letter dated 22 March 2001. It is my conclusion that "Dieudonne" is actually a nickname for the free-trader Guillaume Desjarlais, who had a trading post at Lesser Slave Lake, and is recorded in both the 1899 Half-Breed Commisssion, and the 1901 Athabasca District Census as living with his family at Lesser Slave Lake.

37 Ray et al., *Bounty and Benevolence*, 152–53.

38 A copy of the letter is on file in Aboriginal Land Claims, Alberta Aboriginal Affairs and Northern Development, Edmonton Alberta, and departmental staff provided additional information regarding the letter. Patricia Bartko, Aboriginal Land Claims, Alberta Aboriginal Affairs and Northern Development, Edmonton, to the author. Letter dated 22 March 2001.

39 See RG10, Indian Affairs, vol. 3708, file 19,502, Dieudonne Desjarlais to Edgar Dewdney, 4 February 1890 as quoted in Ray et al., *Bounty and Benevolence*, 153, 276n9.

40 Ray et al., *Bounty and Benevolence*, 154.

41 The complaints recorded by northern Natives during this period included the drunkenness and immorality of the gold-seekers; the use of poisoned bait to kill fur-bearing animals in addition to overhunting by incoming white hunters and trappers. René Fumoleau, O.M.I., *As Long as This Land Shall Last: A History of Treaty 8 and Treaty 11* (Toronto: McClelland and Stewart, 1974), 46–55.

42 Only the first three points of a much longer disposition are quoted here. According to René Fumoleau, "this affidavit was sworn in duplicate and sworn in the presence of S.A. Dickson, Commissioner for Oaths, in Edmonton, on November 1, 1937. One copy was sent to Ottawa, the

other copy is retained at RCMAFS, file: Indiens-Traité avec eux." See Fumoleau, *As Long as This Land Shall Last*, 74–75, 103n99.

43 Fumoleau, *As Long as This Land Shall Last*, 74–75.

44 PAC, RG15, Dept. of the Interior, B-1a, vol. 329, file 518:158, Albert Lacombe to David Laird, 22 June 1899, as quoted by Fumoleau, *As Long as This Land Shall Last*, 76,106n100.

45 G. Neil Reddekopp, *The Creation and Surrender of the Beaver and Duncan's Bands' Reserves*. Paper no. 2. Revised May 1997 (Edmonton: Indian Land Claims Unit, Alberta Aboriginal Affairs, 1997), 7.

46 His annuities for 1900 were repaid to him retroactively in 1901. Reddekopp, *The Creation and Surrender of the Beaver and Duncan's Bands' Reserves*, 14.

47 See Reddekopp, ibid., 32–34.

48 Ibid., 334.

49 On migration of the Saulteaux to Moberly Lake, see following sources: Reddekopp, *The Creation and Surrender of the Beaver and Duncan's Bands' Reserves*; a series of oral interviews from *The Peace River Country Research Project* (specifically: Harry Garbitt, Moberly Lake, British Columbia, August 13, 1955; Mr. Harry Garbitt, Moberly Lake, B.C. June 1956; Barney Maurice, High Prairie, Alberta, July 1956; Harry Callahoo, Paddle Prairie, Alberta, July 1956; and Miscellaneous and Personal Notes of Old Timers, interview with W.F. Bredin, on June 12, 1933 by W.D. Albright). A second set of oral interviews and historical notes from the Calverley Collection, compiled by the late Dorothea Horton Calverley of Dawson Creek, B.C., has also been cited. This collection, which is housed in the Dawson Municipal Public Library in Dawson Creek, B.C. has been transcribed and is accessible on a website, called *History is Where You Stand* (http://www.calverley.dawson-creek.bc.ca/calcoll.html). Interviews and historical notes cited from this collection are as follows: "01-146: Mrs. Marcelena Desjarlais of Chetwynd," interview by Lee J. Phillips on 15 March 1973; "01-147: John Dokkie of Moberly Lake," interview by Lee J. Phillips on 6 April 1973; 18-044: Gabriel Leprete of Dawson Creek, from "An Interview with Rick Belcourt (n.d.);" "01-119: The First Treaty-Signing Day in Hudson's Hope," by Dorothea Calverley; "01-120: The Last Treaty-Singing Day in the Peace," by Dorothea Calverley; "01-106: Chief Wabi's Prophecy," by Dorothea Calverley (n.d.); "01-138: Mrs. Caroline Beaudry's Story: Tales of the Stone Age in a Modern Living Room," from a 1973 interview with Dorothea Calverley; "15-09: Early Days Around Chetwynd," Eric Logan.

50 "01-147: John Dokkie of Moberly Lake," Interview by Lee J. Phillips on 6 April 1973.

51 Harry Garbitt was the second husband of Martha Desjarlais, the daughter of "Old Gwillim" Desjarlais. Interview with Mr. Harry Garbitt, Moberly Lake, British Columbia, 13 August 1955.

52 "01-146: Mrs. Marcelena Desjarlais of Chetwynd," interview by Lee J. Phillips on 15 March 1973, in the Calverley Collection, Dawson Creek Municipal Library, Dawson Creek, B.C. (hereinafter known as the *Calverley Papers*).

53 Bill Desjarlais, the son of Gwillim Desjarlais, was born at Lac Ste Anne.

54 "01-106 – Chief Wabi's Prophecy" by Dorothea Calverley (n.d.).

55 Interview with Mr. Harry Garbitt, Moberly Lake, B.C., June 1956. It has been suggested that the reason why the Treaty 8 commissioners had such difficulty in locating Natives to sign the treaty adhesion (which finally took place in 1914) was because the Crees and Saulteau of Moberly Lake were avoiding the authorities. According to Dorothea Calverley, "The Saulteaux and Crees from Moberly Lake had their own reasons for staying away from the authorities. The first are reported to be refugees from the Red River Rebellion and many of the latter from the North West Rebellion in the prairies in 1885. By 1913 'they now express a desire to come under Treaty.'" See 01-119: "The First Treaty-Signing Day in Hudson's Hope," by Dorothea Calverley.

56 Exactly who Gwillim Desjarlais was is a mystery. Because the oral accounts identify him as a Saulteaux from Saddle Lake, it is possible that he is William Desjarlais dit Okanese, one of the Saulteaux from Keeseekoowenin's band at Riding Mountain, Manitoba, who settled on Pakan's Reserve prior to the Rebellion, and who was identified as one of the rebels who accompanied Gabriel Cardinal dit Labatoche eastward after the murder of his son Joseph Cardinal. Although the family of his brother, Pierre Desjarlais dit Okanese, was given land at St. Paul des Métis, as was the family of Gabriel Cardinal, there is no record of William Desjarlais dit Okanese having settled there.

57 See David W. Leonard, "Introduction: Charles Mair and the Settlement of 1899," in Mair, *Through the Mackenzie Basin*, xi–xl: xxviii–xxix.

58 Fumoleau, *As Long as This Land Shall Last*, 76.

59 *Edmonton Bulletin*, 25 September 1899. As quoted in Fumoleau, *As Long as This Land Shall Last*, 76–77, 103n103.

60 Joe Sawchuk, Patricia Sawchuk, and Theresa Ferguson, "The Métis Settlements," in Sawchuk et al., *Métis Land Rights in Alberta*, 187.

Chapter 8

1 That this ethnic revitalization movement is occurring at the grassroots level, and proliferating without the sanction or "blessing" of the officially-recognized provincial and federal aboriginal organizations testifies to its strength and resilience.

Appendix 1

1 The many confusing references in the scholarly literature pertaining to three different men named Antoine Desjarlais are cases in point. Two of these men were *Canadien*; one was métis. But the references for Antoine

Desjarlais in the different sources suggest that the editors have amalgamated the information for different men into one. See the appendices, and the footnotes elsewhere, for an extended discussion of "the Antoines."

2 For further information on this collection, see Owens and Roberto, *A Guide to the Archives of the Oblates of Mary Immaculate.*

3 See Jeffrey S. Murray, *A Guide to the Records of the Métis Scrip Commissions in the National Archives of Canada* (Ottawa: National Archives of Canada, 1996), iii–iv. Indexed summaries of Métis scrip records can now be accessed and searched on-line at http:// www.collectionscanada.ca/archivianet/02010507_e.html (accessed 10 May 2004).

4 For further information, see Peter Gillis, David Hume, and Robert Armstrong, comps., *Records Relating to Indian Affairs, RG10* (Ottawa: Public Records Division, Public Archives of Canada, 1975).

5 See Louis Aubry, *Recueil heraldique des bourguemetres de la noble cité de Liège* (Liège: J. P. Gramme, 1720), 8, 9, 40, 45, 48, 53, 143, 191, 376–78. *Annuaire de la noblesse de Belgique* (1900), 102–23; see also *Annuaire de la noblesse de Belgique* (1864), 313–16. See John DuLong, *Genealogical Notes*; see also personal correspondence, Howard K. Thomas, Washington, D.C., to Ken De Jarlais, Champlin, Minnesota dated 10 July 1985. Copies of correspondence in collection of the author.

6 Desjarlais family file, *Picton Papers*, St. Boniface Historical Society, St. Boniface, Manitoba.

7 Louis-Joseph Doucet, Montreal to L'Abbé Pierre Picton, St. Boniface. Letter dated 27 January 1946. Desjarlais family file, *Picton Papers*, St. Boniface Historical Society, St. Boniface, Manitoba.

8 See Anton J. Pregaldin, "Mottin and St. Cin Families." *French-Canadian and Acadian Genealogical Review* 3, no. 1 (spring 1971): 62–63.

9 See "Noms des homme qui ont été mariée par les Missionaires Catholiques depuis l'etablissement de la Mission de la Rivière Rouge en 1818 jusqu'an 15 Fevrier 1831." Undated MS, from the *Red River Collection*, Add. MSS 345, British Columbia Provincial Archives, Victoria, B.C. (Joanne J. Hughes, transcriber).

10 See Merk, *Fur Trade and Empire*, 20.

11 See letter of Fr. Pierre Picton, St. Norbert, Manitoba to Monsieur Coté, dated 12 September 1947, where he discusses the family of Joseph Desjarlais and Okimaskwew, noting that another researcher, with whom he has corresponded, "Il ne m'a pas fournir aucun reuseignement sur la famille d'Antoine Desjarlais qui etait dans la même région et dans la même période." Desjarlais family file, *Picton Papers*, St. Boniface Historical Society, St. Boniface, Manitoba.

12 See PRDH, Record #727141; *Baptismal Record of François Desjarlais*; and PRDH, Record #548536; *Burial Record of François Jarlais*.

13 See William Conolly's District Report for the year 1821–22 in HBCA 1M71 B/115/A/5, *Lesser Slave Lake Post Journal 1821–22.*

14 See p. 5 of *St. Boniface Church – Manitoba, Canada – Photocopies of Original Records Saved from Fire – June 6, 1825 – November 25, 1834.*

Undated MSS in the collection of the Geneological Forum, Portland, Oregon. Copy courtesy of Geoff Burtonshaw, Calgary, Alberta.

15 See "Early Baptisms at St. Peter's Church, Mendota, MN," *Lost in Canada?* 3, no. 1 (January 1977): 41. See also M. M. Hoffmann published version of the Baptismal Register of St. Raphael Cathedral Dubuque, Iowa in *Minnesota History*, March 1927. This information courtesy of Mary Black-Rogers, Edmonton, Alberta, as recorded in her data notebooks of 1985. Mary Black-Rogers, Personal Collection.

16 See Nicks, "Native Responses to the Early Fur Trade at Lesser Slave Lake," 285, 290. See also Provincial Archives of Alberta, Oblate Archives, *Fort des Prairies, Registre de Baptêmes, Mariages, Sepultures 1842–1851*.

17 See "Communications," at http://www.genealogie.umontreal.ca/en/main.htm (accessed 10 March 2004).

Appendix 2

1 "The Most Frequent First Names," in *Programme de récherche en démographie historique* (PRDH), *The Population of Quebec before 1800: Demography–History–Genealogy* (website): http://www.genealogy.umontreal.ca/en/main.htm (accessed 10 March 2004).

2 Ibid.

3 Flandrin, *Families in Former Times*, 11–13.

4 Jetté, *DGFQ*, 1091–1094.

5 Ibid., 1167.

6 See PRDH.

7 Several entries make reference to the involvement of male members of the Cardinal family in fur trading prior to 1730 (i.e., engagé Ouest; marchand de fourtures; engageur Ouest; marchand bourgeois). See Jetté, *DGFQ*, 197–98.

8 Giraud, *The Métis in the Canadian West*, 2:322.

9 See Jetté, *DGFQ*, 471 (for information on the Gatignon dit Duchesne family), and 586 (for information on the Imbaut dit Matha family).

10 The burial record for Josephte Cardinal, Joseph Cardinal's métis daughter, in the Lac La Biche parish registers states "... nous sousigné prêtre avons inhumé le corps de Josette Cardinal décédée il y a quatre jours âgée d'environ quatre-vingt-dix ans, [ninety years] femme de Desjarlais." See burial record for Josephte Cardinal, dated 4 May 1875, in "Registre de Baptêmes, Mariages, Sépultures de Notre-Dame des Victoires du Lac La Biche, 1853–1885," OA, PAA.

11 Please see the excellent overview of Métis practices vis-à-vis names and nicknames in Diane Paulette Payment, "The Free People – Otipemisiwak" – Batoche, Saskatchewan 1870-1930 (Ottawa: National Historic Parks and Sites Service, Environment Canada, 1990): 60-64.

12 The Ojibwa and Cree had virtually identical naming practices, with only slight variations. Several contemporary and historic descriptions exist which document naming ceremonies, which were community events. See,

for example, David G. Mandelbaum, *The Plains Cree: An Ethnographic, Historical and Comparative Study* (Regina: Canadian Plains Research Centre, 1979), 140–42; Duncan Cameron "The Nipigon Country: 1804," in L.R. Masson, *Les Bourgeois de la Compagnie du Nord-Ouest: Recits de Voyages, Lettres et Rapports Inedits Relatifs au Nord-Ouest Canadien* (2 vols). (1889–90; reprint, New York: Antiquarian Press, 1960), 2:252–54; Peter Grant, "The Sauteux Indians," in Masson, 2:324–25. Hallowell, *Ojibwa of Berens River, Manitoba*, 12–13; Landes, *The Ojibwa Woman*, 2–3, 11, 13–14; and Laura Peers and Jennifer S. H. Brown, "'There is No End to Relationship among the Indians': Ojibwa Families and Kinship in Historical Perspective," *The History of the Family – An International Quarterly* 4 (2000): 529–55.

13 French traders are known to have made it to the Rocky Mountains before Finlay, but only Finlay's surname survives of the earliest Montreal pedlars who formed unions with Native women in the Rocky Mountains. Other European surnames in the region are a product of later unions with North West Company, and later Hudson's Bay Company, employees. W. S. Wallace, "The Pedlars from Quebec," *The Canadian Historical Review* 4 (December 1932): 392–94.

14 In April of 1848 Paul Kane became acquainted with a band of Assiniboines living in the vicinity of the Hudson's Bay Company fort at Rocky Mountain House. They were led by their head chief Mah-Min ("the Feather"), and a second chief named Wah-he-joe-tasse-e-neen "The half-white Man" [*sic*]. See Kane, *Wanderings of an Artist Among the Indians of North America*, 289.

15 Morton, *Journal of Duncan M'Gillivray*, 36.

16 See Mandelbaum, *The Plains Cree*, 146–48, 294–95.

17 An earlier record of a trading chief bearing a similar name is that of the Flemish "Bastard," a chief of Dutch and Iroquois ancestry in colonial New York State, the son of a "Hollander" and a Mohawk woman. See Blair, *The Indian Tribes of the Upper Mississippi Valley and the Region of the Great Lakes*, 1:157.

18 See Peers and Brown, "'There is No End to Relationship among the Indians'," 533–35.

19 The children of a mixed-blood woman and an Ojibwa man possessing a *dodem* would immediately have clan membership, while the children of a mixed-blood man and an Ojibwa woman would not. Only if their children married Ojibwa possessing *dodems* would the descendants of this family branch acquire a *dodem*. According to Melissa Meyer, the Minnesota Chippewa attempted to adapt their clan system to accommodate the increased numbers of métis people within their communities. "Some suggest that the appearance of the Eagle clan for those of Anglo-Anishinaabe descent and the Maple Leaf clan for those of Franco-Anishinaabe descent represented atttempts to accommodate doodem-less mixed-bloods with clans of their own." See Melissa Meyer, *The White Earth Tragedy: Ethnicity and Dispossession at a Minnesota Anishinaabe*

Reservation, 1889–1920 (Lincoln: University of Nebraska Press, 1994), 122.

20 The Plains Cree is divided into several loosely organized groups, described in terms of their geographical and ecological locations. The Rabbit Skin People occupied the region between the Assiniboine and Qu'Appelle Rivers, while the Calling River People lived along the Qu'Appelle Valley. The Touchwood Hills People occupied the area between the Touchwood Hills and Long Lake. The House People hunted along the South Saskatchewan in the vicinity of Fort Carleton, while the Parklands People lived to the east of the House People. The River People lived between the North Saskatchewan and Battle Rivers, while the Beaver Hills People occupied the region between the North Saskatchewan River and the Battle River. The western bands (the Beaver Hills, House, Parkland, and River People) are known collectively as the "Upstream People," while the eastern bands (the Calling River People, the Rabbit Skins, and Touchwood Hills People) are known as the "Downstream People." See Mandelbaum, *The Plains Cree*, 10–11.

21 See RG15, Dept. of the Interior, Series D-II-8-c, vol. 1335, Reel C-14948, Scrip Claim of Marguerite Belanger, born 1842 at Carleton, daughter of Pierre Belanger alias *Chiymistiwasis* (Métis) and Anne (Indian).

22 As historian Sherry Farrell-Racette observed, the ermine is a fur-bearing animal that is "white in the winter, and brown in the summer," hence the name Ermineskin, which would aptly describe the complexion of a *métis* person whose skin would tan in summer and pale in winter!

23 See RG15, Dept. of the Interior, Series D-II-8-c, vol. 1334, Reel C-14946. Scrip claim of Frederick Ballendine (b. 1860), son of Ermine Skin (adopted son of Peter Ballendine) and Jane Belanger (Métis).

24 This relationship is identified in Beal and Macleod, *Prairie Fire: The 1885 North-West Rebellion*, 209.

25 In the biography of Poundmaker, he is identified as the son of Sikakwayan (Skunk Skin), a Stony Indian, and a mixed-blood mother. Mistawasis is also identified as his maternal uncle. If this is the case, Poundmaker's mixed-blood mother must be a woman with the surname Mistawasis dit Belanger. A further confirmation of the links between Poundmaker and the Mistawasis dit Belanger family can be found in RG15, Dept. of the Interior, Series D-II-8-c, vol. 1335, Reel C-14948, Scrip Claim of Caroline Belanger (b. 10 June 1869 at Carleton), the daughter of William Belanger or Ah-ya-tas-kew (Métis) and Marie Skunk-Skin (Métis). The actual relationship is not clear though it does suggest that Poundmaker and Caroline Belanger could be cousins. See also Hugh A. Dempsey, "Pitikwahanapiwiyin (Poundmaker)," *DCB*, 11:695–97.

26 When conducting a search of scrip records bearing the name Belanger, additional surname aliases identified for Belanger included Chimistiwasis, Mistawassis, Mistawasis. See RG15, Dept. of the Interior, Series D-II-8-c, vol. 1335, Reel C-14948. Scrip claim of Peggy Belanger (b. Eagle Hills, 1858), daughter of Mistawassis Belanger.

27 See RG15, Dept. of the Interior, Series D-II-8-c, vol. 1363, Reel C-14997. Scrip Claim of Alexis Piche alias Bob-Tail, born 1826 on Saskatchewan River, son of Piche (Métis) and Opeh-tah-she-toy-wishk (Métis). Married 1849 at Pigeon Lake to Catherine Pierre. See also See RG15, Dept. of the Interior, Series D-II-8-c, vol. 1363, Reel C-14997. Scrip claim of Alexis Piche alias Bob-Tail, heir to his deceased daughter Angele Piche, daughter of Alexis Piche alias Bob-Tail and Catherine Cardinal. See also RG15, Dept. of the Interior, Series D-II-8-c, vol. 1363, Reel C-14997. Scrip claim of Catherine Piche (b. 1828 at Lac La Biche). Father Pierre Eia-io-wew (Métis) and Catherine Cardinal. Married 1849 at Pigeon Lake to Alexis Piche.

28 See RG15, Series D-II-8-c, vol. 1363, Reel C-14997. Scrip claim of Louis Piche or Piyeskakkitoot, heir to his deceased wife Susanne Mondion Cardinal, daughter of Laurent Cardinal and Marie Mondion.

29 See RG15, Dept. of the Interior, Series D-II-8-c, vol. 1363, Reel C-14997. Scrip claim for Eugene Piche, or Wah-we-he-nam (b. 1846 at Moose Lake). Father: Kees-te-nap Piche (Métis) and Mother: Ke-na-we-ematt (Métis). Married, 1868 at Lac La Biche to Eliza Cardinal.

30 See RG15, Dept. of the Interior, Series D-II-8-c, vol. 1351, Reel C-14976. Scrip Claim of Rosalie House, daughter of Baptiste Piche, Mother Betsy Natawahpekao.

31 See Coues, *Manuscript Journals*, 2:553–54.

32 See Coues, *Manuscript Journals,*, 2:622, for references to Grand Bâtard and Little Knife.

33 All of these aliases appear in scrip affidavits, fur trade documents, and parish records interchangeably. The surname Jacknife is common on the Elizabeth/Fishing Lake Métis Settlement in Alberta.

34 Patricia Forbes and Muriel Holland Smith, eds., *Harrap's Concise French and English Dictionary*. Edited by Helen Knox (London: Harrap, 1984), Part 2 (French–English): 44.

35 Edward S. Rogers and Mary Black Rogers. "Method for Reconstructing Patterns of Change: Surname Adoption by the Weagamow Ojibwa, 1870–1950," *Ethnohistory* 25: 319–46.

Bibliography

Primary Sources

Archives Nationales du Quebec, Québec City (ANQ)

British Columbia Archives

Red River Collection (MSS 345)

Geoff Burtonshaw Genealogical Collection, Calgary

Registre de la Mission St. Florent au Lac Qu'Appelle. Vol. 1 (1886–1881)
(Photocopy of original parish record)
    Ancien Registres de St. Boniface 1825–1834 (photocopy of original record)
Register of Baptisms, Marriages and Deaths – St. Francis Xavier Church
    – Manitoba, Canada – 1834–1851 (photocopy)
Register of Baptisms, Marriages and Deaths – St. Francis Xavier Church
    – Manitoba, Canada – 1836–1863 (photocopy)

Glenbow Archives, Calgary

C.D. Denney Papers
Peace River Country Research Project 1837–1956 (Margaret and Isobel Loggie
    Papers)

Hudson's Bay Company Archives/Provincial Archives of Manitoba, Winnipeg (HBCA)

B.63/a/1-9 Fort Ellice Post Journals 1793–1867
B.89/a/4-31 Ile-à-la-Crosse Post Journals 1819–1861
B.89/a/32-35 Ile-à-la-Crosse Post Journals 1862–65
B.94/a/1-3 Jasper House Post Journals 1827–1831
B.104/a/1-2 Lac La Biche Post Journals 1799–1820
B.115/a/1-3 Lesser Slave Lake Post Journals 1817–1820
B.115/a/4-6 Lesser Slave Lake Post Journals 1820–1823
B.115/a/7-9 Lesser Slave Lake Post Journals 1825–1831
B.115/e/1-5 Lesser Slave Lake – District Reports 1819–1823
B.190/a/1 Fort St. Mary's Post Journal 1818–1819
B.190/a/2-3 Fort St. Mary's Post Journal 1819–1821
B.224/a/1 Fort Vermilion (Peace River) Post Journal 1802–1803
B.224/a/2-7 Fort Vermilion (Peace River) Post Journals 1826–1840
MG.1/c6/a-b Journal of Occurrences at Fort Ellice, 1856–1859
MG.2/c38 Peter Garrioch Journal, 1843–1847
MG.2/b5/2 Red River Settlement – Red River Correspondence

Latter-Day Saints Archives, Family History Center, Salt Lake City (LDS)

#1031749 Québec – St-François-du-Lac – Comte Yamaska
Index to Parish Registers 1687–1876
#1290059 Québec – Vercheres – Ste-Trinité de Contrecoeur
Parish Registers 1744–1819
#1290060 Québec – Vercheres – Ste-Trinité de Contrecoeur
Parish Registers 1819–1845
#1298969 Québec – Saint-Maurice; Trois Rivières Église catholique – Immaculée
    Conception
BMD (1634–1749)
#1902787 Missouri – Église catholique St. Ferdinand de Florissant
Marriage Register 1794–1973
#1902788 Missouri – Église catholique St. Ferdinand de Florissant
Register of Baptisms 1790–1993, Marriages, 1813–1821
Deaths 1822–1870

Missouri Historical Society, St. Louis (MHS)

Papers of the St Louis Fur Trade

Part One: The Chouteau Collection, 1752–1925
Part Two: Fur Company Ledgers and Account Books

National Archives of Canada, Ottawa (NAC)

#M866 Québec – Église catholique de Varennes (BMD 1693–1800) – extraits/
    extracts.
#C – 3024 Québec – Église catholique de St. François-du-Lac, comté de Yamaska
    (BMD 1687–1836) – extraits/extracts.
#C – 2899 Kaskaskia – Notre Dame de la Conception (BMD 1695–1834)
    – registre/register.
RG10 (Indian Affairs)
NAC, RG10, Indian Affairs – Vols. 1569–1682. Saddle Lake Agency, Alberta,
    1885–1912. *Indian Agent's Letterbooks, 1885–1912.*
NAC, RG10, Indian Affairs – Vols. 9413–9418. *Treaty Annuity Paylists, Treaty
    Six, 1879–1885.*
NAC RG10, Indian Affairs, Series B-8-M, Vol. 10038. *List of Halfbreeds Who
    Have Withdrawn From Treaty June 1, 1888.*
RG15 (Department of the Interior)
NAC RG15. Department of the Interior, *Index to Métis Scrip, 1885–1900.*
NAC RG15. Department of the Interior, *Métis Scrip Records, 1885–1900*, Vols.
    1325–1327, Brazeau – Desjarlais.
NAC RG15. Department of the Interior, *Métis Scrip Records, 1885–1900*, Vols.
    1327–1328, Denomme-Desjarlais – Gosselin-Gullion.
NAC RG15. Department of the Interior, *Métis Scrip Records, 1885–1900*, Vols.
    1343–1344, Deschamp-Desmerais.
NAC RG15. Department of the Interior, *Métis Scrip Records, 1885–1900*, Vols.
    1475–1477.

Programme de recherche en démographie historique (Université de Montréal) (PRDH)

Provincial Archives of Alberta, Edmonton (PAA)

Oblate Archives MI 11-12.
Fort des Prairies, Registre de Baptêmes, Mariages, Sepultures 1842–1851. Acc: 71.220; Item: 5214; Boite: 255.
Notre Dame des Victoires, Lac La Biche. BMD 1853–, Lac La Biche, ACC. 71.220 (parish records).

St. Boniface Historical Society, Winnipeg

"Absents-curatelles de Personnes Absentes du district de Montréal du 03-09-1794 – 30-03-1830" (unpublished manuscript).
Pierre Picton Papers

Published Primary Sources

Abel, Annie Heloise. *Tabeau's Narrative of Loisel's Expedition to the Upper Missouri.* Norman: University of Oklahoma Press, 1939.
——. *Chardon's Journal at Fort Clark 1834–1839.* Pierre, SD: Department of History, State of South Dakota, 1932.
Alvord, Clarence W. *The Illinois Country, 1673–1818.* Springfield, IL: 1920.
——. *Kaskaskia Records, 1778–1790.* Springfield, IL: Illinois State Historical Society, 1909.
——. *Cahokia Records, 1778–1790.* Springfield, IL: Illinois State Historical Society, 1907.
——. *Illinois and Louisiana Under French Rule.* Cincinnati, OH, 1893.
Alvord, Clarence W., and Clarence E. Carter. *The New Régime, 1765–1767.* Springfield, IL: Illinois State Historical Society, 1916.
——. *The Critical Period, 1763–1765.* Springfield, IL: Illinois State Historical Society, 1915.
Archives Nationales du Québec. "Les Congés de Traite Sous le Régime Français au Canada," *Rapport de l'archiviste de la Province de Québec pour 1922–23.* Quebec: 1923.
——. "Répertoire des Engagements Pour L'Ouest." In *Rapport de l'archiviste de la Province de Québec pour 1930–31.* Quebec: 1931.
Archives Nationales du Québec. "Répertoire des Engagements." In *Rapport de l'archiviste pour 1942–43.* Quebec: 1943.
——. "Inventaire des Biens de La Succession de L'Honerable Luc De Chap Ecuyer Sr. De LaCorne." In *Rapport de l'archiviste pour 1942–43.* Quebec: 1943.
——. "Répertoire des Engagements." In *Rapport de l'archiviste pour 1943–44.* Quebec: Redempti Paradis, 1944.
——. "Recensement des Habitants de la Ville et Gouvernement des Trois-Rivières," *Rapport de l'archiviste pour 1946–47,* 12–13.
——. *Table des matières des rapports des Archives du Québec.* Quebec: Roch Lefebvre, 1965.
Blair, Emma Helen. *The Indian Tribes of the Upper Mississippi Valley and the Region of the Great Lakes* (2 vols.). Cleveland, OH: Arthur H. Clark, 1912. Reprint: Lincoln and London: University of Nebraska Press, 1996.

Cameron, Duncan. "A Sketch of the Customs, Manners, and Way of Living of the Natives in the Barren Country About Nipigon." In Vol. 2 of L. R. Masson, *Les Bourgeois de la Compagnie du Nord-Ouest* (2 vols.). New York: Antiquarian Press, 1960, 239–300.

Carrière, J. M. "Life and Customs in the French Villages of the Old Illinois Country (1736–1939)." Canadian Historical Association, *Historical Reports 1939*: 34–47.

Coues, Elliott, ed. *The Manuscript Journals of Alexander Henry the Younger and David Thompson 1799–1816*. (2 vols.) Reprint ed.: Minneapolis: Ross & Haines, 1965.

Cowie, Isaac "Editorial Notes." *The Journal of Daily Occurrences at the Hudson's Bay Company's Fort Ellice, Swan River District – From 1st May 1858 to 27th April 1859*: 39. Unpublished manuscript on file, Provincial Archives of Manitoba, Winnipeg.

Denissen, Révérend Frère Christian. *Genealogy of the French Families of the Detroit River Region, 1701–1911*. (Frederick Powell, ed.). (2 vols.) Burton Historical Collection, Detroit Public Library. Detroit: Detroit Society for Genealogical Research, 1976.

Erasmus, Peter. *Buffalo Days and Nights*: as told to Henry Thompson (reprint ed.). Calgary: Glenbow Institute, 1999.

Faribault-Beauregard, Marthe F. *La population des forts français d'Amérique (XVIIIe siècle)*. (2 vols.) Montreal: Bergeron, 1982–84.

Fleming, R. Harvey, ed. *Minutes of Council Northern Department of Rupert Land, 1821–31*. Toronto: Champlain Society, 1940.

Grant, Peter. "The Sauteux Indians." In L.R. Masson, *Les Bourgeois de la Compagnie du Nord-Ouest* (2 vols.). New York: Antiquarian Press, 1960: 2: 303–66.

Harpole, Patricia C., and Mary D. Nagle, eds. *Minnesota Territorial Census, 1850*. St. Paul: Minnesota Historical Society, 1972.

"Index of names of Claimants to Share in the grant of Scrip to original white settlers who came to the Red River country or to the North-West Territories, between 1813 and 1835, inclusive, and their descendants, not being Halfbreeds, who were alive on the 26th May, 1874" (transcript). *Manitoba Free Press*, 16 January 1911.

Kalm, Peter. *The America of 1750: Peter Kalm's Travels in North America*, ed. Adolph P. Benson, (2 vols.). 1937. Reprint, New York: Dover Publications, 1966.

Kane, Paul. *Wanderings of an Artist Among the Indians of North America*. Edmonton: Hurtig, 1974.

Lamb, W. Kaye. *The Journal of Gabriel Franchère*. Toronto: Champlain Society, 1969.

List of Halfbreeds Who Have Withdrawn from Treaty June 1, 1888. Unpublished manuscript in possession of the author.

Luttig, John C. *Journal of a Fur Trading Expedition on the Upper Missouri, 1812–1813*, ed. Stella M. Drumm. St. Louis: Missouri Historical Society, 1920.

Masson, L. R. *Les Bourgeois de la Compagnie du Nord-Ouest* (2 vols.). New York: Antiquarian Press, 1960.

McDermott, John Francis, ed. *Old Cahokia: A Narrative and Documents Illustrating the First Century of Its History*. St. Louis: St. Louis Historical Documents Foundation, 1949.

Morton, Arthur S., ed. *The Journal of Duncan M'Gillivray of the North West Company: at Fort George on the Saskatchewan, 1794-5*. 1923. Reprint, Fairfield, WA: Ye Galleon Press, 1989.

Munnick, Harriet Duncan, comp. *Catholic Church Records of the Pacific Northwest: St. Paul, Oregon, 1839–1898* (Vols. 1, 2, and 3). Portland, OR: Binford & Mort, 1979.

Munnick, Harriet Duncan, comp. *Catholic Church Records of the Pacific Northwest: St. Louis Register, Vol. 1 (1845–1868); St. Louis Register, Vol. 2 (1869–1900): Gervais Register (1875–1893); Brooks Register (1893–1901).* Portland, OR: Binford & Mort, 1982.

Munnick, Harriet Duncan, ed. *Catholic Church Records of the Pacific Northwest – Vancouver – Vols. 1 and 2 and Stellamaris Mission.* St. Paul, OR: French Prairie Press, 1972.

Nasatir, A. P. *Before Lewis and Clark: Documents Illustrating the History of the Missouri, 1785–1804.* Lincoln: University of Nebraska Press, 1990.

Nute, Grace Lee. *Documents Relating to Northwest Missions, 1815–1827.* St. Paul: Minnesota Historical Society, 1942.

Olson, Edna M., comp. *Index to the St. Charles County, Missouri Marriages, 1792–1863. Recorded in the Saint Charles Borromeo Catholic Church of St. Charles and in the Saint Francis Catholic Church of Portage Des Sioux* (reprint ed.). St. Charles: Author, 1969.

Pease, Theodore Calvin, and Ernestine Jenison, eds. *Illinois on the Eve of the Seven Years' War.* Collections of the Illinois State Historical Library, Vol. 29. Springfield, IL: Illinois State Historical Library, 1940.

Pease, Theodore Calvin, and R.C. Werner, eds. *The French Foundations, 1680–1693.* Springfield, IL: Illinois State Historical Library, 1934.

Programme de récherche en démographie historique (PRDH) – website – http://www.genealogy.umontreal.ca – l'Université de Montréal, Québec.

Programme de récherche en démographie historique (PRDH). "The Most Frequent First Names." In *The Population of Quebec Before 1800: Demography-History-Genealogy* (website): http://www.genealogy.umontreal.ca/en/main.htm. Author: 1999.

Registre de la Mission St. Florent au Lac Qu'Appelle, Vol. 1 (1868–1881) and Vol. 2 (1881–1887). Photocopies of original parish records, Geoff Burtonshaw Genealogical Collection, Calgary, Alberta.

Register of Baptisms, Marriages and Deaths – St. Francis Xavier Church – Manitoba, Canada – 1834–1851. Extracted from photocopy of original records. Portland, OR: Genealogical Forum, n.d.

Rich, E. E., ed. *Journal of Occurrences in the Athabasca Department by George Simpson, 1820 and 1821, and Report.* Toronto: Champlain Society, 1938.

Williams, G., ed. *Andrew Graham's Observations on Hudson's Bay, 1767–91.* London, ON: Hudson's Bay Record Society, 1969.

Wood, W. Raymond, ed. "Journal of John Macdonell, 1793–1795." Appendix. In Provo, Daniel J. *Fort Esperance in 1793–95: A North West Company Provisioning Post.* Reprints in Anthropology, Vol. 28. Columbia, MO: Department of Anthropology, University of Missouri, 1984: 81–13.

Secondary Sources

"Absents – Curatelles de Personnes Absentes du District de Montréal du 03-09-1794 – 30-03-1830." Unpublished manuscript on file, St. Boniface Historical Society, Winnipeg.

Adair, E. R. "France and the Beginnings of New France," *Canadian Historical Review* 25 (September 1944): 246–78.

——. "The Evolution of Montreal under the French Regime." *Canadian Historical Association Report*, 1942: 20–41.

Allaire, Gratien. "Officiers et marchands: les sociétés de commerce des fourrures, 1715–1760," *Revue d'histoire de l'Amerique français* (hiver 1987): 409–28.

——. "Fur Trade Engagés, 1701–1745." In Thomas C. Buckley, ed. *Rendezvous: Selected Papers of the Fourth North American Fur Trade Conference, 1981*. St. Paul, MN: North American Fur Trade Conference, 1981: 15–26.

Altman, Ida, and James Horn, eds. *"To Make America": European Emigration in the Early Modern Period*. Berkeley: University of California Press, 1991.

Anderson, Gary Clayton. *Kinsmen of Another Kind: Dakota-White Relations in the Upper Mississippi, 1650–1862*. Lincoln: University of Nebraska Press, 1984.

Andrew Historical Society. *Dreams and Destinies: Andrew and District*. Andrew, Alberta: Author, 1980.

Annuaire de la noblesse de Belgique (1864).

Arima, Eugene. *Blackfeet and Palefaces: The Pikani and Rocky Mountain House*. Ottawa: Golden Dog Press, 1995.

Asch, Michael. "Kinship and Dravidianate Logic: Some Implications for Understanding Power, Politics and Social Life in a Northern Dene Community." Unpublished paper, Department of Anthropology, University of Alberta, 1993.

Aubry, Louis. *Recueil heraldique des bourguemetres de la noble cité de Liège*. Liège: J.P. Gramme, 1720.

Auger, Roland J. "Judith Rigaud," *French-Canadian and Acadian Genealogical Review* 9, nos. 1–4 (1981): 21.

Babcock, D. R. *Lesser Slave Lake: A Regional History*. Unpublished manuscript on file, Historic Sites Service, Historic Sites and Cultural Facilities Division, Alberta Community Development.

Baergen, W. P. *The Fur Trade at Lesser Slave Lake, 1815–1831*. Unpublished MA Thesis, University of Alberta, 1967.

Barry, Louise. *The Beginnings of the West: Annals of the Kansas Gateway to the American West, 1540–1854*. Topeka: Kansas State Historical Society, 1972.

Barth, Fredrik, ed. *Ethnic Groups and Boundaries: The Social Organization of Cultural Difference*. Boston: Little, Brown and Co., 1969.

Bartko, Patricia. "Desjarlais Information." Unpublished research document on file. Aboriginal Land Claims, Alberta Aboriginal Affairs and Northern Development, Edmonton, Alberta.

Baxter, Angus. *In Search of Your Canadian Roots: Tracing Your Family Tree in Canada*. Toronto: Macmillan of Canada, 1978.

——. *In Search of Your Roots: A Guide for Canadians Seeking Their Ancestors*. Toronto: Macmillan of Canada, 1978.

Beal, Bob, and Rod Macleod. "The North-West Rebellion" (encyclopedia entry). *The 1999 Canadian Encyclopedia: World Edition*. Toronto: McClelland and Stewart, 1998.

——. *Prairie Fire: The 1885 North-West Rebellion*. Edmonton: Hurtig, 1984.

Beckett, Jeremy R. "Kinship, Mobility, and Community Among Part-Aborigines in Rural Australia." In Ralph Piddington, ed. *Kinship and Geographic Mobility*. Leiden: E.J. Brill, 1965: 7–23.

Belting, Natalie Maree. *Kaskaskia Under the French Regime*. Urbana: University of Illinois Press, 1948.

——. "The French Villages of the Illinois Country," *Canadian Historical Review* 24 (1943): 14–23.

Billon, Frederick L. *Annals of St. Louis in its Territorial Days, From 1804–1821*. St Louis, MS: Nixon-Jones, 1888.

——. *Annals of St. Louis in its Early Days Under the French and Spanish Dominations*. St. Louis, MS: Nixon-Jones, 1886.

Binnema, Theodore, Gerhard J. Ens, and R. C. Macleod, eds. *From Rupert's Land to Canada: Essays in Honour of John E. Foster*. Edmonton: University of Alberta Press, 2001.

Birkett, Patricia, ed. *Checklist of Parish Registers, 1986*. Ottawa: Manuscript Division, Public Archives of Canada, 1987.

Bishop, Charles A. *The Northern Ojibwa and the Fur Trade: An Historical and Ecological Study*. Toronto: Holt, Rinehart & Winston, 1974.

Boas, Franz. *Race, Language and Culture*. New York: Free Press, 1940.

Bosher, J. F. "La Rochelle's Primacy in Trade with New France, 1627–1685." In *Business and Religion in the Age of New France – 1600–1760: Twenty-Two Studies*. Toronto: Canadian Scholars' Press, 1994: 109–41

——. "The Family in New France." In *Business and Religion in the Age of New France – 1600–1760: Twenty-Two Studies*. Toronto: Canadian Scholars' Press, 1994: 93–106.

Bradford, M. E., and J. M. Hanson. "Lac La Biche." In Patricia Mitchell and Ellie Prepas, eds. *Atlas of Alberta Lakes*. Edmonton: University of Alberta Press, 1990.

Brown, Jennifer S. H. "Fur Trade as Centrifuge: Familial Dispersal and Offspring Identity in Two Company Contexts." In Raymond J. DeMallie and Alfonso Ortiz, eds. *North American Indian Anthropology: Essays on Society and Culture*. London: University of Oklahoma Press, 1994: 197–219.

——. "Linguistic Solitudes and Changing Social Categories." In Carol M. Judd and Arthur J. Ray, eds. *Old Trails and New Directions: Papers of the Third North American Fur Trade Conference*. Toronto: University of Toronto Press, 1980: 147–59.

——. *Strangers in Blood: Fur Trade Company Families in Indian Country*. Vancouver: University of British Columbia Press, 1980.

——. "Company Men and Native Families: Fur Trade Social and Domestic Relations in Canada's Old Northwest." Doctoral dissertation, University of Chicago, 1976.

Brown, Jennifer S. H., and Elizabeth Vibert, eds. *Reading Beyond Words: Contexts for Native History*. Peterborough, ON: Broadview Press, 1998.

Brown, Jennifer S. H., W. J. Eccles, and Donald P. Heldman, eds. *The Fur Trade Revisited: Selected Papers of the Sixth North American Fur Trade Conference, Mackinac Michigan, 1991*. East Lansing: Michigan State University Press, 1994.

Brown, Jennifer S. H., and Robert Brightman, eds. *"The Orders of the Dreamed": George Nelson on Cree and Northern Ojibwa Religion and Myth, 1823*. Winnipeg: University of Manitoba Press, 1988.

Brown, Margaret Kimball, and Lawrie Cena Dean, eds. *The Village of Chartres in Colonial Illinois, 1720–1765*. New Orleans: La Compagnie des Amis de Fort de Chartres, 1977.

Brunet, Michel. *French Canada and the Early Decades of British Rule 1760–1791*. Ottawa: Canadian Historical Association, 1981.

Bull, Sam. *100 Years at Whitefish 1855–1955* (typescript, unpublished). Glenbow Archives, Calgary, Alberta.

Bumsted, J. M. *The Red River Rebellion*. Winnipeg: Watson & Dwyer, 1996.

Burguière, André, and François Lebrun. "The One Hundred and One Families of Europe." In André Burguière, Christiane Klapisch-Zuber, Martine Segalen, Françoise Zonabend, Eds. *A History of the Family, Vol. 2 – The Impact of Modernity* (Sarah Hanbury Tenison, trans.). Cambridge, MA: Belknap Press of Harvard University Press, 1996: 11–94.

Burguière, André, Christiane Klapisch-Zuber, Martine Segalen, and Françoise Zonabend, eds. *A History of the Family: Vol. 2 – The Impact of Modernity*. Cambridge, MA: Belknap Press of Harvard University Press, 1996.

Burley, Edith I. *Servants of the Honourable Company: Work, Discipline and Conflict in the Hudson's Bay Company, 1770–1879.* Toronto: Oxford University Press, 1997.

Burns, Edward McNall, Philip Lee Ralph, Robert E. Lerner, and Standish Meacham. *World Civilizations: Their History and Culture* (vol. 1 – 7th ed.). New York: W.W. Norton, 1986.

Burt, A. L. "The Frontier in the History of New France." *Canadian Historical Association Reports 1940:* 93–99.

Caldwell, Norman Ward. *The French in the Mississippi Valley, 1740–1750.* Urbana: University of Illinois Press, 1941.

Cameron, D. E., and J. H. Gibson. "The Dream of Peter Shirt." In *Scarlet and Gold,* vol. 10 (1928): 86–88.

Campeau, Lucien. "Jean Juchereau de La Ferté." In David M. Hayne, ed. *Dictionary of Canadian Biography.* Vol. 2. Toronto: University of Toronto Press, 1969: 400.

Carrière, J. M. "Life and Customs in the French Villages of the Old Illinois Country (1763–1939)." *Canadian Historical Association Reports,* 1939.

Champagne, Juliette. *Lac La Biche: Une Communaute Métisse au XIXeme Siècle* Unpublished MA thesis, on file in the Department of History, University of Alberta, Edmonton, 1990.

Charbonneau, Hubert. "Le comportement démographique des voyageurs sous le régime français." *Social History/ Histoire Sociale* 11/21 (May 1978): 120–33.

Charbonneau, Hubert, et al. *The First French-Canadians: Pioneers in the St. Lawrence Valley.* Newark, DE: University of Delaware Press, 1993.

Chartrand, Réné. "Introduction." E. Z. Massicotte, ed. *Canadian Passports, 1681–1752.* Originally published in *RAPQ* 1921–23, with a supplement from *Bulletin des Recherches Historiques,* Vol. 32, 1926. Reprint, New Orleans: Polyanthos, 1975.

Choquette, Leslie P. *Frenchmen Into Peasants: Modernity and Tradition in the Peopling of French Canada.* Cambridge, MA: Harvard University Press, 1997.

——. "Recruitment of French Emigrants to Canada, 1600–1760." In Ida Altman and James Horn, eds. *'To Make America': European Emigration in the Early Modern Period.* Berkeley: University of California Press, 1991: 131–71.

Collet, Oscar Wilkes. *Index to St. Louis Cathedral and Carondelet Church Records.* St. Louis: Missouri Historical Society, 1918.

Conrad, Glenn R., and Carl A. Brasseaux, eds. *A Selected Bibliography of Scholarly Literature on Colonial Louisiana and New France.* Lafayette, LA: Center for Louisiana Studies, University of Southern Louisiana, 1982.

Cook, Ramsay. "Cabbages Not Kings: Towards an Ecological Interpretation of Early Canadian History." *Journal of Canadian Studies* 5, no. 4 (Winter 1990–91): 5–16.

Corvisier, André. *Armies and Societies in Europe.* Abigail T. Siddall, trans. Bloomington: Indiana University Press, 1979.

Cowie, Isaac. *The Company of Adventurers.* Toronto: William Briggs, 1913.

——. "Editorial Notes." *The Journal of Daily Occurrences at the Hudson's Bay Company's Fort Ellice, Swan River District – From 1st May 1858 to 27th April 1859:* Unpublished manuscript on file, Provincial Archives of Manitoba (PAA), Winnipeg.

Craver, Rebecca McDowell. *The Impact of Intimacy: Mexican-Anglo Intermarriage in New Mexico, 1821–1846.* Southwestern Studies Monograph Number 68. El Paso: University of Texas Press, 1972.

Culbertson, Thaddeus A. *Journal of an Expedition to the Mauvaises Terres and the Upper Missouri in 1850*, ed. John Francis McDermott. Washington, DC: Smithsonian Institution, Bureau of American Ethnology, Bulletin no. 147, 1952.

Davidson, Gordon Charles. *The North West Company*. New York: Russell & Russell, 1967.

Davis, Richard Clark, ed. *Sir John Franklin's Journals and Correspondence: The Second Arctic Land Expedition, 1825–1827*. Toronto: Champlain Society, 1998.

Dechêne, Louise. "Jacques Testard de Montigny." In David M. Hayne, ed., *Dictionary of Canadian Biography*. Vol. 2. Toronto: University of Toronto Press, 1969: 625–27.

——. *Habitants and Merchants in Seventeenth-Century Montréal*. Montreal: McGill-Queen's University Press, 1992.

Demallie, Raymond J., ed. *Handbook of North American Indians – Vol. 13 – Plains* (Part 2 of 2). Washington, DC: Smithsonian Institution, 2001.

DeMallie, Raymond J., and Alfonso Ortiz, eds. *North American Indian Anthropology: Essays on Society and Culture*. Norman, OK: University of Oklahoma Press, 1994.

Dempsey, Hugh A. *Big Bear: The End of Freedom*. Vancouver: Douglas & McIntyre, 1984.

——. "Pitikwahanapiwiyin (Poundmaker)." In Francess Halpenny, ed., *Dictionary of Canadian Biography*. Vol. 11. Toronto: University of Toronto Press, 1982: 695–97.

Denig, Edwin Thompson. *Five Indian Tribes of the Upper Missouri: Sioux, Arikaras, Assiniboines, Crees, Crows*. Norman: University of Oklahoma Press, 1961.

Dickason, Olive P. *Canada's First Nations: A History of the Founding Peoples From Earliest Times* (2d ed.). Don Mills: Oxford University Press, 1997.

——. "From 'One Nation' in the Northeast to 'New Nation' in the Northwest: A Look at the Emergence of the Métis." In Jacqueline Peterson and Jennifer S. H. Brown, eds. *The New Peoples: Being and Becoming Metis in North America*. Winnipeg: University of Manitoba Press, 1985: 19–36.

——. *The Myth of the Savage and the Beginnings of French Colonialism in the Americas*. Edmonton: University of Alberta Press, 1984.

Doucet, Mme. Louis-J. "Généalogie de Gerlaise-Desjarlais," from *Memoires de la Société Généalogique*, Vol. 7. Montréal: Société Canadienne Français, 1956: 78–91.

Douville, Raymond, and Jacques Casanova. *Daily Life in Early Canada* (Carola Congreve, trans.) London: Macmillan Co., 1968.

Drumm, Stella M. *Down the Santa Fé Trail and Into Mexico: The Diary of Susan Shelby Magoffin, 1846–1847*. New Haven, CT: Yale University Press, 1926.

Duckworth, Harry W., ed. *The English River Book: A North West Company Journal and Account Book of 1786*. Montreal: McGill-Queen's University Press, 1990.

DuLong, John. *Genealogical Notes* N.d. In collection of the author.

"Early Baptisms at St. Peter's Church, Mendota, Mn." In *Lost in Canada?* 3, no. 1 (January 1977): 41–42.

Eccles, W. J. *The French in North America, 1500–1783* (rev. ed.). East Lansing: Michigan State University Press, 1998.

——. "François-Marie Perrot." In David M. Hayne, ed., *Dictionary of Canadian Biography*. Vol. 2. Toronto: University of Toronto Press, 1969: 540–42.

——. *France In America*. Markham, ON: Fitzhenry & Whiteside, 1972.

——. "The Social, Economic, and Political Significance of the Military Establishment in New France." *Canadian Historical Review* 52 (March 1971): 1–22.

——. *The Canadian Frontier, 1534–1760.* New York: Holt, Rinehart & Winston, 1969.

Elliott, John Huxtable. *The Old World and the New, 1497–1650.* Cambridge: Cambridge University Press, 1970.

Ens, Gerhard. "Dispossession or Adaptation? Migration and Persistence of the Red River Métis: 1835–1890" *CHA Historical Papers 1988*: 120–44.

Ens, Gerhard. "Desjarlais Family – Land Holding Red River." Unpublished manuscript, n.d., in the collection of the author.

Erasmus, Peter. *Buffalo Days and Nights*: as told to Henry Thompson (reprint ed.). Calgary: Glenbow Institute, 1999.

Fagan, Brian. *The Little Ice Age: How Climate Made History 1300–1850.* New York: Basic Books, 2000.

Fisher, Robin, and Kenneth Coates, eds. *Out of the Background: Readings on Canadian Native History.* Toronto: Copp Clark Pitman, 1988.

Flanagan, Thomas. "Louis Riel and the Dispersion of the American Metis," *Minnesota History* 49, no. 5 (spring 1985): 183–90.

Flandrin, Jean-Louis. *Families in Former Times: Kinship, Household and Sexuality.* Cambridge: Cambridge University Press, 1979.

Forbes, Patricia, and Muriel Holland Smith, eds. *Harrap's Concise French and English Dictionary.* Revised and edited by Helen Knox. London: Harrap, 1984.

Foster, John E. "Wintering, the Outsider Adult Male and the Ethnogenesis of the Western Plains Métis." *Prairie Forum* 19, no. 1 (spring 1994): 1–13.

——. "Indian–White Relations in the Prairie West During the Fur Trade Period – A Compact?" In Richard Price, ed. *The Spirit of the Alberta Indian Treaties.* Edmonton, Alberta: Institute for Research on Public Policy, 1987.

——. "Some Questions and Perspectives on the Problem of Métis Roots." In Jacqueline Peterson and Jennifer S. H. Brown, eds. *The New Peoples: Being and Becoming Metis in North America.* Winnipeg: University of Manitoba Press, 1985: 73–91.

Foucault, Michel. *Discipline and Punish: The Birth of the Prison* (2d ed.), Alan Sheridan, trans. (Originally published in France as *Surveiller et Punir: Naissance de la prison*; Paris: Gallimard, 1975); New York: Vintage Books, 1995: 3–69.

Fournier, Marcel. "Belgian Immigration to Canada from its Origins Until 1765" [unofficial translation of an article originally published in *L'Intermediare des Genealogistes*, Brussels, No. 265 (Jan.–Feb. 1990).

Friesen, Gerald. *The Canadian Prairies: A History.* Toronto: University of Toronto Press, 1987.

Friesen, Jean. "Magnificent Gifts: The Treaties of Canada With the Indians of the Northwest, 1869–70." *Transactions of the Royal Society of Canada*, series 5, 1 (1986): 41–51.

French, B. F., ed. *Historical Collections of Louisiana, Part I.* New York: Wiley & Putnam, 1846.

Fumoleau, René, O.M.I. *As Long As this Land Shall Last: A History of Treaty 8 and Treaty 11.* Toronto: McClelland and Stewart, 1974.

Gagnon, Ernest. *Choses D'autrefois feuilles éparses.* Québec: Typ. Dussault & Proulx, 1905.

Gagnon, Serge. *Quebec and Its Historians: 1840–1920.* Montreal: Laval University Press, 1978.

Genealogy in St. Louis (database online) http://genealogyinstlouis.accessgenealogy
.com

Gillis, Peter, David Hume, and Robert Armstrong, comps. *Records Relating to
Indian Affairs – RG10.* Ottawa: Public Records Division, Public Archives of
Canada, 1975.

Giraud, Marcel. *The Métis in the Canadian West* (2 vols.), trans. George
Woodcock. Edmonton: University of Alberta Press, 1986.

——. "France and Louisiana in the Early Eighteenth Century." *Mississippi Valley
Historical Review* 36, no. 4 (1949–50): 657–74.

Gleach, Frederic W. "Controlled Speculation: Interpreting the Saga of Pocahontas
and Captain John Smith." In Jennifer S.H. Brown and Elizabeth Vibert, eds.
Reading Beyond Words: Contexts for Native History. Peterborough, ON:
Broadview Press, 1998: 21–42.

Godbout, Archange. *Généalogie de la famille Testard de Montigny.* Montreal:
Beauchemin, n.d.

——. "Nos Ancêtres Au XVII Siècle." Province de Québec, *Rapport de l'archiviste
de la province de Québec,* 1956–57.

——. O.F.M. "Jean Daigle dit Lallemand." *Mémoires de la Société généalogique
canadienne française,* t. 4, Janvier 1950: 12.

Goosens, N. Jaye. "Indians of the Fort Ellice Region." Unpublished manuscript on
file, Historic Resources Branch, Province of Manitoba (March 1976).

Goubert, Pierre. *The Ancien Régime – French Society: 1600–1750.* New York:
Harper and Row, 1973.

Goulson, Cary F. *Seventeenth-Century Canada: Source Studies.* Toronto:
Macmillan of Canada, 1970.

Government of Alberta. *Reports, Evidence, etc. Re: The Report of the Royal
Commission to Investigate the Conditions of the Half-Breed Population of
Alberta.* Edmonton: Department of Lands and Forests, 1935.

Gray, John S. "Honoré Picotte, Fur Trader." *South Dakota History* 6, no. 2 (spring
1976): 186–202.

Greer, Allan. *The People of New France.* Toronto: University of Toronto Press,
1997.

——. *Peasant, Lord, and Merchant: Rural Society in Three Québec Parishes,
1740–1840.* Toronto: University of Toronto Press, 1985.

——. "Fur Trade Labour and Lower Canadian Agrarian Structures." *CHA
Historical Papers 1981*: 197–214.

Guillemette, André, and Jacques Légaré, "The Influence of Kinship on Seventeenth
– Century Immigration to Canada." *Continuity and Change* 4, no. 1 (1989):
79–102.

Guyon, Louis. *Étude généalogique sur Jean Guyon et ses descendants.* Montreal:
Mercantile Printing, 1927.

Gutmann, Myron P. *War and Rural Life in the Early Modern Low Countries.*
Princeton, New Jersey: Princeton University Press, 1980.

Hafen, LeRoy R., ed. *French Fur Traders & Voyageurs in the American West.*
Lincoln: University of Nebraska Press, 1997.

——. *The Mountain Men and the Fur Trade of the Far West* (10 vols.) Stanford,
CA: Academic Reprints, 1954.

Hallowell, A. Irving. *The Ojibwa of Berens River, Manitoba: Ethnography into
History.* Edited with Preface and Afterword by Jennifer S.H. Brown. New
York: Holt, Rinehart & Winston, 1992.

——. *Contributions to Anthropology: Selected Papers of A. Irving Hallowell.*
Chicago: University of Chicago Press, 1976.

——. "Northern Ojibwa Ecological Adaptation and Social Organization." *Contributions to Anthropology: Selected Papers of A. Irving Hallowell.* Chicago: University of Chicago Press, 1976: 334–36.

——. "Ojibwa Ontology, Behavior, and World View," from *Contributions to Anthropology: Selected Papers of A. Irving Hallowell.* Chicago: University of Chicago Press, 1976: 383–85.

——. "Ojibway World View and Disease." *Contributions to Anthropology: Selected Papers of A. Irving Hallowell.* Chicago: University of Chicago Press, 1976: 391–444.

——. *The Role of Conjuring in Saulteaux Society.* Philadelphia: University of Pennsylvania Press, 1942: 27–29.

Hareven, Tamara K. "The History of the Family and the Complexity of Social Change." *American Historical Review* 96, no. 1 (February 1991): 95–124.

Hartz, Louis. *The Founding of New Societies.* New York: Harcourt, Brace & World, 1964.

Hatt, Ken. "Ethnic Discourse in Alberta: Land and the Métis in the Ewing Commission." *Canadian Ethnic Studies* 17, no. 2 (1985): 64–79.

Healy, W. J. *Women of Red River.* Winnipeg: Russell, Lang and Co., 1923.

"Henry Cardinal Sr. Interviewed About the Time of the Signing of Treaty 6." Saddle Lake Indian Reserve, *O-Sak-Do: Treaty No. 6 Centennial Commemorative Tabloid, Saddle Lake Indian Reserve, Alberta Canada – July 1976.* Saddle Lake, AB: Author, 1976: 12–13.

Hill, J. J. "Antoine Robidoux, Kingpin in the Colorado River Fur Trade, 1824–1844." *The Colorado Magazine* 7, no. 4 (July 1930): 125–32.

History is Where You Stand (Web site). http://www.calverley.dawson-creek.bc.ca/calcoll.html

Hoerder, Dirk. "Ethnic Studies in Canada from the 1880s to 1962: A Historiographical Perspective and Critique." *Canadian Ethnic Studies* 26, no. 1 (1994): 1–18.

Hope, Adrian. "Into the Great Lone Land: The History of the St. Paul Half Breed Reserve." In Saddle Lake Indian Reserve, *O-Sak-Do: Treaty No. 6 Centennial Commemorative Tabloid, Saddle Lake Indian Reserve, Alberta Canada – July 1976.* Saddle Lake: Author, 1976: 25.

Houck, Louis. *The Spanish Regime in Missouri.* Chicago: R.R. Donnelley & Sons, 1909.

_____. *A History of Missouri From the Earliest Explorations and Settlements Until the Admission of the State Into the Union* (3 vols.). Originally published St. Louis, 1908. Reprint ed. New York: Arno Press, 1971.

Huel, Raymond J. A. *Proclaiming the Gospel to the Indians and the Métis.* Edmonton: University of Alberta Press and Western Canadian Publishers, 1996.

Hughes, Catherine. *Father Lacombe, The Black-Robe Voyageur.* Toronto: McClelland and Stewart, 1920.

Hughes, Stuart, ed. *The Frog Lake "Massacre": Personal Perspectives on Ethnic Conflict.* Toronto: McClelland and Stewart, 1976.

Igartua, J. E. "The Merchants of Montreal at the Conquest: Socio-Economic Profile." *Histoire Sociale/ Social History* 8, no. 16 (November 1975): 275–93.

——. "A Change in Climate: The Conquest and the *Marchands* of Montreal." *CHA Historical Papers* (1974): 197–214.

Innis, Harold A. *The Fur Trade in Canada*. Toronto: University of Toronto Press, 1956: 188–200.

Jaenen, Cornelius. *The Belgians in Canada*. Ottawa: Canadian Historical Association, 1991.

———. "Miscegenation in Eighteenth Century New France." In Barry M. Gough and Laird Christie, eds. *New Dimensions in Ethnohistory: Papers of the Second Laurier Conference on Ethnohistory and Ethnology*. Hull, QC: Canadian Museum of Civilization, 1991.

———. *The French Relationship with the Native Peoples of New France and Acadia* Ottawa: Research Branch, Indian and Northern Affairs Canada, 1984.

———. "French Attitudes Toward Native Society." In Carol Judd and A.J. Ray, eds. *Old Trails and New Directions: Papers of the Third North American Fur Trade Conference*. Toronto: University of Toronto Press, 1980: 59–72.

———. *The Role of the Church in New France*. Toronto: McGraw-Hill Ryerson, 1976.

Jetté, René. *Dictionnaire généalogique des familles du Québec: des origines à 1730*. Montréal: University of Montreal Press, 1983.

Jones, Siân. *The Archaeology of Ethnicity: Constructing Identities in the Past and Present*. London and New York: Routledge, 1997.

Kavanagh, Thomas W. "Comanche." In Raymond J. Demallie, ed. *Handbook of North American Indians – Vol. 13 – Plains* (Part 2 of 2) (Washington: Smithsonian Institution, 2001): 886–906: 886–87.

Kellogg, Louise Phelps. *The French Régime in Wisconsin and the Northwest*. Madison: State Historical Society of Wisconsin, 1925.

Lambert, James H. "Québec/Lower Canada." In Brook M. Taylor, ed. *Canadian History: A Reader's Guide – Vol. 1 – Beginnings to Confederation*. Toronto: University of Toronto Press, 1994: 112–83.

Landes, Ruth. *The Ojibwa Woman*. First published in New York by Columbia University Press, 1938. Reprint Edition: Lincoln and London: University of Nebraska Press, 1997.

Landry, Yves. "Gender Imbalance, Les *Filles Du Roi*, and Choice of Spouse in New France." In Bettina Bradbury, ed. *Canadian Family History: Selected Readings*. Toronto: Copp Clark Pitman, 1992: 14–32.

Landry, Yves, and J. Légaré. "The Life-Course of Seventeenth-Century Immigrants to Canada." *Journal of Family History* 12, no. 1–3 (1987): 201–12.

La noblesse Belge: Annuaire de 1900 (1903).

Lavender, David. *The Fist in the Wilderness*. Garden City, NY: Doubleday, 1964.

Leach, E. R. *Pul Eliya: A Village in Ceylon*. Cambridge: Cambridge University Press, 1961: 66, as quoted in Fred Plog and Daniel G. Bates, *Cultural Anthropology* (2d ed.). New York: Alfred A. Knopf, 1980: 256.

Lecompte, Janet. "Introduction: Voyageurs and other Frenchmen in the American Fur Trade." In LeRoy R. Hafen, ed. *French Fur Traders & Voyageurs in the American West*. Lincoln: University of Nebraska Press, 1997: 9–26.

———. "The Chouteaus in the St. Louis Fur Trade." In William R. Swagerty, ed. *A Guide to the Microfilm Edition of Research Collections of the American West: Papers of the St Louis Fur Trade*. St. Louis: Missouri Historical Society, 1991: xiii–xiv.

Leonard, David. "Introduction: Charles Mair and the Settlement of 1899." In Charles Mair, *Through the Mackenzie Basin: An Account of the Signing of Treaty No. 8 and the Scrip Commission, 1899*. Introductions by David W. Leonard and Brian Calliou. Reprint. Edmonton: Edmonton and District Historical Society and University of Alberta Press, 1999: xi–xl.

———. *Delayed Frontier: The Peace River Country to 1909*. Calgary: Detselig, 1995.

Lesage, Germain, O.M.I. *Manereuil: Fondateur de Louiseville 1665–1672.* Louiseville, QC: Presbytère de Louiseville, 1966.

——. *Histoire de Louiseville 1665–1960.* Louiseville, QC: Presbytère de Louiseville, 1961.

Lessard, Renald. "Louis Picotte." In Francess Halpenny, ed., *Dictionary of Canadian Biography.* Vol. 6. Toronto: University of Toronto Press, 1987: 642.

Lewis, Hugh M. "Pierre Isadore Robidoux." In *Robidoux Chronicles: French–Indian Ethnoculture in the Trans-Mississippi West.* Electronic document copyright Hugh M. Lewis 2002 at http://www.lewismicropublishing.com/Publications/RobidouxFrames.htm

L'Imprimeur de sa Majesté la Reine. *Table des Matières des Rapports des Archives du Québec.* Québec: Author, 1965.

Lunn, A. J. E. "The Illegal Fur Trade Out of New France, 1713–1760." *Canadian Historical Association Report*, 1939.

Lussier, A. S. "The Métis: Contemporary Problems of Identity." In Antoine S. Lussier and D. Bruce Sealey, eds. *The Other Natives: The/Les Métis.* Winnipeg: Manitoba Métis Federation Press, 1978, 187–92.

Lussier, Antoine S., and D. Bruce Sealey, eds. *The Other Natives: The/Les Métis.* Winnipeg: Manitoba Métis Federation Press, 1978.

MacGregor, James G. *Father Lacombe.* Edmonton: Hurtig, 1975.

Macleod, Margaret Arnett. *Cuthbert Grant of Grantown: Warden of the Plains of Red River.* Toronto: McClelland and Stewart, 1963.

Macpherson, Elizabeth. *The Sun Traveller: The Story of the Callihoos in Alberta.* St. Albert, AB: Musée Heritage Museum, 1988.

Mair, Charles. *Through the Mackenzie Basin: An Account of the Signing of Treaty No. 8 and the Scrip Commission, 1899.* Introductions by David W. Leonard and Brian Calliou. Reprint. Originally published: Toronto: William Briggs, 1908. Copublished by: Edmonton and District Historical Society and University of Alberta Press, Edmonton, 1999.

Malone, Dumas, ed. *Dictionary of American Biography.* New York: Charles Scribner's Sons, 1935.

Mandelbaum, David G. *The Plains Cree: An Ethnographic, Historical and Comparative Study* Regina: Canadian Plains Research Centre, 1979.

Marks, Constance R. "French Pioneers of Sioux City and South Dakota." *South Dakota Historical Collections* 4 (1908): 255–60.

Massicotte, E.-Z. *Canadian Passports, 1681–1752.* New Orleans: Polyanthos, 1975.

——. *Montréal sous le régime français: Répertoire des Arrêts, Edicts, Mandements, Ordonnances et Règlements conservésdans les Archives du Palais de justice de Montréal, 1640–1760.* Montreal: G. Ducharme, 1919.

——. "Repertoire des engagements pour l'Ouest conservés dans les Archives judiciares de Montréal (1670–1778)."Archives Nationales du Québec, *Rapport de l'archiviste de la Province de Québec pour 1929–30* Quebec: Author, 1930.

Masson, L. R. *Les Bourgeois de la Compagnie du Nord-Ouest: Recits de Voyages, Lettres et Rapports Inedits Relatifs au Nord-Ouest Canadien.* First published 1889–90. Reprint Edition: New York: Antiquarian Press, 1960.

Mathieu, J. "Mobilité et sédentarité: stratégies familiales en Nouvelle-France," *Recherches sociographiques* 28, nos. 2–3 (1987): 211–17.

McCullough, Edward J., and Michael Maccagno. *Lac La Biche and the Early Fur Traders.* Edmonton: Canadian Circumpolar Institute, 1991.

McDermott, John Francis, ed. *Frenchmen and French Ways in the Mississippi Valley.* Urbana: University of Illinois Press, 1969.

McDermott, John Francis. *The French in the Mississippi Valley*. Urbana: University of Illinois Press, 1965.

McDermott, John Francis, ed. *The Early Histories of St. Louis*. St. Louis: St. Louis Historical Documents Foundation, 1952.

McDonnell, Roger. *Paper on Band Formation Used as Supporting Evidence in the Bill C-31 Litigation*. Unpublished manuscript on file, Department of History and Classics, University of Alberta, n.d.

McDougall, John. *Saddle, Sled and Snowshoe: Pioneering on the Saskatchewan in the Sixties*. Toronto: William Briggs, 1896.

——. *Forest, Lake, and Prairie: Twenty Years of Frontier Life in Western Canada, 1842–62*. Toronto: Ryerson Press, 1895.

McLean, W. J. "Tragic Events at Frog Lake and Fort Pitt During the North West Rebellion." In Stuart Hughes, ed. *The Frog Lake "Massacre": Personal Perspectives on Ethnic Conflict*. Toronto: McClelland and Stewart, 1976: 244–95.

McManus, John. "An Economic Analysis of Indian Behavior in the North American Fur Trade." *Journal of Economic History* 32 (1972): 36–53.

McMorran, G. A. *Souris River Posts and David Thompson's Diary of His Historical Trip Across the Souris Plains to the Mandan Villages in the Winter of 1797–98*. Souris, MB: Souris Plaindealer, 1953.

——. "Souris River Posts in the Hartney District." In J.A. Jackson and W.L. Morton, Eds. *Papers Read Before the Historical and Scientific Society of Manitoba* – Series III, Number 5. Winnipeg: Advocate Printers, 1950: 47–62.

Melnycky, Peter. *A Veritable Canaan: Alberta's Victoria Settlement*. Edmonton: Friends of Fort Victoria Historical Society, 1997.

Merk, Frederick. *Fur Trade and Empire*. Cambridge, MA: Harvard University Press, 1968.

Metis Association of Alberta. *Origins of the Alberta Métis: Land Claims Research Project, 1978–79*. Edmonton: Author, 1979.

Meyer, Melissa L. *The White Earth Tragedy: Ethnicity and Dispossession at a Minnesota Anishinaabe Reservation, 1889–1920*. Lincoln: University of Nebraska Press, 1994.

Michel, Louis. "Varennes et Verchères, des origines au milieu du XIX siècle: état d'une enquête." In J. Goy and J.P. Wallot, ed. *Evolution et éclatement du monde rural*. Paris: ACLU des hautes études en sciences socials; Montreal: University of Montreal Press, 1986.

Milloy, John S. *The Plains Cree: Trade, Diplomacy and War, 1790–1870*. Winnipeg: University of Manitoba Press, 1988.

Milot, Charles-Arthur. "Un Picotte Aventureux." *Bulletin Société d'Histoire de Louiseville*, 5 Mars 1989.

——. "Famille Picotte." Family group sheet, n.d.

Miquelon, Dale. *New France 1701–1744: 'A Supplement to Europe'*. Toronto: McClelland and Stewart, 1987.

——. *Society and Conquest: The Debate on the Bourgeoisie and Social Change in French Canada, 1700–1850*. Vancouver: Copp Clark, 1977.

Mitchell, Patricia, and Ellie Prepas, eds. *Atlas of Alberta Lakes*. Edmonton: University of Alberta Press, 1990.

Molloy, Maureen. "'Considered Affinity': Kinship, Marriage and Social Class in New France, 1640–1729," *Social Science History* 14, no. 1 (spring 1990): 1–26.

Moogk, Peter N. *La Nouvelle France: The Making of French Canada – A Cultural History*. East Lansing: Michigan State University Press, 2000.

——. "Reluctant Exiles: Emigrants From France in Canada Before 1760." *William and Mary Quarterly* (3rd series) 46, no. 3 (July 1989): 463–505.

Morris, Alexander. *The Treaties of Canada With the Indians of Manitoba and the North-West Territories*. Reprint. Originally published in Toronto by Belfords, Clark & Co., 1880. Reprint ed.: Toronto: Coles, 1971.

Murphy, Edmund Robert. *Henry De Tonty: Fur Trader of the Mississippi*. Baltimore, MD: Johns Hopkins University Press, 1941.

Murray, Jeffrey S. *A Guide to the Records of the Métis Scrip Commissions in the National Archives of Canada*. Ottawa: National Archives of Canada, 1996.

Nagel, Joane. *American Indian Ethnic Renewal: Red Power and the Resurgence of Identity and Culture*. Oxford: Oxford University Press, 1996.

Neufeld, Peter Lorenz. "The Notable Michael Cardinal Family," *Indian Record* 49, no. 1 (January 1986): 20–21.

——. "The Clear Lake Indian Cemetery," *The Minnedosa Tribune* (Minnedosa, MB) 3, no. 50 (Wednesday March 2, 1994): 30.

——. "Keeseekoowenin," Francess Halpenny, ed., *Dictionary of Canadian Biography*. Vol. 13. Toronto: University of Toronto Press, 1994: 537–38.

Nichols, Roger L. "Historians and Indians." In Roger L. Nichols, ed. *American Frontier and Western Issues: A Historiographical Review*. Westport, CT: Greenwood Press, 1986: 149–77.

Nichols, Roger L., ed. *American Frontier and Western Issues: A Historiographical Review*. Westport, CT: Greenwood Press, 1986.

Nicks, Trudy. "Native Responses to the Early Fur Trade at Lesser Slave Lake." In Bruce Trigger, Toby Morantz, and Louise Dechêne, *'Le Castor Fait Tout': Selected Papers from the Fifth North American Fur Trade Conference, 1985*. Montreal: Lake St. Louis Historical Society, 1987: 278–310.

——. "Demographic Anthropology of Native Populations in Western Canada, 1800 -1975." Doctoral dissertation, University of Alberta, 1980.

——. "The Iroquois and the Fur Trade in Western Canada." In C.M. Judd and A.J. Ray, *Old Trails and New Directions: Papers of the Third North American Fur Trade Conference*. Toronto: University of Toronto Press, 1980: 85–101.

Nute, Grace Lee. *The Voyageur*. St. Paul: Minnesota Historical Society, 1955.

——. "Introduction." Grace Lee Nute, ed. *Documents Relating to Northwest Missions, 1815–1827*. St. Paul: Minnesota Historical Society, 1942: xi–xix.

Nute, Grace Lee, ed. *Documents Relating to Northwest Missions, 1815–1827*. St. Paul: Minnesota Historical Society, 1942.

Ouellet, Fernand. *Economy, Class, and Nation in Quebec: Interpretive Essays*. Toronto: Copp Clark Pitman, 1991.

——. "Economic Dualism and Technological Change in Quebec, 1760–1790." In Fernand Ouellet, *Economy, Class & Nation in Quebec: Interpretive Essays*. Jacques A. Barbier, ed. and trans. Toronto: Copp Clark Pitman, 1991.

——. "Ruralization, Regional Development, and Industrial Growth Before 1850." In Fernand Ouellet, *Economy, Class and Nation in Quebec: Interpretive Essays*. Jacques A. Barbier, ed. and trans. Toronto: Copp Clark Pitman, 1991.

——. *Lower Canada 1791–1840: Social Change and Nationalism*. Toronto: McClelland and Stewart, 1980.

Owens, Brian M., and Roberto, Claude M. *A Guide to the Archives of the Oblates of Mary Immaculate: Province of Alberta-Saskatchewan*. Edmonton: Missionary Oblates, Grandin Province, 1989.

Owram, Doug. "'Conspiracy and Treason': The Red River Resistance From an Expansionist Perspective." In R. Douglas Francis and Howard Palmer, eds. In *The Prairie West: Historical Readings* (Edmonton: Pica Pica Press – Textbook division of the University of Alberta Press,): 167–84.

Palmer, Howard. "History and Present State of Ethnic Studies in Canada." From *Research on Ethnicity in Canada*. (n.d.): 167–83.

Pannekoek, Frits. *A Snug Little Flock: The Social Origins of the Riel Resistance of 1869–1870*. Winnipeg: Watson & Dwyer, 1991.

Payment, Diane. *"The Free People – Otipemisiwak" – Batoche, Saskatchewan 1870–1930*. Ottawa: Minister of Supply and Services Canada, 1990.

Peers, Laura. *The Ojibwa of Western Canada, 1780 to 1870*. Winnipeg: University of Manitoba Press, 1994.

Peers, Laura, and Jennifer S.H. Brown. "'There is No End to Relationship Among the Indians': Ojibwa Families and Kinship in Historical Perspective." *The History of the Family – An International Quarterly* 4 (2000): 529–55.

Perrault, Claude. "Nicholas Perrot." In David M. Hayne, ed. *Dictionary of Canadian Biography*. Vol. 2. Toronto: University of Toronto Press, 1969: 516–19.

"Peter Shirt Remembers: Memories of Early Days on the Reserve," Saddle Lake Indian Reserve, *O-Sak-Do: Treaty No. 6 Centennial Commemorative Tabloid, Saddle Lake Indian Reserve, Alberta Canada – July 1976*. Saddle Lake, AB: Author, 1976: 7–10, 30–31.

Peterson, Jacqueline. "Many Roads to Red River: Métis Ethnogenesis in the Great Lakes Region." In Jacqueline Peterson and Jennifer S. H. Brown, eds. *The New Peoples: Being and Becoming Métis in North America*. Winnipeg: University of Manitoba Press, 1985: 37–71.

Peterson, Jacqueline, and Jennifer S. H. Brown, eds. *The New Peoples.: Being and Becoming Métis in North America*. Winnipeg: University of Manitoba Press, 1985.

Peterson, Jacqueline, and John Anfinson. "The Indian and the Fur Trade: A Review of Recent Literature." In William R. Swagerty, ed. *Scholars and the Indian Experience: Critical Reviews of Recent Writing in the Social Sciences*. Bloomington: Indiana University Press, 1984.

Phillips, Paul Crisler. *The Fur Trade* (2 vols.). Norman: University of Oklahoma Press, 1961.

Piddington, Ralph. "The Kinship Network Among French-Canadians." In Ralph Piddington, ed. *Kinship and Geographic Mobility*. Leiden: E.J. Brill, 1965: 145–65.

Piddington, Ralph, ed. *Kinship and Geographic Mobility*. Leiden: E.J. Brill, 1965.

Pinay, Donna. "The History of the File Hills Farming Colony," *Saskatchewan Indian* 4, no. 6 (July 1974): 16.

Pittman, Philip. *The State of the European Settlements on the Mississippi*. London, 1770; repr. by F.H. Hodder, ed.; Cleveland, 1906.

Plog, Fred, and Daniel G. Bates. *Cultural Anthropology*. (2d ed.) New York: Alfred A. Knopf, 1980.

Podruchny, Carolyn. "Sons of the Wilderness": Work, Culture and Identity among Voyageurs in the Montreal Fur Trade, 1780–1821. Unpublished PhD dissertation, University of Toronto, 1999.

Pregaldin, Anton J. "Mottin and St. Cin Families." *French-Canadian and Acadian Genealogical Review* 3, no. 1 (spring 1971): 62–63.

Price, Richard, ed. *The Spirit of the Alberta Indian Treaties*, 2nd ed. Edmonton: Institute for Research on Public Policy, 1987.

Provo, Daniel J. *Fort Esperance in 1793–95: A North West Company Provisioning Post*. Reprints in Anthropology, Vol. 28. Columbia, Missouri: Department of Anthropology, University of Missouri, 1984.

Provost, Honorius. "Claude Auber." In David M. Hayne, ed. *Dictionary of Canadian Biography*. Vol. 2. Toronto: University of Toronto Press, 1969: 72.

——. "Robert Giffard de Moncel." In David M. Hayne, ed. *Dictionary of Canadian Biography*. Vol. 2. Toronto: University of Toronto Press, 1969: 330–31.

Qualey, Carleton C. "Ethnic Groups and the Frontier." In Roger L. Nichols, ed. *American Frontier and Western Issues: A Historiographical Review.* Westport, CT: Greenwood Press, 1986: 199–216.

Ray, Arthur J. "Indians as Consumers in the Eighteenth Century." In Carol Judd and A.J. Ray, eds. *Old Trails and New Directions: Papers of the Third North American Fur Trade Conference.* Toronto: University of Toronto Press, 1980: 255–71.

——. *Indians in the Fur Trade: Their Role as Hunters, Trappers, and Middlemen in the Land Southwest of Hudson's Bay.* Toronto: University of Toronto Press, 1974.

Ray, Arthur J., Jim Miller, and Frank Tough. *Bounty and Benevolence: A History of the Saskatchewan Treaties.* Montreal: McGill-Queen's University Press, 2000.

Ray, Arthur J., and Donald Freeman.*'Give Us Good Measure': An Economic Analysis of Relations Between the Indians and the Hudson's Bay Company Before 1763.* Toronto: University of Toronto Press, 1978.

Reardon, James Michael. *George Anthony Belcourt: Pioneer Catholic Missionary of the Northwest, 1803–1874: His Life and Times.* St. Paul, MN: North Central Publishing, 1955.

Reddekopp, G. Neil. *The Creation and Surrender of the Beaver and Duncan's Bands' Reserves.* Unpublished manuscript on file, Indian Land Claims Unit, Alberta Intergovernmental and Aboriginal Affairs, March 1996, revised May 1997.

Rich, E. E. "Trade Habits and Economic Motivation Among the Indians of North America." *Canadian Journal of Economics and Political Science* (1960): 35–53.

Robidoux, Orral Mesmore. *Memorial to the Robidoux Brothers Who Blazed the Western Trails for Civilization: A History of the Robidouxs in America.* Kansas City, MO: Smith-Grieves, 1927.

Robinson, Doane. *A History of the Dakota or Sioux Indians.* Minneapolis: Ross & Haines, 1967.

Rogers, Edward S., and Mary Black Rogers. "Method for Reconstructing Patterns of Change: Surname Adoption by the Weagamow Ojibwa, 1870–1950." *Ethnohistory* 25: 319–46.

Rotstein, Abraham. "Trade and Politics: An Institutional Approach." *Western Canadian Journal of Anthropology* 3 (1972): 1–28.

Rowand, Evelyn. "The Rebellion at Lac La Biche." *Alberta Historical Review* 21, no. 3 (1973): 1–9.

Roy, A. *Inventaire des greffes des notaires du Régime français.*

Roy, Régis, and Gérard Malchelosse. *Le Régiment de Carignan: Son Organization et son Expédition au Canada (1665–1668).* Montréal: G. Ducharme, 1925.

Saddle Lake Indian Reserve. *O-Sak-Do: Treaty No. 6 Centennial Commemorative Tabloid, Saddle Lake Indian Reserve, Alberta Canada – July 1976.* Author, 1976.

St. Boniface Church – Manitoba, Canada – Photocopies of Original Records Saved from Fire – June 6, 1825 – November 25, 1834. Undated MSS in the collection of the Genealogical Forum, Portland, Oregon.

St. Louis Genealogical Society. *Earl Fischer Database of St. Louisans.* Electronic database at http://www.rootsweb.com/~mostlogs/efdb/index.htm. St. Louis: Author, 1999.

St. Louis Genealogical Society. *Catholic Marriages St. Louis, Missouri 1774–1840.* St. Louis: Author, n.d.

St.-Onge, Nicole J. M. "Variations in Red River: The Traders and Freemen Métis of Saint-Laurent, Manitoba." *Canadian Ethnic Studies* 24, no. 2 (1992): 1–21.

Saunders, Richard M. "The Emergence of the *Coureur de Bois* as a Social Type." *The Canadian Historical Association Historical Reports, 1939*: 22–33.

Sawchuk, Joe. *The Métis of Manitoba: Reformulation of an Ethnic Identity.* Toronto: Peter Martin Associates, 1978.

Sawchuk, Joe, Patricia Sawchuk, and Theresa Ferguson. *Métis Land Rights in Alberta: A Political History.* Edmonton: Métis Association of Alberta, 1981.

——. "The Métis Settlements." In Joe Sawchuk, Patricia Sawchuk, and Theresa Ferguson, *Métis Land Rights in Alberta: A Political History.* Edmonton: Métis Association of Alberta, 1981: 187–214.

Scharf, J. Thomas. *History of Saint Louis City and County, from the Earliest Periods to the Present Day Including Biographical Sketches of Representative Men* (2 vols.). Philadelphia: Louis H. Everts & Co., 1883.

Schenck, Theresa M. "The Cadottes: Five Generations of Fur Traders on Lake Superior." Jennifer S. H. Brown, W. J. Eccles, and Donald P. Heldman, eds. *The Fur Trade Revisited: Selected Papers of the Sixth North American Fur Trade Conference, Mackinac Michigan, 1991.* East Lansing: Michigan State University Press, 1994: 189–98.

Service, Elman R. *Primitive Social Organization: An Evolutionary Perspective* (2d ed.). New York: Random House, 1962.

Smith, Donald B. *Le Sauvage: The Native People in Quebec Historical Writing on the Heroic Period (1534–1663).* Ottawa: National Museums of Canada, 1974.

Soc.genealogy.french. Internet newsgroup.

"Some St. Louis Divorces and Separations (1808–1863)" (http://genealogyinstlouis .accessgenealogy.com/dldivorces.htm), *Genealogy in St Louis* (website). (http: //genealogyinstlouis.accessgenealogy.com).

Sprague, D. N., and R. P. Frye, comp. *The Genealogy of the First Métis Nation: The Development and Dispersal of the Red River Settlement, 1820–1900.* Winnipeg: Pemmican, 1983.

Stanley, George F. G. "Gabriel Dumont's Account of the North-West Rebellion." In Antoine S. Lussier and D. Bruce Sealey, eds. *The Other Natives: The/Les Métis* Winnipeg: Manitoba Métis Federation Press, 1978: 147–75.

——. *The Birth of Western Canada: A History of the Riel Rebellions.* 1936; reprint, Toronto: University of Toronto Press, 1992.

Stonechild, Blair, and Bill Waiser. *Loyal Till Death: Indians and the North-West Rebellion.* Calgary: Fifth House, 1997.

Sulte, Benjamin. *Mélanges Historiques.* Montréal: G. Ducharme, 1922.

——. *Histoire des Canadiens-Français.* Montreal, 1882.

Sunder, John E. *The Fur Trade on the Upper Missouri, 1840–1865.* Norman: University of Oklahoma Press, 1965.

Surtees, Robert J. "Canadian Indian Policies." In Wilcomb B. Washburn (ed.) *Handbook of North American Indians – History of Indian-White Relations* (vol. 4). Washington: Smithsonian Institution, 1988: 81–88.

Swagerty, William R. "Marriage and Settlement Patterns of Rocky Mountain Trappers and Traders." *Western Historical Quarterly* 11, no. 2 (April 1980): 159–80.

——., ed. *Scholars and the Indian Experience: Critical Reviews of Recent Writing in the Social Sciences.* Bloomington: Indiana University Press, 1984.

——. "General Introduction." In William R. Swagerty, ed. *A Guide to the Microfilm Edition of Research Collections of the American West: Papers of the St Louis Fur Trade.* St. Louis: Missouri Historical Society, 1991.

——, ed. *A Guide to the Microfilm Edition of Research Collections of the American West: Papers of the St Louis Fur Trade*. St. Louis: Missouri Historical Society, 1991.

Swagerty, William R., and Dick A. Wilson, "Faithful Service Under Different Flags: A Socioeconomic Profile of the Columbia District, Hudson's Bay Company and the Upper Missouri Outfit, American Fur Company, 1825–1835." In Jennifer S.H. Brown, W. J. Eccles, and Donald P. Heldman, eds. *The Fur Trade Revisited.: Selected Papers of the Sixth North American Fur Trade Conference, Mackinac Island, Michigan, 1991*. East Lansing: Michigan State University Press, 1994: 243–67

Tanguay, C. *Dictionnaire généalogique des familles canadiennes depuis la fondation de la colonie jusqu'à nos jours* (7 vols.). Montréal: 1871–79.

Tanner, Helen Hornbeck. "The Career of Joseph La France, *Coureur de Bois* in the Upper Great Lakes." In Jennifer S. H. Brown, W. J. Eccles, and Donald P. Heldman, eds. *The Fur Trade Revisited*. East Lansing: Michigan State University Press, 1994: 171–87.

——, ed. *The Settling of North America: The Atlas of the Great Migrations Into North America from the Ice Age to the Present*. New York: Macmillan, 1995.

Taylor, Brook M., ed. *Canadian History: A Reader's Guide – Vol. 1: Beginnings to Confederation*. Toronto: University of Toronto Press, 1994.

Thistle, Paul C. *Indian-European Trade Relations in the Lower Saskatchewan River Region to 1840*. Winnipeg: University of Manitoba Press, 1986.

Thomas, R.K. "Afterword." In Jacqueline Peterson and Jennifer S.H. Brown, eds., *The New Peoples: Being and Becoming Metis in North America*. Winnipeg: University of Manitoba Press, 1985: 243–51.

Thorne, Tanis. *The Many Hands of My Relations: French and Indians on the Lower Missouri*. St. Louis: University of Missouri Press, 1996.

—— "People of the River: Mixed-Blood Families on the Lower Missouri." Doctoral dissertation, University of California, Los Angeles, 1987.

Tousignant, Pierre, and Madeleine Dionne-Tousignant. "Luc de la Corne." In Francess Halpenny, ed. *Dictionary of Canadian Biography*. Vol. 4. Toronto: University of Toronto Press, 1979: 425–28.

Trudel, Marcel. *The Beginnings of New France, 1524–1663*. Toronto: McClelland and Stewart, 1973.

Trudel, P.E., O.F.M. *Généalogie de la famille Trudel(le)*. Montréal: Sourds-Muets, 1955.

Trudelle, T.A. *Le premier Trudelle en Canada et ses descendants*. Québec: Brousseau & Desrochers, 1911.

Turney-High, Harry Holbert. *Château-Gérard: The Life and Times of a Walloon Village*. Columbia, S.C.: University of South Carolina Press, 1953.

Tyler, Kenneth J. "Kiwisance (Cowessess, Ka-we-zauce, Little Child)." In Francess Halpenny, ed. *Dictionary of Canadian Biography*. Vol. 11. Toronto: University of Toronto Press, 1982: 477–78.

Upshur, Jiu-Hwa L., et al. *World Civilizations: Their History and Culture* (vol. 1 – 7th ed.) New York: W.W. Norton, 1986.

Van Kirk, Sylvia. "'What if Mama is an Indian?' The Cultural Ambivalence of the Alexander Ross Family." Jacqueline Peterson and Jennifer S.H. Brown, eds. *The New Peoples.: Being and Becoming Métis in North America*. Lincoln: University of Nebraska Press, 1986: 207–17.

——. *Many Tender Ties: Women in Fur Trade Society, 1670–1870*. Winnipeg: Watson & Dwyer; Norman: University of Oklahoma Press, 1983.

Verney, Jack. *The Good Regiment: The Carignan-Salières Regiment in Canada, 1665–1668*. Montreal: McGill-Queen's University Press, 1991.

Wallace, Joseph. *Illinois and Louisiana Under French Rule*. Cincinnati: R. Clarke, 1893.

Wallace, William Swilling. *Antoine Robidoux 1784–1860: A Biography of a Western Venturer* Los Angeles: Glen Dawson, 1930.

——. "The Pedlars From Quebec." *Canadian Historical Review* no. 4 (December 1932): 387–402.

Wallot, Jean-Pierre. "Religion and French-Canadian Mores in the Early Nineteenth Century." *Canadian Historical Review* LII (March 1971): 51–91.

Weber, David J. *The Extranjeros: Selected Documents From the Mexican Side of the Santa Fe Trail 1825–1828*. Santa Fe: Stagecoach Press, 1967.

——. *The Taos Trappers: The Fur Trade in the Far Southwest, 1540–1846*. Norman: University of Oklahoma Press, 1971.

Weilbrenner, Bernard. "Nicholas Juchereau de Saint-Denis." In David M. Hayne, ed. *Dictionary of Canadian Biography*. Vol. 2. Toronto: University of Toronto Press, 1969: 401–402.

White, Richard. "Introduction." In Emma Helen Blair, trans., ed. and ann., *The Indian Tribes of the Upper Mississippi Valley and Region of the Great Lakes*. Originally published: Cleveland: Arthur H. Clark, 1911. New Edition: Lincoln: University of Nebraska Press, 1996: 1–7.

Whitten, Norman E. Jr. "Ethnogenesis." David Levinson and Melvin Ember, eds. *The Encyclopedia of Cultural Anthropology*. New York: Henry Holt and Co. 1996: 407–10.

Wien, Thomas. "Canada and the *pays d'en haut*, 1600–1760." In Brook M. Taylor, ed. *Canadian History: A Reader's Guide – Vol. 1 – Beginnings to Confederation*. Toronto: University of Toronto Press, 1994: 32–75.

Williams, G., ed. *Andrew Graham's Observations on Hudson's Bay, 1767–91*. London: Hudson's Bay Record Society, 1969.

Williams, Scott. "First Company San Luis de Ilinuenses Militia" (1999). *Time Portal to Old St. Louis* (website). http://members.tripod.com/oldstlouis/stluismilitia.htm

Wishart, Bruce. "Archaeology on the Souris River: Fort Desjarlais" (a four-part newspaper article, n.d.). Manuscript on file at the Provincial Archives of Manitoba, Winnipeg.

Wolfart, H.C., and Freda Ahenakew. *The Student's Dictionary of Literary Plains Cree*. Winnipeg: Algonquian and Iroquoian Linguistics, 1988.

Wood, W. Raymond, and Thomas D. Thiessen. *Early Fur Trade on the Northern Plains: Canadian Traders Among the Mandan and Hidatsa Indians, 1738–1818*. Norman: University of Oklahoma Press, 1985.

Woods, Patricia Dillon. *French-Indian Relations on the Southern Frontier, 1699–1762*. Doctoral dissertation, unpublished. Ann Arbor: Michigan State University, 1980.

Index

....

Cardinal, St. Paul "Menoomin," 165, 168
Cardinal and Piche families intermarriage, 233
Cardinal as surname, 226–28
Cardinal dit Labatoche, Gabriel, 147
Cardinal dit Mustatip, Catherine (a.k.a. Catherine Pierre), 233
Cardinal family, 181
  rebel supporters, 164
  treaty Indians, 164
Carignan-Salières Regiment, 2, 23, 33, 46
  encouragement to marry, 28
  formation of, 24
  as immigrants to New France, 26–28
  notoriety in France, 25–26
Carondelet, 56
Cavelier, Pierre, 39
censitaires, 28, 32–34, 37, 39–42, 44–45
  definition, xv
Census enumeration (illustration), 142
Cerré, Gabriel, 62
Cerré, Pascal, 65
Chaboillez, Charles, 77
Champlain Society publications, 211
Chatillon, Rosalie. See Hardy dit Chatillon, Rosalie
"Child" (Mistawasis), chief, 128
children. See also métis children
  lives of, 11
  marriage contracts stipulations, 31
  mortality, 22
  responsibility for, 36
Chouteau, Auguste, 7, 56, 67, 73
Chouteau, Pierre, 65
Chouteau family, 60
Christianity and Christianization, 6, 8, 113, 167. See also missions and missionaries
  Athabasca vs. Red River, 140
  bad for business, 7
Christie, Alexander, 132
Clark, William, 65
Columbia Fur Company, 65
Columbia region, 93, 98

Comanche kidnap legend, 72
communities, Native, 1885, 153
community, 46
  Métis and Indian concepts of, 167
Compagnie des Indes, 46
congé de traite, 34, 49, 77, 79
  widows, 35
"conjuring," 104–5, 268n90
Conolly, William, 93, 95–97
  scaling back privileges to freemen, 94
Contrecoeur, 41
Cook, Henry, 134
Cornwall, James K, a.k.a. "Peace River Jim"
  affidavit on Treaty 8 negotiations, 187–88
Coté, J. A., 190
country marriage, 5, 63–64, 66, 255n33. See also marriage à la façon du pays
  kin obligations of, 231
  regularization, 72, 113–14, 123
coureurs de bois, xv, 3, 37, 54
Courtoreille, Kathleen
  Rebellion story, 192
Cowie, Isaac, 136, 137, 145
Cree, 102, 120, 163, 206
  Duncan Tustawit's Cree Band, 191
  métis ancestry, 232
  as middlemen in fur trade, 103
  open letter to John A. Macdonald, 148–52
  petition for treaty at Slave Lake, 186
  Woods Cree, 166, 191
Cree/North West Mounted Police confrontation, 153
Creole
  definition, xv
  families, 63–64, 72–73
cultural identity
  definitions, 1
Cumberland House, 119

....

Dakota Indians, 3, 131
De Gerlaise, Antoine, 44
De Gerlaise, Jean-François, 44–45, 48–50

Desjarlais, Eliza, 160
Desjarlais, Eloi (b. 1770), 67, 256n46
Desjarlais, Eloy, 63
Desjarlais, François, 82, 119, 219,
        262n23
    integration into Métis parish, 139
    move to Baie St. Paul, 121
Desjarlais, François (b. 2 Jan. 1820),
        220
Desjarlais, François (Muscowequan
        Reserve), 173
Desjarlais, François "Peaysis," 147,
        160, 177–78, 207–8
    band of, 146, 178, 194, 207
    joined rebel cause, 157
Desjarlais, Frederick "Keh-kek"
        (Hawk), 146, 161, 163, 204,
        274n39
    cultural identification as Cree, 126,
        180
    first settler, Andrew, Alberta, 180
    John McDougall's description of,
        126–28, 128–29
    kinship network, 128, 130, 139
    riding a buffalo (illustration), 127
    withdrawal from treaty, 180
Desjarlais, Guillaume
    free trader, 182–83
    insanity, 183
Desjarlais, Gwillim
    "promised land" dream, 191–93,
        290n56
    refused treaty, 193
Desjarlais, Hélène, 64
Desjarlais, Isabel, 185
Desjarlais, Jean-Augustin-Baptiste (b.
        1733), 50
Desjarlais, Jean-Baptiste, 64
Desjarlais, Jean-François. See De
        Gerlaise, Jean-François
Desjarlais, Jean-Marie, 182
    scrip application, 191
    took treaty, 191
Desjarlais, Joseph (b. 29 Jan. 1810),
        61–62
Desjarlais, Joseph (b. 3 Sept. 1754), 2,
        4, 82–83, 85, 90, 222
    affiliation with North West Co., 84

begging for assistance, 96–97
    burial, 121
    contact with Quebec relatives, 90–91
    country marriage to Okimaskwew,
        80–81, 201
    died, 1833, 120
    entered fur trade as an independent,
        77–78
    kin relationship to Toussaint Lesieur,
        79
    left Lesser Slave Lake region, 119
    trading licence, 76, 78
Desjarlais, Joseph (engagé), 49–50
Desjarlais, Joseph Jr., 85–86, 122, 147,
        163, 221
    country union with Josephte
        Cardinal, 233
    remained in Athabasca, 119, 204
Desjarlais, Joseph (married to Marie-
        Josephte Hervieux), 76–77
Desjarlais, Josephte, 222
Desjarlais, Julie, 67–68
    divorce, 71
Desjarlais, Louis (b. 1730), 45, 49–50
Desjarlais, Louise (b. 12 Nov. 1823),
        219
Desjarlais, Madeleine, 173
Desjarlais, Marcel ("Gwiwisens"), 85,
        119, 132, 201, 204, 276n55
    measles, 92
Desjarlais, Marie, 163
Desjarlais, Marie-Anne, 60
Desjarlais, Marie-Josèphe, 63
Desjarlais, Marie-Madeleine. See De
        Gerlaise, Marie-Madeleine (b.
        1725)
Desjarlais, Martial. See Desjarlais,
        Marcel
Desjarlais, Paul, 60
Desjarlais, Pierre-Amador (b. 1740), 45
Desjarlais, Pierre-François, 49–50
Desjarlais, Rosine, xi, xii
    Industrial School, 173
Desjarlais, Thomas, 85
    measles, 92–93
Desjarlais, Thomas (son of Baptiste
        "Penawich")
    and family, Lebret, 174

half-breeds. *See* Métis; métis

Hallowell, A. Irving, 100, 102, 104–5

Hamelin, Alexandre "Azure," 157, 162–63

  kin relations with Big Bear's band, 163

Hamelin, Marie Desjarlais Blondion, 164

Hardy dit Chatillon, Rosalie, 60

Harmon, Edward, 134

"Harry Legs." *See* Desjarlais, Antoine (b. ca. 1792)

Hayter Reed's memorandum, 171–72

  impact on Desjarlais family, 170

Henry, Alexander the Younger, 83–84, 233–34

Hervieux, Marie-Marguerite, 76

Hervieux dit Lesperance, Marie-Josephte, 62

hivernants, 83, 144, 201

House People *(wasahikanwiyiniwak)*, 232

Howse, Adam, 157

Hudson's Bay Company, 3–4, 6–7, 12, 130, 132, 186

  amalgamation with North West Company, 82, 93, 111, 202

  ascription of aboriginal identity, 109

  attempts to control freemen, 94, 201

  competition with North West Company, 90, 92

  divide and conquer policy, 209

  monopoly, 134–35

  new policies after 1821, 109

  punitive 1825 operating policies, 99, 203

  "Retrenching System," 111

Hudson's Bay Record Society, 211

Hugonard, Father, 173

Hunter, Thomas, 161

hunting and fishing rights

  Treaty 8, 189

hunting bands. *See* boreal forest hunting bands

hunting territories, 97, 102–3

  usufruct dominance, 107

Illinois country, French settlements, 57

Illinois settlements, 50

  fur trading and subsistence agriculture, 54

  lifestyle after British conquest, 54, 56, 58

  migration to St. Louis, 56

  social hierarchy, 54

Imasees (Big Bear's son), 154

indentured labour, 2

Indian

  definition, xvi

Indian Act

  amendment re ammunition, 175

Indian Affairs Documents, 216–17

Indian girls, 69

Industrial School, Lebret, 173–74

Iron Head, chief, 152

Iroquois

  attacks, 25–26, 40–41, 45

  engagés, 5

  freemen, 86, 89

  suppression of, 46

  treaty with, 41

Jackfish Lake, 128

Juchereau, Jean, 32

Juchereau, Nicolas, 32

Ka-qua-num's band, 147, 160

  acceptance and sale of scrip, 193

Kaketa, Marie, 123

Kane, Paul, 125

Kankakee, Illinois, 66

Kaskaskia, 54, 59, 62

keelboat, 63

Keeseekoowenin's reserve, 165

Keh-kek. *See* Desjarlais, Frederick "Keh-kek" (Hawk)

Kehewin's band, 155, 160

Kennedy, Robert, 90–91, 93

Keskayiwew. *See* Bob Tail, chief; Piche, Alexis

Ketawayhew Reserve, 172

kin-based "communities of interest," 17

Lebret, Industrial School at, 173
  Roman Catholic mission at, 135, 172
Ledoux, Eusebe, 130
Leduc, Paul, 49
Lefebvre, Jean-Baptiste, 49
LeGardeur, Marguerite, 38
LeMaître, Marie, 38
LeMaître-Auger family, 49
LeMaître dit Lamorille, Antoine, 38
LeMaître dit le Picard, François, 38
LeMaître family, 37, 39, 45
LePine, Jacques. *See* Maret dit LePine,
  Jacques
Lesage, Jean-Baptiste, 44
Lesieur, Charles, 62
Lesieur, François, 62
Lesieur, Joseph, 62
Lesieur, Toussaint, 62, 79
Lesieur family, 62, 80
Lesperance, Marie-Josephte. *See*
  Hervieux dit Lesperance,
  Marie-Josephte
Lesser Slave Lake, 86
  migration from St. Paul des Métis,
    184
  scrip, 189–90
  trading store, 182
  Treaty 8, 187
Lesser Slave Lake Post Journal, 84–85,
  87, 89–90
Lesser Slave Lake region, 84
Letremblade, Paul. *See* Guyon dit
  Letremblade, Paul
Lewes, John Lee, 85–86, 94, 99
  definition of "freeman," 82
  friendship with Tullibee, 88
  patronage of Desjarlais family, 86
  transferred to Columbia, 93
Lewistown, Montana, 136
Liège, Principality of, 23, 29
Liguest, Pierre Laclède, 56
liquor
  gifts of, 112
liquor trade, 7, 114, 116, 201
literacy, 23, 29, 81
Little Black Bear, 173
Little Hunter's band, 146, 164, 180

Little Knife, 164, 234
Little Prairie, 56, 62
Logan, Thomas, 134
Lottinville, Aurélie Picotte, 66
Louis XIV, king, 25, 30
Louisiana, 4
  became British territory, 51
  definition, xvi
  migration to, 53
  trading licences, 56
Lower Canada. *See also* New France;
    Quebec
  agricultural crisis, 199
  economic crisis, 267n79
  newly created province, 198
  "loyal" bands, 178–79

....

Macdonald, John A., 148
Le Maigre (trading chief), 101
Malchelosse, Gérard, 23
Maminonatan, chief, 152
mangeurs du lard, xvi
Manitoba, 8
Marais, Marin, 41
Marest dit Labarre, Marin, 44
Maret dit LePine, Jacques, 32
marital relations *à la façon du pays,*
    3–4, 7
Marque, Marin de la, 50
marriage, 42, 51, 63–64, 123
  Athabasca country, 72
  as business, 67–72
  contracts, 31–32
  Early Modern Europe, 22
  endogamous nature of, 68
  intermarriage, 48
  intermarriage (Cardinal and Piche
      families), 233
  intermarriage (métis children into
      local aboriginal bands),
      122
  intermarriage with Indians in
      aboriginal bands, 92
  marital alliances, 43–45, 48
  Mexican wives, 70
  New France, 31–32

Treaty Four, 144
Treaty Five, 144
Treaty Six, 144
withdrawal from treaty, 178–80
métis children, 61, 69
    baptism, 63–64, 113–14, 202,
        253n18, 254n32
    cultural closeness to Cree, Saulteax,
        or Chipewyan cousins, 122
    estrangement from white society, 73
    financial provisions for, 64
    social respectability, 64, 73
    St. Louis area, 200
métis wintering families
    intimate exposure to both cultures, 91
métissage, 3, 35, 202
métisse, 60, 173
Mexico, 70
Michel Reserve, 180
Michilimackinac, 50, 59
Mission Bay, 123
missions and missionaries, 7, 113, 139.
        See also headings for individual
        missions and missionaries
    British opposition to, 7, 113
    formation of Métis identity, 7
    interfaith rivalries, 116, 126
    lack of facility in Native languages,
        116–17
    Methodist, 124
    Protestant, 116
Mississippi Valley, 54
Missouri branches of the Desjarlais
        family, 219
Missouri fur-trading territories
    proximity to settlements, 63
Mistawasis, chief, 163, 232
Mistawasis band, 160
Mistihai'muskwa. *See* Big Bear
Mitche Cote. *See* Desjarlais, Antoine
        (b. ca. 1792)
Mitchell, John, 177, 178–79
mixed-blood children. *See* métis
        children
Moberly Lake, 192–93
Moberly Lake Reserve, 192–93
Molloy, Maureen, 30

Mongrain, Louison, 166
Monkman, James, 134
Monkman, Joseph, 134
monogamy, 63
Montana, 143
Montour, Nicholas, 77
Montour, Robert, 134
Montreal, 28, 51, 67
    fur trade, 3, 5, 46–47, 53, 199–200
    Iroquois raiders, 41
    population, 47
    prominent outfitters, 77
Moose Mountains, 130, 204
Moral, Antoine. *See* Desjarlais dit
        Moral, Antoine
Morin, Antoine, 134
Morris, Alexander, 141
    description of Métis, 142–44
La Mothe-Saint-Héray, 25
Moving Stone Lake, 146
murder of Joseph Cardinal
    impact, 160, 161
    incitement to revolt, 160
murders at Frog Lake, 155
Mus-ke-ga-wa-tik (Wah-sat-now) band,
        146
Muscowequan Reserve, 172–73
Muscowequan's band, 145
Mustatip, Catherine. *See* Cardinal dit
        Mustatip, Catherine (a.k.a.
        Catherine Pierre)

··········

Naming practices, 223–35
Napitch (Cree woman), 123, 179
négociants, 48, 53, 199
New France, 197
    Canadien society, 46
    entrepreneurial *ethos,* 101
    fur trade, 3, 5, 34–35, 39, 47–48,
        50, 197
    immigrants, 27
    importance of family, 197
    policy of intermarriage, 35–36
    population, 26
    seigneurial system, 33, 37, 45
New Madrid, 56, 62

Cree and Saulteaux of the North
West Territories, 144
Desjarlais signatories to, 145
métis, 144
Treaty Five, 143
métis, 144
Treaty Six, 148, 169
Cree, Chipewyan and Assiniboine,
144
Desjarlais signatories, 146
métis, 144
native disillusionment, 148–52
no provision for scrip, 206–7
open letter from Cree and Stoney
bands, 148–52
Treaty Seven, 207
Treaty Eight, 169, 186–91
Desjarlais signatories, 190–91
government reasons for, 187
hunting and fishing rights, 189, 208
identity decisions for Native peoples,
194
J. K. Cornwall's recollections, 187–88
Métis scrip, 9, 195
separation of Indians and Métis, 208
Treaty of Paris, 51
treaty paylists, 14
Trois-Rivières, 45
as centre for fur trade, 37, 46
Iroquois raiders, 41
settlement of, 28
Trottier des Ruisseaux family, 117
Trottier Desruisseaux dit Pombert,
Joseph, 49
Trottier Desruisseaux dit Pombert,
Pierre, 49
Trottier dit Beaubien, Michel, 42, 44
Trottier dit Desruisseaux, Antoine, 42
Trottier family, 42
Trudel, Jean, 28, 32
Trudel, Jeanne, 28, 31, 42, 245n47
Trudel, Marguerite (Thomas), 28–29,
32
Trudel, Philippe, 28
Tullibee, 80, 83, 85, 94, 100, 201
designated trading chief, 86–87
friendship with John Lewes, 88

left Lesser Slave Lake region, 119
loss of trading chief status, 95, 99
measles, 92
participation in Cree war expedition,
97
remained in region of Carlton House,
119
Turtle Mountain, 136
Chippewa, 136
Métis, 131
Tustawits, Duncan, 191
Two-Lance, chief, 66

....

Unions à la façon du pays. See
marriage à la façon du pays
Upper Missouri Outfit, 65–66, 131
U.S. government
treatment of Métis culture, 73

....

Vankoughnett, Lawrence, 152, 187
venereal disease, 93, 100
Vésina, Jacques, 32
Victoria Settlement, 162
Methodist mission, 124
Vincent, John, 134
violence, 7, 80, 92, 109, 126, 155
Athabasca region, 202
as cause of emotional detachment, 22
gifts of liquor and, 112
Rupert's Land, 112
visions, 104
The Voyageur (Nute), 2
voyageurs, 2, 12, 38, 197
cohabitation with Native women, 36
(See also country marriage;
marriage à la façon du
pays)

....

Wabamun, Antoine. See Desjarlais dit
Wabamun, Antoine
Waddens, Jean-Etienne, 79
Wambdi Autopewin (Eagle-Woman-
That-All-Look-At), 66
Wandering Spirit, 160

raid on Indian Agency at Frog Lake,
154–55
wasahikanwiyiniwak, 232
Wetchokwan. *See* Cardinal, Louison
"Wetchokwan"
White Earth House, 83
white prisoners. *See* McLean, W. J.
Whitefish Lake, 126, 146, 176, 180
    mission and agricultural settlement,
124
Whitford, William, 183
widows
    congé de traite, 35, 249n90
Wilkie, Bapt., 134
William, chief, 152
wintering, 4–5
    Athabasca hinterland, 83
    hivernants, 83, 144, 201
    with Indian bands, 108
Woodpecker, Chief, 152
Woods Cree, 166, 191

. . . .

Yamachiche, 60, 62, 79
Yamaska, 41
Yanktonais, 131
Young, Harrison, 157
Yukon gold fields, 187